Uncommon Education

The History and Philosophy of Prescott College
1950s through 2006

Samuel Nyal Henrie

contributions by students, alumni, and faculty

Melissa Doran, contributor and editor

Libby Rasmussen, editor

Uncommon Education: The History and Philosophy of Prescott College, 1950s through 2006

Published by Wheatmark®
610 East Delano Street, Suite 104
Tucson, Arizona 85705 U.S.A.
www.wheatmark.com

Publisher's Cataloging-In-Publication Data

Henrie, Samuel Nyal.
Uncommon education : history and philosophy of Prescott College / Samuel Nyal Henrie.

p. : ill., map, charts ; cm.

Includes bibliographical references.
ISBN: 978-1-60494-021-3 (pbk.)

1. Prescott College--History. 2. Education, Higher--Aims and objectives--United States. 3. Education--Study and teaching--United States. 4. College environment--United States. I. Title.

LD4572.P742 H46 2008
378.791   2008923589

Cover photo: new student orientation patrol, hiking in
Escalante Canyon, southern Utah.

Contents

◇◇◇◇◇◇◇◇

PART II

EDUCATION AT PRESCOTT COLLEGE: PHILOSOPHY AND PRACTICE 157

PART III
DISTINCTIVE CURRICULAR PROGRAMS AND PROJECTS 203

Part IV

PART V
HUMOROUS, OUTRAGEOUS AND TOUCHING ACCOUNTS OF PRESCOTT COLLEGE LIFE AND ADVENTURES 361

Ode to Prescott College

By Steve Matthews, Class of 1972

I fell in love once, not with a woman (and not with a man)
but with a college (of all things).
It wasn't a one-sided affair
as I knew the people and the buildings and the land
and they knew me.
It wasn't exactly the ideal romance, either;
it ended too soon.
Some might find it
a bit odd or ridiculous,
this falling in love with a college
(of all things), but it isn't, and really,
it wasn't the college I was in love with,
but the life.
Young, idealistic, intelligent, unsure
and struggling for maturity.
I found a way of life I truly loved.
Oh no, it wasn't perfect. In fact, it was just
a beginning, that first year, but I was on the move.
I was going to change (and I have, I did).
Now my love is gone.
She didn't abandon me, though. I was the one to leave.
I'm still a bit in love, however,
and someday I hope I'll return.
Yes I fell in love once, I truly did.

Acknowledgments

◇◇◇◇◇◇◇

I would like to thank the members of the Prescott College faculty and staff of all divisions and locations who have provided essential information about the various projects and events in the history of Prescott College. So many people have contributed to this book it is not possible to mention them all.

Students have taken major responsibility in every phase of producing this book. Their viewpoint as students and participants in the College community has been vital to the creation of a firsthand and balanced treatment. It is an important component of a Prescott College education to demonstrate competence through professional quality work, and they have certainly fulfilled that expectation. I wish to thank them and acknowledge their indispensable contributions.

Melissa Doran researched and authored several excellent pieces in the book which appear under her byline. She gathered stories and photographs and lent her considerable journalistic and editorial talents to almost every aspect of the project. Melissa was also a contributor to a preliminary publication, *The Five Worlds of Prescott College*, which has appeared in various forms during the past two years. Libby Rasmussen has served as technical and content editor, and helped select photographs. She played a leading role in the organization and layout of the book in its final form according to the publisher's standards. Travis Patterson offered his photography to be used in the book.

When I first took on this project I put out a general call to the community requesting submissions. Those who responded with their histories and stories are all included under their bylines and are an invaluable addition to the information, balance, and flavor of this book.

Cathy Church, Assistant to the President, has been a partner in creating the Prescott College Archives. While they were students, Lori Tella, Matthew Sicher, Dana Launius, and Krista Cole helped process and conserve these records. Tom Brodersen of the Information Commons (library) has created an archive of photographs, Catalogs, and other media, and some special documents. The Oral History Project was initiated by Rick Taylor, alum and former staff librarian. This continuing project contains interview recordings and transcripts of Jim Stuckey, Ann Dorman, Joseph Griffin, Hal Lenke, Betsy Boulding, Dan Garvey, Bob Harrill, Annabelle Nelson, Noel Caniglia, Joan Clingan, and Walt Mendelssohn. Public Relations Director Mary Lin and the Alumni Office staff provided some of the short pieces written by graduates from every period. Cathy Boland and Lucy Kemper and Vice Presidents Steven Corey and Joel Hiller were all very helpful in supplying recent data on the finances of the College and Corporation. I wish to acknowledge and thank all of these alumni, colleagues, and coworkers.

Ryan Flahive and Scott Anderson of the Sharlot Hall Museum Archives professional staff deserve many thanks for helping find information of the founding and first years of Prescott College, from the 1950s through 1975. The Museum Archives proved to be a rich and important source. Nancy Cannon, a volunteer archivist at the Museum, who processed the Franklin Parker records and papers, was very helpful. Ann Parker and Ethel Lytle, wives of the most active founders, also provided essential insights and documentation.

I am indebted to Keegan and Warren Miller for the graphs and tables in the Money chapter, and owe my appreciation to Warren Miller and Hayley Love of Wheatmark for overall editing.

Finally, I wish to thank my wife, Angie Henrie, a retired Curator of Education from the Sharlot Hall Museum, for her assistance with early Prescott history, and for being my faithful support and critic.

In acknowledging all who have contributed to this research, writing, editing and production of this book, I also take responsibility for any errors in facts or interpretations.

Introduction

◇◇◇◇◇◇◇

Prescott College's achievements and extraordinary educational experiments have made a meaningful contribution to higher education. The College succeeded at a time when several similar new colleges failed. By swimming against the current and coming up breathing, Prescott College has spawned a vibrant mythology that has become an integral part of the school's character. This is not surprising; all significant human endeavors naturally accumulate a mythos that communicates their beginnings, purpose, and accomplishments. However, oral tradition tends to drift through processes of forgetting and confabulation. In the case of Prescott College, the real events surpass the color and adventure of the oral mythology that has grown up over the years.

The College has existed as a concept for sixty years and a real organization for over forty. Only a few of the founders of the 1960s and '70s are still available to perpetuate the authentic stories, yet legends live on in heroic and emotional tales told at ceremonial occasions or around campfires. Indeed, Prescott College does have a worthy creation myth that is often retold, but it always begins with the school's second creation in the mid-1970s. Accounts of the college's original creation in the 1950s and '60s are fading. Few now recall and fewer still mention how the College was designed in the minds of its original founders and how the citizens of Prescott banded together to give physical and educational form to that dream.

Because the College has been a pioneer, it is important that a history be recorded. Putting the history into writing can help preclude further drift. In this book I have tried to create an account of the beginnings and development of the whole organization, which has many components, from its first conception to around 2005. In a certain sense it is increasingly difficult to record history the closer one gets to the present. There is far too much information regarding the last decade, and it becomes difficult to select what to focus on and how to interpret it. Over time, successive generations will want to get the most accurate story. They will appreciate this record, and extend it.

I am not quite certain whether I chose to write this history or if the history chose me. Prescott College is maturing and it was time for someone to consolidate its mythos. Since I have been deeply involved in the life of the College for most of the years reported in this book, people within the community and outside it were beginning to ask me questions about the past. Being an accommodating person, I always tried to give complete answers. Some responded, "I only want to know that date—not the whole history of the West and the city of Prescott, history of the field of higher education, etc." This sort of exchange left us both frustrated. Ten years ago the faculty voted to change my status and assignment somewhat, allowing me more time to do research and writing. About five years ago, the Dean of the resident program in which I am a faculty member suggested that I should write a book about the history and philosophy of the College. And the rest, as they say, is history.

I came to Prescott to teach and not to divide my time between teaching and administration as I had for the previous decade. Joining Prescott College's very small faculty allowed me to be fully involved and to participate in many of the crucial decision at every phase of the school's development. I was on the faculty of the College for most of the years reported in this book, and this experience has some very decided advantages that purely archival research can't match. When I read materials from the archives my memory fills in factual and sensory details, and I understand the context in which events occurred.

The potential disadvantage of having an internal player write a history is that of the subjectivity. All of us see what is happening around us through a personal lens, and it might be suspected that only an "outsider" could be objective. By my personal epistemology, I do not believe that objectivity can exist, except in certain aspects of mathematics. Everyone's point of view is selective. When framing a history, thousands of choices must be made as to what should be included, what should be left out, and how events should be interpreted. I feel that a person with direct experience can actually make those decisions more competently and fairly. However, I am sensitive to the possibility that the book could reflect too many of my perceptions and interpretations of events. To insure integrity, I have reread hundreds of publications of the College, studied reports and audits from every year, carried forth the Oral History Project, and submitted chapters to others to read. To balance my own interpretations I have included pieces written by other faculty members and by alumni and current students.

This experience has confirmed the truth of the notion that an historian has to answer the same questions that a teacher does: what is the information of most worth to readers? What is important, unique, noteworthy, and provident for them to learn? A historian can only record the tiniest sample of what has happened. To inform their choices, historians work to elucidate specific themes. The four themes I have used to guide me are:

The vision and the remarkable educational innovations that have been undertaken by Prescott College in order to live by its own educational philosophy at every level.

For significant periods the College attempted to operate at the faculty, financial and administrative, and policy levels in ways that applied the values taught in classroom and field settings, namely—***community, equality, social justice, self direction, and environmental responsibility***. Students learn by example, and creating a community and school has provided thousands of experiential learning opportunities. At the College the phrase "walking your talk" has epitomized this approach to running the school. In these pages I will present an overview of how and why these experiments were created and eventually modified—or in some cases abandoned.

Prescott College as an important pioneer in several fields of education.

Innovations in Education at the College include (a) unique liberal arts degree-granting programs at the BA, MA and PhD levels, (b) experientially based teacher education and credentialing programs, (c) teacher preparation and credentialing extended to such underserved populations as bilingual American Indians (taught on reservations) and bilingual Hispanic populations in the border region, (d) outdoor education, for which the College is probably best known, and (e) environmental and sustainability education.

The evolution of Prescott College through stages, adapting to internal and external pressures, and to financial circumstances.

Institutions change over time, because society is dynamic. What succeeded in the past may not be relevant at later stages, as evidenced in Prescott College's continuous search for identity. Financial history may not be so visible on the surface, but it has a dramatic impact on the philosophy, direction, and often on the very life or death of a college. After attempting to synthesize operational/philosophical history with financial history, I decided to present these two aspects separately. The narrative history is presented chronologically in Part I, and the financial history is arranged thematically in Part IV.

How people learn. This theme addresses the importance of small colleges like Prescott, despite their inefficiency.

A small college has to find means to deliver a comprehensive liberal arts education through a very limited curriculum. Prescott College has accomplished this by freeing students to learn in a more open structure, insisting

on self-direction, and encouraging and relying on the students themselves to
become the synthesizers.

These themes have guided my selection of what to include in this history. It is my hope that the events and programs not directly discussed will be
evident by association and inference.

This book is the product of four years of research and drafting. When
I began the project I believed that writing and collating this history would
take only one year. I did not realize that the various records relating to the
College were so dispersed and that I would have to assume the mantle of an
archivist. The College has a present-minded and future-oriented culture. At
the time I believed that it would be difficult to find enough material to fill
and document a small book.

I soon discovered that historical materials of all kinds existed, but they
were stored in dusty shelves and closets of different College buildings, old
forgotten file cabinets, stacks of boxes in community members' garages
(including mine), and in other obscure places. I put out requests in all our
newsletters asking for any pictures, news clippings, founding documents—
anything that would open a window into the College's past. Over the next
three years the growing archives received boxes of organizational and financial reports and also scrapbooks full of black and white photographs, yel-
lowing news clippings, student writings, forgotten College newsletters and
announcements—disparate materials from every period of the history.

Much was not of general interest, but there were nuggets of gold dispersed throughout. A large space in the basement of the College's Sam Hill
Warehouse was provided and a dozen four-drawer legal sized file cabinets
were scrounged from all over the campus. More than thirty storage boxes full
of materials were hauled to the work room and a crew of work-study students
under my direction began to sort them and put them into the file cabinets,
labeling files and drawers according to a provisional system and keeping lists
on worksheets.

It quickly became apparent that other archives had been collected at
the College. The Publications department and Alumni Office had been fil-
ing photographs for decades and most had been reduced to slides or digital
jpg files. They also had cabinets full of College media including Catalogs of
all programs and copies of the excellent alumni magazine, *Transitions*. The
business office had student records and audits in both electronic and paper
formats going back fifteen years—earlier paper records were stored in a commercial facility. The Information Technology department had been data mining for eight years and had megabytes of student and program data stored
electronically. And one of the professional staff of the Library had initiated

an oral history archive, with recorded interviews of some of those who were founding faculty and alumni. At the same time, I discovered that another substantial body of records was archived at Sharlot Hall Museum, a regional historical institution located in Prescott. These were from the first decades and included the personal papers of some of the founders of the College.

These details are presented to paint the picture of how the Prescott College Archives were put together. At the time of this writing these records have been disorganized again, due to a building project that co-opted the space I used as a workroom and file storage area. Those who have done similar organizational tasks will immediately understand. The Archives went from a condition that seemed to be a scarcity of historical information to a nearly unmanageable glut.

Most of the research into the conceptualization and founding of the College, from the mid-1950s through 1975, was researched using the Archives at the Sharlot Hall Museum in Prescott, Arizona. Sharlot Hall Museum is an agency of the State of Arizona, and is the repository of extensive archival records of Territorial Arizona and regional history. Many of the original founders of Prescott College left their papers and documents to the Museum's Archives Department, so they would be preserved and made available to the public. These Archives consist of hundreds of files containing reports, letters, maps and photographs, legal documents, audits, and financial reports. Some Sharlot Hall Museum records concerning College finances are sealed until the year 2064.

The majority of the research into the years 1975 through the time of this writing (2005-06) was done using materials from the Prescott College Archives as well as my own papers and the interviews from the Prescott College Oral History Project. For financial data after 1997, current records held in the College Business Office were used. A reference section and bibliography has been included in this book for the convenience of those who wish to dig deeper.

Finally, it is often difficult to appreciate where you are until you acknowledge where you've been. This work has changed me. I am much more cognizant of the many important contributions of my colleagues, of the long-range effects of day to day decisions, and of the awesome complexity of creating and operating a college.

Sam Henrie

PART I

Historical Narrative

This section presents a chronological narrative of the history and philosophy of Prescott College in four phases. First is the founding period, before 1966. The second describes the College while it occupied the campus six miles north of Prescott, opening its doors to the charter class in 1966 and closing down in December of 1974.

To distinguish the first and second phases, the terms "original College" or "old College" have been used.

The third phase is the reestablishment of the College in downtown Prescott under another corporate entity, Prescott Center for Alternative Education (PCAE), between January 1975 and 1999. The fourth is marked by the acquisition and use again of the original corporate entity, Prescott College, Inc., and is characterized by the expansion of the new campus in town, building new facilities and expanding programs to include a doctorate in sustainability education.

Phases three and four are often distinguished by the use of the term "new College." At the time of this writing (2006) Prescott College has its largest student body to date—approximately 1000 enrollees, facilities in Prescott, Tucson, and Sonora, Mexico, and four active divisions offering a large variety of educational options to its students who range from first-time freshmen to people in their middle and later years.

Dedication of Bronze Statue of Bucky O'Neill, Spanish-American War Hero
from Prescott. July 4, 1907, Prescott Town Square.
Courtesy of Sharlot Hall Museum Archives.

An Ideal Place for a College

In 1934, at the depth of the Great Depression, young Franklin Parker had recently been called to lead the Congregational Church of Prescott. Driving around in his new home town, he turned to his spouse and said, "This is the ideal location for a college."[78]

It was a beautiful town built around creeks that flowed from the surrounding mountains forested with fragrant pines. Although elegantly laid out around a central square and county courthouse like small towns in the East, Prescott still had a frontier flavor and an appealing Western ruggedness. At the time they arrived, there were barely six thousand residents, but to the Parkers, it was the future and it looked full of promise.

Prescott wasn't just picturesque with its tree-lined streets and Victorian houses, it had a splendid history. It had been chosen by Abraham Lincoln in 1863 to be the first capital of the Arizona Territory. The already mature town of Tucson in the south had been the first option, but on learning that rich deposits of gold and silver had been discovered in and around Prescott, Lincoln chose Prescott as capital to secure these resources for the Union. Prescott was also within a protective distance of the nearby military post of Fort Whipple and not in the lap of the pro-Confederate sympathizers of the south. After the close of the Civil War, Tucson and Prescott wrangled over the location of the capital and it moved back and forth between the two towns until 1889, when Prescott lost the distinction permanently.

The mines began to peter out in the early twentieth century, but the ranchers, farmers, and businessmen who had moved into Prescott to support the miners were well established and the community was thriving on its own resources. As the seat of Yavapai County, Prescott continued to have significant importance, but it remained isolated as the national web of highways developed. It wasn't on the way to anywhere.

Prescott was a part of the bigger Arizona scene, however, and around the time that the Parkers were reconnoitering their new home in 1934, Arizona was making important changes that were to lead to unprecedented growth.

In 1929 the Navajo Bridge had been built, making it possible to cross a tributary of the Colorado River. Prior to that time, an upper section of Arizona, called the Arizona Strip, was inaccessible to the rest the state without a several hundred mile detour through Nevada or the Navajo reservation. With the completion of the highway across the new Hoover Dam in 1935, and bridges being built across the lower Colorado, Arizona became connected to the states of California, Nevada, and Utah, and on into the national transportation network.

As Reverend Parker built his congregation and worked to fulfill his ministry, he watched Arizona blossom. Irrigation projects that had started earlier with the building of Roosevelt Dam were continuing to expand and were boosting Arizona's growing agricultural economy by making hundreds of thousands of acres in central Arizona available for cultivation. During World War II huge allotments of federal money were invested in war industries and air bases, bringing industrialization to Arizona. Then, after Germany and Japan surrendered to the Allies in 1945, came the enormous postwar boom.

Prescott, being off the main highway and isolated from the action, was peripheral to the dramatic growth taking place in Arizona. The field of education, however, was one arena that could be entered where seclusion would be an attraction, and the leaders of Prescott began to dream about how to have their community become a recognized center for quality higher education.

This interest in education was not new to its founders or the people of Prescott. In the 1860s the little settlement was named after an eminent historian of the nineteenth century, William Hickling Prescott, and one of the first public buildings was a log cabin schoolhouse, a replica of which has been preserved on the grounds of Sharlot Hall Museum. In the 1870s two schools were established: a parochial school called St. Joseph's Academy, and the Prescott Free Academy, which Governor John C. Fremont called "the finest school in the territory."[81]

Now, in the expanding postwar economy of the 1940s and 1950s, there were fresh possibilities, and the establishment of an institution of higher education became the ambition of Prescott's town leaders.

The first attempt was led by the largest local Baptist congregation, and was supported by the Chamber of Commerce. In May of 1947 the Baptist General Convention of Arizona in cooperation with the Chamber of Commerce incorporated a liberal arts college in Prescott and leased a half section of land for a campus. They named their college Grand Canyon College, and operated out of the Prescott Armory facility on Gurley Street for two years. Although a fundraising drive was carried out under the auspices of the Chamber of Commerce, not enough money was raised to pay the mortgage on the land and operate the college. In 1949 a 160-acre cotton field was donated to the Baptist Convention in northwest Phoenix (Glendale), an area that was growing rapidly. The Baptists took the opportunity and moved Grand Canyon College to Phoenix.

Vic Lytle, who was second only to Franklin Parker in the creation of Prescott College, related the conversation he had with Parker after Prescott lost Grand Canyon College to Phoenix. "I was manager of the Chamber of Commerce then. I was standing with Franklin [Parker] on the sidewalk, lamenting the loss of the college. He said: 'There isn't any reason this has to be a dead issue. I think the Congregational Church would look on this favorably.'"[77] Franklin took the bit between his teeth and began promoting the idea, writing letters and speaking about the creation of a college whenever an occasion presented itself.

Caption: Lytle receives first check for Prescott College, Feb. 28, 1963

To bring in the Congregationalists was not an unusual idea. As a Congregationalist minister, Parker was well aware of the church's illustrious history in American higher education. When Parker began to promote his dream of a "Harvard of the West" many may have wondered what Harvard, in Massachusetts, had to do with a new college to be located in a little city in the mountains of Arizona. Parker knew the connection.

Harvard (1636) and Yale (1701) are both Congregationalist schools. In fact, close to fifty of the finest colleges and universities in the United States were sponsored by individual congregations with the help of Congregationalist regional conferences. Over a third of these schools, eighteen in fact (and when you count Prescott College nineteen), were named by the local churches with the name of their own town or city, indicating they were joint projects with the churches and town leaders—for some examples: Amherst, Oberlin, Beloit, Atlanta University, and Elton. The Congregationalists were also dedicated and effective abolitionists. After the Civil War they were instrumental in founding the great colleges for black students such as Howard and Fisk Universities as well as several smaller colleges.

Upon being questioned concerning what might be expected of the Congregational Churches and organization that might prove of benefit to the founding of a small college in Arizona, Chairman Parker responded that he believed two great assets were to be contributed by the Congregational Fellowship: "One, the seventy-five years of history of the churches in Arizona with a respected standing and a definite sense of responsibility, two, the long tradition of the Congregational Fellowship in the establishment of some forty-seven colleges throughout the United States."[73] It is clear in all his statements that Parker felt he could rely on the Congregational Church's strong history of developing educational institutions to help him create a school in the West.

Values Linking Congregationalist and Prescott College Philosophies

There is more than the work of Reverend Franklin Parker and the quarter-million-dollar grant the Congregationalists provided over the first decade to connect Prescott College and its original sponsor. Much in Prescott College derives either directly or indirectly from Congregationalism. As a religious movement in America, Congregationalism has gone by many names and has spawned a range of other religious groups. In the three and a half centuries since they settled in New England, the group has joined with many other Protestant conferences including their latest nationwide fusion with the United Church of Christ. Throughout all these organizational changes, however, the core of their creed remains constant.

The central plank of their philosophy and practice, that which distinguishes them most clearly, is **self-direction**. Each *congregation is indepen-*

dent and self-governing. In parallel fashion, the authorizing documents and literature of Prescott College always contain a phrase pointing up that the school is *independent and unaffiliated.* Since 1975, each stakeholder—student, alum, faculty member, employee, etc.—is a voting member of the authorizing corporation—whether Prescott College, Inc., or Prescott Center for Alternative Education, Inc.

Another plank of the Congregationalist way is that they allow great latitude in interpretation of the truth. No doctrine or fixed interpretation can be imposed on members of the congregation—or, indeed, on anyone. Prescott College has a parallel attitude toward learning: self-directed learning. Prescott students are not treated as empty vessels to be filled up by their teachers, to provide information for them to memorize and recite in tests and papers. As much effort is put into helping students gain their own modes of learning and follow their own interests. Another similar value that they share is called service or involvement by the Congregationalists and experiential or service learning by Prescott College.

Indeed it was to a meeting held by the Congregationalists in Prescott that the very beginnings of Prescott College can be traced. Parker, in describing this event said, "In 1955 we celebrated the 75th anniversary of the Congregational Church in the Southwest. The Arizona Association met in Prescott to help mark the observance. ... Out of a discussion of the Men's Group an idea was talked over, and they brought into the meeting of the entire group ... the possibility of at least looking into ... a [private] college in the Southwest."[73]

The members of the Arizona Association of Congregational Churches who attended this celebration approved of the idea and authorized establishing a College Survey Committee. Then Parker, after consulting with Charles W. Pine, moderator of the Arizona Association, asked some of those who had liked the idea of a college in the Southwest to gather on Thursday, January 26, 1956. This first meeting of the Survey Committee was held in the Aluminum Room of the Westward Ho Hotel in Phoenix with the Reverend Charles Franklin Parker as chairman.

The College Survey Committee concluded by assigning Parker the task of creating committees to study various possible resources available, general campaign and promotional procedures, and realistic goals as to the economical size or the operation of a college.

According to Parker, "The idea rocked along, and then rather bogged down. ... In August, 1959, the Phoenix Kiwanis Club asked me to speak and it was at that time that I decided to make one final thrust on the college idea. The Arizona Republic not only picked up the idea in a good story but also editorially, and the results gave a new spark to the idea … this had real influ-ence on the Board of Home Missions [of the Congregationalists' Western Conference] to encourage them to have a financial survey made." [76]

Seeking guidance, Parker contacted the National Education Body of the Congregational Christian Churches. Dr. Wesley A. Hotchkiss, then execu-tive director of higher education, and Dr. Howard Sprague of the United Church of Christ Homeland Ministries, then treasurer of their educational board, both of New York City, were enlisted and became key players in advis-ing and working with Parker.

Sprague made several recommendations: the new college should hire a fundraising firm, shoot for at least $3,000,000 *from the local community*, then go to the extended region of the Southwest in a phased campaign to raise ten to fifteen million dollars. Sprague also suggested that the United Church of Christ should be tapped for significant funds. He predicted that 75% of the funds raised would come from only fifteen wealthy individuals and founda-tions. And he cautioned that if the campaign were not to reach its stated goals, those who did contribute would be turned off for future contribution for at least ten years. [82]

Following Sprague's advice the conference hired a fundraising company to carry out a feasibility study. Sprague recommended the Cumerford Cor-poration, a new fundraising firm of St. Louis and Denver, apparently associ-ated with the development of religious institutions. Their research consisted of interviewing more than 350 people by telephone, direct mail, or in per-son. Interviewees included church ministers, business and professional men and women, the "power structure" of major centers, corporation executives, foundation heads, and representatives of nearly every level of civic, frater-nal, or social organizations in major communities throughout Arizona, New Mexico, and Southern California.

Cumerford's conclusion was that "Prescott would be an excellent loca-tion and … Arizona and the Southwest would be able to support the kind of institution of higher education that could take its place among great schools founded by the Congregationalists." [16, 74] The Arizona Association, thus en-couraged, resolved that it would lend its influence to support the founding of such a college in Prescott.

With this encouraging report and a green light from the regional church conference and leaders from throughout the state and the town, a Leadership Council was set up by Parker, Lytle, and several other influential citizens. Lytle was appointed Chairman of the Board and Parker was the Director. One of the first acts of the Council was to register Prescott College with the Arizona Corporation Commission as a nonprofit educational corporation on March 8, 1960, and the College was underway.

Even before this Council was underway however, Parker was using his considerable promotional talent to sell the idea, and gearing up for a fundraising campaign of major scope. Continuing to follow the advice of Sprague and Hotchkiss, Parker wrote a letter to the Conference College Committee of the Arizona Association asking for an initial grant of $100,000 and a pledge of $50,000 per year for the following ten years. Also, several letters and fundraising reports from 1960 indicate that Parker was trying to raise funds in Southern California from the churches there for "Christian Education." His letters argue that funds in the millions of dollars are being raised for New College in Sarasota, Florida, but not for Prescott College. And he asked to be considered because Prescott was, after all, located in the West.

Sprague and Hotchkiss of the Homeland Ministries Board again encouraged Parker and Lytle to engage Cumerford to conduct a "needs assessment" to determine how much money would be necessary, and how a campaign should be structured to raise those funds in the Southwest. This round, the firm recommended a minimum figure of $4,500,000 to $5,000,000 to be raised in a period of one year, starting immediately in 1962. But it was recognized that five million might not provide the cushion needed to build the campus and open the doors.

The records show that the ultimate fundraising goal depended on who was speaking or writing at the time. Those with more fundraising experience considered $10,000,000 to be a realistic goal. Others with more college administration experience thought at least $15,000,000 would insure the new College had a healthy start. But all the consultants and planners agreed that at least $1,000,000 had to be raised locally to start with, to "prime the pump." In contemplating these money estimates, the reader should be aware that a dollar in 1962 had the purchasing power of $6.38 in 2005. Therefore, the Founding Fund goal was comparable to asking for more than six million dollars in 2005 value, which is a stiff request.[73]

Dr. Parker and Vic Lytle open Prescott College Founding Fund Office

The Prescott College Founding Fund

On March 21, 1962, the Prescott College Founding Fund was created as a legal financial entity, and the local Prescott campaign was officially launched, with the goal of raising $1 million. *"It's up to you in '62! To Open the Door in '64!"* was the slogan with which Parker introduced the town to the concept of creating a "Harvard of the West." His absolute conviction of the benefits of a new college was contagious, and before long, almost everyone was convinced that a private, four-year liberal arts college would be a prime asset for the community.[23]

So, while still serving as the head pastor of the local Congregationalist Church, Parker took on the difficult task of creating a college, proving the words he had said when he described himself as a "man of the cloth," but also a savvy "operator." [55, 56]

There was never a doubt in Parker's mind that this new college would be first class, with a faculty of "such quality as to be without apology" and with

Miss Prescott College looks on Mt. Everest Funding Goal May 3, 1962
photo by Ken Shake

only the very best and brightest students. Almost every day the local news outlets extolled the benefits. The faculty would be stimulating, "a culture of music and other arts will appear," and "the community will vibrate with vital meaningful vigor." "Intellectual people seek intellectual climates."[22]

Victor Lytle mentioned at the time that he did "help foster the Baptist College as Chamber of Commerce manager but never had toward them a feeling such as I have on this college. Franklin [Parker] has laid a fine and firm groundwork—and there has been a careful step by step progress— through the Association, the Conference, the Arizona Council of Churches and the Home Board." The board of directors decided at its first meeting of 1962 that "the primary project for the year is the opening of Prescott College as soon as possible"; this was emphasized by Jack Reuter, president of the Prescott Chamber of Commerce. They put all their support into helping reach the $1 million mark. Everyone knew that the $1 million local goal was only the beginning of the $15 million needed to actually build the college, but it would be a show of "community spirit" that would give outside donors the confidence to pledge their support as well.

In order for the Prescott community to come together and raise $1 mil-

Parker, Lytle, and Supporter View First Model of Campus Buildings (later abandoned for more modernistic architecture)

lion for the creation of this new college, it was important that Parker and those devoted to Prescott College make clear the benefits it would bring to the community. Victor H. Lytle, President of Prescott College, Inc., published a series of question-and-answer articles in a booklet designed to answer the community's frequently asked questions regarding the building of the college, its financing, and its purpose.

In these articles he explained that economically, the formation of Prescott College (with a student body of 1,000) would bring an additional yearly income of $3,000,000 to the town, that every major cultural and scientific area in the country has grown around a seat of learning, and that "contributing to the future of the area and to the improvement of the moral fibre, character and intellect of the citizens of tomorrow … is a job for everyone who has and is benefiting from the privileges of America."[22]

The president of the Chamber of Commerce added to this sentiment when he stated that, "It is our considered opinion that nothing would benefit Prescott economically as much as Prescott College—no single industry or recreation attraction—nothing would benefit as much in dollars and cents." And that "We believe that every business and professional man will have returned to him many times over the amount he invests in Prescott College." The townspeople had done their math. They knew that all the students that the College drew in would be bringing their checkbooks with them, adding an estimated $3 million to the Prescott economy each year. This was an opportunity not to be missed.[23]

The community wholeheartedly embraced the idea of a college in their town and joined in the fundraising. Groups and individuals devised unique and creative ways to raise money. Two College benefit balls were held by the Yavapai Cosmetologist Association. Mrs. Hale Tognoni, a widely known sculptress from Phoenix, donated the money she made from the sale of her religious statues. The young people of Prescott jumped on the Prescott College bandwagon as well, in hopes that someday soon they might attend this prestigious new institution. The local 4-H groups got in on the action by donating and creating "competitive pledges." The Chino Valley Go-Getters Club donated $100, challenging other local clubs to do the same, and even donated the money earned from the sale of a prize calf. Other schools, such as St. Joseph's Academy, also responded with $100 donations. A quarter-page news photo shows Parker and several supporters gesturing toward a billboard with a giant thermometer imposed upon a profile of Mt. Everest; it claims they were within $200,000 of the summit. In another news photo, Miss Prescott College was perched above the back seat of a Lincoln Continental convertible, waving to the July 4th Parade crowd.

Funding Headquarters in Downtown Prescott

By August 1 of 1962, the Founding Fund reached its goal. The town of Prescott showed its enthusiastic support by going above and beyond the $1 million goal, albeit mostly in pledges, within a matter of a few short months.

The number of pledges to the Prescott College Founding Fund was around 700, with the average donation of $1,191. And many anonymous donations of up to $50,000 were received. Counting everything—including over $300,000 in cash, vacant lots, mining claims, stocks and bonds, a classic rodeo saddle, a concert piano that needed some refurbishing, the prize calf— by August 29, 1962, there were 1,199 pledges totaling $1,048,062.

This was all achieved within a matter of months. Everyone understood that the $1,000,000 local goal was only the beginning of the millions needed to actually build the College. Now they hoped for $4-5 million from the Southwest and various other national resources to cover the balance.

The Leadership Council continued to be chaired by Parker until he was officially recognized as *Founding* President of Prescott College, Inc., in 1962. Under his and Lytle's leadership, several planning and development councils were set up—Academic, Administration, Campus Land and Physical Plant Construction, and Funding and Endowment—all peopled with local volunteers recruited for their prestige or special skills.

SECURING LAND FOR A CAMPUS

While the fundraising feasibility study was going on, the Campus Land Committee and Prescott leaders, including Lytle, Dr. Taylor Hicks, and Atty. John Favour, were addressing the question of campus. In the late fifties, parties interested in creating a college for Prescott had made inquiries regarding the use of a National Guard rifle range six miles north of town and were told it was never used–that it was cheaper to send the Prescott unit to the Phoenix range for training than to maintain the one in Prescott. Following this possibility, Parker and Lytle made inquiries at the state level. In answer the Committee received a letter, dated November 25, 1959, from Governor Fannin. According to Parker, "From there, the Governor got word to the National Guard. We found out the range didn't belong to the National Guard but to the Army, and in further negotiations we learned that all branches of the military had to say they didn't want the land. Both Governor Fannin and Barry Goldwater gave lots of help in these negotiations … Stewart Udall was a great help. … He had appointed as his legal counsel an Arizona boy, Max Edwards, who had lived in Prescott at one time. So a letter from Fannin to Edwards brought rapid results. Morris Udall also helped a lot at the last in bringing the final results. In fact, there was excellent cooperation from all." A little later, Arizona's other senator, Carl Hayden, also gave support.[67, 78]

The original ambition of the Committee was to secure the square mile of land (640 acres) that had been the rifle range, but due to a couple of interven-

Founders at Site of Future Campus

ing complications the campus site ultimately ended up comprising 483 acres. First, after the preliminary approval of federal land patents, the Committee was then required to cede several acres of land on the east side for the development of Willow Creek Road. Then, in 1963 there were serious problems holding onto the title to forty acres in the center of campus. Luckily, city, state, and federal agencies at the highest levels came to the aid of the College to resolve these matters. These events are described and documented in *Money Matters Part I.*

The outcome of this epic that began with a simple inquiry at the National Guard office was that the College had ownership of almost a square mile of beautiful wild land. An equally important outcome was that some of the most important and influential people gained a knowledge of the pioneering concepts going into the creation of Prescott College.

With support growing in Arizona and among the Congregationalists and $1 million pledged from the community, and land being secured, Prescott College was on its way. At that point Parker resigned his position as Minister of First Congregational Church, after twenty-nine years of service, in order to dedicate his full time to the founding of Prescott College.

Parker's next goal was to produce a symposium. He began networking

Student Rock Climber on Granite Dells Near Campus
(with Granite Mountain ten miles in the background)
photo by Travis Patterson

nationally to identify and invite one hundred leaders with state and national status in higher education, finance, government, philosophy, and religion.

Southwest Is a Great Place for a College

When newly arrived, Franklin Parker saw great promise in Prescott as a place to create a great College, and his vision proved prescient. Yet he did not fully appreciate all of the educational opportunities the region offered. The Southwest presents a spectacular and unique natural endowment, an unparalleled opportunity for study and research in the natural sciences and human cultures.

Within a day's travel from Prescott one can reach the Grand Canyon carved out of the spectacular high plateau by the Colorado River, most of the famous sandstone canyons and natural bridges painted in all shades from deep purple to creamy pink, two giant man-made lakes and many creeks, small rivers, and lakes, a major fourteen-thousand-foot volcano, (Mt. Humphreys), the famous Meteor Crater, dense alpine forests, two types of deserts and Death Valley, some of the best and most demanding hiking and mountain bike trails, hundreds of square miles of wilderness and the clear, wide blue sky that cowboy songs extol.

A little farther to the south one enters the State of Sonora, Mexico, and then reaches the Sea of Cortez, an incomparable body of water for almost any purpose. Prescott College has developed a field station for study and research on the Eastern shore near a necklace of islands sometimes called the northern Galapagos because of their uniquely evolved wildlife. Whales of several species feed and breed in channels close to the station, as do porpoises, sea lions and seals, and innumerable species of sea birds, fish, shellfish, cephalopods, and myriad life forms that make up a fertile ocean.

The Southwest is also a center for American Indian life and a prime place for the study of cultures. Arizona is home to twenty-two American Indian Tribes, Nations, and Communities and twenty-one federally recognized reservations. More than 30% of the land base is under some form of legal Indian jurisdiction. The majority of the quarter million American Indians living in this state prefer to reside on tribal reservations, according to the 2000 Census, which is not typical of Native American people in the rest of the country. Both native traditions and archeological research indicate that ancient origins of these tribes differ, some people spreading into the Southwest from Canada, others from the Great Plains. Many tribes are related to the pueblo peoples of Mexico and to the Aztecs. Still others migrated to this region from the Pacific coast. Some of these peoples have lived here for over ten thousand years while others came into the Southwest only just before the Spanish. A large area in the northeast of the state is the territory of the Navajo (Diné), the most populous tribe in the United States, and such famous tribes as the Hopi and Apache are centered here. The city of Prescott encompasses one of three reservations of an ancient Southwest tribe called the Yavapai, a name derived from their word "enyaeva" meaning sun, and "pai" meaning people.

Roundup, 1958, at Ranch near Prescott's Old Campus
Courtesy of Sharlot Museum Archives.

Symposium: The Philosophical Foundation of Prescott College

◇◇◇◇◇◇

To understand what was discussed at the Symposium held in 1963 is to understand the underpinnings of Prescott College. The importance of this Symposium cannot be overemphasized, because the document it produced became the fundamental reference for Mackenzie Brown, first Dean of the College, for President Ronald Nairn, who put together the original College and for President James Stuckey, in recreating the College in 1975. And it has also served as a guide for many other leaders and the community.

Parker was remarkably successful in his efforts to enlist the highest level national and state leaders in higher education, finance, government, philosophy, and religion. Eighty-six of the one hundred who were invited were able to attend. Those unable to attend contributed to the proceedings through correspondence. Everything was recorded and transcribed. The full conference report was published a year and a half later by Prescott College under the title *Emergence of a Concept: A Dynamic New Educational Program for the Southwest*, edited by Charles Franklin Parker, Library of Congress Catalog No. 65-24271. A copy of the 154-page document is available for loan through the Prescott College Library.

Parker first brought aboard one of the superstars of higher education, Dr. Laurence M. Gould, the retired president of Carleton College, known for its academic quality. Gould sat on the Board of Trustees of the Fund for the Advancement of Education, established by the Ford Foundation. It was Gould who helped Parker secure a grant of $15,000 as partial support to mount the conference on the grounds that it would lay the philosophical and practical foundation for an exceptional college to serve the Southwest, and also lead the way to educational reform nationally. (In 1962 a dollar had the purchasing power of nearly six and a half dollars in 2005.[86] The grant was thus equivalent to well over $80,000.) The three-day conference was held at Camelback Inn in Phoenix, Arizona, November 7 through 9, 1963.

Notable Educators Take Break Between Meetings

Among the participants were such brilliant and influential individuals as Hugh Odishaw, ScD, Executive Director, Space Science Board, National Academy of Sciences; Daniel E. Noble, ScD, Executive Vice-President in Charge of Communications, Semiconductor, Solid State, and Military Electronics Divisions, Motorola, Inc., Phoenix, and eight other leaders in the fields of science and industry; Walter R. Bimson, LLD, Chairman of Board, Valley National Bank, the largest statewide financial institution; W. W. Dick, Arizona State Superintendent of Schools and Arthur M. Lee, PhD, representative of the Governor of Arizona; James D. MacConnell, EdD, Director of School Planning Laboratories, Stanford University, Palo Alto, California; Sterling M. McMurrin, PhD, former U.S. Commissioner of Education and author of the Philosophy section of Encyclopedia Britannica; Henry R. Luce, LLD, Editor-Publisher of Time-Life, Inc.; J. Edward Murray, Managing Editor of the Arizona Republic, Arizona's largest newspaper; John M. Jacobs, owner of Jacobs Farms, Phoenix, representing the ranching and farming establishment; D. Mackenzie Brown, PhD, Chairman of Asian Studies,

University of California at Santa Barbara; Pauline Tompkins, PhD, General Director, American Association of University Women; A. B. Schellenberg, Member of Board of Regents, Arizona Universities and Colleges; James M. Goddard, LLD, Executive Director, Council of Protestant Colleges and Universities; Wesley A. Hotchkiss, PhD, General Secretary, Division of Higher Education and the American Missionary Association, Board of Homeland Ministries, United Church of Christ (Congregationalists); and sixteen others representing educational leadership in several faiths; John Y. Begaye, Director of the Department of Health, Education, and Welfare for the Navajo Tribe; nineteen college and university presidents or their representatives, including those of the three state universities of Arizona; nine professors who were recognized as outstanding educators and experts in the fields to be discussed in the Symposium; and a number of business people and community leaders from Prescott and other Arizona cities.

The format was a three-day symposium to design the unique academic goals of a new institution and, in Parker's words, "to transplant an educational tradition some three hundred years old, growing out of New England, to the locale of the Southwest, with its own peculiar overlays of culture, long heritage and emerging opportunities." Added to this was the emphasis on projecting concepts to meet the conditions of a new century and employing the most advanced teaching techniques and methods.[89]

Dr. Parker introduced the opening session with their charge: "to lay the philosophical and educational foundations for a top-tier institution of the quality and influence, continuing the long tradition of excellent colleges and universities founded by the Congregationalists (United Church of Christ) beginning with Harvard (1636) and Yale (1701) and continuing with over fifty schools including Smith, Dartmouth, Williams, Amherst, Oberlin, Mount Holyoke, Howard, Elmhurst, Wellesley, Pomona, and UC Berkeley."

They were asked to create a vision of a college that would train a new generation of leaders with the skills, moral foundation, and vision to promote peace and well-being among the world's peoples, and with the foresight to attack such looming problems as environmental degradation, poverty, overpopulation, etc. They were told by Parker that "plans are in progress, therefore, for the establishment of a proper educational program and for the development of an adequate plant to house the academic community." And he then invited them to consider serving in a more permanent role in the future College.

SUMMARY OF THE SYMPOSIUM'S RECOMMENDATIONS AND
CONTROVERSIES

The following account of the three-day symposium is presented by quoting the actual words of the participants as much as possible. Their words reflect the wealth of professional experience they brought to the task and their diverse points of view. Their statements, however, show the extent to which they truly sought to create a unique educational institution. While there were points of controversy, more often there was consensus. All references in this section are from **Emergence of a Concept.**

The participants articulated three principles they would use to guide the creation of the school relative to the teaching/learning process. Wesley A. Hotchkiss calls this "THE DIDACTIC," which included 1) The Principle of Unity, 2) The Principle of Respect for the Disciplines, and 3) The Principle of Flexibility. [p. 40]

The Principle of Unity was conceptualized as "a seamless coat of knowledge," quoting the great American philosopher Alfred North Whitehead. The participants agreed that they were not happy about the tripartite division (arts, humanities and sciences). They hoped to create "a bridge between the so-called two cultures, the *hard* sciences and the humanities." [ref. John W. Dodds, p. 106] The customary departmental and divisional structure of curriculum was radically reexamined and ultimately decided against in their pursuit of an education emphasizing the interrelationship of knowledge. To implement this approach it was decided that there would be a single faculty, with no individual departments or divisions between the humanities, social sciences, and natural sciences. Student knowledge of the relationships among various disciplines would be stressed. The term *interdisciplinary curriculum* was repeated throughout the conference. They agreed that "essential courses should be taught as entities and not be fragmented into irrelevant particles offering only partial views of great themes in human learning." [Karl Dittmer, p. 51] Another related theme was that the artificial separation of the sciences and humanities should be done away with.

In place of conventional departments there should be an integration of curricular programs. Programs were not to be isolated, or taught in a vacuum, but instead they should "work together to provide students with a broad, conceptual understanding of the world. [Parker, p. 2] Later a speaker expressed his hope that "if all can be kept under a general division which deals with man and society, I think we have some possibility of eliminating much of the friction which now exists [between disciplines]." [Brown, p. 56]

As to content, the core and unifying element of the curriculum should be the study of a number of civilizations or cultures regarded as entities of knowledge and human experience. As to process, the programs must foster "not only the depth of [students'] mastery, but also [their] knowledge of interdisciplinary relationships ... a student should choose a culture or civilization, namely American culture, European civilization, Hispanic-American culture or Asian civilizations, and study one of these intensely enough with appropriate language skills to be able to demonstrate in written and oral form in his senior year his vision of the total structure of knowledge and understanding." Noting the "proximity of the Indian cultures" to Prescott College, Brown said, " we would hope that it would be possible in Prescott College to have on the faculty and in the student body those who have first-hand knowledge of the Indian cultures so illustrative of the principle of unity of values and outlook, so necessary in a healthy civilization." [Brown, p. 104]

Dr. Mackenzie Brown, who subsequently became the first dean of Prescott College, expanded on the first principle of UNITY as it applies to social sciences, saying, "When we get a group of people together in the social sciences and attempt to solve problems of man's relationship to society, we sometimes find the experts working at cross purposes. The economist may feel out of his depth in political problems, or, if he gets into them, he gets into them as a virtual incompetent. This conflict and friction eventually seem to result in a very vicious system of departments and departmental interests. If you look at most of our great universities you would be apt to find an amazing provincialism among the faculties of the social sciences. They lose sight of the overall problem and simply attempt to build power and prestige and influence and budgets and numbers of faculty for their own particular department ... I hope in this discussion of social science that we can think of it as a single problem, a problem of how to understand man's relationship to society, without the ridiculous specialization which is so often developed in different departments." [Brown, p. 55]

In another discussion, Dr. Brown expanded this view to include the *hard* sciences. "It seems to me that with the problem of civilization you have to come back to the conclusion that science by itself cannot exist. This is the great problem of our times, that you cannot determine by scientific means those values which are most significant for our culture ... I would like to suggest that the Academic Advisory Council examine a curriculum based on depth of coverage and emphasizing problem solving and reasoning rather than be concerned with the presentation of all the facts known. Specifically, in chemistry I would look at the English or Australian curricula, also the program at Earlham College. What can be learned from these in planning a new program? I would also endorse independent work, laboratory or field and library studies, and above all, readings (like St. John's), a schedule and curriculum that would encourage and *demand* reading time for the students on their own—for example, something like a period of two to four weeks twice a year for reading." [Karl Dittmer, p. 52]

In the summation of the conference they stated, "*Our first conclusion* was that there should be a single faculty for Prescott College, eliminating not only individual departments but even the academic divisions between science, the humanities and the social sciences. Faculty members would retain titles appropriate to their disciplines, such as professor of geology or chemistry or history or Latin, but there would be no administrative breakdown. We were unable to find any acceptable divisions within the social sciences since the entire area deals with the problem of man and society, even though we recognize the absolute necessity of individuals having thorough mastery of one particular approach to the study of society. Going beyond this, we found the same interdependence and interrelationship with the humanities, and we believe that a knowledge of the history of science will demonstrate to anyone that this intimate relationship exists with the physical sciences as well." [Brown, p. 103] [also see p. 138]

The Principle of Respect for the Disciplines followed directly after the Principle of Unity. Though this second principle seems to contradict the first, the participants insisted, "Our emphasis upon the interrelatedness of knowledge must not obscure the necessity for mastery of subject matter in depth. … The fact that there is free and uninhibited movement between the disciplines does not mean that the major branches of learning lose their identity in some kind of generalized education."[Hotchkiss, p. 40]

Dr. Noble, who directed research at Motorola, quoted the American philosopher Alfred North Whitehead: "The race which does not value trained intelligence is doomed." Henry R. Luce of Time-Life responded, "Dr. Noble is undoubtedly right that the liberal arts college today would be archaic unless it had a very heavy stress on mathematical and physical sciences. Well, so it is. But I would also like to remind you that one of the greatest, perhaps the most characteristic slogan of the Greeks … who made a leap forward in brain power with the uses of the intellect, reason and mind was about character—character is a man's destiny."

Dr. Brown cited some relevant research: "Harvard University Medical School did a study three years ago of the success in Harvard Medical School of its entering students. They divided the students for control purposes into two groups. One was composed of students who had liberal arts training, a four-year liberal arts training, as distinguished from the other group composed of graduates of schools providing a tightly organized scientific curriculum in the traditional mode of preparing for zoology, genetics, biology, chemistry, physics, and so forth. They found that the students prepared in what I would call the narrow or traditional hard scientific curriculum did better in the freshman year of medical school than the students who had broader training in the humanities and language and fine arts and history—the liberal arts generally. But in the second, third and fourth year of medical school at Harvard the group of students trained more liberally, more broadly, did better than the students more narrowly trained. There's a similar study that has been done at Johns Hopkins Medical School in the last few years." [Brown p. 57]

When the discussion turned to the sort of faculty who could be expert in their disciplines yet teach in an interdisciplinary way, it was observed that "one of our functions in a liberal arts college is to continue the liberal education of the highly trained but narrow specialists who come to us with PhD degrees—to teach on the faculty. Why must a teacher be reeducated when he becomes a member of the faculty? Would it have been possible, had he gone to Prescott College, to avoid over-specialization?" [Brown, p. 56]

This second principle does seem to contradict the first principle, and therefore gets slighted in the Symposium. But specialization and disciplines do receive attention later when the science panel reports its curriculum recommendations. In other words, the conference did not solve the perennial conflict between the hard sciences and humanities. What we see is the emergence of three competing models: (a) liberal arts traditionalists who want to repackage conventional curriculum, calling it innovation; (b) scientists and engineers who want to have a seven-year curriculum in mathematics and specialized science so the students can be prepared for careers in industry; and (c) social scientists who want to create an experiential and research-based division in the curriculum to understand contemporary society, with various emphases on different civilizations. It should also be noted that studies of North American Indian cultures surrounding Prescott, particularly their previous cultures—as in archeology or anthropology—adds another and different element, since these are tribal cultures, not civilizations. Such discrepancies tended to be papered over in the conference. Then again, the symposium was only three days long and provided very little time for resolution of long standing academic issues. However, such issues would inevitably arise in the development of the on-the-ground College.

The Principle of Flexibility further cemented Prescott College's unique place in the collegiate world. This principle was based on the premise that each student is responsible for his or her own education. It applied not only to choice of courses, but also the progression through the program and ultimately the graduation process and requirements. The participants agreed that students must graduate on the basis of "demonstrating competence, not merely through passing courses and gaining credits." "The arrangement of the curriculum, the methods of teaching, and the sequence of courses must be designed with utmost flexibility to allow for the individuality of the student. … It must be assumed that no student will progress at the same rate as all the others through all the branches of knowledge. The usual classification of students as freshmen, sophomores, juniors and seniors will need to be reexamined." [Hotchkiss, p. 40]

There must be flexibility of curriculum as well as unity so that individuals within the community would feel free to develop their particular interests, talents, and abilities. This sense of flexibility would depend upon the intimacy of relationships between faculty and undergraduates. This leads also "to the conclusion that there must be a large degree of flexibility within the academic system in terms of classes and lectures, and particular professors would be given this freedom to establish their courses along the lines that they thought to be most suitable for this particular environment." [Hotchkiss, p. 41]

It is the purpose of Prescott College to "bridge the gap" between the past and the future, between the cultural and scientific influences on our civilization, between the contemplative and measurable influences on our thought processes, and between the subjective and objective points of view.

"The degree to which this purpose is fulfilled will be measured only by the degree to which the graduates of Prescott College will be prepared to contribute to the development of civilization." Intrinsic in this concept was a future-thinking curriculum that would allow students to explore and connect to their society and environment in a deep and meaningful way. [Brown, p. 138]

The intent was to provide students with "a unique perspective of society as a whole and the individual within that society. The curriculum is based upon the conviction that human affairs can neither be understood nor solved by compartmentalized minds. [Parker, p. 2] The educational process of the college should be based upon the learning experience of the student. This means that the student must be motivated, must motivate himself, to seek an understanding of himself, his society, and the natural world. This is a highly individual process, and the function of the faculty should be not to teach in the conventional sense of imparting facts, but to enable students to learn. A belief was expressed that "with adequate resources for individual studies, the student can assume the responsibility for a large part of his own education under competent leadership." [Gores, p. 61] Independence could be fostered by "telling them what you want them to study and telling them to go study it and come back and tell you what they found out." [Welch, p. 77]

Dr. Welch questioned whether this approach was feasible from a practical point of view, and Brown suggested, "After examining [the student], the reading he has done, his capacity to exhibit competence and depth in a particular field, we would get together and certify that this individual was entitled to the equivalent of so many credits or so many years in this or that subject." "Therefore, the student's progress, his rating and his program should be determined by intimate personal contact with the faculty dedicated to teaching in the best sense." [Brown, p.59]

The concern was raised that such a policy might tend to confine the undergraduates to Prescott or to colleges of a similar nature [i.e., limit their ability to transfer credits to traditional colleges]. The response given was, "For general purposes undergraduates would be expected to participate within this total environment for a period of at least two years." [Gordon, p. 68] By then they would have the tools to follow special interests. At this point there were dissenting voices from the science group and others who believed more than two years of in-depth study would be needed to gain competence in their particular fields. The science and mathematics panel ultimately recommended a minimum of seven years to earn a BS degree.

Earlier Dr. Brown had asked, "What do we mean, then, when we say that we don't want to have the specialized training interfere with liberal education? What do we mean by a liberal education? If we can come to some conclusion as to that, then all of our talk about a liberal arts college, a liberal education and all our concern about specialization interfering with a student's understanding of our society will have meaning." [Brown, p. 56]

Another line of disagreement with the principle of flexibility arose when a participant asked whether students are good judges of what they need. One response was that the Prescott College curriculum and process should be structured and organized to (a) provide knowledge (including self-knowledge, a knowledge of others, a knowledge of the physical and biological world, a historical view of man's social, intellectual, and artistic achievement, and a knowledge of religion and philosophy), (b) provide intellectual skills (including language, critical thinking, and mathematics), and (c) help students develop a social consciousness and personal philosophy. [Odishaw, p. 108]

Dr. Brown said, "I would disagree with you from this point of view—as a cultural historian. Pardon me for bringing that in, but this is where I get my point of view. We fail to realize that the individual is a product of his culture. Now the older generation always looks to the prior culture in which they developed and says, 'These are the things that college students ought to have.' They fail to look at the current culture in which we are living and fail to realize that it is the total impact of our culture that produces the college student and not the college itself."

SPECIFIC CURRICULUM RECOMMENDATIONS

When a collection of ambitious college professors and administrators are given the opportunity to write the specifications for a new curriculum, their wishes (and perhaps their frustrations) can become unrealistic. To use the old cliché, they are like kids in a candy store.

What follows are highlights quoted from the curricular recommendations of the three panels dealing particularly with curriculum—Social Sciences, Humanities, and Physical Sciences—which were presented in the final plenary session.

Sample of Recommendations from the Humanities Panel

Modern languages: "Because here we are in a particular area where Spanish is obviously the … language that should be understood … in order to understand the influence of the Spanish culture, [students should] reach a high level of fluency in speech and writing. In other words do what a language is supposed to do, communicate with other people who are able to speak and write it. Within the section of modern languages we would have German, French, and Spanish." [John W. Dodds, p. 106]

Literature: " … We would like to see the study of world literature itself. We would like to see the courses being offered such as survey courses in the humanities, in Western civilization, in the history of great ideas, and in American civilization. We would conceive of courses in contemporary issues which might be helpful to seniors." [Ernst Gordon, p. 69]

Fine Arts: "When we discussed the creative arts we felt that there was a very real place for them within the curriculum, but we felt, however, that the creative arts should be combined with regular academic courses." [Ernst Gordon, p. 69]

Sample of Recommendations from the Social Science Panel

Study of Civilizations: "We suggest, too, that in line with this idea of a cognate major there should be special programs in the various civilizations, such as Eastern civilization, and this would again have to be limited, I think, to something like Hindu civilization or Chinese civilization or to the Islamic civilization or to European civilization." [Ernst Gordon, p. 69]

History: "Yes, certainly we should say not only American civilization but Latin American civilization. In the area of history we included the suggestion that there be a course in the history of science with lab demonstrations and that laboratory demonstrations could be in the form of film and also experiments carried on within the lab or laboratory itself." [Hotchkiss, p. 70]

Sample of Recommendations for the Physical Science Panel

Physics and Chemistry: "A year of chemistry, general chemistry, I would hope to see somewhere in the physics program. A year or semester of what might be called chemical physics where you would do atomic structure, where you would do statistical mechanics, and where you would do chemical physics, solid state, metals." [Keller, p. 72] "A year of mechanics, a semester or a year of optics." [Odishaw, p. 72]

Brooks: "Are you thinking also that physics would be required of all students in the program as a general rounding?" Welch: "Yes." [pp. 71-74]

"Another specific ingredient applicable in this approach would be to mix the literature and science together—for example, by reading Roger Bacon and looking at it as literature but at the same time showing how the development of scientific thought took place. If you could mix this into the physics curriculum you just might turn out the best kind of physicists that ever got turned out." [Welch, p. 73]

One panel member went so far as to project that "Prescott College could, fifteen years from now, be known as the institution in the country that would be considered the ultimate place to go for physics." [Taylor Hicks, p. 72]

Other sciences:

"A year of biology; at least three years of mathematics." [Odishaw, p. 72] One participant attempted to synthesize by saying that through the entire curriculum they would be teaching thinking skills: "Let us try each of the items I listed yesterday—investigation, analysis, understanding, synthesis, organization, and communication." [Welch, p. 76]

General Introduction—First Year Requirement

Dr. Odishaw: "Furthermore, the first summer before the first academic year, we're going to pull these students in for about three months and give them a rigorous course in review of grammar and a lot of composition, and we're going to give them a program in the review of mathematics. We hope that they will come to us with something like an equivalent of a half-year in calculus." [p. 82]

Dr. Gould: "Well, not as juniors out of high school." [p. 83]

Dr. Odishaw: "Yes, that's the hope." [p. 83]

There were also different opinions as to who should decide what the curriculum content would be "… this would be left as an exercise for the Board of Trustees and other committees to explore." "The pattern of curriculum should be left to faculty." [Dodds, p. 106]

The participants realized there was no consensus. The following statement was made in the concluding session. "The only specific curricular recommendation which we are prepared to make is the offering in the freshman year of a course which will demonstrate to the entering student precisely what is meant by the term education. This would specifically deal with Western civilization and would be designed to illustrate the intimate relationship between the humanities, sciences and social sciences in the origin and development and progress of our civilization." [Brown, p. 104]

Clearly the bridge between the sciences and humanities had not been built in this Symposium. And that is not surprising. As we will see, this issue plagued the College in its first incarnation, and continues to be a problem in academia at large.

COLLEGE LIFE OUTSIDE THE CLASSROOM

The second overarching theme of the Symposium was life at the new College outside the classroom, what could be called the ethos of the College community and its individual members. Hotchkiss [p. 40] termed this aspect "THE EXISTENTIAL," and introduced it by saying, "Once Prescott College has agreed upon intellectual and academic excellence in its didactic life, it still will not be the kind of institution we have in mind unless it orders its entire life in such a manner that the profound meaning of the academic community begins to inspire, inform and ennoble all of its members. It is this critical area of meaning, purpose, and self-identity which is in crisis in present-day education. This is the intuitive ground upon which the college stands which determines its intellectual posture. This is the climate within which the students can discover their personal destinies and their own reasons for being."

Dr. Gould led a discussion about what constituted a Christian college, "There is no such thing as Christian physics or Christian mathematics or Christian economics, but there is such a thing as an atmosphere in which those and similar subjects may be taught. Such values do not require to be presented as absolute laws but rather as practical guides helpful in the reinforcement of the *ethos*. The code of action [later called "The Honor Code"] which has been understood and accepted voluntarily by all is the moral discipline which makes the intellectual task of the college not only feasible but actual. [As an example,] "The law of evolution may be a law capable of being scientifically demonstrated. It is, however, a law of the Creator operating within our particular planet." [from a paper by Hotchkiss, p. 50]

"The need for the recovery of the ethical dimension of cultural and academic life is obvious in these days when the estrangement between science and morality has left us without a place in the universe and with nowhere to go but annihilation." [from a paper by Hotchkiss, p. 50]

LACK OF CONSENSUS ABOUT THE ETHOS OF [THE] NEW COLLEGE

From discussions regarding the College's ethos that were interspersed throughout the conference, it is clear that there was some confusion about the kind of college they were planning—what tradition would it follow or create?

Wesley A. Hotchkiss, representing the Division of Higher Education of The United Church of Christ (and Congregationalists) who had been instrumental in authorizing studies and setting up the Symposium, expressed the view that "Prescott College ... has chosen to identify itself with a certain rather well-defined tradition of the liberal arts and sciences, and it is within this heritage of humane learning that it proposes to make its contemporary contribution to education." He then cites traditions of higher education in Massachusetts Bay Colony (Reverend Cotton Mather, eighteenth century), the palace school of Charlemagne (ninth century) maintaining that the idea of the "college" clearly descended to them through the schools of the prophets of ancient Israel, and the Greek academies of the classic age, comparing them to their current effort. Hotchkiss then states: "And now, Prescott College, in the nation's most rapidly expanding region, will be the newest embodiment of this intellectual tradition. Any innovating Prescott College will do will be based upon such a massive substructure of heritage that even the most radical departures can be made with confidence. Upon this foundation the college can build with security its most thoroughly contemporary educational structure." [Hotchkiss, p. 39] Parker commented: "One statement is that Prescott College is *related* to the Congregational churches. It says it will be church related though not church controlled. Now, this is a very, very uncharted country, this business of what is church related but not church controlled." [Shannon, p. 63]

Other participants emphasized they believed they were designing a "New College" pointed toward the future, and experimenting with the latest and best learning techniques and technologies. Alvin C. Eurich, PhD, Vice President of the Fund for the Advancement of Education, Ford Foundation, which had paid for this symposium, presented an excellent eight-page essay in which he lays out the major trends in higher education in the twentieth Century. He implied that Prescott College would advance the trend of future-oriented education, in its view of the needs and potential of students, the best new learning psychology, new models of teaching, and an *experimenting* or experiential teaching environment. He compared it to "institutions such as Bennington, Goddard, and Bard ... colleges which take pride in the fact that no two of their students followed the same course of study." Parker responded: "I am not afraid of innovation. I don't like innovation for the sake of innovation. I'm not afraid of it, and I frankly am not fearful even of accrediting agencies and all the rest that goes with it, if we are prepared to prove by objective measurement the value of the thing we are doing."

Professor Brooks added, "This could be sort of a modern Meiklejohn or Black Mountain sort of experimentation in education. Maybe you shouldn't use the word "experiment" because this is not [well understood], but let's say a different attitude on the part of the faculty, less awareness of the status symbol because they wouldn't necessarily be concerned about that, or shouldn't be, as much as they should be about the students ... whose progress and whose broadening and whose advance in the subject field is their concern."

PRACTICAL RECOMMENDATIONS FOR THE SYSTEMS AND PROCESSES OF THE NEW COLLEGE

Thus far this summary of the Symposium has attended the more philosophical side of designing a new college. What follows are samples of comments from participants regarding the organization and operation of the College.

Type and Selection of Students:

"Elites—capable of high quality pre-professional training in academia, business, government." "*Superior* people who would make their mark. My experience with college students in regard to these issues is that they are not so much irreligious as that they are [not] theological, and I think we're dealing here with the question of semantics." [see John W. Dodds, pp. 105-106]

"When we draw on our student body and recruit our freshman, sophomore and other classes, some of the students will have come in with no idea of what they really want to do except that they want to keep in the swim—to be in college because of the social advantages or to be exposed to learning in a general sense." [Brown. p. 56]

"In the selection of students, the panel believes that the College Board Examinations should be used if for no other reason than to afford a general basis for comparison, but the college should develop its own qualifying written examination and that it should conduct careful interviews with all prospective students." [Odishaw, p. 111]

"And in order to define liberal education we are going to have to say something about the values we are seeking. The student should be proficient in the use of words and numbers; these are the two fundamental disciplines, it seems to me, in a liberal arts college. The mastery of these will unlock bodies of knowledge to him later and will give him, when he finishes the liberal arts training, the meanings—I hesitate to say the 'techniques,' but that's really the concept of the word—the techniques for addressing himself to later problems that come up in professional school, law school, in life." [Shannon, p. 57] In essence he is saying that the College needs Writing Certification and Math Certification for graduation.

Size of Student Body

"Do you think it can be done with a group larger than eight hundred or one thousand?" [Brown, p. 61] It is intended that the school will have a student body of some 800-1,200 students. [Odishaw, p. 108] A small student body is necessary if we are to train them for leadership and dedicated service and as seekers after truth, and to prepare them to confront the new dynamic duties of societal change which are now emerging.

Duties of the Dean

"The principal task of the college's academic dean must be the very careful choice of faculty: men of competence and breadth. Appointments should be made in a given discipline (e.g., professor of English, etc.) but that there should be a single faculty—or, at the most, a faculty in the sciences and a faculty in the humanities." [Odishaw, p. 111]

The Teacher's Role and Student-Teacher Ratio

"Begin with some first-rate generalists rather than specialists. Particular professors would be given this freedom to establish their courses along the lines they thought to be most suitable for this particular environment. [Dodds, p. 105]

"The average liberal arts college in the United States has about one faculty member for fifteen to eighteen students. Large universities quite often run one faculty member for twenty students or more. Now I think you could do, with that faculty-student ratio, what we were talking about today. You might have to have a slightly higher type of faculty member, and consequently you might have to pay each faculty member a little more money than you pay your instructors and assistant professors in the large universities. But I don't think the cost would necessarily be exorbitant." [Gores, p. 61]

Dr. Odishaw addressed the commonly made comparison between American and British schools. Americans have been more effective " ... in pumping information through lecture techniques, etc., while the English "lead students to communion with great minds." He went on to speculate: "Suppose we went all the way to the extreme of the tutorial approach and the professor saw each student two times a week for a one-hour session [as in the great English universities]. ... In Cambridge there is the tutorial system and a student really reads original papers. He has to dig into the literature himself, and he comes into direct communion with the great minds—the great scholars of the past and with [help of] the tutor." [Odishaw, p. 80] He acknowledged that Americans use the term tutor differently, that at Cambridge a tutor is full faculty member. This led to a discussion of faculty load, office hours, and student-faculty contact hours, thus skirting the issue of quality that was Dr. Odishaw's main point. The question of whether undergraduate teachers should do research then arose, and created vigorous discussion but remained unresolved.

"Let's get away from a narrow notion of courses. Regarding lecturing, I don't feel lectures are necessary in an undergraduate school in that the books are available." [Welch, p. 83]

"Pardon me, what about student loads? These panelists consider lecture time as learning time—very traditional view of students as empty vessels to be filled up with knowledge. You could cut down on the classroom time." [Brooks, p. 78]

Grading/Reporting Systems

Dr. Gordon: "Let me summarize the work of the Humanities Panel: In order to preserve the character and personality of the college, in order to insure that we have the right kind of professors and graduates, we have to think seriously about the whole matter of testing, evaluation and grades. It has been suggested that we should think in terms of the evaluation of the student by the members of the faculty as being the final determining factor in this matter. The admission of undergraduates would certainly include the use of the present tests, but we ought to think in terms of how some evaluation can be made of them personally in addition to those tests. As far as grades are concerned, we feel that we should not think in terms of numerical grades but should think in terms of honors, passes and failures. It was also suggested that in order to insure that undergraduates are coming to better understanding of a subject, able to analyze a subject and able to communicate facts in a reasonable way, that there needs to be greater reliance upon the use of essays in each particular field and the avoidance of what may be called examsmanship [with] the possibility of de-emphasizing formal tests and examinations but perhaps bringing in outside examiners like Swarthmore system." [Hall, p. 84]

"The panel felt that the normal approach of courses, examinations, grades, and credits was undesirable. Objective assessment, discipline and flexibility suggested that some compromise approach should be studied without eliminating the teacher's appraisal of the student. Perhaps a simplified scheme of comprehensive examinations in each discipline would provide an objective test to complement the teacher's appraisal. [Like Oxford and Cambridge.] Comprehensive examinations in a discipline also afford flexibility in the advancement of a student: he should be given the opportunity to take such an examination at any time he feels qualified so that he may advance at his own rate and with the least stress feasible."

Facilities and Classrooms

"It is likely that it is useful for us to say there are two kinds of [instructional] spaces—teacher to student, student to student, as long as we know beforehand how they will be arranged. ... in what size groups, whether it is eyeball to eyeball, or seminar, or standard class or large group ... then the second kind of space is where people will be dealing with things (labs, rehearsal spaces, etc.)—the people versus the thing space. It is apparent in the direction in which education seems to be moving ... to the point where the student will be given access to facts from inanimate things." [Hotchkiss, p. 42]

Dr. Hicks: "It might be well to have a statement that while we recognize the growing tendency toward these mechanical devices we would hope that the college would stress the tutorial-student relationship or something to that effect."

A Dissenting Voice

"I would have an auditorium and it would hold one thousand students and I would have a lecture by a member of the faculty, and I would wish that he would be an inspiring and brilliant lecturer for all one thousand students because I think he would give a better lecture. I think the problem of lecturing to a small class leads to an inferior lecture. There is less compulsion, even of a psychic kind, of a lecturer and it is impossible to lecture to a small group like this if you imagine breaking down into small groups of about ten." [Odishaw, p. 80] Another disagreed by saying, lectures are not efficient—that is why we have texts.

Library—to be open 24 hours a day 7 days a week

"So I need a library that breathes, that is diurnal, that gives and grows daily. Now how do I get that?" [Gores, p. 43]

"'Library' broadly defined is a good honest word, and the donor who is seeking instant immortality understands what a library is. So, don't depart from the word library; don't call it a communication center or something like that. It is a library. It has, of course, papyrus in it, but it also has the other carriers of information." [Gores, p. 43]

Dr. Hotchkiss: "This idea of the library as the center has tremendous symbolistic meaning. To me it's incredible that any of our colleges could have been built under any other concept, actually."

Academic Ritual

"Because the College has culture of its own, it must dramatize and celebrate its cultus on ceremonious occasions. Prescott College must, from its inception, give serious attention to its liturgical dramas, those occasions of high solemnity when its academic community recalls its origins and acknowledges its sovereign Veritas. [Note—veritas is in the Harvard seal—and means "truth" in Latin] [Hotchkiss, p. 41]

Note: Despite this archaic language, the College has found its rituals like graduation baccalaureate, welcome back from orientation, etc., very important in creating a sense of community and of the individual student's identity.

Some of the Do-Nots Taken Directly from the Symposium Manuscript

(a) Do not emulate state colleges.

(b) Do not be pre-professional in the vocational sense of the word.

(c) Do not be withdrawn from the world; therefore, think in terms of what conferences can be supported on the campus that would include outside lecturers and would include the town of Prescott itself and the whole neighborhood.

(d) Do not seek multiple accreditations—regional, rather.

(e) Do not trade on the climate as part of the faculty's salary. Be honest about this and be sure that adequate salaries are paid.

(f) Do not set the natural sciences above the humanities.

Prescott College as an Innovative Leader in Higher Education

"In conclusion and in short, the entire process of learning at Prescott College should be one of freedom, student initiative, spontaneous growth, rigidly judged by a faculty insisting upon seriousness of purpose and depth of achievement." [Brown, p. 104]

"Our goal would be a graduate who understands and appreciates the civilization which produced him and has the capacity to understand it and to appreciate other cultures and to contribute to his own culture as a responsible representative of it, as one who is committed to the preservation of its best traditions and to furthering its continued progress." [Brown, p. 104]

"The students and the faculty should together constitute a company of scholars. Without artificiality, for some subjects must be regarded as well-defined disciplines in themselves, the panel recommends proper use of an interdisciplinary approach. More specifically, the panel believes that the college should emphasize the tutorial approach in the relationship between students and faculty." [Odishaw, p. 111]

"We have chosen to be bold and to pioneer. We have ignored certain inhibitions such as the pressure of graduate schools upon the content of curricula and the problem of acceptance of our students by other institutions. We are confident that if the faculty and program are sound, our students and curricula will be accepted on our own terms." [Brown, p. 103]

Dr. Parker expressed his hope that the new Prescott College would be a beacon of change in higher education. "This Academic Symposium for Prescott College has been prepared in the belief that this plan may commend itself to others, both those in the process of establishing new institutions for higher learning and to those seeking new methods and changed patterns within the field." [Parker, Preface, p. v]

A Shift in Paradigm: From New England to the West Coast

◇◇◇◇◇◇◇

Before the Symposium, Parker was generally considered leader of the effort to create the College, as indicated in this article in the *Phoenix Gazette* (March 5, 1963):

"The Arizona Senate last week paid deserved tribute to Dr. Charles Franklin Parker, the Prescott clergyman who left his pulpit last December to devote full time to a projected Arizona private college. His leadership has made possible the start of construction some time this year on the new Prescott College, which will transplant some of the New England education tradition to an Arizona city ..."[65]

The tribute by the Arizona Senate was well deserved. Parker had pushed the project far in the eight years since 1955 when it was first discussed by a few leaders of the town. The College had been incorporated; a Founding Fund had raised $300,000 in cash and valuable gifts and collected over $1,000,000 in pledges; the townspeople of Prescott were solidly in support of "the Harvard of the West"; national and state leaders in the Cogregationalist/United Church of Christ conferences (which had founded forty-seven outstanding schools) were in support; a fundraising company had been hired; the Symposium had been a great success, bringing together education, business, and government leaders from all over the United States; and Arizona's senators and governor were aboard.

Cumerford Corporation, which had done the feasibility study, was employed to expand the fundraising campaign to the rest of Arizona, and the Southwest, with the goal of raising at least five million dollars. Cumerford asked Parker to move to Phoenix for a short period to organize the Arizona development campaign based on the network of Christian churches and support organizations, and hoping for substantial support of the well-placed Symposium participants from Phoenix. Although Parker's wife, Jo, had suffered a heart attack the previous year, and they had just purchased a home near the College's tract of land, the Parkers made the move. They rented out their new home and found an apartment in Phoenix. Parker also took on the task of editing and publishing the Symposium report, *Emergence of a Concept*, and also editing and publishing the College newsletter, *Progress*.

This was definitely a high point; every aspect of the Prescott College project seemed to be prospering. But the last two assertions of the reporter were not reflections of the developing reality. One could say the recent Symposium had deflected the route of the future College away from New England, and they would not break ground that year as was hoped. It would take at least two additional years to get the College ready. In fact, the school had yet not fully secured titles to the tracts of land, although that was in process, and the original architects' drawing would soon be scrapped. Even if the townspeople had raised the full million *in cash* there would not have been enough money to "open the doors in '64," as the Leadership Council had promised. They were looking at at least a two-year delay.

New College Administration; Dean Brown far left and President Nairn far right.

The Symposium ended on November 9, 1963, and the next two and a half years was a period of significant transition. The changes began with a series of appointments of nationally prominent educators and philanthropists to the Board of Directors of Prescott College, Inc. Laurence Gould, former president of Carleton College, who was serving in a faculty position at the University of Arizona, Tucson, continued as Chairman of the Board.

Newly organized committees of local leaders were busy with all the projects needed to create the college. One committee was securing deeds to acquire tracts of land to fill out campus acreage, through grants and purchases. Another was working with new San Francisco architects to design the grounds, infrastructure, buildings, and facilities. Mackenzie Brown was working with other consultants and academic volunteers to create a curriculum that would reflect the recommendations that came out of the Symposium. A finance committee was creating a business model and seeking funds from local sources. A development committee was collecting pledges and seeking new sources of support. To report on these developments, a public relations committee was working with news people, and they eventually put out a printed periodical entitled Prescott College Progress.

Practical and Philosophical Contradictions Reveal Themselves As New College Is Designed

As these projects moved forward, the many issues and contradictions brought up as theoretical issues during the years of dreaming and planning now had to be resolved pragmatically. This stimulated an evolutionary process that can be discerned in several important changes in the orientation for the College within the world of higher education. At this point, the attention of the College's leadership crossed the continental divide. Instead of attempting to model it on the great colleges and universities of the East and Midwest, they now looked to the West. Its developing curriculum and teaching-learning processes began to reflect ideas from the University of California at Santa Barbara and the Rand Corporation. The College also crossed the divide of centuries, moving forward in time to the present—and even into the future—fifty years into the future. While the "Harvard of the West" was still around, the new catchphrase was "Educating leaders for the twenty-first century."

The traditional administrative hierarchy in which a well-heeled Board of Trustees (guardians) sits above an administration, which watches over academic departments, where the teaching of well established "subjects" carefully divides the intellectual world into medieval categories, was overturned. In its place, a model for dynamic interdisciplinary teams of professional educators, scientists, and artists arose who had input into a "flat" organization.

A physical expression of the change taking place can be seen in architectural plans. The College abandoned its first architectural plans, which depicted prominent and traditional structures hierarchically located, guarding lawn-covered quads.

New architects from San Francisco were engaged to create a campus based on the *think tank* model—small, low buildings consciously designed to accommodate a "flat" organizational structure and blend into the natural setting.

The educational objective of this new plan was to accommodate instructional methods that involve a close working relationship between faculty and student through allowing for convenient physical juxtaposition of faculty offices, classrooms, seminars, and conference rooms. It was hoped that each course would feature, in part at least, seminar and conference procedures to take advantage of a relatively small student body and a faculty chosen for this form of instruction.

The high-desert ecosystem that existed on the campus land would be disturbed as little as possible, so that natural life flowed organically without artificial barriers. The campus itself would be a learning laboratory for studies of natural plant and animal communities.

Cultural insularity and orientation to European and American post-conquest societies began ceding ground to a focus on cultural and regional studies of the Southwest, Latin America, and Southeast Asia. The original privileged position of the Christian religion, and the specific connection with the Congregationalists, was weakened. Religious idealism was broadened as a theme—and flowed into conceptions like world citizenship, the "honor conscience," role of religions in history and humanities, and even interest in world religions like Buddhism. There would be a minister on faculty, but that teacher could be from any of the world's religions, not specifically a Protestant or American. (As eventually happened, the first professor of religion was a Catholic priest and an expert on East Asia.)

Brown had asked in the Symposium: "Are you in favor of the establishment of a chair of world religions?"

A discussion ensued in which they spoke of various concepts of religion, including Navajo views of the nature of God and Nature. Brown articulated a consensus: "We need integrated teachers without departmentalized minds. There is no differentiated subject matter. The study of life is important." As Brown had said, in the new curriculum, religion would be integrated in every study and particularly studies of physics and biology.

It had become clear in the Symposium that there might be an incompatibility between the *Principle of Flexibility* and a classic curriculum. It had been agreed by all "that we cannot break with the tradition of the past." Then the concern was expressed that students might not wish to study Latin and two or three languages. Some argued that ignoring the teaching of classics in a college such as Prescott would be to take a vote against the classics and to suggest that they were irrelevant in the twentieth century. No real consensus was forged, but they contented themselves with the declaration: "we believe we have to keep the door open, and, while we're keeping the door open, we may be realistic about it and realize that we don't have adequately trained students at this moment who are capable of taking a full course in the classics. Therefore, we suggest that there should be at least instruction in Latin, in ancient history, and in the introduction to classical literature through the various excellent translations." This dilemma continued throughout the nine year span of the original College, to its detriment.[8]

Brown Becomes Dean, and Nairn Chosen to Be President

In February 1965, Dr. D. Mackenzie Brown, who had served as academic consultant for the previous year, was appointed Dean of the College by the Board. This made official the break with the old conception of college. Prescott College would move away from the traditional models of higher education: it would become a school oriented toward contemporary and future curricula, experimental and experiential philosophy and methodology.

Dr. Ronald C. Nairn, who was in some ways Brown's protégé, was chosen to be the first *operational* President. A press release issued by Vic Lytle, on behalf of the PC Board of Trustees, dated March 24, 1965, announced his appointment. In the first paragraph they also recognized "the vision and initiative which Dr. Charles Franklin Parker brought to the task of preparing the way for the new college," therefore "the Board has conferred upon him permanent title of Founding President." Nairn's biography was released for publication through several outlets; the following is from the College publication, *Prescott College Progress*:

> Dr. Nairn is a Professor of Political Science at the University of California at Santa Barbara. He holds a B.A. degree from the University of Canterbury in New Zealand and the M.A. and PhD degrees from Yale University.
>
> He is recognized as an authority on Southeast Asia, and his forthcoming book on the sociological and political problems of foreign aid in the area will be published shortly by the Yale University Press. A further study on issues of ideological confrontations in Southeast Asia is in preparation.
>
> Dr. Nairn was formerly the New Zealand representative on the South East Asia Treaty Organization (SEATO). He has lived with the Hill tribes of Thailand and Laos and has traveled more than 50,000 miles in the remote interior of these disputed areas. He has an intensive knowledge of Southeast Asia countries generally as a result of World War II experience and subsequent diplomatic and research activity in the region.

During his service on SEATO Dr. Nairn had close personal relationships with diplomatic leaders in the United States and other member countries in that organization. He is also a consultant for the Rand Corporation, an organization responsible for preparing international studies for the United States government.

The new President will undertake his duties soon after leaving the University of California (Santa Barbara) at the end of this academic year. His primary educational interest is in the small liberal arts college which he feels to be an essential element in modern higher education, wielding an influence in the intellectual and public life of the Western world far beyond the number of students and faculty involved in this educational segment.

Among his other responsibilities as President of Prescott College Dr. Nairn will be immediately concerned with the initiation of the building program to be started shortly on the attractive 240 acre site north of Prescott. [44]

This announcement was actually incorrect in terms of campus size. At this point there were nearly 400 acres. It also underplays the importance of the Rand Corporation affiliation. Rand was then one of the most important think tanks in the world, and was involved in higher education. Rand is still a major force in research into social change, future studies, and projections for such clients as major universities, the U.S. government, and military and multinational corporations.

At his installation, Nairn also paid tribute to Parker and the Board, saying, "I am inspired by the plan of this college which has been so ably conceived and initiated by Dr. Parker and the Trustees. I look forward to a challenging educational experience at Prescott and hope that the Founding President will continue to have an active interest in the success of the work which lies ahead.

Changing of the Guard

The new leadership was very disappointed by Cumerford's and Parker's fundraising results and tended to blame it on Parker, as indicated in several letters and memos to him. In response to a particularly unkind letter, Parker wrote to the Board, "Since I was not a party to the discussions with President Nairn prior to his election by the Board, and since I do not have at hand his memorandum of March 25, 1965, I am only now aware of the matters referred to therein."

Parker responded defensively in his own long memo dated June 24, 1965, acknowledging that Cumerford's plan had not produced the five million dollars everyone had hoped for in order to open the College in proper style. He reminded the Board and Nairn of the million dollars in pledges that hometown campaign had produced, saying he had personally transmitted $785,522 from Phoenix. He apologized for not having been able to penetrate the "power structure" of Phoenix, and he agreed that Nairn's proposal to go to large donors was now the strategy they must take. He pledged himself to work hard with the contacts he had in hand and "raise every dollar that I can."[67]

Shortly after receiving Parker's memo, the Board reiterated Parker's permanent title of Founding President, and formalized an action taken earlier at its meeting on March 13, 1965, awarding him an annual stipend of $15,000. "You will also be entitled to reasonable and actual expenses subject to provisions set in each year's operating budget. While your general responsibilities have substantially decreased, the Board felt that your past experience should enable you to continue with fund raising activity on a significant scale. With this expectation in mind, the Board concurs that you should continue to live in Phoenix and approves continuance of your rent subsidy at its present rate."

Clearly the Board and Nairn wanted to confirm the change in presidency and retire Parker as gently as possible. Parker commanded much respect and affection in Prescott and among those working so hard to build the College. It illustrates his fine character that he continued to work for the College. He sent letters to all the planning councils and symposium participants and major donors announcing that "a time to which we have long looked has come! President Ronald C. Nairn and his family are now arrived in Prescott and a new day of reality has come in the life of Prescott College." The letters were sent out between July 23 and August 8.[68]

If Parker's feelings had been somewhat soothed, Nairn, in his blunt fashion, rubbed salt in the wound by sending a memo demanding that Parker refrain from interacting with any of the new fundraising contacts he was making.

Not to excuse Nairn's bad manners, this rather insensitive treatment of a founder can be understood by taking into account the truly disappointing results of the Southwest-wide effort. The Archives contain many versions of their plans, and it is clear the fundraising plan that they had first attempted, to raise money mostly through church contacts, failed. Finally Parker gave up that plan, and apparently sent Cumerford home. Parker then concentrated on opening up what he called "the establishment" in Phoenix. This was a more promising approach, but it was too late to earn the needed dollars by 1965; the college's opening was growing closer. Letters and memos in both archives indicate that the new president, Nairn, had little patience for small-scale fundraising. He boasted, "I don't know how to ask for less than a million dollars." Expanding the insult, Nairn then asked Parker to locate indefinitely in Phoenix and not return to Prescott.

Parker responded just as bluntly, "As far as the Parkers are concerned, Prescott is our home." He assured Nairn he would remove himself altogether from administration of the College when they returned to Prescott. He also said he would give a full accounting of fundraising and donors, to James E. Patrick, Campaign Chairman. He offered to continue editing *Progress*. He concluded by saying, "I think I should say that we do not feel that I would be the one to seek to direct a hot high pressure campaign in Phoenix . ...." After a few months, Parker closed the Phoenix office, shipped cabinets full of fundraising campaign records to Prescott, and then moved back. Later in reminiscence he wrote, "We have come a long way in the past eleven years when no one really thought that a college in Prescott would come into being. These have been times of disappointment and joy, near defeat and finally attainment. I have had my part. I have run my lap in the race."

Nairn Launches Larger Scale Fundraising Effort, and Internal Austerity

Nairn's new President's Council was announced in *Prescott College Progress #3*,[44] August 1965.[70] This body, composed of twenty-two very influential business and political leaders, was headed by Barry Goldwater, who was a five-term U.S. Senator from Arizona (1953–65, 1969–87) and the Republican Party candidate for President in 1964. Some of the members had also been members of the Symposium group, and all were obviously chosen because they had access to big money. Here are some of the members: Lorna Lockwood, Chief Justice of the Arizona Supreme Court; Henry Luce, Editorial Chairman of Time-Life; David C. Lincoln, President of Bagdad Copper Corp.; Walker McCune of the McCune Foundation, Inc.[80]

Simultaneously Nairn imposed an austerity regime as indicated in this memo of July 14, 1965, which read: "Soon Prescott College will promulgate its operating budget. This must be allied with the capital commitments arising from the other immediate problem of plant activation. I need not tell you that relative to the expenditures which lie before us, our financial resources are desperately slender. There is a necessary and foreseen commitment for every penny. In this note I wish to stress two things. Firstly, every possible step must be taken to conserve funds both in your daily and long term operations. Secondly, I would ask for your understanding when I seemingly make demands upon you to exercise economies. Here the reason is not economy for economy's sake. Rather it is economy geared to bringing Prescott College to life, an event which you will agree is in the interest of all of us."

Nairn spent much of that year building recognition for the College and himself, and courting large-scale donors with the advice and assistance of Barry Goldwater and other influential leaders. Brown was building the faculty, many of whom came on board during that year to help design the curriculum and academic processes. Frank Mertz, a talented businessman, was hired to create the business office and oversee building and other functions.

A news release by Brown, dated November 26, 1965, named two Arizona students the first accepted for the Charter Class, and promised the Charter Catalog would be published by September. Registration was set for Monday-Tuesday, September 26-27.

On August 21, 1965, the Board of Directors signed a contract with Tanner Construction Co. to begin building. Breaking ground on the new campus was a celebration for the town of Prescott and for everyone who had contributed. There were just fourteen months left for building before students would arrive on campus.

Preparing for the opening was exhilarating, a period of great expectations, but the excitement masked the serious problem of inadequate funds. The Cumerford feasibility study had indicated they would need to raise between five and ten million dollars just to open, and at least a million of those dollars should come from local sources in order to "prime the pump." A million dollars from local donors had been pledged; however, only a portion of this money was in the bank when Nairn took over. Despite a well organized fundraising campaign carried out by the Congregationalist Church and town leaders, the bigger money pump hadn't worked as planned. Nairn had abruptly dropped the efforts to raise money through churches and small-scale fund drives. His pursuit of bigger fish had some success.

THE FOUNDING OF YAVAPAI COLLEGE

In the meantime, the town turned its attention to the founding of Yavapai College, which would be very important for Prescott, and would fulfill many of the dreams the townspeople had about a place for their own children. It was affordable because it was publicly financed through county taxes. It offered traditional academic preparation in a two-year pre-university curriculum, and vocational training, retirement classes, sports and arts activities, and venues for cultural enrichment. Much of the energy that could have gone into Prescott College went into Yavapai College.

CHANGES IN DIRECTION BECOME CONSOLIDATED

The College departed significantly from its original conception as a Christian-oriented local school as a result of the broad-based academic horsepower of the Symposium. The changes instituted in the two and a half years after the Symposium were irreversible, yet there is no indication in the archives that anyone noticed or was not in accord with the new directions. Before the Symposium, Parker had assumed he would serve the college in some important role, possibly as its president or board chairman, but he accepted his diminished position with apparent good will. In the process of reorientation, the dreams and expectations of the town were absorbed into a larger conception of what a college is, whom it should serve, and how it should look and feel. The College was still named *Prescott* College. It was still an object of the town's attention and pride. But their belief that the College would serve the town as an educational center and school for their own children seemed to have slipped through their fingers. Many of the donation pledges were never paid. It was clear that Prescott College would be opening to, and serving, a very specialized out-of-town clientele.

AUTHOR'S TRIBUTE TO DR. CHARLES FRANKLIN PARKER

Dr. Charles Franklin Parker, the Founding President of Prescott College, was a leader possessed of a transcendent vision: a great institution serving the Southwest in the tradition of Harvard, Yale, and fifty other schools established by the Congregationalists in America. He had the drive to realize his dream and launch an educational institution with a progressive mission to educate leaders for the twenty-first century.

Parker was born in Albany, Missouri, on December 15, 1902, into a third-generation pioneer family. He graduated from the University of Missouri in 1929 and entered the Chicago Theological Seminary, where he received a Bachelor of Divinity degree in 1932 and was later honored with a Doctor of Divinity degree. Parker came to Prescott, Arizona, in 1934 to serve as head pastor of the First Congregational Church, where he served until 1963, when he retired from the ministry to dedicate his full time to the creation of Prescott College. During his service as minister he was also involved in church and town development, state and national educational government and education. He organized the Yavapai Cooperative Parish through which four new Congregational Churches in the Prescott vicinity were established. He was the exchange preacher to Britain on the American British Exchange Program in 1962. He was often called on to be Chaplain in the Arizona State Legislature, and was Chaplain to the G.O.P. state conventions of 1952 and 1956. He was a leader in the International Committee for Underprivileged Children and president and campaign coordinator of the Arizona Society for Crippled Children. He was governor of the Southwest District Kiwanis and served as Grand Prelate of the Knights Templar of Arizona and the Sovereign Red Cross of Constantine. In 1960, he was named Prescott Man of the Year and was awarded a gold medallion for outstanding community and statewide service by the University of Arizona. A recognized authority on Southwest history, he was a prolific writer, publishing many articles and two books of inspirational literature.

Parker was a man of big infectious dreams and prodigious energy. Victor Lytle, who moved to Prescott the same year as the Parkers—and was a partner in founding the College—described Parker as a "consummate politician." Jim Stuckey, the fourth president, enlisted Parker to help reestablish the College in 1975. Parker described himself to Stuckey as a "man of the cloth," but he went on to say he was also a "savvy operator." Prescott's local Sharlot Hall Museum has a voluminous collection of Parker's papers, including his work in establishing Prescott College.

At a Board-sponsored dinner in 1965 celebrating Parker's leadership in founding Prescott College, Lytle commented, "I think Franklin has been too modest—these things [gaining church and secular support, establishing the corporation, securing the campus land, raising $1 million in pledges] didn't happen by accident. Franklin laid a fine and firm groundwork and there has been a careful step by step progress."

I met him toward the end of his life. He was still an imposing figure of medium height, with silver hair and the face of a friendly bulldog. He was an avid talker, a philosopher, and a promoter in one.

Dr. Parker died at the age of 80 on August 22, 1983, after a long illness.

The Original Prescott College, 1966-72

◇◇◇◇◇◇

A Great Adventure to Prepare
Leaders for the Twenty-First Century

Prescott College was opened to the charter class of eighty students on September 26, 1966. A small student body of enthusiastic students on a brand new campus set in the natural piñon and chaparral generated an electric atmosphere. They came from every area of the country, one from East Asia.

Less than a third of them were from the Southwest, and only a few from Arizona. Some came for adventure, but many came to gain the knowledge and tools to contribute to a new and better world. They were to be the charter class and to help create a new kind of school. They had been recruited with the idea that this was no ordinary college, that the curriculum was revolutionary, and that the new faculty was the best, and they wanted to believe it. They were bright and creative, and eager to move into to their dorm suites, explore the pristine wild environments, kick a soccer ball around the "polo field," and investigate the horse stables, gossip with their new friends, stand on central hill and gaze at the spectacular sky—and to get started. Everything was new. It was nothing less than the embryo of a College of the Future.

As recently as the previous year, Nairn had been predicting a charter class of around 250 students. But in the fall of 1966 the College facilities and organization really were not ready to receive many more than 80. There were just as many other people working on campus—construction workers and technicians, cooks and maintenance workers, office staff, administrators, and faculty.

At the inauguration celebration for Nairn, held on October 23, 1966, many "notables" were brought to the campus, including the dean of the College of Liberal Arts, University of Arizona, the presidents of Arizona State University and Northern Arizona University, as well as delegates from

regions	states	student #s	% of total
Prescott	Hometown AZ	19	7.3%
Rest of state	Non-Prescott AZ	33	12.7%
Reservations	Arizona (Native Americans)	2	0.8%
Subtotal all Arizona			20.8%
West Coast	California, Hawaii	45	17.4%
Upper Midwest	Missouri, Iowa, Kansas, Minnesota, Wisconsin, Michigan, Illinois, Indiana, Ohio	29	11.2%
Lower Mountain West	Colorado, New Mexico	27	10.4%
Northwest	Oregon, Washington, Alaska	22	8.5%
D.C. area	D.C., Virginia, Pennsylvania, Maryland	15	5.8%
Lone Star	Texas	14	5.4%
Eastern Elites	New York, New Jersey, Connecticut, Rhode Island	13	5.0%
Southeast	Oklahoma, Arkansas, Tennessee, Kentucky, West Virginia, No. Carolina, So. Carolina, Georgia, Florida, Alabama, Mississippi, Louisiana	12	4.6%
Upper New England	New Hampshire, Maine	12	4.6%
Upper Mountain West	Idaho, Utah, Wyoming, Montana, Nebraska, So. Dakota, No. Dakota	8	3.1%
Left-over Desert	Nevada	4	1.5%
Overseas	Tibet, Taiwan, New Caledonia, Nigeria	4	1.5%
		259	

Table 1. Where Prescott College Students Came From, 1966–71

twenty-three other colleges and universities throughout the nation. Board Chairman Dr. Laurence M. Gould and President Nairn dedicated the College to its purpose and its future. [44]

Nairn, the new face of the College, was a dynamic but enigmatic figure. He was considered by some who knew him socially as gracious, urbane, well educated, witty, and talkative. Anne Dorman, who worked with him as a student intern, said her main impression of him was of "a super promoter—the kind of guy who could make things happen."[50] He certainly had no interest in rural Prescott, Arizona, as a place to live, and as soon as the College could budget for it he built a fine President's House on a ridge above the working campus, with a vista of the rolling, wild hills, and a picture window facing west to take in the spectacular Arizona sunsets.

New Buildings Almost Ready

The students soon settled into the routine of the college. Small classes with an open seminar style were the most common format, but this was not the only mode. Field work and laboratory sessions were also an integral part of their program. As much as feasible, the school was self-governing and operated through an ethical code called the Honor Conscience. There were no exam proctors to watch for cheating and no monitors for the dormitories—the students were asked to set reasonable and respectful rules. And food services, grading systems, internal communications were openly available to everyone. The library was open twenty-four hours every day under the trust of the students. It operated open stacks and students were authorized to check books out and in with no security system. This Honor Conscience System was a self-pledged and self-enforced standard of ethics requiring personal integrity and academic honesty of all students. The campus wasn't locked up tight. A student could have access to the auditorium at any time where a practice piano was available. The system was made possible by the fact that the campus was located off a main road about six miles from town, making it a relatively isolated and contained community, so there was a sense of security and little concern about abuse of the system coming from without the campus. The language about Honor Conscience does not appear in Catalogs after 1969, but the spirit of honor and respect was established. With the 1970 Catalog such issues were referred to the Community Advisory Committee, an elected body of students, faculty, administration, and trustees who gathered regularly to discuss and make recommendations to the President on any area of concern within the academic community.

CREATING A CULTURE AS WELL AS AN ACADEMIC PROGRAM

As the months passed, the College became its own diverse world with its unique stories and crises, each student finding a personal interest or cause. On large urban campuses, burning issues of justice and peace were more proximate, because the military draft and the Vietnam War were in progress. At Prescott College students' advocacy idealism tended to revolve around environmental rather than political or social causes. Students reserved their protests for conservation issues such as demonstrating about the bulldozing of the over-hundred-year-old junipers and scrub oaks on campus. They had no stories about attending big anti-war rallies or Woodstock-like events, but many stories about running out of water for a few hours, encountering mountain lion or elk in the forest, almost stepping on a coiled rattlesnake on the trail, getting lost by taking the wrong fork in a remote side canyon. While students were learning the same basic materials as their friends in conventional schools back home, they felt they were learning in a setting and by a methodology they couldn't have anticipated.

In 1966-67, when student protests throughout the country were at their height, college-aged people everywhere were feeling less inhibited and more self-empowered to express radical opinions and veer from traditional mores. While there were many very conservative students on the campus, a few

Dorms with Natural Landscaping

of the new students experiencing their first time away from home became "instant hippies," meaning wearing thrift store clothes and going barefoot. One professor barred students from class unless they were properly shod and dressed. But as Noel Caniglia, a charter class student, recalls, "It doesn't take very many hippies [to project that image] when you're in Prescott, Arizona, in the late '60s, early '70s. ... It was a cultural mismatch."[61]

Many people in town were excited to have the new College underway, but many more felt they had lost their College to out-of-towners. It wasn't just the look of the new students walking around town; there had been no vigorous recruiting or offering of scholarships to local students. While a hundred or so Prescott people worked and made their living at the campus and the school brought money into the community, Prescott's young people were not in attendance. Prescott College had ceased to be "Prescott's college."

Local perception of Prescott College somehow evolved into a half-myth that it had become a playschool for the rich and famous. It is true that many students came from privileged families and had attended private high schools, but the majority of them were middle class and some had worked for long periods to save money in order to come to this special College.

It is true that the College had it own polo field and stable. In Arizona ranch country, a polo field smacked of elitism. But the students didn't play polo; instead they used that square of lawn for soccer games. There were regular weekend and late-afternoon soccer games. And the students eventually organized an official Prescott College team and entered into the Arizona state tournament. Miraculously, one year Prescott College defeated the three state universities and won the championship. The stable owned a few horses that were not offered as pastime for the leisured wealthy, but were used as an

Campus L-shaped Pool; Field House and Soccer Green in Background

integral part of the curriculum and were the first experience most students had had working with animals. To pay expenses, the horses were rented out at a modest fee, and were occasionally used for equestrian outings.

The campus also had a swimming complex north of the central courtyard. The pool was at least as large as an Olympic pool, but styled like an L-shaped resort pool so it could not be used to swim exercise laps or races. Real sport diving would be dangerous—the board was too short and the pool too shallow. Yet as a showpiece it was very well built with ample decks, pool furniture and bath house facilities. With typical creativity, outdoor action classes and white water enthusiasts made constant use of the splendid L-shaped resort pool by practicing kayak maneuvers like Eskimo rolls, and launching themselves—in their kayaks—off the snub-nosed eight-foot diving board. Of course, sunbathing and socializing took place there year round.

Along with the fun of being a charter class on a new campus and the added stimulation of being part of the '60s generation, Prescott College students were offered a chance, and indeed pushed, to develop their individuality. In the second half of the Symposium, Parker had called it "THE EXISTENTIAL," and those discussions not only encompassed religious impulses, morals and ethics, ambitions, desire to serve, and respect for peoples' rights, but also an appreciation of individual difference. This essential dimension of "the existential" acknowledged students' need to find and develop their personhood. Carl Rogers's book *On Becoming a Person* had become the standard for personal growth movement literature in the 1960s. Prescott College adopted one of Rogers's lines as a slogan: "Education is a Journey, Not a Destination."

Student Studying on Granite

1966-67—First Year's Curriculum

Despite all of the rhetoric about futuristic curricula and interdisciplinary study in the Symposium Report, ***Emergence of a Concept***, the actual curriculum offered to the students of the charter class was highly conventional, as is evident in the 1966 Charter Catalog and Bulletins. The curricular offerings were organized into the three traditional divisions: (1) Humanities, (2) Natural Science, and (3) Social Sciences. However, the text of the Charter Catalog does promise interdisciplinary or multi-disciplinary study: "Anthropology, with all its traditional interests in cultural variability, culture history, language, race, and human evolution is a prime integrator of much that is important concerning man and his manifold behaviors" (Robert Euler); "As a mediator between feeling and thought, Art has always expressed man's most intimate concerns, his judgments, values, and religious beliefs" (Fred Sommer); " ... religious studies ... is concerned with the basic premises and philosophical foundations of the great civilizations and is integrally related to the disciplines of history, philosophy, anthropology, science and the arts" (Mackenzie Brown). The charter year was the first opportunity to have a student body and a full faculty working together. They designed a sweeping change, the structure of interdisciplinary centers resembling small university graduate institutes.

Amid All the Ferment over Higher Edification, a New School Politely Thumbs Its Nose at Tradition

by Jerry Eaton, 1967

The solemn strains of "Pomp and Circumstance" will not be heard at graduation ceremonies at Prescott College this month because there will be no graduation.

Even if there were (impossible because this private liberal arts school in its first year accommodates freshmen only), "Spanish Flea" or "King of the Road" or "Concerto No. 2 in C Minor" by Rachmaninoff conceivably might be substituted for the traditional processional music.

Such a departure, such a detour from the routine would cause no uplifted brows because Prescott College politely thumbs its nose at tradition.

This is quite appropriate, because it was conceived as a "community of scholars" to combat the "academic schizophrenia" of the twentieth century. It scorns tradition in many ways, including curriculum, architecture, student-teacher ratio, and viewpoint on mankind. Academic departments have been eliminated—junked—and students plug in their intellectual batteries to four major areas—anthropology, language and literature, science and systems, and civilizations.

The twenty-two brown slump block buildings on the 240-acre [*sic.*] site six miles north of Prescott complement rather than dominate the environment. They are designed to serve the needs of the school and not dictate them.

Prescott College has a philosophy of "rigidity be damned" in architecture. A building used for one purpose today may be pressed into operation for something else next week or next month or next year. The cafeteria, for example, will be converted to an arts center. Architects designed it with an easy transition in mind in keeping with guidelines established for every building on campus.

Besides a curriculum designed to produce what Dr. Buchanan Cargal, dean of the college, terms "cultural revolutionaries" and architecture subordinate to function, Prescott College prides itself on a low student-teacher ratio, 5 to 1 this year.

The fifteen faculty members are what Dr. Ronald C. Nairn, the forty-three-year-old founding president, calls "the best money can buy." Then he continues as he stabs a finger toward your chest for emphasis, "And don't think money isn't important to teachers. Tales about dedicated teachers content to work for peanuts are ridiculous."

Teachers are as free as the students and almost as uninhibited. Although classes average 1 1/2 hours in length, the professors may talk 20 minutes or beyond 90 minutes. They encourage comments from students, verbal interaction in class, healthy debates, and an occasional argument to let off steam.

"We don't break life into fifty-minute units," Cargal said. "In addition to flexible scheduling, we are blessed as a private college in not being compelled to furnish what is required by popular demand like the state universities. The central and comforting aspect of a private school is that it can discriminate."

The Socratic method of teaching, which has poked its head up periodically since the Golden Age of Greece, is embraced and tenderly kissed by Prescott College. Cargal qualifies as the Socrates of the campus, teaching a mathematics class that has only two students.

Prescott College refuses to allow its students to specialize themselves into extinction. Faculty members say the mechanism for survival and leadership tomorrow is flexibility. They try to teach students to see the world as a whole, to realize that the body of knowledge is indivisible and that a particular field of study is but a part of civilization.

"A discipline or a profession is understood within its cultural context," Cargal said. "Maybe the student likes poetry, but a poet is only half real if he doesn't know the meanings of the world he's writing from."

Nairn, a native Irishman who was reared in New Zealand and lived in Asia, leaned back in a plush blue chair in his office, studied some modern art framed on the walls and said in a clipped British accent:

"I became president here because this is a new college. It is free to take fresh approaches, free to improvise and experiment. Old colleges can't innovate, they don't change and neither do many of the intellectuals within their walls." Nairn, an acknowledged expert on Southeast Asia and a former professor of political science at the University of California, designed the campus, supervises some of the construction, travels thousands of miles soliciting funds to operate the College, and even teaches a couple of classes.

A New Zealand Air Force fighter pilot twice wounded in World War II, Nairn scoffs at statements of students that the college is loaded with money. He concedes, however, that he anticipates a balanced budget in the mid-1970s with an average faculty salary of $24,000. Gifts totaling high in the six figures have been showered on Prescott College by some of the more prominent families and individuals in the nation.

The national organization of the Congregational Church helped get the school started with a grant of $250,000, but has no tangible control of the College. Prescott citizens raised $1 million, and there was a grant of $600,000 from the Kettering Fund, controlled by the Kettering family of Denver and Ohio.

Walking outside the administration building, Nairn gestured toward a rolling plain, once an Indian battleground, sweeping north and east and into a ranching valley.

"Someday this college will have five campuses, one hundred and eighty buildings, and eighteen hundred students," he said. "We won't construct multistory giants to perpetuate our ego. I feel we have the space to build a great number of classrooms in which small groups will meet. Eventually, this will be a self-contained campus with a main street, post office, variety stores, bowling alley, and other buildings."

The library, which now has around 10,000 volumes, will eventually have 300,000. Material on tape will give it the equivalent of one million books.

In its first year, Prescott College has barely scratched the surface of its master plan, but it has created an atmosphere of academic and personal freedom that stamps it as a novel experiment in education.

The seventy-five freshmen come from fourteen states and two foreign countries, pay an annual tuition of $2,500, live in three-bedroom buildings on campus and call professors by their first names. They savor the freedom given to them, including an open dormitory policy in which boys and girls can visit and study together.

Students are permitted to have pets in their rooms, they can check out library books for indefinite periods (a privilege that delights them) and they are spared some of the agony of sweating out grades. Teachers assign students an S for satisfactory, a U for unsatisfactory or, in the case of exceptional scholarship, honors.

Students complain about being a bit lonely, but they'll have company next year when they become sophomores and the enrollment spurts to 225 with the addition of the new freshman class. Their junior year, 1968, enrollment will swell to 1,000. Prescott College will have the full four classes and around 1,500 students in 1969, and the first graduation will be in the spring of 1970.

Then, as now, the anthropological viewpoint will be emphasized in the curriculum and students will work to understand the totality of relationships composing a community or culture or state. Religious and philosophical premises and foundations are linked to the most modern and complex developments in science, technology, art, and social institutions.

"We're trying to give the student an overview, a wider perspective about mankind evolving," Cargal said. "We want him to see the whole puzzle and not just a piece of it. Every attempt is made to relate how civilizations arose, why they place values on certain things and how they relate to one another."

Students consider the curriculum stimulating and the faculty highly competent, but not infallible. They are encouraged to ask questions and present their views during class.

"I don't mind speaking up if I feel I have something intelligent to say," said John Carlisle Lockwood, twenty-two, "I think the most important thing about this college is that it wants the students to express their thoughts verbally and in writing."

Lockwood sat with three other students who chatted for an hour after lunch in the carpeted handsome dining room.

"Just say I have no address right now," Lockwood said. "I like to move around. I may stay here another year, maybe two—who can tell?"

Across from Lockwood, who wore Levis, a dress shirt with tail out, and sandals, sat Stan Jones, twenty, a bearded young man from Phoenix.

"I knew when I inquired about Prescott College that it was the place for me," he said. "In some ways, such as academic freedom, it's too good to be true."

Anna Johnson, eighteen, of Chattanooga, Tenn., said she felt unsure of herself in her first weeks at Prescott College. "It took a lot of the students here a semester to get used to the College's way of presenting material and the sort of relaxed way of doing things," she said. "I guess maybe some of them didn't take the College as seriously as they should have. I was accustomed to receiving grades and I felt I didn't really know where I stood here."

Ed Cooper, twenty-one, of Scottsdale, said he turned to Prescott College when he became "disgusted and disillusioned at Arizona State University."

Cooper said he unsuccessfully tried to persuade his fraternity to admit a Negro. "When I failed, that pretty well finished me as far as Arizona State was concerned," he said. "I sought a college I thought might regard humanity in a more enlightened manner." However, there are no Negroes enrolled at Prescott College.

Lockwood and Cooper visited a friend in an apartment after concluding their conversation in the dining room. Their friend, a red-bearded youth who formerly attended the University of Arizona, was listening to a recording of a folk tune describing a cockroach walking in a bean can.

The three students talked about the guitar technique in the recording and then Cooper excused himself to study in the library. He waved at a student studying on the floor in a corner near a book stack and chatted as he hunted books to help him write a report on Greece, a country he hopes to visit next year.

"Some students sort of feel they're hiding out here at Prescott College, like they're retreating from the world," he said. "Maybe some of us are backing away for awhile to get a better look at ourselves, but we know we have to return to the outside world. There aren't many of us [students] over twenty-one, but those of us who are go into Prescott for fun and games. Big deal—there isn't much to do in Prescott, so we drink beer."

Lockwood wandered into the library, too, and he and Cooper discussed Prescott College's honor code. Cooper said that, boiled down, the code means "no drinking on campus, no drugs on campus, and no promiscuity on campus."

While some students may consider Prescott dull, their impact on the town has been negligible. Most of the students are kept busy by a social schedule at college that includes parties, banquets, dances, receptions, intramural sports, horseback riding (the college has its own stables and corral), hikes, fishing, and skiing.

Scholarship, however, is the crown prince of the campus, the sun around which the students revolve. One student remarked, "My folks aren't shelling out $2,500 a year for amusement. They want results and I'm expected to produce."

The curriculum is enticing, but challenging, too. Students attend classes in art of literature, religious traditions of the American Indian, Hispanic civilization, Asian civilization, art and aesthetics, anthropology, drama, natural science, real numbers, and dance.

Although courses in religion are taught as they relate to civilizations, Nairn questions the relevancy of the church in society today. The church and education may be two lost souls on the highway of life, he says.

"Education doesn't know where it is going except, perhaps, vocational education," he said. "In education and everything else, we are the most dynamic and rapidly changing society in history. We are the people in ferment."

If education in general is lost in an intellectual wasteland, Prescott College in particular forges ahead, lantern in hand, to provide light in the darkness, Nairn says.

"We feel we know where we're headed and we are particularly challenged to help the student gain a sensible comprehension of culture."

In a rugged, rural environment, students at Prescott College are learning how to live in a society that is becoming increasingly more computerized and mechanistic.

"The computer is a language, but it does not solve intellectual problems," Nairn said. "It extends them, however, and here is its intellectual importance. The computer has a language of its own and I seriously suggest that scholars had better learn the language before this century is over. Similarly, science has always been a language; math is a supreme language.

"Now, if our contemporary culture in science is technologically oriented, why do we still insist that college German is a 'must' to an understanding of Goethe, but exhibit a pristine reluctance to learning mathematics, which I suggest might be essential to the understanding of our culture?"

To cope with the advance of technology, Prescott College seeks teachers aware of the computer and who are artists, theologians, psychologists, and sociologists. So-called "well rounded" professors are hard to come by, but Nairn feels he has them. The institution's charter faculty includes teachers from Stanford, Yale, Princeton, and Cornell. There also are professors from Spain and Belgium.

While language is taught on a new level and related to other disciplines, the basic pattern applies to all four teaching and research centers at the college.

Students are being taught systems that are inherent in a technological culture, whether they are systems of the corporation, the bureaucracy, or jet aircraft.

"Our life is somewhat fused with systems in this technological culture and yet at the undergraduate level, little is being done to incorporate the implication and nature of systems in an educational plan," Nairn said.

To those who say Prescott College has made an auspicious start in curriculum to prepare students for the twenty-first century, Nairn retorts, "You haven't seen anything yet—huh!" He tacks on the word "huh" to sentences to drive home a point.

Next year he intends to offer a course titled Peasantry and Existentialism. Another new course, Science and the Roman Catholic Church, will be taught by a Franciscan priest released by his order to teach. They will be additions to the Center for Comparative Civilization, which views the Western world and Asia from the standpoint of land form, climate, ethnic patterns, and ecology. Study of these land areas receives particular emphasis.

Nairn, a representative to the Southeast Asia Treaty Organization, terms the Center for Comparative Civilizations "the great integrator."

Arizona's wide open spaces, which once inspired a writer to compose the song "Ragtime Cowboy Joe," convinced the College's founding fathers that a private school was an economic possibility in this young state.

On the undulating countryside, facilities were built for less than half the national average cost—less than $2,500 per student. The climate also was utilized toward cost reduction. In the average college facility, some 30 percent of the floor space is occupied by corridors, stairways, lift-ways, and cul-de-sacs. With single story structures, stairs and lifts are not needed.

"The tax-free status (of Prescott College) offers a potential cost reduction of significant proportions as opposed to regular contracting," Nairn said. "Because of our prolific use of land and our sprawling campus we have managed to blend buildings with flora and terrain. Often, we have adjusted building sites to save a tree, and the results have been a high degree of natural beauty in the campus construction."

What Nairn saves on buildings, he spends on people—the faculty. Many leading educators across America applied for positions at Prescott College, and Nairn hired those he considered the most competent.

"People are more important than things at a college," he said. "Teachers are more important than buildings. Without a knowledgeable faculty, a college is a hypocrite."

Prescott College is concerned first and last with a student's scholarship. It will never participate in intercollegiate sports, Dean Cargal said.

"Students aren't chosen on the basis of how much they weigh or whether they are tall enough to stuff a basketball," he said. "It is hard enough to find academically motivated students, much less recruit athletes."

"It's machines and societies and sciences. What I'm talking about is a new and unique synthesis of the humanities, social sciences and natural sciences, and technology."

For a youngster, Prescott College is quite a promoter; a salesman with a ten-gallon hat. Nairn says securing money is one of his most important responsibilities. To obtain it, he visits the individual donors from whom come 80 percent of the funds to operate private schools in this country. Foundations, industry, and other organizations contribute the remainder.

Advertising conscious, the college lures students with such copy as: " … We're looking for the young man or woman who wants to meet tomorrow's world head on instead of escape from it—the kind of person who, when the days get windy, yearns for wings instead of shelter. Prescott wants the 'C' student with determination, the 'B' student with leadership potential, the 'A' student with concerns wider than his books.

"If you already have 'all the answers,' if you are now about to close your mind and open your mouth and start thinking in slogans, we can't teach you anything. But if you are willing to make a real commitment to prepare your-self to the best of your ability for a meaningful and effective life in a troubled but promising world, let us hear from you."

If the advertising copy is successful and if projections of enrollment are correct, Prescott College will reach the maximum 1,800 students in six years.

What then—what about the student-teacher ratio, the curriculum defy-ing the traditional?

"We won't become trapped in our bigness," Nairn said. "This college was created, among other reasons, to stimulate mental gymnastics between teacher and student, to give both of them a voice that is loud and clear, to help the individual to blossom."

Nairn squinted at the rolling land on which future buildings of the col-lege will rise.

"We won't permit the college to have more than 1,800 students," he said. "If it appears it will exceed that number—well, the answer is obvious."

He paused, shrugged, and then said: "We just might build another col-lege."

Interdisciplinary Programs:
1967 through 1973

◇◇◇◇◇◇◇

*"What I learned at Prescott College was
to read, to write, and to think."*
GERALD REED, GRADUATING CLASS OF 1975

The second year opened with well over a hundred new recruits, increasing the student body to 172. In contrast to the conventional charter year curriculum, the second was innovative and well organized around the three principles of unity, respect for the disciplines, and flexibility that had been outlined in the Symposium.

In place of the conventional departmental structure, the curriculum was organized into four interdisciplinary "Teaching and Research Centers" designed to foster new modes of teaching and learning, to help the College break out of the traditional lecture and reading—test and grade—process so ensconced in conventional schools. The Centers were organized around real-world critical issues. They forged links between such fields as environmental sciences, societal studies, systems theory, natural sciences, civilizations, writing, literature, and the arts. By triangulating on the same set of issues, scholars, artists, and scientists with diverse training could cooperate in the atmosphere of a think tank, laboratory, or field station. Real research by teachers working with students promoted initiative and self-direction.

The evolution of Prescott College's original curriculum was quite complicated.

Table 2 outlines the development of the various components, entities, centers, programs, and consolidations that came, and sometimes went, over this period. Hopefully it will help to place the narrative in context.

	CURRICULUM CONFIGURATION	HISTORICAL CONTEXT
1963	From the 1966 Symposium—characteristics of the new college: • mission of preparing young people to be leaders in the 21st century, • ethical/spiritual emphasis, • strong education in the humanities, • address emerging environmental problems, • provide high quality private education for the Southwest and northern Mexico • Prescott College, "Harvard of the West," to assume leadership in higher education in terms of innovative curriculum & teaching/learning methodologies.	Dr. Charles Franklin Parker, Founding President, sets up a conference of state and national community leaders, secures over 500 acres, and raises over $1 million in donations and pledges.
1966-67	Charter Catalog lists traditional subject areas in the three "departments" of **Humanities, Natural Sciences**, and **Social Sciences**: Art, Biological Science, Dance, English and Comp. Lit., Historical Studies, Mathematics, Physical Science, Religious Studies, French, and Spanish	College opens with 80 students on a new campus still under construction; Dr. Ronald Nairn, first Operating President.
1967– 1975	Leadership Institute Established Outdoor Action/Wilderness Exploration Program begins. Orientation for all new students. Leadership Institute manages orientation and outdoor programs, experiential self-directed educational methods.	Receive substantial support from DeWitt Wallace, Reader's Digest Foundation. Much favorable national publicity.
1967– 1975	Four "Centers" created (somewhat like Departments): Civilizations Center / Systems Center / Language & Literature Center / Anthropological Studies Center	Curricular stability. Faculty and student body remain small. Tension around "classical" vs. "new" educational paradigms.
1970-75	Fifth Center added—The Center for the Person, patterned after "The Center for the Study of the Person" founded by Carl Rogers in La Jolla, California. Wilderness Orientation put under management of "5th Center."	Several new faculty members brought in from La Jolla and other parts. Received financing from Charles F. Kettering II
1971– 1973	Nairn and Board set up two more separate corporate entities—the Corporation and the Schole. When added to The Leadership Institute (with Outdoor Action), and Prescott College (which was the umbrella for all of the curricular Centers), there were now four entities, located on campus.	Arizona Corporation Commission accepts petition to change the name of the corporation to "The Prescott Institutions, Inc." Nairn appointed Chancellor. Two major donors pass away.

	CURRICULUM CONFIGURATION	HISTORICAL CONTEXT
1973-74 and 1ˢᵗsem 1974-75	The FRED committee recommends collapsing the four entities into one College with many more "liberal" features. Board recombines all entities and regains Prescott College name and corporation. First Year Curriculum tried—eight one-month blocks for new students.	"Prescott Institutions" prove too expensive. Arab Oil Embargo produces rocketing interest rates. Campus closed Dec. 18, 1974. Bankruptcy filed Jan. 1975.

Table 2. Permutations of "Old" Prescott College's Curricular Offerings, 1963–1975

THE TEACHING AND RESEARCH CENTER FOR LANGUAGE AND LITERARY STUDIES

The largest of the four, this Center encompassed literary studies and written and oral expression; reading of literature was essential. Communications of all types were studied. This center was charged with helping students improve their skills in oral and written communication—although all four Centers had this mission. This Center sought to identify the elements and processes of communication in the arts, as they exist in electronic technology, in social intercourse, in the world of advertising and all media. It encompassed the languages of sense, form, visual, symbolism, and myth. This included computer language, studies of media, science and technology—especially mathematics—new linguistics, mythic and symbolic aspects of art and religion. It also embraced some studies of cultures and societies, particularly Hispanic civilization. A surprising detail is that the study of foreign languages was not placed in this Center, but rather was in the mission of the Civilizations Center.

In a report to the Board, Nairn acknowledges that the Language Center encountered some difficulties because it "encompassed many diverse ideas and personalities. Each seems to have its own idea about how things ought to go and this is fine as long as there can be dialogue rather than the view, 'if it does not go my way, I will take my marbles and go home.' Nevertheless, the issue of the Center's main thrust seems to be resolving itself. ..." Nairn goes on to praise the newly appointed director of the Center: "He has come forth with some remarkable ideas and methodologies. These seem to be obtaining faculty support ... as the Center is developing, it is focusing around Literature, History, Religion, Art and Philosophy. ... I might add here, however, that within Philosophy I naturally include Science and Formal Logic. After a fairly difficult year, I have great hopes that this Center has found its feet."[46]

The Teaching & Research Center for Systems

Systems theory has always been a guiding aspect of civilizations in one form or another, but in the 1960s the "Systems Approach" was being applied in practically every intellectual, industrial, commercial, and sociological/ psychological field, as exemplified by the work of Kurt Lewin in his theory of social change.[87] The Center's mission in the new curriculum was to help students learn to carry out "rational analysis and decision making," and "provide a platform for interdisciplinary study of physical, symbolic, engineering, technological, social, institutional, economic and political systems … as well as the relationships between human and natural systems." At a deeper level, students and faculty at the Systems Center intended to open up studies of chaos and order in both physical and human realms; an area that did not generally enter the conventional higher education curriculum until the 1990s. "The effort in Systems is concerned with the human success and failure to produce order from chaos, and with the human relationship to order and chaos in the physical universe."[40]

According to Nairn, in practice the Center for Systems concentrated mainly on mathematics, chemistry, and to a much lesser degree, physics. This is borne out by reading the actual course offerings over three years. However, more advanced students were delving into the aspects mentioned above though independent studies and research projects.[46]

The Teaching and Research Center for Studies in Civilization

The mission of this Center was to study and teach the common features of most civilizations as well as differences that distinguish them. Students carried out interdisciplinary investigations, blending economic, political, sociological, and religious studies. Those who chose to complete their graduation competences in this Center were required to complete five core studies: World Cultures, Western Civilization, English Language and Literature, The Technological Society, and two quarters of either Art or Music. Then they concentrated on applied social/political investigations. Examples of courses (which they called offerings) demonstrate the interdisciplinary work done in this center: Religion in Confrontation; Violence, Revolution, and War; Liberty, Equality, and Justice; The Technological Society. As discussed in the Symposium, the whole College's program was intended to be centered around the study of civilizations—including American—contemporary technological society, American Indian, Hispanic, and South Asian. An issue that shows through in their literature is the distinction between the concepts of a culture and a civilization. This reveals the political correctness of the day when Native American and other groups were attempting to restore their ethnic roots.

Southwest and Mexican Hispanic culture provided an opportunity to bridge between the Centers. Spanish language instruction was located in the Civilizations Center, and was prerequisite to doing off-campus studies in Latin America or Iberia. The synthesis of Native American cultures with that of early Spanish settlers and Catholic missionaries produced a unique laboratory to investigate how disparate cultures clash and then integrate—or fail to do so—which was of interest to the Systems Center, as well as to the Anthropology Center. The proximity of Mexico with its opportunities for outdoor action in the Sea of Cortez also linked the Civilizations Center to the rest of the College.

There was no emphasis then on political activism and involvement in ongoing movements and issues. They studied social change at the Center, but at a distance, as scholars and observers of the contemporary scene. When activist involvement happened it was done by individual students and faculty, not under sponsorship of the College. A few students who aspired to political and social change lamented about a sense of isolation, of being "out of the mainstream."

The Teaching and Research Center for Man and Environment

For its first year, 1967-68, this center was called "the Center for Studies in Anthropology." Thereafter it was designated "the Teaching and Research Center for Man and Environment," although its strongest curricula continued to be in anthropology and field work in Southwest archeology. Promi-

Student Archeologists Uncover Pit House

nent in their mission statements was "to bring together the concepts and tools of Archaeology, Physical Anthropology, Social Anthropology, Geology, and Biology in the objective study of man and man's relationship to the environment. The word "objective" was crucial here, and was meant to draw a distinction between hard (meaning data-driven) science and soft (meaning subjective or ideology-driven) sciences like sociology, psychology, etc. They identified four areas of study: man as an organism, the culture of man, the society of man, and man's relation to his natural environment. After the students had sufficient background, the disciplines listed above were applied to studying critical problems in government, industry, public health, colonial and native administrations, and the impact of Western Culture and technology upon American Indians and the "underdeveloped" nations of the world.

A prized and unique aspect of this Center was that field schools at the undergraduate level were carried out in all of the disciplines listed above, most of them in late spring and summer. A student wrote, "For 15 days we were submerged in the geology, biology, anthropology of the area. ... We learned about our entire environment because we wanted to and it made sense. It is courses like this that fulfill the purpose and promise of Prescott College— combining learning with actual out-of-classroom experience. Courses and experiences like this serve not only as the 'invitation to life' a college must be, but serve also as another basis for ecological and environmental awareness that is the paramount goal for survival on earth."[84]

The Center for Man and Environment had a close relationship with departments and institutes at Southwest universities and the Museum of Northern Arizona. Arizona not only is home to over twenty tribes, but also has literally thousands of archeological sites that have not been adequately researched. The arid climate has preserved a rich record of occupation and cultures, spanning many thousands of years. Because the Southwest has the fastest growing population in the United States and laws require that developers carry out surveys to discover whether important sites exist before they build, there is a great deal of archeological research needed. Prescott College had highly competent teams of scientists to fill such contracts. To name a few of their projects, the Center worked on sites on Prescott College campus, on Black Mesa (Hopi reservation), and the Sundown Site, in Williamson Valley. Their research in Williamson

Dr. Robert Euler and Class at Dig Site

Valley centered on a large mound, approximately sixty-five feet in diameter, that served as a burial center. This was prior to a series of federal laws that prohibited the study of ancient human remains without tribal approval.[91] In a report to the board, Nairn's assessment was that "this Center is by far our greatest success. It is doing extraordinary things. We should be proud of it. … The field schools associated with the Center are blooming. We will commence this year to examine specific ecology studies and probably begin to emphasize environmental management."[46]

In a recent oral history interview, Anne Dorman, who was a student in that era, estimated that there were about twenty-five students every year who were professionally interested in anthropology and graduated through that Center.

CHALLENGE DISCOVERY/OUTDOOR ACTION.

Probably the most famous and enduring aspect of Prescott College has been the Outdoor Action program (which has been known over the years by various other titles—Challenge Discovery, Outdoor Leadership, Adventure Education, etc.). The College was the first degree-granting institution that brought together world-class outdoor adventurers, the Outward Bound philosophy, and a funding source adequate to establish and sustain it. This very popular program quickly became an essential component of Prescott College that has continued for forty years without interruption.

Elements of the Program were being developed in 1967, but the first Catalog to list some of its activities was 1968, in which Roy Smith is designated as Director of Outward Bound and Outdoor Action Program. "Mr. Smith has an international reputation in mountaineering, with outstanding climbs done in East Africa, Iceland, Switzerland, France, the Italian Dolomites, and the Andes." The principal benefactor was the DeWitt Wallace Foundation. Wallace was the owner-publisher of *Reader's Digest* magazine. He funded the program from its beginning and his sizable contributions continued for eight years until 1974, which was the final semester of the "old" College. Nairn wrote in a 1968 brochure, "It is our belief at Prescott College that through the medium of the mountains, the sea, canyons and rivers, the qualities of style, compassion, integrity, responsibility, and leadership can be fostered and encouraged. This facet of education is very often overlooked in our universities and colleges in America. When a student hangs by a rope down the side of a mountain to rescue a fellow man, it is difficult to measure how much that student has grown. A student making a decision on how the rest of the group will run a rapid in the inner gorge of the Grand Canyon is assuming a greater responsibility than any football or basketball player ever takes, and greater than any college professor can ever expect of him. Through these types of activities which are real, unavoidable, concrete and definable, a student truly begins to understand what integrity, compassion, responsibility and leadership really mean. The inner man is revealed and becomes known in times of stress. These experiences allow a student to adopt attitudes and form values which are realistic and can stand the abrasion of time. More important in these activities, it is the student's assessment of himself that counts. Students know by their approach, attitude, and performance whether they have failed or succeeded. I see the student as measuring himself only against his own potential and not necessarily against his peers. Above all, willingness to try counts far more than ability to accomplish." (Note: Nairn was a New Zealander, and in the British tradition he uses the word "man" generically for both sexes together. Women students participated fully and on an equal basis in all outdoor adventure programs at Prescott College from the beginning.)

KURT HAHN, FOUNDER OF THE OUTWARD BOUND MOVEMENT

Kurt Hahn was an influential educational philosopher educated in Germany who believed that rigorous activities in a healthy outdoor environment would enhance students' intellectual capacities and moral character. When the Nazis took control of Germany in the 1930s Hahn was incensed by their unethical and destructive regime, and he was not reluctant to make his view known. Soon he was imprisoned; but because of his prestige and good connections he was exiled to England, where he continued his work founding a number of educational programs based on the principles of wilderness education in rural areas of Northern England, Scotland, and Wales. In 1941, Hahn and colleagues founded the Outward Bound Foundation and the first school. The school developed a wilderness orientation component very similar to Prescott College's. In 1955 the movement went international, and programs were established in Germany, Austria, the United States, New Zealand, Singapore, Canada, Hong Kong, and Belgium. There are several Outward Bound schools in the U.S.; the first—established in 1963—was the Colorado school, which worked with Prescott College to design and carry out the Freshman Wilderness Orientation.

WILDERNESS ORIENTATION PROGRAM

The first Freshman Wilderness Orientation took place between September 3 and 29, 1968, under the auspices of the Challenge Discovery Program, working in conjunction with the Colorado Outward Bound School. In the Catalog of 1968, orientation was not listed as part of the curriculum; however, in the "Student Life" section, Wilderness Orientation is mentioned and it appears to be extracurricular. It is unclear whether all freshmen participated that year, or it was optional. In a separate brochure it says, "It is the purpose of the Freshman Orientation program to provide students with concrete, definable, realistic, and unavoidable experiences—experiences which provide challenges that speak to the problems of students in our contemporary society, that speak to developing the perspective of man that is vital to being an adult; experiences of success that, in themselves, give the individual a sense of competence; to see new human possibilities developed through determination and the will to prevail. The orientation program is not going to be easy. Many aspects of the program have been designed to be strenuous. Emphasis is placed on overcoming difficulties such as fear, hunger, and loneliness, as a means of encouraging a reassessment and a fresh view of oneself. Nevertheless, students are not stressed beyond their

Skit during Preparation for Orientation
photo by Travis Patterson

capacities, although they will encounter stress up to their capabilities."

The brochure describes the actual process: "For most of the program, students will be in wilderness areas using sleeping bags and with little more equipment than the early explorers had who passed this way hundreds of years ago. At all times students will be in groups of ten under the guidance of experienced instructors who have been members of Mountaineering Expeditions and Exploratory teams in remote areas of the world. Faculty and other members of the College administration will also engage in part of the program." Organizing and carrying out a twenty-six day wilderness experience for young people who may never have traveled in the wilderness, never carried and prepared their own food, nor created an interdependent microcommunity was not easy. Those leading the groups were well trained in all outdoor skills. They had explored the whole itinerary, identified and explored evacuation routes, and located where safe water could be found every day, etc. It takes a great deal of skill and leadership, and the leaders were carefully chosen and prepared to handle all foreseeable danger and contingencies.[42]

The Solo was the centerpiece of new student orientation. This is a three-day experience in which each student is placed in a location alone, with only a sleeping bag, water containers, a notebook and pencil, and other minimal gear. Unless there is a medical reason, the student is asked not to take food. The group leaders check on each student at least once each day. The solo experience is modeled on such transformational practices as the Native American "vision quest" in which the subject searches for his destiny. One student described her solo in Paria Canyon as a time when "I got to know myself better, enjoyed being alone and the challenge of remaining alone for three days and nights, the experience of knowing what it is really like to be hungry and really being a part of nature. ... As a result of orientation I feel I can undertake and accomplish almost anything I want to do or have to do throughout life...." Another had a different experience, "The solo was pure hell for me, but it was worthwhile. I could have gone back so easily, but I didn't. For once I didn't back out, and now maybe I'll be able to take the next bad thing that happens."[84]

Each person has had a different experience, but most have written about the solo as an episode that set them on a path of self-knowledge and self-direction. Solo has been described as an "orienting" process, but in a sense its purpose has been to disorient new students, to help them break out of stereotypical practices like the conventional lecture and textbook memorization, tests, and competing for grades rather than seeking knowledge and skills. Students return from Freshman Orientation ready to take over their own educations.

The Teaching and Research Center for the Person

The Center for the Person was added in 1970 at the insistence of a major donor and board member who was very interested in innovative education, Charles F. Kettering II. He controlled a major fortune through the Kettering Family Foundation, and had been active in supporting innovative education all through the 1960s. Mr. Kettering joined the Prescott College Board in 1967 and took a major interest in the College's innovative teaching goals and methods. However, there was one area of educational innovation that the College had not pursued, and that was the study of humanistic psychology.

Nairn and many faculty members had been dismayed by what was happening on many urban campuses—anti-war protests and student activism in support of the sexual revolution, the drug culture, dropping out, the hippie life style, etc.—and they uncritically connected such new social phenomena with the "humanistic psychology movement" led by important academic and popular writers such as Carl Rogers, Abraham Maslow, Rolo May, and many others. Nairn is quoted as making one of his rash pronouncements, "The day a psychologist sets foot on this campus is the day I leave."[60]

Kettering was more up with the times and knew that many leading institutions of higher education were pursuing growth psychology and contemporary social movements. He convinced the board to bring these elements into the curriculum. They were essential if Prescott College were to fulfill its mission of preparing leaders for the twenty-first century. All of these and still other factors combined to produce a radical change in upper middle class college student populations. Privileged youth were creating new values and lifestyles, and also attempting to find their way through the labyrinth of conflicting values as they created them. Prescott College had been less affected than large urban schools, because of its emphasis on outdoor leadership programs. Nevertheless, Prescott College students felt a need to participate in some way. While they had avoided the draft and service in the war, they had friends who did serve and some who were wounded or killed. They felt a duty to support protests and find their own issues. All of this had profound educational implications, and the faculty was divided between those who could be called conservative and progressive.

When the new "Fifth Center," the Center for the Person, was made official in 1970, an administrator and a few teachers were recruited to get it started. The Outdoor Action Program and Orientation were moved into the Center. Dance and some social programs were also moved there. Honor Conscience and personal growth processes, group process, alternative educational theories, and other "non-disciplinary" subject matter were assigned to the Center. It had been the hope of many students and faculty that the new center would be a safety valve, venting the pressure building up between those faculty who saw quality in terms of rigorous pursuit of established disciplines (although with a gloss of interdisciplinary rhetoric), and those faculty who were attempting to promote change (sometimes with an attitude of "change for the sake of change"). For example, half of the faculty saw Outdoor Action as a deviation from academic learning, a version of extracurricular activity not worthy of transcripted credit, while a growing segment of the faculty—including the President—saw it as a very important element in academic learning and character development, thus central to the curriculum.

The curriculum framework of the Center for the Person consisted of four basic programs: **(1) Introductory Process,** which included Wilderness Orientation and the various academic and community orientation activities that were required of all students. **(2) Community Life,** which was administered through a Community Advisory Committee, an elected body of students, faculty, administration, and trustees who gather regularly to discuss and make recommendations to the President on any area of concern within the academic community. The Advisory Committee functioned primarily through three subcommittees: Resources, Student Affairs, and Curriculum.

Additional activities included the Environmental Defense Committee, various religious services and activities, student-organized dances, parties, and cultural events, and a Communications Office through which students produced a weekly newspaper, a magazine, and a monthly calendar enabling the community to keep abreast of all scheduled activities. And the Honor conscience ethical code was supervised by the Center. (3) **Self-Progression Program,** through which students develop self-knowledge, productive study habits, ethical commitments through courses, workshop, service projects; and (4) **Outdoor Action Program**.

The Center for the Person was also seen as a place to put courses and activities that the more structured faculty didn't want to deal with, but many students wanted.

The Center's mission statement in the 1970 Catalog states, "The purpose of this Center is to help students design and accomplish a strategy for their academic and personal lives. Areas of primary attention within the Center are: To develop the awareness that physical and intellectual growth are not only interrelated but interdependent; To project the student into the world beyond the College and, on an individual basis, equip the student to deal with that world; To induce self-awareness, confidence in one's ability, and a willingness to be accountable for one's actions."

Unfortunately the hope that adding a "Fifth Center" would soothe philosophical tensions within the faculty was not realized.

FROM *TIME* MAGAZINE FRIDAY, OCTOBER 11, 1968

21ST CENTURY FRONTIER

Freshman orientation is a trifle more strenuous than listening to a series of welcome speeches. Instead, incoming students, both male and female, strap on forty-pound packs and spend three weeks hiking through dry, bramble-strewn canyons and scrambling down 165-foot cliffs; for three days, they must live on their own, surviving on nothing but water. In addition, they paddle kayaks and canoes for 95 miles around a wind-chopped lake, struggling to keep afloat during cloudbursts and camping overnight on the rocky shore.

The explanation for Prescott's rigorous "wilderness course," declares the school's president, Ronald C. Nairn, is that "man is a part of nature. Millions of years of his evolutionary history are rooted in life as a hunter, a nomad, an adventurer. Deep facets of personality and emotional needs are tied to his past. Urban industrial society increasingly fails to meet these needs." Gritty native spirit is only one part Prescott's unique educational program. The college has junked traditional academic departments and installed a system of wide-ranging integrated courses that bridge the gap between humanities and the sciences. The curriculum concentrates on great ideas rather than an accumulation of facts. The object is to help each student create his own world view, relate classroom concepts to his own life and become what one school official calls "a cultural revolutionary."

Unfettered by Tradition. When Prescott opened its doors in 1966, it was conceived as a private, four-year liberal arts college "unfettered by any tradition that would limit its opportunity to relate itself dynamically to the emerging 21st Century." That goal was explored at a symposium of 100 educators and businessmen sponsored by the Ford Foundation, resulting in funds for construction of the college's 43 buildings on 640 acres of rolling plain six miles north of Prescott, Ariz. Though present enrollment is only 186, Prescott plans to expand to a maximum of 1,000 by 1978.

All Prescott's students take a heady curriculum in four areas: anthropology; language and literature; civilizations; systems. The language and literature program includes a study of the cinema as well as courses on the Christian tradition and comparative mythology. The study of systems at Prescott starts with an analysis of logic and mathematics, branches off into astronomy, physics, chemistry, psychology and political science. The anthropology department deals with man's relationship to his environment, to his culture, and to himself. It ranges from courses in geography and geology to zoology—all backed up by six weeks of field work in the nearby desert. In their first trip to the desert, Prescott students unearthed pueblo ruins left by predecessors of the Hopi Indians in A.D. 1100.

To the Limits. Prescott's most novel enterprise is the outdoor sports program. Convinced that students need more than the artificial competition of games, Prescott has abandoned traditional team sports. Instead, it has adopted the techniques developed by Outward Bound, an international program of more than twenty wilderness camps that stresses adventure, challenge and self-sufficiency.

Touched by Layne Longfellow
by Steve Matthews, Class of 1972

What I carried away from solo (besides a month of numb feet) and the trip in general was a bit of psychological endurance. I believed then (and still do now) that I could endure almost anything. In fact, daily frustrations are trivial when I recall those long, cold hours at Purgatory Flats. On several occasions this realization has been the cue for undertaking arduous but necessary projects.

The second experience I'd like to describe is an intellectual one. Layne Longfellow was giving a talk about his educational philosophy (one of a series of lectures by Prescott College sponsored by a Center of the Person education class). Layne began his presentation by describing his childhood in Appalachia and some of his later college experiences.

The honesty and openness with which he spoke, and the revelation of personal changes (leaving behavior modification at the University of Michigan to live off the land in Alaska and ultimately work with Carl Rogers in California) brought the entire audience to a psychological high. After the talk many of us remained, hypnotized as it were. Questions were asked and meaningful dialogue continued. At one point Layne walked over to the piano and played some of his compositions. I recall being so absorbed in the experience that I missed dinner and spent the rest of the evening "coming down to Earth." Aside from stimulating further exploration of psychology, Layne's presentation confirmed a philosophic approach to education and human behavior that has stayed with me through undergraduate and graduate study.

With that single lecture, Layne probably had the greatest impact on my life of any professor I have known. Other instructors provided academic and affective support, but not on issues more fundamental than those touched by Layne.

Nairn's Grand Plan and the Decline of the Original College

◇◇◇◇◇◇◇

With the addition of the Teaching and Research Center for the Person in 1970, the College would seem to have achieved its two paramount goals as articulated in the Symposium: (1) the DIDACTIC, i.e., building a high quality interdisciplinary instructional program and (2) building an EXISTENTIAL program that attended to the emotional and character building aspects of college life. The Five Centers were settling in and had gained the loyalty and enthusiasm of a progressive student body, which had grown to nearly 300 students despite substantial increases in tuitions. As the first to embrace Outward Bound in its curriculum, the College attracted national attention. Its Wilderness Orientation innovation was photographed and heralded in newspapers and other media. *Time* magazine[83] featured it and Charles Kuralt dedicated a spot in his nationally broadcast television series, "On the Road."[92]

It seemed that the five Centers and the Outdoor Action curriculum were Fhealthy, despite internal quarrels that intelligent adults should have been able to resolve. The Board of Trustees was in support and apparently willing to stick with the College as it pursued its next tasks—expanding the student body, creating a sustainable financial base, finishing and paying for the new campus. Large-scale gifts were coming in, and a small-scale yearly appeal was -bringing in supplemental revenue. The Board was looking at ways to build Ban adequate endowment to see the College through hard times that might eventuate. In other words, the Prescott College experiment seemed to be heading in the direction of success.

However, there were partially hidden philosophical and financial issues beneath the surface. Although launching the Fifth Center would seem to have been the best way to settle the academic standards and legitimate curricular content arguments, these squabbles continued unabated. A possibly apocryphal story illustrates the widening gap between the "new humanists" and "academic traditionalists." The chairman one of the Centers is reported to have proposed that the full faculty, dressed in their academic gowns and mortarboards, would meet and greet the freshmen returning from Wilderness Orientation at the entrance of the campus in order to impress on them that Prescott College was a serious academic institution. One faculty member expressed the thought of several when he said that Orientation spoiled the students for any serious academic learning, and the faculty had to lose three weeks reconditioning students to the classroom. It is difficult to interpret these stories. Perhaps after Orientation some students were more outspoken and independent. It has been suggested that many of the young men grew beards while in the wilderness and didn't shave them upon returning. Some new students affected the style of "nature's children," often going barefoot during the mild and beautiful fall weather of Prescott. The orientation leaders, who were professionally trained for that job, were not necessarily academics, and critics suggested they conditioned the more impressionable to feel the life of study and subordination to an authoritative faculty teacher was not necessary.

> The title of the experience "Wilderness Orientation" is quite accurate, but it could also be called "disorientation," because it allowed young people to experience a different environment that was not the creation of modern humans. It allowed them to experience a lifestyle more like that which our nomadic ancestors lived for a hundred thousand years or more. Conservatives were uneasy about this momentary return to primitivism—even those who had dedicated their careers to the study of older cultures.[61]

The Prescott Institutions

There was an equal and opposite reaction to such criticisms. Other faculty criticized the "conservatives" for wanting to teach only half of the person, the rational mind. These "humanists" were more interested in exploring the ways to expand the self. Each faction gave different interpretations to words coming out of the Symposium, like freedom, self-direction, spiritual growth, and individuality. One must consider all of this against the backdrop of the Vietnam protests, sexual revolution, drug culture, and the *real* hippie movement happening in urban centers and on large campuses. Another story from this era illustrates the conflicting philosophies. The "traditionalists" developed a contract based on the Honor Conscience that they wanted all students to sign. Obviously, the purpose was to set some rules for behavior, as is done in many elementary and prep schools. Most students were incensed by this effort, which seemed to them to fly in the face of trust and freedom. They recruited a faculty member to advise them, formed a protest group, and marched to the president's office. The traditionalists had to back down, but there was little effort to resolve the issues involved. Another possibly apocryphal story is that Nairn stood in a faculty meeting in which they were quarreling over these issues, and told them to get along together, and do what he wanted, or he would "fire the whole lot of you and hire a new faculty!" While such stories seem to be outside the customary civility between faculty members, it is well known that quarrels did exist and were never satisfactorily resolved. For example, it became commonplace for faculty of the first four Centers to call the new Fifth Center the "fifth wheel," implying it was illegitimate or useless. Philosophical and operational conflicts between and within student bodies and faculties was nothing new in the world of academia, particularly during the late 1960s and early 1970s, rather it was almost to be expected. Few participants in the College expected it to undermine the school, since everything else was going well.

A careful study of the speeches and actions of the Board and Nairn around 1970 indicates an important turning point in the history of the College was coming. The Board and Nairn were planning an extensive reorganization. The picture came into focus with the issuing of a thirty-seven page proposal written by Nairn. His narrative began with an account of how he sought a new vision for the College:

> I spent this summer back in … that pleasant, congenial region of Northwest Thailand; I found I had time to think. A short visit to old friends and environs at the monastery of Chiengdao was most helpful. Uppermost was concern for Prescott College and its future. This, however, could not be detached from the future of private education in the U.S.A. in general.
>
> [Nairn had analyzed the problem and concluded that] the future for the small private college was indeed bleak. … These institutions have shown enormous resiliency [and] no doubt they will die hard. But a massive acceptance of faith is required to assume that many will survive. …
>
> [Nairn recognized] twin afflictions affecting the small, independent, liberal arts college … curriculum and money [and noted] We at Prescott College have, over these past five years, had remarkable success in raising funds. But we still fell far short of what was needed. Neither could I see the real needs being met by my fundraising efforts.

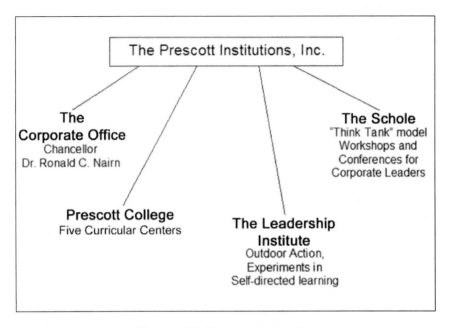

Figure 1. The Prescott Institutions

A new approach to financing was obviously needed and that is what this plan is all about. [29]

    The College was to be divided into four pieces: (1) a Corporate Office, (2) Prescott College, (3) the Leadership Institute, and (4) the Schole.

    In 1972, just six years after the College had opened to students, the Board asked the Arizona Corporation Commission to grant a new corporate name, which it did: *The Prescott Institutions, Inc.* By this means a new corporate office was created and the feuding parties were further separated. Nairn was elevated to overall leadership, as President of the new Corporation, and Chancellor of the other Institutions.

(1) The Corporate Office

This new entity, which was commonly referred to as *the Corporation*, was not a school per se, but a sort of holding company that became the administrative arm and central financial management structure for the three other Institutions, which were schools. The Board of Directors was responsible for the new corporation, for financial management, for management of the campus, and for any other revenue-enhancing schemes that might be devised. The Prescott Institutions, Inc., was incorporated as a nonprofit corporation just as the College had been, but that status did not preclude earning money.

Nairn did have money-making schemes in mind that could be done through the Corporation. For example, Nairn's office was developing a plan for renting out the college campus in the summers to a group called Western Resources. Through this partnership, the campus would become host to various summer camps and conferences.

(2) Prescott College

Prescott College became a subset within the Corporation. Functionally it remained virtually the same, with its five Curricular Centers. It did lose some of its more futuristic curricula and methodology, and the outdoor action programs that had caused some of its traditionalist members so much consternation. The visible effects of this change were to open a separate office for the College and for Nairn to appoint a president, Jack Dougherty, from the faculty. Various management functions such as bookkeeping and maintenance were transferred from the College to the Corporation, thus freeing the College to concentrate on academics. Technically, *Prescott College* now had its own board of directors, which was interlocking with the main corporate board of directors.

(3) The Leadership Institute

The outdoor leadership group had been quietly evolving since 1968 when connections were made with the Western Resources Conference, Challenge Discovery, and Colorado Outward Bound. Roy Smith, an internationally known outdoor educator was brought on board. The new Leadership Institute was small but had an office and its own separate board, including Willi Unsoeld, the famous mountaineer and spokesman for outdoor education. Those faculty and staff who had managed the outdoor programs for the College were transferred from the Center for the Person to the Leadership Institute. In 1971-72 and 1972-73 the Leadership Institute enrolled just over twenty students each year, the majority of them transferred from the College, but a few were new recruits. Being so small, it could not support its own registrar, and so students of the Institute actually received Prescott College credits and degrees. Field courses included some amazing adventures such as ascending to the summits of Mount McKinley and Mount Kenya in Africa, sea kayaking and sailing in the Sea of Cortez, rafting and white water kayaking in dangerous rivers, and mounting expeditions in Alaska, Mexico, and Africa where they traveled on foot through big game areas.

Impressive as such expeditions were, the main work of the Leadership Institute during the academic year was to provide high quality, demanding studies for students who were mature enough to design and follow their own chosen directions. These studies could be in any field—pre-engineering, wildlife management, creative writing, etc.—but they were fully designed by the student, working with an advisor and studying with mentors. All credits were awarded on the basis of completing a contract, which demanded rigor and freed students from taking any prescribed courses. Most Institute students did complete courses at the College, and some completed work at other institutions.

The first professor recruited for the Institute from outside the College was Dr. James Stuckey (who later became the president of the "new College," PCAE, in 1975). He described his first semester teaching: "Well, in the Institute, I taught some courses, I even taught a couple courses for the College, and we moved back and forth—so I was teaching psychology, I was teaching learning theory. I don't think I taught math at that time, though I did some independent studies. But we were doing independent studies in everything." Although Dr. Stuckey had recently completed a PhD he found this kind of teaching to be a rich education for himself. "I spent large amounts of time talking to students and thinking and writing about how learning works, how education works, how you package learning activities into a higher education curriculum, how you package it in a way that's palatable to people who come from all kinds of places, many of them, you know, with enough money, legitimately to be spoiled, and then wacky. You know the young people who just hadn't grown up as I had in some fairly rigid channel and … they just sort of believed they could do pretty much anything." He found that these young people could do exceptional work since they had the freedom and resources they needed. With the Outdoor Action programs safely tucked away within their own Institute, teachers and students were free to experiment. Innovative ideas such as learning contracts and portfolios, brought to the college by the president's assistant, Lee Maynard, and a stronger emphasis on self-direction were introduced. Instructors from Carl Roger's Center for the Study of the Person were brought into the Institute and also the Center for the Person. Academic rigor and experiential learning were blended with continued research on the latest in learning theories. Jim Stuckey stated that the Leadership Institute at this time was "the ground zero of education." These "dangerous" experimental ideas would soon be transformed into the core methodology of Prescott College.[56]

(4) The Schole

The Schole was designed to employ the campus and some of the faculty to conduct conferences and short courses for corporate executives, businessmen, government officials, and others who needed an in-depth preparation in order to work with Asian businesses and governments. It was to be modeled on the sorts of institutes attached to various colleges and universities, for example, the Asia Institute attached to the University of Melbourne. With East Asia as a focus and his own credentials, Nairn believed he could enhance the College's standing and earn money for the budget. Professional training could be offered for business people. An added attraction of the Schole would be providing exciting, if less demanding, wilderness experiences or horseback expeditions for a more mature and affluent clientele who would be attending the Schole programs. Eventually, certain areas of research could be housed at the College through the Schole. It was an interesting concept, but events removed the the financial backing, particularly the tragic death of Charles F. Kettering II.

Dr. Nairn's four institutions model was put into effect for two years. Robert Harrill, who later was given the duty of closing the College, commented, "It was a college of about four hundred people with four administrations, offices, distinct stationery, and three boards. The costs were unbelievable. The College remained operating at over a half a million dollar debt, the Schole was operating many thousand dollars in the red, and the Leadership Institute was just barely breaking even. The College was beginning to drown in debt and Dr. Nairn's fundraising effort was no longer bringing in the money that it used to. When they came to visit, his donors were not seeing the 'Harvard of the West,' a glittering citadel of erudition and character building, they saw a bunch of hippies walking around barefoot, and of course there were plenty who weren't, but that's who you see, so the money started drying up."[50]

It is not entirely clear why this new and overly complex organizational structure was designed and put into effect. The previous configuration with five Centers would certainly have been sufficient to manage a school with just 284 students in 1971 and 448 in 1972. And yet, the Board and Nairn were determined to plow ahead with this third reorganization. There are several stories and theories that attempt to explain it, and they will be reviewed very briefly.

One theory involved the confidence Nairn had in his own fundraising abilities, or the relationship the College had developed with their most generous and capable donors, particularly with Charles F. Kettering II. The rumor circulating was that Kettering had guaranteed the College while it was getting established to the level of four or five million dollars. (Taking into account inflation, as per the CPI, that would be equivalent to twenty-five to thirty million dollars at the time of this writing (2006). Tragically, Kettering was killed in an auto accident in December 1971. The Kettering Family did not share his enthusiasm for Prescott College, and they withdrew any pledges. Within a few months a second important board member and donor, George Farnham, passed away. But it was too late to reverse course.

A story that circulated, possibly told by Nairn, was that he had a moment of enlightenment while vacationing and hiking in Thailand, and foresaw that the College would be caught up in an economic downturn. His moment of revelation told him that he should create additional revenue streams for the College project. The Prescott Institutions was his attempt to prepare. Historically, the OPEC oil embargo of 1973-74 disrupted U.S. and world economies, and inadvertently contributed to the economic failure of the College.

Another widely held supposition was that Nairn was restless and tired of working at ground level, solving the day-to-day issues that all college presidents face. Nairn felt he could do more for the College operating at a national and international level. His method of escaping to the higher level was to delegate day-to-day operations to the three executives he appointed to run the institutions. The fact is that Nairn was seen on campus less often after 1972.

THE FRED COMMITTEE REFORMS

Board weighs program overhaul for Prescott Institutions was the headline of an article that appeared in the Arizona Republic after the December board meeting of 1972-73. From the text: "A major revamping of the program at Prescott Institutions was proposed at a meeting of the board of trustees. They are considering an overhaul of the school's administration that would abolish all departments and reestablish a more progressive liberal arts philosophy."[85]

During 1974, a quasi-secret committee was formed with the knowledge and encouragement of the Board. It was composed of a few administrators and teachers—and probably students knew about it. They did not know what to call it, until someone said "let's call it FRED." The FRED Committee soon found out how serious the financial condition of the Prescott Institutions was. Costs of running the institutions with four senior administrators, each with an office and staff, were unsustainable. Considering all options, the FRED Committee eventually recommended that each of the Institutions be consolidated with the College or shut down, and that the corporation retrieve its original name, Prescott College, Inc. They further recommended that the five Centers in the College should be administratively combined, although they should remain functionally separate. Through all of the reorganizations, the Centers as a mode of curricular organization were the most stable element, and they remained in place from 1967 to 1974.

For a few months in 1972-73, Bob Euler was both head of the Man and Environment Center and president of the College. In the May 5, 1973, Board meeting, Chancellor Nairn's resignation was accepted and a retirement agreement was presented to him which he found unacceptable. It was subsequently re-negotiated, and in the October 6 meeting a final agreement was reached and was authorized by the Board. In the interim he was being paid.

Euler took a position at the Grand Canyon and left the College. Facing a deepening financial crisis, the Board turned to Frank Mertz, who had been business manager from the beginning. He accepted the post of interim president. Mertz was a conscientious man with a degree and excellent skills in business. Prior to joining the College, he had been in the top management of Franklin College. Although he held a BA in philosophy, he readily admitted that he did not have the academic credentials to be a college president. His educational philosophy aligned very well with that expressed in the Symposium. He took on the position knowing he had a rapidly fraying financial situation to face, and he realized he had to look for help wherever he could find it—while at the same time reassuring students, faculty, and donors that the College was on its way upward. Layne Longfellow, the charismatic chairman of the Center for the Person, became vice-president for curriculum. Bob Harrill, a research chemist who had been chairman of the Systems Center, became vice-president for administration. They formed a small and compatible team that was given the charge to get the College under control and live within the budget.

The new management team, under Mertz's leadership, took two types of rational actions. They put the College on an austerity budget, cutting costs by deferring some maintenance and laying off adjunct teachers and some service staff. The Board additionally took decisive steps to consolidate the debts (see Money Matters Part I).

In 1973-74 the Centers were combined in terms of curricular organization, and Longfellow launched the last innovation, a special "First Year" curriculum for all new students. This concept had been in play since the Symposium, but never followed up. Longfellow's design was loosely based on the Colorado College model of a full academic year consisting of nine one-month, one-course blocks. Most of the faculty participated, and First Year presented a wide variety of subjects and topics. Some students were very enthusiastic, since it provided an overview of the whole College and acquaintance with many faculty members. As usual, there were also critics. One faculty member quipped that First Year would provide an excellent foundation for navel gazing and underwater basket weaving. While a full First Year curriculum for all students has not been used again, its lasting contribution has been the incorporation of three one-month blocks in to the yearly schedule, which has continued since 1975.

Along with Euler, most of the other anthropology teachers began to leave the faculty, and the excellent anthropology and archeology programs ended. Their lasting accomplishment was to lay the groundwork for College's Environmental Studies Program, which has also been a very key component of the College's curriculum since 1975.

Within a period of only eight years, five extensive curricular, administrative, and organizational restructurings had taken place. A national economic downturn occurred, curtailing the success of the annual fundraising effort, and Prescott townspeople's support of the College had been reduced. But the College was still managing to skirt the cliff of the financial canyon. Remarkably, the majority of the students did not seem very worried about an impending fiscal collapse. Or perhaps they were so busy with their studies and outdoor activities that they did not put up a commotion.

In the spring of 1974 the College received a final installment from the Wallace Foundation and a substantial gift from a parent of two students. Delaying payments and other economies sufficed to get through the summer. In August tuitions came in, but by October operational bank accounts were empty. Frustratingly, the College had many thousands of dollars sitting in restricted accounts, second semester tuitions, employee withholding benefits, and the like, all of it unavailable until after January 1, 1975. It was illegal to spend a penny before that date. Mertz was again pleading with the utility companies and suppliers to extend credit to the College until the first of the year. Mertz felt the Board members could and should donate to or lend the College enough money to cover the deficit until the first of the year, and he believed he had a plan to finish the year and then put the College on a firmer basis. At a Board meeting in October he was forced to give an honest report of the College's dire financial situation, and lay out his plan. He told of the sacrifices he and others were making. Instead of the help he expected, he later gave an account of Board members who were "stabbing him in the back," and of his own personal grief. Within a short time, Mertz was replaced as President by a VP, Bob Harrill.

Mertz had revealed more at the Board meeting as well. A member of what he called the Religious Charismatic Movement, he prayed for the College constantly. At the meeting he confided that he had had a prophetic dream that indicated he would receive a call from someone who would help them save the College. The next day he did receive a call that led to a contact with a Chicago foundation with what seemed impeccable credentials. When he spoke with the director, Hal (Harry) Lowther, Mertz was told that it was the mission of foundation to save foundering schools of merit. This eventually led to negotiations and Lowther and his wife, Dr. Barbara Phillips, came to Prescott to work out a contract. She was to take over the presidency of the College; her foundation would supply the funds needed to finish the year, while the foundation looked for more permanent support.

Lowther wrote checks from the Phillips Foundation checkbook to pay insurance, utilities, suppliers, and faculty and staff paychecks. The checks were given to their intended recipients and then deposited with the recipients' endorsements. Within weeks, this momentary bubble burst. The foundation wasn't what it seemed, and soon the couple was demanding that the money in the same restricted bank accounts be turned over to them immediately to cover the checks Lowther had written. Harrill and the Board refused, of course. By late December, over $200,000 in bogus checks signed by Lowther were being returned by the banks for collection, and no other *saviors* of the College had appeared. Therefore, in the middle of the night of December 17, 1974, the Board met in an unannounced executive session. Harrill had to review with them all the unpaid bills, and the one that was most alarming was that the College's liability insurance was lapsing. If anyone were seriously hurt on campus or in field classes, the trustees would be individually liable. They realized they had two options: to come up with over $200,000 that night, or close down the College. They chose the latter option, and told Harrill to do it the next day, which was just two days in advance of the school calendar date for closing.

The morning of December 18, 1974, was crisp and beautiful on the Prescott College campus. Several end-of-semester cultural presentations and celebrations were underway, and most people were in a holiday mood. As faculty arrived, they found notes taped to their office doors: "There will be no classes today. Go directly to the auditorium for an emergency meeting." By ten o'clock the hall was filled with teachers, students, and staff, and buzzing with nervous chatter. Interim President Harrill arose and made a simple announcement: the Board had met the previous evening and decided the semester would be ending two days early; it was necessary to vacate the campus as quickly as possible. Those who were present have different recollections of the exact hours by which faculty, students, and others had to remove their possessions from the campus, but the deadlines were impossibly short, a matter of hours. Within a day the front gate would be padlocked, and no one but the guards and other officials would be allowed to enter. Harrill did his best to explain the reason—that the doors could not stay open because the bank accounts were exhausted. A tense discussion erupted. *Had the Board declared bankruptcy?* Not at this point. They intend to raise funds during the holidays for the spring semester. *What happened with the plan to bring in the Lowthers?* They had backed out—the Board was conducting an investigation. *Would our paychecks be made good?* Not immediately. *What will happen to outdoor equipment and other stuff we can't get off the campus?* We don't know. Find a truck. *How can you expect us to clear out of the dormitories immediately? Where will we go? My plane ticket is for Sunday.* The gate will be locked by four o'clock. Stay with off-campus friends. Call the airlines and change your tickets. Call your parents. Do the best you can.

Meanwhile, the telephone lines were jammed. Parents reacted with shock and every emotion from concern to sympathy to anger. Local hotels and motels were filled. Cars and pickups loaded with students, luggage, backpacks, skis, research files, and books shuttled back and forth to town. Word went out to local and Arizona media, to the national syndicated news media, and to community newspapers as far away as Providence, R.I. Soon articles were appearing in major newspapers like the New York Times, including the Chronicle of Higher Education.

PC Future Unknown—Foundation Agreement Questioned

from The *Paper* (a Prescott weekly) 12-24-74

The future of 10-year-old Prescott College remains unknown and certainly not bright this week in the wake of a series of events that indicate the Illinois-based foundation that was to pay the bills is unable to do so.

Phillips Research Foundation and the Institute for Educational Development, a Phillips corporation, had agreed to pay all operating costs from mid-November to Dec. 15, including payroll.

However, all checks issued bounced and the amount of bad checks issued could reach $150,000.

Bob Harrill, acting PC president, ordered the campus closed last Wednesday, two days before the scheduled Christmas vacation break. Hamilton Wright, president of the PC board of trustees, said this week "it is extremely doubtful that the college will open for the second semester Jan. 20."

Principals in the foundation and IED are Harry Allen Lowther Jr., 53, chairman of IED, and his wife, Dr. Barbara Lowther, head of the foundation. Lowther admitted Friday that he has been convicted twice of securities fraud and is currently on probation.

Wright said Friday he had asked the U.S. attorney's office to investigate the circumstances in which $124,000 in checks written by Lowther to pay college bills were rejected by the banks. He also said Lowther will be sued for that amount.

Wright said Lowther attempted to transfer funds from the college to the institute's account but "diligence" on the part of Valley Bank and United Bank officials prevented it. Wright said up to $400,000 in college funds would have been involved if the banks hadn't intervened. Much of the total represents student tuition for the second semester.

The Lowthers approached PC officials in November and expressed a willingness to assist the financially strapped institution. Wright said the Lowthers agreed to pay all bills for a month and have an interest payment deferred until next May. Wright said "they have not lived up to the agreement" and, speaking for himself, Wright added he would have no further dealings with the Lowthers or the IED and the Phillips foundation.

The college has been mired in financial difficulties since it opened.

The Lowther-Phillips apparent swindle created a national scandal, and many commentators found their manipulation an easy hook on which to hang the story of the College's closedown. The story engendered much sympathy and some help for the College. At the time, those who heard it were inclined to blame the whole financial problem on the Lowther-Phillips team. The fact is that, in the end, they never got a cent of the College's money. In an ironic twist, Mertz's night vision did save the College. The whole fiasco took enough time to allow the College to finish the fall semester. It is still a mystery how the pair was able to gain control of a prestigious foundation and operate for a couple of years in this fashion, victimizing schools and charitable foundations. Because it is a mystery, and a spin-off of Prescott College history, Melissa Doran has written a mystery-styled account which is included in this book (see "Hal Lenke, Private Eye," by Melissa Doran).

The Board was not able to raise enough money to float the second semester; only a token effort was made by most of them. They had closed the College for good. Lawyers were now totaling up the debts and assets, and finalizing arrangements for the Wilson Foundation to take over the sale of the campus and assets. At least one trustee was inquiring into the Lowther-Phillips team, to see if they could be prosecuted. For a portion of the students and their parents, an emergency search for another college placement was underway. For several faculty and most of the staff and administration, it was a time to scramble for alternative possibilities and income. For them, all of the excitement, idealistic dreams, and real accomplishments had come to an abrupt end. The 565 acres of land, the campus buildings worth over five million dollars, the excellent library, and even students' second semester tuitions, were locked up in the bankruptcy.

But for about half of the faculty and students, an exciting adventure was being launched in living rooms and coffee shops.

Prescott Center College (PCAE) from 1975 to 1984

◇◇◇◇◇◇◇

In that fateful community meeting the morning of December 18, 1974, after the shock of the bankruptcy announcement subsided, one faculty member, then another stood to say that the College isn't a physical plant and campus land—it is the people who learn and teach here. It is the academic and spiritual community. Other facilities could be arranged. Those who spoke felt that for the benefit of the students, the College could, and should, finish out the year one way or another. Memories vary about the exact sequence of events that day. But it is generally held that Hal Lenke, faculty chairman, called a faculty meeting for the afternoon, with the agenda—to set up a communication network for everyone connected with the school, and to arrange a community gathering to develop a plan for the remainder of the school year. Word went out to all faculty, staff, and students who could be reached to assemble on the College's polo (soccer) field.

Not all of the approximately five hundred students and faculty and staff could get there, but those who could, gathered and listened to faculty members including Jim Stuckey, Sam Henrie, Carl Tomoff, Hal Lenke, and others give reasons to support the school and the students who were to graduate in the spring. The community was easily convinced, as everybody in attendance was already prepared to go to battle for the College. They divided into small groups to discuss alternative facilities and plan how programs could be continued. When they regrouped to report their ideas, they realized that keeping in touch once they had left for winter break would be a problem, so a "communication fund" or the "start-up fund," as Jim Stuckey called it, began. A hat was passed and everyone was asked to contribute whatever they had in their pockets. The collection amounted to $235. From the viewpoint of financial history, this fund could be considered the original endowment for the second version of the College.

Plans were discussed for proceeding over the holidays. Questions concerning who would be in town or who would be able to help by telephone were asked. Another meeting was set for the next day to take place in the large living room of Stuckey's home.

During the next weeks an intensive round of meetings in faculty homes and downtown coffee shops was held. The group—students, faculty, and staff—was determined to see the College continue, and they hammered out the details. Faculty and staff members, and even some students, volunteered for assignments as registrar, heads of curricular programs, student recruitment, and other committees. Several students gave up their winter break to stay in Prescott and help.

In early January of 1975, the founding group of faculty and students met in the home of former College President (1972-73) Jack Dougherty and decided to incorporate a new school to carry on the work of Prescott College. They elected Dr. James M. Stuckey as their president. With the pro bono help of a lawyer, the group prepared the papers to create a new educational vehicle. On January 28, 1975, the incorporation of the nonprofit educational entity, Prescott Center for Alternative Education (PCAE) was finalized. The eleven volunteer incorporators served as the first Board of Directors. The corporation was PCAE, the new school's official name was Prescott Center College. So the beginnings of Prescott Center College were well underway when its predecessor, Prescott College, Inc., officially went out of business on January 31, 1975.[3,35]

SELF-DIRECTION AS A FINANCIAL AND GOVERNANCE PROPOSITION

Democratic Governance

Relieved of the anxiety that had pervaded the atmosphere of the "old College" during its final semester, the Prescott Center community banded together. Initiative and self-responsibility had always been major principles in Prescott College philosophy, but at the "old Prescott College" there had been a structural contradiction that negated this philosophy. Now the community members matched their action to their philosophy by creating their own corporation. They were resolute in the determination that this new legal entity belonged to them. There was a powerful feeling of communal and financial ownership, and a new sense of effectiveness.

There had been an underlying feeling that had they been allowed some input in the former Board's governance, the College might have been saved. Therefore, the founders set about to create a new type of corporate bylaws that would guarantee community control. There was no wish to create a copy of the traditional structure that could empower another autonomous board of outsiders, however well motivated and affluent, with fiduciary and policy-making powers to control the new College through a president they would appoint. This was a radical position that did not fit comfortably into the framework of customs and laws that govern nonprofit corporations.

The incorporators were aware that in the structure of conventional nonprofit corporations those who held the financial control and set overall policy, the board of directors and president, operated in a top-down manner. Board members were analogous to owners of the former College in that they were fully authorized to decide how the property of the College should be used or disposed of. In Prescott College the board hired and supervised the president, and they could set policy in every aspect of the operation. By convention and law, those who had been charged with carrying out the educational programs, the staff, faculty, and students, were subordinate in terms of ultimate decision making. While their recommendations were often asked for, and sometime listened to, functionally they were just paid workers. Unlike *for-profit* corporations that are controlled by the votes of their investors, *nonprofit* corporations cannot be controlled by the votes of those whose investment was their hard-won expertise and degrees as well as their life-energy. In nonprofits they have no vote.

PCAE adopted very different bylaws, in which trustees were to be nominated in an open process and elected by vote of all who had a role in the Prescott Center—students and alumni, staff, faculty, administrators, and present and past board members. The first PCAE Board consisted of those who had signed the papers to create the new corporation. Within months, the community elected a board that represented all segments, including local friends of the College.

New Fiscal Policy

Prescott College had seemed invincible to everyone because it had attracted so much national and regional attention for its innovative philosophy and curriculum. But all the faith and good will that existed could not overcome the fact that in the real world of money, when an organization runs out of cash and credit so that it becomes insolvent, it is forced to close its doors. The founders of PCAE had lived through that experience and learned a lesson about the unyielding reality in the world of money. As they created a new set of principles and policies, they built in a prohibition of paying for operations through borrowing. The new policy had various names: *no debt*, *in the black*, or *pay-as-you-go*.

When tuition and gift income did not equal budgeted expenditures, the budget was reduced. In moments of shortfall, when other expenditures were cut to the bone, paychecks were delayed or even reduced by mutual consent. Reserved funds like IRS and FICA withholding were never dipped into.

Bookkeeping was conscientious, and regular audits were contracted, even though account figures were very small. One reality that kept the College's managers on target with this no-debt policy was the fact that the new corporation, and its College, were tainted with a poor credit rating resulting from the bankruptcy of their predecessor. PCAE and the Center College claimed to be the full successor of the old college, and merchants and lending institutions took them at their word.

During the first semester of PCAE, even when the odds were so fully stacked against the continuation of the College for the next semester, only a few of the faculty looked elsewhere for jobs. After the bankruptcy, twenty-six out of thirty-one faculty members returned. Stuckey, as their new president, provided a center for this new *co-op college*. He was a creative and charismatic leader and although thoroughly qualified, Stuckey jokes that he was elected president because "I was single and had a pretty good sized house and more importantly had a big living room, so most of the meetings happened in my living room." He also stated that the other major reason he was elected was because he was the "middle man," he was not aligned with any faction, although he admitted he did enter as faculty in the Leadership Institute. His expertise was learning, and to "develop tools to help students be more self-directed, to build their own rigor into their academic work."[56]

Prescott Center College opened mid-January 1975 in the basement rooms of the historic Hassayampa Inn, which was located in the center of downtown Prescott and was closed for business at the time. The rooms were rented to the College for the token amount of $120 per month. The school had additionally been granted access to a collection of classroom and laboratory facilities at Yavapai College, the local two-year community college. PCAE petitioned the bankruptcy court representative for all student records to be removed from the old campus, and Yavapai College was willing to safely house student records.[37]

One hundred ninety-six students had returned to Prescott for the second semester at the new Prescott Center. Not all were required to pay tuition. Almost twenty percent of the returning students had paid for the full year, and their second semester tuitions were absorbed into the bankruptcy, a loss to them and to the new Center. Prescott Center agreed to honor their tuition and enroll them without further payment. The income for that semester was excruciatingly small. A scant $251,124 had to stretch to pay most of the teachers of the former College. The student-faculty ratio was probably the best in the country, about four to one.[34]

As a new corporation, PCAE was not accredited and would have to go through the lengthy accreditation process to become so. However, there were over sixty seniors at Prescott College who had been working on their final projects, as well as up to fifty other seniors who had already finished but had not been able to participate in a graduation ceremony to receive their earned degrees. These students had taken all or most of their coursework at Prescott College when it was accredited.

Dr. Herman Bleibtreu, a member of the former Board and the Dean of Liberal Arts at the University of Arizona in Tucson, formed a small committee of his U of A colleagues who supported the school's plan to finish the academic year. They convinced the former Board members of Prescott College to approve 105 accredited degrees for those students who were scheduled or had the possibility to graduate in the spring of 1975. News accounts of the time indicate that Dr. Bleibtreu had to engage in various rounds of negotiation with the College's accrediting association, North Central Association of Schools and Colleges (NCA), to convince them. North Central refused his first request, but Bleibtreu persisted, and was ultimately permitted to make out and backdate the accredited degrees. These were signed by Frank Mertz, the last President of Prescott College, and were held "in escrow" at the University of Arizona in anticipation of a spring 1975 graduation. It may be the first and last time accredited degrees have ever been held "in escrow" in the world of higher education. Toward the end of May, the bankruptcy representative opened the campus, and a very emotional graduation ceremony was held outdoors on the polo (soccer) field. At the graduation ceremony Bleibtreu blamed the Board for failing the college, but mentioned that "Prescott College has turned out more individuals and individualists than any place I've ever known. Prescott College lives on in these people."[30]

Prescott Center College's First Full Year in the Hassayampa Inn, 1975-76

It is one thing to start a new college after years of planning, fundraising, campus building, and curriculum planning, and quite another to start at a moment's notice in the basement of a hotel. There was a lot of brave talk and sincere eagerness, but many uncertainties remained about funding, students returning in the fall of 1975, recruiting new students, and every aspect of the new corporation and College. Some of the faculty and staff who had joined in the emergency semester and signed up to finish the year in order to graduate as many seniors as possible were not sure they wanted to continue after that was accomplished. About half of the 196 students who enrolled in the Center College for that final semester had graduated. There were hopes that some of the other 250 who had not enrolled in the spring would return if the new College were underway, hopes that they had not committed themselves elsewhere. The Prescott College Archives contain many expressions of the reservations people felt along with the optimism engendered by the prospect of making a new beginning. Alum Ed Miller wrote a glowing letter to his fellows describing the events of closing the old campus and starting the new College, which contained such phrases as: "This brought out the overwhelming positive energy during stress situations for which Prescott College people are famous," and "the spirit of Prescott College is too great to die."[84]

As the summer progressed, decision after decision committed the group to continuing. For example, there was a surplus of about $7,000 from PCAE's last spring semester and the community voted to invest it into recruiting, instead of splitting it and closing up shop. Stuckey said that, at this point, "We were certainly willing to talk about anybody's idea that had any semblance of reality." The college was running outdoor adventure trips, including raft trips down the Grand Canyon, for "friends of the college," which included anybody willing to write a check. Stuckey continues, "What we were trying to do was build friends through that process, to introduce them to the competence of students in life and death situations, and in fact build a mailing list and a donor list."[56] And according to the *Chronicle of Higher Education*, the Center was considering "running outdoor programs for students at *straight* [conventional] colleges."[13]

A new Catalog was created portraying all that had happened. Prize-winning Southwest landscape photography and photos of classroom and field courses were selected and sent to the printers, who produced a Catalog more beautiful than that of the final year on the big campus. By July those who were tepid left and there was no issue; Prescott Center would open.

At that point a new question arose: How many students would really enroll and pay tuition? The admissions volunteers were producing hundreds of hand-written letters, and others were calling former and prospective student by phone. Lists were kept, but it was decided that deposits would not be required that year. It was first come first served.

With a goal of 300 students, a cautious budget was formulated based on 180 students. To be prudent, Stuckey also had a secret budget in case there were only 100 students. On registration day in early September the faculty and staff were expectantly milling around the Hassayampa Inn dining room waiting for the results. By the end of the day 49 full-time and 8 part-time students had registered. So the fall semester of 1975 opened with a tiny number of students.

Operating on the assumption of 180 students, a budget had been drawn up that would pay faculty "not a good salary, not even a decent salary, but a subsistence salary." However, with less than a quarter of the hoped for number of students, everything including the secret budget was "thrown out the window."[56]

During spring semester 1975, when the goal had been to finish the year,

money had been distributed according to the immediate need of each employee and family, as an emergency plan to keep the school afloat. Over the
summer it had been agreed to retain all staff and faculty who wished to stay at
a reasonable salary. When only 57 students reenrolled in the 1975 fall semester, those plans had to be scrapped, and another emergency plan was formed.
Those the Board considered to be essential staff and faculty were offered a
very meager "full time" nine-month salary. Those who had additional sources
of income were asked to accept payment as "half time, half-pay" teachers,
with reduced class loads and decreased advising and administrative duties.

Loss of the grand campus of the old College was certainly a major factor in the decline from around 450 students in 1974 fall semester to only
57 students in the fall of 1975. An even more important factor was the loss
of accreditation. This did not reflect on the educational program, but it had
a direct impact on student recruitment and retention. Some of the students
(and more likely their parents) were uncomfortable with the suspension of
accreditation, but wanted to continue at the new Center College.

Ingenious Approaches to Recreating the Program on a Much Reduced Scale

To address the problem of lack of accreditation, contacts were made with
a number of small alternative colleges. Various arrangements were considered, including purchase of PCAE by another College that was accredited,
or creating a federation of small colleges under joint ownership with joint
accreditation. Prescott Center College soon affiliated with Johnston College,
the alternative college of the University of Redlands in Southern California.
Students of both Colleges could take classes at either, receiving transferable
credit and accredited degrees through Johnston. Students did take courses
at the affiliate for an enrollment period or so, but no Prescott students are
known to have graduated from Johnston.

There was no recruitment budget, so the College was constrained to depend on small ads and word-of-mouth to get out its message. The admissions "office" consisted of a desk operated mostly by students, who answered
inquiries with personal letters, explaining they were in the process of creating
a new kind of college.

The most surprising phenomenon was the type and quality of students
who enrolled when the "lifeboat" College emerged. Accreditation had been
suspended, classes met in dilapidated and crowded facilities, equipment or
vehicles were inadequate or nonexistent for laboratory or field work as well
as for library research, yet the College continued to attract exceptional students. Students who had good academic records, or had developed their own
businesses, traveled to Prescott at their own expense to see what was really

going on, and usually enrolled enthusiastically. One example was a student body officer of a branch of the State University of New York (SUNY) who decided to spend her last two years at Prescott College, knowing she would receive a non-accredited degree. Most of the new recruits had at least one year of college credits and were on average a couple of years older than typical new classes at traditional institutions. Beyond these details, the new students were adventurers, mature in their commitment to learn, eager students, and often outdoor athletes.

The College reduced to a fifth of its former student population and with no real campus or library, had to take seriously its slogan, "The Southwest Is Our Classroom." The eight fresh incoming students were hurriedly whisked off on wilderness orientation while the returning students gathered to design their study programs. They wanted to go to Prescott College. Stuckey recalls, "So there we were, sitting on the basement floor of the Hassaympa Hotel, a dungeon-like setting, and all the students saying this is what we want to do."[56]

One option considered that semester was to relinquish the College's designation as a liberal arts institution offering a BA degree and become an institute for Southwest environmental studies offering a BS degree. After serious deliberation most students decided they were interested in a balanced, interdisciplinary education and the BS alternative was put aside. This made

Rugged Prescott Center students

it necessary to strengthen the social sciences, humanities, and arts curricula, which was done as opportunities allowed.

The returning students eagerly registered for classes and field studies that were already planned and ready to go, and for the number of registrants there was a wide variety of offerings. More importantly they were going to be allowed to be involved in developing curriculum.

The community worked as a team to create the curriculum, convening periodic planning sessions called *curriculum symposia*. Classes and field work were suspended for a day or two while everyone—students, faculty, and staff—designed the courses and field projects, and specified necessary facilities and financing for at least two years in advance.

Experience outside the traditional classroom, whether in the wilderness or urban settings, was an integral feature of the curruculum. Students became directly involved in current social and environmental issues. Members of the faculty with training in sociology, philosophy, history, economics, psychology, and anthropology mentored students as they examined the implications of conflicting ideologies, economic forces, rural life, utopian models, community building, urban problems—all from a perspective of environmental concern.

Projects emcompassed work with the City of Prescott—land use and development studies for planning departments; internships teaching in the local school system; counseling assistance through the local guidance clinic. Other opportunities consisted of working for desert reclamation in Wickenburg (restoring the desert to its pregrazing stage); environmental impact studies; studies of the tourist influence in a Mexican seaside town; weekend Desert Studies where students could work as faculty assistants observing and photographing wildlife, leading trail rides; field work in art composition within the art community of Rancho Linda Vista just north of Tucson.

Prescott College students and faculty members could pop up almost anywhere in the wilderness and in the civilized world. Engaged in experiential learning, or working in service projects, they operated with what Hal Lenke called a "campus in dispersion." Within weeks of the reopening, returning students set out on nine separate expeditions, ranging from the Sea of Cortez to a field study in Hell Canyon examining the existence of God. Students were engaged in land restoration and art projects throughout the state. The students also continued to serve as Prescott's mountain rescue team, continuing in the tradition of saving lives.[57]

Wilderness Orientation was required of all new enrollees and consisted of a three-week expedition through Southwestern rugged terrain. For students with a major interest in adventure and skills training, or who wished to acquire credentials in professional wilderness leadership, there was a solid program in outdoor action.

Courses were listed alphabetically, because the College was not departmentalized and most courses were interdisciplinary. Credit was given at the level of the student's performance and competence in the subjects. These and all courses were jointly planned by faculty and students together in a yearly symposium, based on the individual graduation plans of students.[39]

Drawing on the effort and ideas of all involved, the College was able to resolve issues that had arisen earlier from disparate and conflicting philosophies—issues that had plagued the former College. What was exceptional in the pre-bankruptcy era was preserved. Such features as interdisciplinary and experiential study, wilderness orientation and the outdoor program, and equal dedication to scholarship and innovation were reemphasized. New approaches were also instituted, creating a new synthesis. The College entered into an extended period of poverty and educational innovation, with a remarkably consistent philosophy and practice. The principal foundation stones of this philosophy were:

Student self-direction and experiential learning

People understand and retain what they learn if they choose it, structure it, operate out of internal motivation, and put it into practice in the real world. This principle was applied broadly, not just in the classroom or field studies. Students participated as equals in designing their own graduation programs—no predetermined lists of courses were handed out. It is a safe assumption that no two students ever graduated with identical transcripts. Self-direction was also applied institutionally. Students were members of equal standing on all curriculum, management, and planning committees. Students were also elected to the new Board of Directors, not as representatives of the student body, but as equal participants in their own right. College was the place and time to be a full person in every respect.

Graduation on the basis of demonstrated competence and breadth, not by accumulation of conventional credits

This practice was based on two principles—first, that students are individuals who have different talents and interests, and the Carnegie unit credit systems of graduation leads only to detrimental "cookie cutter" standardization, and second, that credits and grades are inherently flawed indicators, as illustrated by such phenomena as grade inflation. The community believed that *internal* motivation to learn the material and skills would lead to genuine learning, as contrasted with working for *extrinsic* rewards like grades, credits, and GPA scores. The College's philosophy held that learning *by the numbers* leads to superficiality, and that putting badges of achievement between the learner and learning is a distraction. Therefore the portfolio system of digesting learning in more personal terms, thinking on paper, and reporting learning to teachers and mentors replaced the old lecture-test method.

The term *Competence* replaced the conventional idea of a major. Competence meant that students should demonstrate a grasp of the history and literature, major theories and bodies of knowledge, skills and ethics of their fields, and that they could *apply that learning* in the real world. The term *Breadth* replaced minor, to indicate that students should demonstrate themselves to be liberal artists, participants in the literature, arts, and cultural life of their own society, and in most cases of other cultures. The word *demonstrate* in the sentences above meant that it was the responsibility of each candidate to convince a graduation committee that she or he had accomplished at least the BA level of competence in terms of academic learning, but also of experiential learning, and of application of their learning to real life issues. This kind of learning was accomplished through completion of courses and independent studies, but just as importantly through hands-on research, service and management projects, and artistic creation. Credit was only granted through completion of learning contracts, whether in courses or independent studies. The students' self-designed graduation programs culminated in meaningful senior projects, often comparable to MA theses.

One distinct advantage Prescott Center College enjoyed was very small classes. Classes were not cancelled when there were only three or four students, and the largest class was about fourteen. This educational format quickly proved itself through producing high quality learning and encouraging self-direction. In many ways the Center operated more like a good graduate school, and carried out research and service projects locally, throughout the Southwest, and soon in Latin America.

As the months went by and the Prescott Center continued to subsist and carry out an effective educational program, the benefits of bankruptcy and loss of accreditation began to accumulate. It was finally possible to distill a coherent educational philosophy and clarify issues that were papered over in the former College. After some intense give and take, a new synthesis was created in which environmental and liberal arts studies were to be equally emphasized. The operation of the Center was truly focused on education. Its work became simple, transparent, and direct, and it succeeded, with a very small budget. The faculty members who chose to remain with the struggle were well qualified progressive thinkers, and fully involved. Students were able, indeed were required by circumstances, to function as adults responsible for their own education and for the progress of the whole community. Both faculty and students were intent on following the philosophy to which they had recommitted and worked to develop: 1) self-direction, 2) real experience, and 3) competence. Competence was the goal of all students, and the core of their program was determined by the route they chose to take to reach that competence.

THE BEGINNINGS OF A CAMPUS

Although the community had agreed that a college consists of people and not buildings, it was clear that a building to house the college would still be beneficial. The College had been operating out of the basement of the Hassayampa Inn, and had considered buying it, operating the hotel and restaurant and using the facility, but didn't have the funds. Facilities committees continued searching for not only a suitable new campus, but the money with which to buy it.

In the spring of 1977, the money came through a series of old friends and connections that led to a meeting between Stuckey and the director of the Fleischman Foundation, a politically conservative, multi-million dollar fund. Stuckey met with the director in his office in Boulder, Colorado, and wove an elaborate story of the college mixing "part Ron Nairn's initiative and what America needs and leadership and so forth, and part communitarianism and collegialism." Two weeks later the college received a grant of $37,000, its first major fundraising success.[56]

Shortly after receipt of the grant fate intervened again, this time through a well-timed newspaper article. Stuckey noticed the front page headline in the Prescott *Courier*, "Golden Key Loses License." Golden Key was an alcoholic rehabilitation center, and formerly the Sisters of Mercy convent, housed at 220 Grove Avenue—a perfect sized building in the middle of Prescott.

After careful consideration of this location and others by the Board, the building was secured and Sister of Mercy Convent was purchased on May 26, 1976, in time to adapt it and be ready for use in the 1977 fall semester. The Convent building now became "Old Main."[55]

Sisters of Mercy Convent Becomes New Campus

DEVELOPMENT OF CURRICULAR PROGRAMS

All of the drastic changes that occurred in just three semesters (spring 1975, then 1975-76)—leaving the grand campus and moving to downtown Prescott, reduction of the student body from about 450 to 200 and then to 50, losing the anthropology faculty and most of the research scientists and traditionalist professors—

were reflected in the curriculum of Prescott Center College. Nevertheless the philosophical and operational character of the College continued. The anthropology work was replaced by an equally strong focus on natural history and field biology with application to environmental conservation. The scholarly approach to history and philosophy turned more toward current developments in U.S. and world cultures and politics—the revolutions of the 1960s. Photography continued, as evidenced by beautiful work in Catalogs and other media. Performing arts learning involved students and faculty participation in local productions and music groups. With the College now located in town, there was increased interest in public and private schools, and internships in local clinics and service organizations. The outdoor action programs, including wilderness orientation, went ahead without a break in stride, but reduced in size. Most of the facilities that were closed on the old campus had counterparts in the town. Most importantly, students and faculty had full access to the Yavapai College library.

To understand how the curriculum evolved during these years, see Table 4.

Adding a Semiresidential Adult Degree Program

The next major undertaking was the initiation of an Adult Degree Program (ADP) in 1978. This extended experiential education and the opportunity to earn a Bachelor of Arts degree to non-resident students. The program was formed in recognition of the growing trend of adults returning to school and realizing that the College's educational philosophy was especially well-suited to this new group of students. For many adults, returning to a traditional college was inconvenient at best, and often impossible. Therefore, ADP was created to fit around work and family schedules, allowing self-directed adults to obtain their degrees by individually designed plans.

Although the program began in 1978 with only eight students, the College had high hopes of transferring Prescott College philosophies to adult education. In 1980, Annabelle Nelson, who had advanced training in this field, joined the staff. With the support of Stuckey, she developed the logistics and methods and established the Adult Degree Program (ADP).

The school now had the beginnings of a campus and a very active curriculum. But it remained tiny for the next decade, growing from 62 to 100 resident students, and adding a non-resident component in 1978 which grew to 60, making the total student body 160 students in 1983-1984. As a harbinger of change, the College was finally granted the use of its original name, Prescott College, by the purchaser of its original campus and corporation, Embry-Riddle Aeronautical University (ERAU). While ERAU retained

	Programs					Description
Jan. thru June, 1975	The "interim" college, called **The Prescott Center,** offers those courses and independent studies that are needed to graduate seniors and to keep the pattern of the Prescott College curriculum together for the rest of the year.					College reincorporates as Prescott Center for Alternative Education—PCAE. Moves into downtown Prescott.
1975-76	First PCAE Catalog lists four Interdisciplinary Programs					About fifty students return for fall, 1975—student-faculty ratio of 3 to 1. New pioneer spirit emerges—all pledge to continue. Jim Stuckey elected President.
	Outdoor Action	Community and Society	Self Awareness and Expression	Environment and Wilderness		
1976-77	Names of programs are refined:					Student body grows slowly—new curriculum configuration emerges as reflected in programs. Purchase of larger building at 220 Grove Ave.
	Outdoor Action	Interpretations of Culture	Human Development: Stages and Processes	Environmental Studies		
1977 thru 1979	New category of curriculum added: Support Offerings					Support offerings added to provide a home for general education in some humanities areas.
	Outdoor Action	Interpretation of Culture	Human Development: Stages and Processes	Environmental Studies	Support Offerings	
1979 thru 1984	Humanities is added as a new program					1980 begins an 11-year period without major changes in the curriculum—College grows steadily. Starts non-resident program (ADP). Full accreditation restored.
	Outdoor Action	Southwest Studies	Human Development	Environmental Studies	Humanities	

Table 3. Curriculum Configuration, 1975-1984

ownership of Prescott College, Inc., its board formally passed a resolution to allow PCAE to use "Prescott College" as its trade name or brand.

CHANGE IN LEADERSHIP

Dr. Stuckey resigned the presidency early in 1983, having led the reestablishment of Prescott College as a viable and growing institution. He held over as president for a few months while he moved into the Adult Degree Program that he had helped found. There, he continued to provide essential leadership in creating dynamic, experiential education throughout Arizona and beyond.

In the summer of 1983, Ralph Bohrson, of the Ford Foundation, was appointed president. His approach to the presidency was different from Stuckey's emphasis on educational innovation. He brought other skills and priorities. He emphasized stability and wanted to move away from any hint of crisis management. He immediately set out goals that were modest but within reach. He reformed the business and student aid systems, and activated a committee for long term planning, which developed plans that guided the College's development for several years. He initiated new contacts with community leaders, joined the Chamber of Commerce and other service organizations, and made the town aware of the College's real and potential contributions to local culture and economy. Finishing candidacy status and getting full accreditation became a priority for Bohrson, and after two years of intense effort by the whole staff and the Board, Prescott College was granted full accreditation on June 22, 1984.

Having achieved accreditation, Prescott Center College's association with Johnston College was no longer necessary, but a friendly and cooperative relationship continued. Increasingly, the College participated in various consortia with other institutions of higher education, and faculty members were given some support in their participation in professional associations, and in research and writing. For example, the community again became a leader in the Association for Experiential Education (AEE).

Moving into the broader academic circles, the Prescott Center College community was surprised to discover that the larger world of higher education knew of this little Arizona college, and were supportive of "The College That Refused to Die." Research done in the late 1970s indicated that during that era approximately 170 small private schools had been forced to declare bankruptcy. Only Prescott College was able to reestablish itself as a viable residential college. And it was even more gratifying to realize that Prescott College was still considered to be a national leader in environmental and outdoor education and in educational innovation in general. The College became a model for other schools, and many institutions throughout the country patterned programs after those of Prescott Center College.

Although Prescott Center College's programs were recognized as innovative and of high quality, lack of accreditation had restrained student recruitment and growth. With full accreditation granted in the summer of 1984 that barrier was down. Prescott College had been reestablished under its original name, and every aspect of the College began to grow.

While the years between 1975 and 1984 had been very challenging, those who had been involved in the struggle, when asked, said they enjoyed it immensely and were proud of their achievement. Prescott Center College had graduated more than 400 students, 90 of them through the non-resident Adult Degree Program.

Accreditation: Lost and Found

◇◇◇◇◇◇◇

The goal of accreditation is to ensure that education provided by institutions of higher education meets acceptable levels of quality. [98]

The original Prescott College had been accredited by North Central Association of Colleges and Schools (NCA). Although Arizona is obviously a Southwestern state and not in the north central part of the United States, Parker and his supporters who had Congregational Church contacts in Chicago and the upper Midwest chose NCA to be their accrediting agent, and initiated the process even before the opening of the College in 1966.

NCA had been founded in 1895 as one of six regional institutional accreditors in the United States. The accrediting arm of the North Central Association, the Higher Learning Commission, like the other five regional accreditors, is not a division of any governmental agency, but has the official recognition of the U.S. Department of Education and the Council on Higher Education Accreditation.

North Central Association through its Higher Learning Commission accredits degree-granting educational institutions in many states. And Prescott College in Arizona was one of them. [97]

Prescott College's accreditation was terminated with the bankruptcy of its nonprofit corporation, Prescott College, Inc., and it could not bequeath its accreditation to the new corporation, Prescott Center for Alternative Education. To North Central, PCAE was an unknown factor.

The new College survived its first semester and graduated a class of 105 seniors with accredited degrees by the skillful finagling of an agreement with the University of Arizona by Henry Bleibtreu, vice chairman of the Prescott College Board of Trustees and the dean of the U of A College of Liberal Arts. He was a member of a three-person committee that sent a proposal to Prescott College's accrediting agency (NCA) asking that they allow seniors of the Prescott Center to graduate with accredited degrees, since the teachers and classes remained the same, and their work had been completed during the time the College was accredited. North Central at first refused, but Bleibtreu convinced the accrediting association to allow a certain number of degrees to be held "in escrow" from when the college was accredited to allow the seniors to graduate with accredited degrees.

Accreditation is not an official license or a legal requirement for the operation of a college. Accreditation associations have no legal enforcement duties, but are organized to provide institutional evaluation services benefiting students, parents, and donors, as well as the schools themselves. Lack of accreditation puts institutions in the position of having to promote their educational services without any recognized agency evaluating and vouching for the authenticity of their programs. Parents and students are put in the quandary of "buyer beware" should the institution of their choice not be accredited. They have no guarantee that the school's programs are as good as the school professes, and they are also aware that degrees from unaccredited institutions are less valuable when applying for acceptance into graduate programs, employment, or any other significant appointment.

When it began in the spring semester of 1975, Prescott Center College was an unaccredited school with no campus, few facilities or books—basically a lot of spirit, but not many of the accoutrements of a functioning college.

Not having accreditation was a serious handicap, and Prescott Center had to make some sort of arrangement for accreditation if it wanted to continue to attract the same high quality students as its predecessor, and to be able to offer respected academic degrees. The solution was provided by Prescott Center joining forces with Johnston College, of the University of Redlands in California. Students of both Colleges could take classes at either and receive transferable credit. This gave the Johnston College students an opportunity to participate in Prescott Center College's environmental and outdoor action programs and allowed Prescott Center students to receive accredited degrees.

Getting the College re-accredited under it own accomplishments was to take a great deal of work, and several more years. In fact, it was nearly ten more years before the school gained full accreditation from the North Central Association.

President Stuckey had made the argument to NCA that some form of accreditation should be allowed the Center since it was really an extension of the former Prescott College, continuing the same programs with the same faculty and many of the same students. A brief accreditation report was put together, and when the College was well settled into the convent building, the team representing NCA was invited to campus.

In 1978 a committee of professors and administrators (from other colleges) representing NCA made their first visit to the campus. At the conclusion of the visit this team issued a report expressing satisfaction with the Center's innovative programs, faculty, and community spirit, and the progress that had been made. They were concerned with the tenuous finances but noted that Prescott Center College had adopted a serious no-debt policy. But they were also concerned with the possibility of burnout, because the level of commitment and effort they observed appeared to them unsustainable. They awarded the Center "Candidate Status," which was the best result that could have happened at that point. This extended the school's period to apply for accreditation through 1984.

The team revisited Prescott Center College in 1980 to determine the school's progress and then again in 1982.

Although the team noted several strengths in the young College, including a strong commitment to its mission, dynamic and individualized teaching and learning activities, and stabilized academic and financial planning, budgeting, and decision making, they determined that their concerns were too great to allow Prescott Center to gain accreditation. Out of the five criteria used for determining accreditation the team felt that Prescott College was solid on four of them and weak on one.

The Criteria are:

1) A clear and publicly stated purpose consistent with the institution's mission and appropriate to an institution of higher education; 2) the institution has effectively organized the human, financial, and physical resources necessary to accomplish its purposes; 3) the institution is accomplishing its educational and other purposes; 4) the institution can continue to accomplish its purposes and strengthen its educational effectiveness; and 5) the institution demonstrates integrity in its practices and relationships.

The visiting team was not convinced that Prescott College had what it took to guarantee long-term sustainability, and would not pass on the fourth criterion. Among their concerns were the overwhelming demands on the faculty that required them to function at or beyond their limits, inadequate salaries, low student enrollments (which were around a hundred at the time), limited financial resources, student pursuit of diverse interests so as to strain available resources, and marginal physical facilities.

Stuckey, who had been appointed president of the new college in the days following the bankruptcy and had worked hard to get the college back on its feet, sent a twenty-four-page memo defending the College against these concerns, citing additional data he felt should be considered. However, the Center still remained on candidacy status.

Two years later, in March of 1984, the NCA visiting team was back. Previous concerns seem to have been taken care of by the College, or were irrelevant this time around, as one by one Prescott College passed each of the five criteria for accreditation. Regarding their mission statement, the team responded that "the institution has clearly and publicly stated its purposes and those purposes are consistent with its mission and appropriate to a post-secondary educational institution. This mission is distinctive in its single focus thrust and its explicit effort to blend learning accruing from experience with learning accrued from more traditional classroom settings."[1] This time, the resources were deemed adequate, including the student population of 154, only fifty more than the last visit when it was believed to be too low. Although financial sources were still a major concern, and the physical resources consisted of only two buildings, one bus, two vans, and an inventory of outdoor equipment, they were solid enough to allow the second criterion to be met. And regarding the fourth criterion, which two years earlier had questioned the College's ability to continue its programs, the team said, "Through its candidacy and since its founding in 1975, Prescott College has shown its commitment to fulfill a distinctive mission and to operate with fiscal integrity. It is doing so now. There are no 'red flags' which might be interpreted to suggest that the efforts of the college to continue to accomplish its purposes will be undermined." In addition, they noted that "There is a mood of planning and preparation for the future permeating the entire college."[1]

Prescott College regained NCA accreditation on June 22, 1984. According to President Bohrson, "It's a vindication of the school's judgment and our programs. ... It is a fitting tribute to those whose devotion to the ideals of this college generated the energy and drive to keep the dream alive despite crushing odds. We exist today thanks to the vision of our founders and the commitment of those who believe it is this college's job to plan and teach for a future world of humane peace, freedom, and justice."[1]

The re-accreditation of the school had been hanging over the College since the bankruptcy. This was final proof that the College had made it. "As nearly as we can find out, there never has been a private college that went out of business, came back again, and regained their accreditation," said President Bohrson.[102]

Despite a decade of struggling and sacrifice, they had regained the respect of the academic world and still managed to keep the original values alive.

Although the college had regained its accreditation, there were still looming concerns that the NCA team had noted, and that still plagued Prescott Center. Top among them were the ever-present financial woes. They were still operating almost solely off of student tuition (seventy-five percent), making the operating budget vulnerable. Most years the College's total intake was only a few thousand dollars more than it was spending. Salaries and benefits for faculty were still low and physical resources were minimal. Even the most recent accreditation reports mention that finances are still "the area of Prescott Center's greatest vulnerability."

Year after year in subsequent NCA visits for the continuation of accreditation, both the concerns and praise continue to sound remarkably similar. The College is routinely praised for its student body, faculty, and staff that are "unusually committed to Prescott's special mission." The 1990 accreditation report notes that the College is distrustful of administrators and the Board due to the previous bankruptcy; "requiring an unusually high degree of consensus before action is taken, this corporate model has spawned an organization which emphasizes participation and responsibility for all." The NCA also reports, "The faculty and staff are dedicated, engaged and passionate about their work. [1990]"[103]

Growth and Conventionalization
1984-1999

◇◇◇◇◇◇◇

With the College now accredited, Bohrson pushed to update the College's mission. Building on the philosophy from the Symposium and the Stuckey era, he organized a committee to frame a new mission statement, and then personally drafted it based on the committee's outline. It was readily approved by the various faculties and went into effect. A new logo was adopted along with the official motto "For the Liberal Arts and the Environment."

There had been a long-running discussion within the faculty dating back

Prescott Center College Community

to the 1970s concerning the actual mission of the College. The debate had stemmed from the College being principally and nationally known for its experiential and multi-disciplinary approach to studies of the environment. It was equally famous, and a pioneer, in adventure education. There was a demand throughout the United States. and the world for graduates from these programs to manage and lead outdoor adventure, recreation, and education programs. But the other programs were not so well known. The College had also developed excellent programs in fine and performing arts. There were many areas of distinction in the other liberal arts and humanities as well, in spite of their experiencing more volatility in terms of curricula and faculty turnover. Although the liberal arts and humanities had been repeatedly reaffirmed, unofficially there was still a strong strain of the old opinion—that the school was mainly an environmental college. The approval of this new mission statement finally put this issue to rest.

MISSION STATEMENT 1984

It is the mission of Prescott College to educate students of diverse ages and backgrounds to understand, thrive in, and enhance our world community and environment.

We regard learning as a continuing process and strive to provide an education that will enable students to live productive lives while achieving a balance between self-fulfillment and service to others. Students are encouraged to think critically with a sensitivity to the human community and the ethics of the biosphere.

Our broad academic program in the liberal arts utilizes classroom work, tutorials, library research, and field studies. Students are expected to demonstrate competence in individually designed study programs and possess a breadth of knowledge beyond their major areas of study.

Our educational philosophy stresses experiential learning and self-direction within an interdisciplinary curriculum. The curriculum integrates philosophy, theory, and practice so that students synthesize knowledge and skills to confront important value issues and make personal commitments.

More specifically, our goal is to graduate people who demonstrate:
- Competence in subject matter and its application to real life situations.
- College-level skills of written communication and essential mathematics.
- The skills necessary to analyze problems and identify and evaluate appropriate information resources.
- Self-direction in learning.

- Integration of the practical and theoretical aspects of human experience.
- Integration of the spiritual, emotional, and intellectual aspects of the human personality.
- Sensitivity to, and understanding of, one's own and other cultures.
- Commitment to responsible participation in the natural environment and human community.

In order to accomplish our mission, the College offers programs that meet the needs of both adult learners and traditional age students in the areas of Integrative Studies, Environmental Studies, Adventure Education, Arts & Letters, Education, Counseling & Psychology, and Cultural & Regional Studies.

Each division—resident, non-resident, alumni, etc.—undertook the project of completely revising all publications, and the marketing team headed by Dirk Jansen received a national prize for the quality of the College's new logo, Catalogs, and other media. Recruitment efforts and national publicity were reorganized and increased, resulting in the combined student body, both resident and off-campus programs, growing by ten percent or more each year. Some programs grew incrementally while others expanded rapidly, and the College spawned new ones when opportunities presented themselves. This phase has been compared to Prescott College's adolescence. It grew by fits and starts because it was a college with many quality professionals of different persuasions, some pulling one way and some another. It went through some trying times but continued to grow and show remarkable promise. The rapid flowering of programs was continually pushing the College to expand its facilities and budget.

An important element of the newly revised mission was to provide education for underserved populations. The first such opportunity came about in 1987, when the College was authorized by the Arizona Department of Education to train classroom teachers and issue Arizona Teaching Credentials. With the support of federal and tribal grants, the College created the Center for Indian Bilingual Teacher Education (CIBTE). Its mission was to prepare Native American bilingual (tribal language and English) teachers through special training and internships on their reservations. At this writing (2005) Prescott College has graduated and credentialed nearly five hundred Native American teachers on the largest reservations, Tohono O'odham and Navajo (Diné) nations, and on several smaller tribal reservations.[11] The teacher-education and credentialing program was expanded to include bilingual Spanish-English candidates when the College opened a small branch in Tucson in 1988 to serve non-resident students in the southern half of the state.

With the adoption of a firm mission statement and accreditation secured, Bohrson next took on the task of organizing and regularizing the College's accounting practices and business functions. The source of about half of the College's revenue was federal grants and guaranteed loans with which students paid tuitions. The Board and administration undertook a careful review of the processes and accounting procedures related to financial aid, ensuring that the College was following the regulations to the letter. As they did this, they also developed new sources for scholarships and loans, thus enabling more students to attend the College.

A major period of growth and expansion had begun. A new long-range plan was in place. The business procedures were regularized. Prescott Center College was safely established and now seemed to be financially secure. With confidence in the foundation upon which the school finally rested, Bohrson retired as president in 1988. The College was able to continue on track and run smoothly because former president Stuckey was willing to fill in for the next several months while a national search for a new president took place.

Feeling that the College's democratic salary practices might discourage well qualified candidates from applying, the Board decided to offer the president compensation at a higher range than for other administrative employees. In 1989, Dr. Douglas North, former vice president of Goddard College, was selected by the Board to be the next president of the College. North was an ambitious and progressive leader and was attracted to new ideas. During his first two years, he energetically pursued several projects at once, building the fundraising potential of the Board, seeking more adequate campus facilities, hiring a director of development and several other high level staff including a new controller, and paving the way for a new master's degree program. Shortly after appointing him the College began differentially raising the salary for all employees. Faculty and staff compensation were still relatively low, but were boosted to be more equivalent to those typically offered by a group of comparable colleges.

Programs: Their Growth and Development

In 1991 Prescott College was approved to offer its first graduate degree. The low-residence Master of Arts Program (MAP) was accredited by the North Central Association of Colleges and Schools. Its charter class of twelve matriculated in January 1992; it graduated its first class in 1993. Low or limited residence means that most of the coursework was carried out by working with mentors off campus. The program first served local students and those in Tucson, but soon had students throughout the country. The

Prescott College model of self-directed, experiential education was a perfect fit for people developing their professional careers by studying at the master's level while still needing to be employed, or for those wishing to enhance their personal lives while having to maintain a household.

According to Dr. Ellen Cole, original director and then dean of MAP, "when the program was first dreamed of and then actually designed, we were thinking specifically of the adult graduate student ready to work creatively and independently. We wanted to free highly competent adult students from the constraints of 'one size fits all' courses and classrooms, enabling them to design unique, individual programs to meet their needs and interests exactly."[27]

The Outdoor Action program that Prescott College had pioneered was not only becoming a legitimate field of study in higher education during the mid 1980s through the mid-90s, it was growing in popularity. The huge jump in student enrollment during these years prompted the Outdoor Action faculty to revamp the program to give it more structure. According to David Lovejoy, the coordinator of the program at that time, "The program stated its goal to become the best undergraduate source of well-trained adventure education and wilderness guides."

As the Outdoor Action program expanded to meet the needs of the growing College, the faculty teaching load increased considerably, necessitating the hiring of a steadily increasing number of instructors and adjuncts. Many of them were alums returning to the College after gaining more experience and training. More Wilderness Orientation guides were also required, and a comprehensive internship program was developed to train additional guides. The Outdoor Action program, along with Environmental Studies, continued to be valuable assets for the school, not only for their wilderness education curriculum but also because of their strong positive presentation to the outside world.

Environmental Studies was the

Professor David Lovejoy Climbing

most visible aspect of the College's national image and was fast becoming the more dominant program. Benefiting from being featured in much of Prescott College's student recruitment materials, the program led the College's growth. In 1992 the College was able to expand its Environmental Studies curriculum through an exciting new research center. The Kino Bay Center offered a base for the College to offer courses such as Marine Biology, Marine Conservation, and Natural History and Ecology of Kino Bay.

The original philosophy and charter of the College called for an interdis-

Environmental Studies at Sea of Cortez

ciplinary curriculum. Specialization and departmentalization were contrary to the purpose for which the College was conceived.[89]

By the second year (1966-67), interdisciplinary centers combined sciences, arts, and humanities, and planned and administered the curriculum. When PCAE had only about fifty resident undergraduate students, a single highly interdisciplinary program was created to handle a complex of liberal arts and humanities programs. By 1980, the curriculum was distributed into five theme groups—Outdoor Action, Human Development, Southwest or Regional Studies, and Humanities or Integrative Studies. As indicated on Table 4 (p. 121), the environmental and outdoor programs were stable, while humanities, human development, social and regional studies, and fine and performing arts went through some reshuffling of names and curricula, particularly toward the end of this period as the College quadrupled in enrollments.

In the case of the humanities and social studies areas, the main cause of these permutations was transience of faculty. Since Prescott College was known nationally for its pioneering outdoor (wilderness) and environmental programs, most teachers in these programs committed for a long tenure or their whole careers. By contrast, faculty in the liberal arts or humanities complex of programs cycled in and out much more frequently. In a thirteen-year period (1990-2002) there was an average of nine faculty members per year teaching in all of the programs combined. Yet twenty-two different individuals taught in these areas during this period, and only one teacher spanned that whole period. This turnover was on balance advantageous. New faculty brought new energy and creative ideas.

Each of these groupings was composed of small, more specialized, curricular areas, which tended to follow the particular interests and training of individual faculty members—along with demand by students. In the humanities areas, a whole subject field was usually "covered" by one teacher,

Julie Munro's Yoga Certification Class
photo by Travis Patterson

so this person had to be both a good scholar and teacher, and at the same time a generalist. **Human Development** offered foundation courses in developmental and personality psychology, professional education and teaching, counseling, gender studies, and peace studies. Students were placed in a rich variety of internships in local clinics and schools, and they carried out many challenging service projects. **Humanities**, as a curricular program, first offered courses and field work in fine arts, performing arts, literature, Spanish language, history, social and regional studies, and religion and philosophy. In 1991, Southwest/cultural and regional studies were set up as a separate group, but in 1995 they were reabsorbed into humanities due to internal disagreements about specialization. The College had grown considerably so that placing so many faculty members under one tent was unwieldy, and in 1997 the fine and performing arts faculty formed as separate program.

The Humanities and Arts programs continued to grow during this period, stabilizing at around eleven faculty members in 1996. The growth did not represent so much the broadening of the curricular areas covered but rather a strengthening of the existing ones in order to meet the increasing demands of students. The faculty adopted writing and mathematics competency standards for graduation. Competence testing and skills workshops were put in place to help students develop writing and mathematics proficiency and as an aspect of graduation requirements. At the other end of the spectrum many students came to the College with well-developed language skills and literary talent. They were encouraged to study serious literature and create their own by writing poetry, fiction, and journalistic pieces, which were published. The

Student Mounting Art Photographs

creative writings and the black and white photography of Prescott College's art and literature students were featured in the *Alligator Juniper,* a literary journal first issued in 1996. The *Alligator Juniper* has been published annually and has received national recognition since its beginning. The students also began forays into newspaper publication, leading to their regional weekly newspaper, *The Raven Review.*

The Prescott Fine Arts Association, the city's theatrical group, provided a readily accessible platform for students studying music and drama and also served as an important bridge between the community and the school. Students and faculty alike performed in drama productions put on by PFAA. Accomplished and apprentice performers were welcomed into community sponsored folk music festivals, and many joined in the local culture of music and dance. Courses in film writing and production (using video equipment) were frequently offered, with students trying their hand at making their own films.

Prescott College has always offered a world-class program in photography and other two-dimensional media. This began at the old College when the faculty included such world renowned artists as David Paladin and Frederick Sommer. Jay Dusard maintained a close relationship with the College, and his magnificent black and white landscape photographs were found throughout the College's Catalogs and other media, while he was achieving fame for his work photographing ranchers, cowboys, and the U.S.-Mexican border people, creating a permanent record of the disappearing Old West. In the late 1990s the visual arts delved into areas like social change and protest documentation, abstraction, and alternative photographic processes, moviemaking, and so forth. As in many aspects of the College, the emphasis has shifted from the fame and output of the faculty artists to the works of students. This reorientation could be seen in the frequent student art and photography exhibitions and auctions, hanging of their works throughout the

Student Telling Tall Tale

College, and the development of gallery space. Under the guidance of faculty, students worked with local artists in visual arts, sculpture, and native crafts. Prescott's beautiful and varied landscapes inspire the many forms of artistic expression that Prescott and the Southwest are known for.

In one of the faculty turnover cycles, several teachers in the human development and social studies areas left the College over a short interval. Humanities was discontinued in 1997 as a rubric and the **Integrative Studies** program took its place, but was soon separated into two functionally separate sub-programs—Human Development and Cultural and Regional Studies. Throughout this whole period the old cliché applied: the more things change, the more they stay the same.

The College motto, which appeared on all its literature, letterhead, even on campus signs and billboards, was "For the Humanities and the Environment." Though the College was not nationally known for its liberal arts program, a perusal of its Catalogs and its media illustrates the exciting and high quality curricula and activities it has created. Another way to articulate this accomplishment is to point out that within the College's interdisciplinary and experiential philosophy every kind of study—in any of the four or five curricular programs—had social, ethical, and esthetical dimensions.

ADDING TO THE CAMPUS

In 1990 the college was considering several campus space options, and Doug North wrote in his report to the Board on May 26, "The very success of the college has put the inevitability of large-scale change into the air" and that there was "a fear that change of this order might destroy the essential spirit of the college."[7]

The "fear" that North was referring to was discomfort with changes resulting from the need to expand the campus in some way to accommodate the growth of the student body and the requirements of larger programs. One possibility of "change" occurred in the form of a unique piece of property in the Granite Dells called Granite Gate. It all came about serendipitously. Jim Stuckey was doing some recreational flying around Prescott in a small plane when he noticed a large building nestled within the giant granite domes called the Dells northwest of the town. His interest piqued, he investigated. He discovered the property consisted of a large, not quite finished three-story resort hotel building on twenty acres that was in receivership and listed for bid by HUD. North and Dean Hiller quickly followed up and both students and faculty visited the site. The College bid one million, a tiny fraction of its worth; an equal bid came in from an investor group in Hawaii that could pay cash. Because Prescott College needed financing, it lost the bid.

Betsy Boulding, a long-tenure Board member, commented that a move

Year	Program columns / Description				Notes
1980	Addition of Humanities program. Cultural & Regional Studies renamed Southwest Studies.				Full accreditation restored, initiates 11 years without major changes in the curriculum—College grows steadily.
thru 1991	Outdoor Action	Southwest Studies	Human Develop-ment	Environmental Studies / Humanities	Starts non-resident program (ADP) and Native American Teacher Education Center (CIBTE).
1991	Southwest Studies changes name to Cultural and Regional Studies and expands mission				Growth and consolidation of programs. New campus centers in Arizona and Mexico.
thru 1995	Outdoor Action	Cultural and Regional Studies	Human Develop-ment	Environmental Studies / Humanities	
1995-96	Cultural and Regional Studies disbanded—merged with Humanities Human Development reduced				Interim Co-Presidency of Hiller and Branham (1996-97)
	OutdoorAction	Human Development	Environmental Studies	Humanities	
1996-97	Outdoor Action renamed Adventure Education				New President, Neal Mangham, appointed 1997. Board of Directors reformed to achieve financial stability.
	Adventure Education	Human Development	Environmental Studies	Humanities	
1997	Humanities divided. One part became Arts and Letters the other Integrative Studies—grouping of Cultural and Regional Studies with Human Development				Resident student body approaches 500. Total college enrollment approaches 1,000+. All non-resident divisions combines into one, called Adult Degree Graduate Programs (ADGP). New President, Dan Garvey, appointed.
thru 2000	Adventure Education	Integrative Studies split into two sub-programs: Cultural and Regional Studies and Human Development	Environmental Studies	Arts and Letters	

Table 4, Curriculum Configuration, 1980–2000

to Granite Gate "would've incredibly changed the college, because it didn't lend itself to the kind of thinking and the kind of people and the kind of learning that was going on at Prescott College. … It's creating a sense of place right here … in the middle of Prescott where students … face reality, learning to live their lives. We give them the tools to function, and urban settings are where people are going to have to function. [We are] creating a place [where we are], instead of lifting us up and putting us in another place." Her thoughts were not off the mark from what many students seemed to think. After visiting the area, when asked to choose whether they would prefer to move to Granite Gate or stay in town, the majority of students voted to stay in town.[51]

The Dalke property was another matter. It was provisionally offered to the College through a bequest arrangement. Dorothy Dalke, a long-time friend and supporter of the College, owned a trust in which she had placed eighty-seven acres of beautiful pine forest land adjacent to the town. She wished the property to remain undeveloped as a green zone, and she felt the College would be able to preserve it, while using a small portion of it for campus facilities. Through 1991-92, Mrs. Dalke's legal advisors negotiated with the College's administration to create a contract by which the College would purchase an insurance policy on her life with her trust as beneficiary. This was to provide the means for the property to be deeded to the college at her demise.[17]

According to Ann Dorman, a Board member at the time, "the Dalke Property gave great hope to people … it had been somewhat donated and so everybody got excited about that, but when you looked at the situation, it was just beyond the scope of what we could manage at the time … the Board and the presidents, the administration always looked at creating a campus before they had a stable financial base."[50]

The growing student body continued to need additional classrooms and offices. Hiller, under the direction of North and the Board, began to purchase more nearby buildings, to join Old Main as part of the campus. Most of these were already under lease and being used by the school. Downtown Prescott is quite compact, and the College also acquired properties that met special requirements, even though they were located a few city blocks from "Old Main." For several years, the College leased the old Elks Opera House downtown for $1 per year plus maintenance costs—which ultimately turned out to be prohibitive. The Sam Hill Warehouse, a large historic building on North Granite Street, was purchased in 1993 and was remodeled as a community center to accommodate large-scale College gatherings. Both the Elks and Sam Hill provided studio and gallery space for the expansion of curriculum in the fine and performing arts.

The Prescott College community has always had an interest in healthy lifestyle, and that included healthy food. In 1994, the Student Union purchased Tubbman's Café, which had originally been the laundry for the hospital that had been operated by the Sisters of Mercy. This fine old building was outfitted as a restaurant-bar and included a full, if small, commercial kitchen. The Student Union organization purchased the facility out of the students' activity funds, and proceeded to remodel it and qualify for a commercial restaurant license. Within months, the students opened a natural food café, called Organic Alley, which soon became an informal campus and community meeting center. The café building also provided a Student Union office

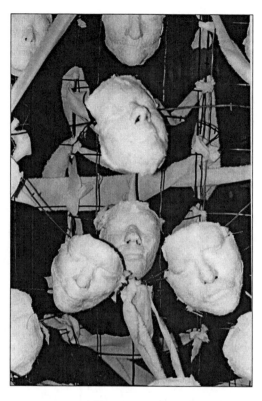

Masks of Identity

and a base for a student-operated Community Sponsored Agriculture (CSA) service that provided fresh organic produce to the college community and local residents.

In 1996 the College added Wolfberry Farm to its campus. The thirty-acre farm, located in the agricultural community of Chino Valley fifteen miles north of Prescott, was dedicated to research and experimentation. The acquisition and use of Wolfberry Farm allowed earlier limited studies in organic agriculture to expand into an extensive agroecology curriculum.

A Shift in Operational Philosophy

At every level there was a tendency to departmentalize and bureaucratize management. Uncoordinated decision making crept in as the College increased in size and spawned new divisions or departments. Fundamental issues surrounding the educational identity of the College emerged. Some segments of the community now felt that terms like "alternative" implied poor quality instruction, or "self-directed" meant loose standards for student performance. Over time as decisions were made, the College adopted more and more elements of the *standard model*—conventional ways of managing students, program planning, evaluation and graduation processes. These decisions were usually based on arguments that traditional practices would be the preferred path to improved standards. For example, formerly banned practices like pre-designing graduation "tracks" were instituted, making students in certain fields complete fixed lists of requirements as in conventional schools. This led to the imposition of quantitative requirements. Conventional credit-counting tended to crowd out qualitative criteria like knowledge of history of the field and acquaintance with the literature and so forth. Counting courses and credits as the main criteria of graduation became the common practice.

Other members of the community continued to hold the unique philosophy created in the Symposium. They suspected that adoption of *standard model* practices had eroded both qualitative standards and the school's emphasis on individualization and self-direction. But the vision of Prescott College as an innovator and pioneer in alternative education was fading, while reversion to convention was in ascendancy. In some cases these changing practices contradicted statements that remained in the College's Catalogs and other media. However, small classes and personal attention, field work, and the infectious enthusiasm of the College's various communities usually concealed and compensated for such disparities, so that the College continued to attract students and faculty who were excited about the small-scale personalized education offered by Prescott College.

There were other factors leading to a shift in paradigms within the College as well. When the College regained accreditation, it became connected to the encompassing world of higher education as never before, so that outside commitments tended to impose onto it the standard model for crediting learning and it tended to follow that standard educational philosophy would be applied. Society is also constantly evolving and changing. The progressivism that characterized the country when Prescott College was born in the 1960s had been severely challenged by a resurgent conservatism, sometimes enticing the College to conform to a variety of more traditional educational practices that were gaining favor nationally. All of these and other factors led to some drift and confusion in the College's philosophy and identity.

Growing Student Body—Increasing Needs

After the College was granted full accreditation in 1984, enrollments grew while at the same time tuitions were raised at rates exceeding inflation. The RDP student body increased from 101 students in 1984 to 370 students in 1994 and tuitions were raised from $3,400 to $9,600 during that period. ADP also increased from 8 students in 1978 to over 200 by 1994, and ADP and CIBTE were both producing significant revenues. Careful money management and good fortune combined so that the insecurities surrounding financial survival appeared to fade away. The more pressing problems seemed to be finding facilities and acquiring equipment to accommodate increasing enrollments and new educational ventures. As result of all this growth, the College budget had increased tenfold from just below $800,000 to almost $8 million by 1994. This amount was just about three times the budget of the "old College" in its most expensive year (excluding campus building costs). And a major part of the bigger budget went to increasing pay to all classified and professional personnel so that pay levels approached industry standards. In considering such money figures, the reader should bear in mind that inflation distorts comparisons over time. In the Money Matters chapters, figures are corrected for inflation by the Consumer Price Index for each year.

Money spent during this period was not carelessly used. It was fully employed in acquiring and servicing a fleet of sixteen passenger vans, renting more buildings for additional classrooms and operational and administrative spaces, purchasing some buildings, and remodeling the convent building. In addition to these local expenses, the College was upgrading the campus center in Tucson and the field research station in Kino Bay, Mexico, as well as an office on the Navajo reservation. There were literally thousands of improvements, small and large, such as developing audio-visual media and teaching equipment, etc.

To pay for these changes, North and the Board set higher goals for student recruitment, increased levels of tuition, and set higher goals for fundraising. Unfortunately the fundraising for unrestricted gifts improved very little—from about $270,000 in 1986-87 to $450,000 in 1994-95, not quite doubling. Restricted giving also remained almost flat. Tuitions revenue increased during that period from about $850,000 to $5.5 million—a multiple of about 6.5 times. The expense budget had thereby increased by a factor of ten while income increased by only a factor of six, creating a significant disparity. (See Money Matters, II.) Under the pressure of this unbalanced budgeting, the fiscal conservatism that had been maintained as a policy since 1975 was seriously eroding. This was not done consciously as a matter of policy. It inched up on the Board and new President. Budgets were planned on anticipated student enrollment and fundraising levels and based on the best case scenarios rather than history or realism.

For three successive years the Board was also in informational limbo. They requested comprehensive audits, but were told that the "books were in transition and were not in shape to support an audit." That explanation seemed questionable, considering that the previous president, Bohrson, was very meticulous in his financial management.

However, it was the case that North had brought in a new controller and manager of the business office. It also appears that a new bookkeeping system was necessary to handle the increasing level of complexity brought on by new divisions like MAP, the on-reservation teacher training program (CIBTE) and other new projects. In fact, the growing deficit was partially obscured by CIBTE grants that appear to have been incorrectly posted as unrestricted revenue for three years (1989-92). Yet almost all of that grant money was earmarked for Native American students' tuitions and administrative and teaching salaries associated with the program, and for that reason could not be used for any other purpose. This all led to a false impression that fundraising was improving.

The financial records from this period are incomplete. The new controller appears to have been incompetent or simply neglectful. At least it is not clear how these growing yearly deficits were bridged across the end of each fiscal year. It is clear, however, that a situation was developing that was similar to that of the "old College," accumulating debt and passing along deficits across the June 30 deadline for reconciling the books. The existing financial records of that period appear to indicate that the no-debt principle had slipped to the point that the College was again in danger.

During the May Board meeting of 1994, President North tendered his resignation, which was accepted. According to Betsy Boulding, long-term Board member from Tucson, "after Doug North left, and a lot of the Board members that Doug had picked [quit] … there wasn't anything much left … Fulton [Wright] and I stayed on to give it [the Board] some continuity and Fulton became President of the Board."[51]

While it was established policy that all professional positions were to be filled through a national search and a community-wide vetting process, the Board felt the College was not ready to open a national search at that time. The Board also was insecure about the financial health of the College. They decided to appoint internal administrators already on board to interim positions to fulfill the presidential functions. Joel Hiller, the dean of the College, accepted the interim position of external president, with the charge to raise funds and represent the College externally. Lady Branham, director of the Tucson operations, accepted the position of interim internal president, with the charge of managing the educational programs, personnel, budgets and other internal affairs.[6]

The new dual presidents soon discovered that North had left the College in an increasingly serious financial predicament. Knowledge of the situation that had been bequeathed to them came up inadvertently but abruptly, triggered by a new federal regulation governing student financial aid. Nearly half of the revenues supporting the College came from financial aid that students used to pay their tuitions (the balance came from their own resources). It had always been essential to maintain certification for the Title IV Student Financial Assistance Program. The very year that Branham began serving as internal president, the US Office of Post-Secondary Education (within Office of Education), which manages federal grants and loans to students, instituted a new regulation. Effective on July 1, 1994, a separate audit of the previous year's financial aid programs had to be submitted by all institutions in order to requalify for the student financial assistance programs. Consequently Branham immediately initiated a two-year audit—both to meet this mandate and to understand in more depth the school's finances. Very quickly the long-term problem with budgeting and financial control became visible.

The accounting was in disarray. Requisite annual reconciliations had not been carried out so the task of sorting out the books was very difficult. After much confusion brought about by incomplete reports, a delayed, mostly complete, financial statement was submitted. Fortunately the Office of Education accepted the report and granted the College temporary certification. The complete audit of fiscal year 1993, which was finally submitted on July 28, 1995, convinced the OE to restore full certification. (For a more detailed analysis of this period see Money Matters, Part IV.)

The dual presidents worked conscientiously so that the potential crisis seemed to be abated by fall 1995. Branham imposed new austerity budgets and corrected issues in the business office. Hiller continued small-scale fundraising and also secured a pledge of half a million dollars from an anonymous donor, which was to be matched dollar for dollar (however, this pledge was withdrawn when the Board decided to open a national search for a president, even though each of the interim presidents was invited to apply). Overall enrollments were up by forty students, and tuition income was up by $500,000.

In 1996, Branham brought a senior-level accountant onto the Prescott College Board whose credentials indicated expertise in community college finances. Ignoring conflict of interest issues, he promptly had himself set up as interim business manager/controller—the third within two years—and took over the College's business office at a significant per diem fee. He told the internal president and executive committee of the Board that his perusal of the books indicated that the College was heading toward insolvency and bankruptcy, and was in imminent danger of losing its accreditation as well as its certification to participate in the government's student financial aid program.

Branham precipitously suspended classes for an afternoon and convened a community meeting to which students, faculty, and administration, as well as local Board members, were invited. This new interim business manager/controller/board member explained his concerns to the whole College, emphasizing that only he had the expertise to "turn the financial train around and keep it from going over the cliff." It was at this same meeting that he told the whole community that the College would have to relinquish its bequest arrangement for the Dalke property. This announcement was made without authorization of the Board and was a stunning revelation to the College community, which put great stock in the prospect of saving the forest from development and building a campus there or at least a field station for environmental studies.

At this point many faculty and students were distracted from their studies to the cause of "saving the College." This board member was also rumored to have contacted North Central Association and the US Office of Education representing himself as the virtual president of a failing college, imploring them not to revoke accreditation or disqualify the College for financial aid. (As noted above, there is nothing in the archives to indicate these agencies were anticipating any such actions.) On February 5, 1996, internal president Branham signed a consulting contract with an out-of-state consulting firm in which he was an owner/partner.[38]

While all of this was happening, the Board's Executive Committee was also developing plans to drastically pare back expenses, including discontinuation of the dual presidency. Contrary to precedent, the spring board meeting (1996) opened and then the Board went almost immediately into executive session, and all non-members were asked to leave. None of the pending decisions were to be presented to the community for discussion. An hour later, when the general session convened, which was open to all of the Prescott College community, a motion was quickly introduced and passed to discontinue the dual presidency, inviting both presidents to apply to a truncated national presidential search. This naturally precipitated political stress in the organization, on top of the supposed financial crisis.

In the meantime the on-campus faculty became aware that through an inappropriate accounting process the deficit was being inflated on the books while in reality savings were accumulating and the money in the bank was adequate to bridge the summer without borrowing. As a result the faculty passed two resolutions and sent them to the Board. The first was a vote of no confidence in the internal president. The second was a demand that the interim business manager/controller/board member be removed from the Board and the business office, and be instructed not to represent himself as "virtual president."[19]

A New Financial and Management Regime

The 1996 summer meeting of the Board of Directors attracted a large audience of community members. All attendees knew that several important changes were likely to be initiated. First the Board confirmed that the dual presidency was ending and set up a formal search for a new president. The internal president resigned from the presidency and from the College. She was thanked for her service, and was given nearly a year's pay as a "golden parachute." The external president was asked to stay on until a new person could be appointed. He was also thanked for his service, and awarded a year's furlough with pay when a new president was in place. The Board listened to the faculty's call for the dismissal of the business manager/controller/*board member*. Although the Board chose not to act on the faculty's request, it precipitated his resignation.

The next major occurrence at the meeting was a proposal from the parents of one of the students, Mr. and Mrs. Norman Traeger. Mr. Traeger, a venture capitalist from Ohio, offered to put the College on the road to financial stability. He pledged a modest donation subject to the condition that he be allowed to restructure the Board membership to include himself and others he trusted and to limit student and faculty Board members to one representative from each group. Other conditions were that he could create and temporarily control a small budget committee, recruit a business manager/controller of his choosing, and participate in the hiring of a new president, chosen from outside the community. There were many questions about this offer, both from the community and Board. Many felt that the confusion of the year had largely been created when the accountant/*board member* had taken over the business office, and now another person was proposing to assume extraordinary authority. For the rest of the day discussions occurred throughout the College as the Board droned through its routine business. By the conclusion of the scheduled sessions, the community and Board came to believe that the offer was sincere—the parents had concern only for the College's survival and would return control of the College to the Board as soon as the financial situation was stabilized. More importantly, the Board believed the plan would bring an end to the chaos suffered the previous year and point the College in a direction of more stable financial management. It amounted to what might be called a "friendly takeover," and the Board accepted.

External President Joel Hiller held things together while an abbreviated presidential search went forward. A new business manager/controller, now designated CFO, was selected and put in place very quickly. This was followed by the appointment of Neal Mangham as president and CEO in January of 1997.

Mangham was the only president in the history of the College who had had experience as a college president. He was capable and worked conscientiously to provide leadership to the whole College, which at the time of his hiring consisted of four divisions, each with its own administration. Working with the new budget committee in their effort to simplify bookkeeping and administration, the Board consolidated all "external" non-resident divisions under one dean, reducing the number of operational divisions to two—RDP and the combined Adult Degree and Graduate Programs (ADGP). Efficiency was gained through this change, and the only downside appears to be the loss of the separate Center for Indian Bilingual Teacher Education (CIBTE). As a result no more grants were requested, and within a short time the number of Native American students being served by the College was reduced by ninety percent.

Mangham was not always part of the decision making, and despite his experience he found managing the College difficult. His role as president was becoming ambiguous because of divided decision making. The reform Board had created another two-headed administration, this time dividing authority between the CEO and the CFO. This new administrative and business leadership didn't last because the relationship was strained; within two years both the new president (CEO) and controller (CFO) had resigned, and new searches were underway. The members of the Board who had intervened to put things straight also left the Board. Another phase had ended and the College had to regroup—again.

This was the point in the Board's evolution when the alumni asserted leadership, effectively replacing internal members (students and faculty) who had been excluded under reformed bylaws imposed by the acceptance of Traeger's offer. The alumni now represented the community membership on the Board of Trustees. Sturgis Robinson, an alum and member of the Board, was appointed interim CEO and served for a year to give the school and the Board an opportunity to systematically contemplate the College's positions and goals while it thoughtfully searched for a president.

ACCOMPLISHMENTS AND CONCLUSIONS

That the past few years had been difficult times can be seen by the high turnover rate of administrators: five different presidents and several different deans in just eleven years, from 1989 through 2000. Politically and financially the College had undergone a great deal of turmoil, but surprisingly during this time the individual programs grew and were doing well, and the student body had expanded from approximately four hundred students in 1984 to well over one thousand in 1998.

The only downside to the growth in the late 1990s was the dispersion of the various programs into their own worlds. No participant in the College was able to personally know everyone involved, or to keep up with what was happening in every aspect and at every venue of the College. Efforts were initiated to bridge gaps in community cohesion through newsletters, e-mails, and open door policies by administrators, a plethora of community clubs, and topical events—all of which helped very much. However, less face-to-face contact tended to produce clusters of participants involved in their particular projects rather than in the overall College and official and spontaneous departmentalization resulted.

Student participation and activities at the College continued to be dynamic and unique. For example, students created a coed college soccer club in 1990, which competed against all-male teams across Arizona, including its rival, Embry-Riddle Aeronautical University, that occupied the old campus with its legendary polo-soccer field. The official uniform was tie-dye, and students played in everything from bare feet or sandals to, sometimes, heavy hiking boots or even cleats. Prescott College students were engaged in such activities as protesting the killing of buffalo and wolves as soon as these reintroduced native animals migrated outside of Yellowstone Park. More than once students retraced the 1869 seven-hundred-fifty-mile pioneering route

Rafting in Rapids

of John Wesley Powell, through Marble and Grand canyons, in whitewater rafts and kayaks.

The most telling and important accomplishment of these fourteen years (1984-1998) was the graduation of almost 1,300 resident students with BA degrees, and 2,300 non-resident ADP students with BA degrees, about 200 MA degrees after 1993, and the granting of about 500 Arizona teaching credentials, a significant portion of these to Native American teachers.

History of Prescott College in Kino Bay

◇◇◇◇◇◇

by Doug Hulmes

Those first coming to the land and waters of Kino Bay and the Midriff Islands of the Gulf as well as the communities of Kino Bay old and new, and the Seri villages of Punta Chueca and Disemboque, are coming upon a landscape that has shaped its plant and animal life as well as the cultural characteristics of its people. The relationships between physical and cultural geography, and the ecology of the sea and desert, create a complex web that you become a part of.

A sense of place for Kino and its surroundings varies for each of its inhabitants, as it will for those who come here to study. Being here will change their perceptions of reality and will bring about changes as well, as has happened for many students, faculty, and researchers. Steinbeck eloquently captures this essence:

> Let's go wide open. Let's see what we see, record what we find, and not fool ourselves with conventional scientific strictures. We could not observe a completely objective Sea of Cortez anyway, for in that lonely and uninhabited Gulf our boat and ourselves would change it the moment we entered. By going there, we would bring a new factor to the Gulf. "Let us go," we said, "into the Sea of Cortez, realizing that we become forever a part of it; that our rubber boots slogging through a flat of eel grass, that the rocks we turn over in a tide pool make us truly and permanently a factor in the ecology of the region. We shall take something away from it, but we shall leave something too." And if we seem a small factor in a huge pattern, nevertheless it is of relative importance. We take a tiny colony of soft corals from a rock in a little water world. And fifty miles away the Japanese shrimp boats are

dredging with overlapping scoops, bringing up tons of shrimps, rapidly destroying the species so that it may never come back, and with
the species destroying the ecological balance of the whole region. That
isn't very important in the world. And thousands of miles away the
great bombs are falling and the stars are not moved thereby. None of
it is important or all of it is.

FROM THE LOG FROM THE SEA OF CORTEZ BY JOHN STEINBECK (1955)

For me, it began in January 1972. It was possibly fate that brought me
to Kino Bay, for I had been planning to study ornithology in Peru. However,
when I learned that the primary focus of the course was to collect and stuff
birds, I withdrew and found a space in Marine Invertebrate Zoology, taught
by a scholarly and inspiring professor, Dr. Jane Taylor. We were joined by
Prescott College Professor Mr. Paul Long, who assisted with the scientific
visual recording of specimens collected during the class. Prescott College
began its presence in the Gulf just three years earlier in November of 1969
when a group of students led by instructors Rusty Baillie and Roy Smith
made the first kayak crossing via the Midriff Islands. Ours, however, was the
first actual Prescott College field course to be held in Kino.

We arrived at two a.m. after a heroic twenty-three hour drive from
Prescott. The two-lane highway between Nogales and Hermosillo was a series of detours around washed-out bridges, lighted in the dark by kerosene
flares. Ghostly shapes of skittish Mexican cattle appeared suddenly out of the
darkness, causing our driver to make sudden stops or swerves to avoid colli-
sions. Looking back, it seems strangely ironic that we crawled out of the vans
and slept on the beach directly in front of what would become the Prescott
College field station twenty years later.

Dawn provided one of the most brilliant sunrises I have ever seen. Its
profound beauty welled up in my soul, and I knew this place would forever
change me, as it did one of my classmates, Gary Nabhan, who would go
on to receive his PhD in Ethnobotany, and win the John Borroughs Award
for his book, *The Desert Smells Like Rain* (San Francisco: North Point Press,
1982). Another student in Jane's second course, Kim Clifton, would become
a major force for sea turtle conservation in the Gulf. After living with the
Seri Indians, where he learned of their hunting practices and the significance
of the sea grass beds in the Inferneo Channel between Tiburon Island and
the mainland, Kim continued his studies at the University of Arizona, where
he published several papers with Dr. Richard Felger, including *Winter Dor-
mancy in Sea Turtles: Independent Discovery and Exploitation in the Gulf by
Two Local Cultures* (1976), and *Sea Turtles of the Pacific Coast of Mexico* (1981).

George Huey, who was also enrolled in one of the first Kino classes, has become a renowned nature photographer. His photographs have appeared numerous times in *Arizona Highways*. Recently he was the photographer for the book *Wild Cactus*, with a foreword by Gary Nabhan. Reflecting on his first experience in Kino, he wrote:

> My original visit to Kino Bay, twenty-five years ago, was not only an introduction to the Sea of Cortez, but also a first taste of Mexico—and it made a lasting impression. My class at Kino led to a connection with fellow student Kim Clifton, who began work on a sea turtle research project there. As a result of that work, a few years later I joined Kim on a World Wildlife Fund sea turtle conservation project, where we found ourselves confronting armed turtle poachers and working with Mexican Marines on an isolated stretch of Mexico's southwest coast. Four years ago the Kino Bay connection resurfaced for me when I was searching for locations to photograph a book about cactus, I remembered two islands off the coast of Kino Bay—Turner Island and Isla Cholludo—and with the help of Prescott College, was able to visit them once again. (Huey and Houk, *Wild Cactus,* Artisan Pub., New York 1996)

Our class was based out of two *casitas* that we rented at Islandia Marina, located on the north end of Old Kino. A group of Seri Indians were living in traditional ocotillo shelters among the dunes 200 yards north of our compound. Pieces of ironwood may still lie scattered beneath the drifting sands mark-

Kino Fisherman's Catch

ing the place where they camped and carved ironwood sculptures for tourists, mainly for the retired snowbirds who annually migrated with their trailers to their wintering grounds in Kino. Some of these "gringos" became friends and sources of valuable information for the students and their projects. One elderly woman was an expert on mollusks and spent hours with Prescott College student Martha Meyers going over her collection of shells.

Old Kino was a dusty, tar-paper shanty town of a few hundred inhabitants. The men and boys worked mainly as fishermen or at the cannery, which closed down shortly after our arrival in

1972 due to declining numbers of fish and shrimp in the Gulf. Out of respect for the culture we were visiting, our female students were required to wear long dresses when they entered the village to shop at the markets.

The decline of fishing caused the Mexicans to seek other ways of making a living. They began producing imitations of the Seri ironwood carvings. Seri ironwood carvings for tourists began during the mid-1960s after a North American doctor purchased a few carvings and suggested that shoe polish paste would bring out the brilliant colors of the wood. Early traders in Seri art (anthropologist Jim Hills, who wrote his master's thesis, *An Ecological Interpretation of Prehistoric Seri Settlement Patterns in Sonora, Mexico*, for ASU, in 1973, and David Yetman, who wrote *Desert by the Sea*), began purchasing and trading for carvings that were then displayed at art galleries and museums throughout the Southwest at a time when interest in Native American art was gaining in popularity. A detailed history of the Seri ironwood carvings and basket making can be found in *People of the Desert and the Sea*, Richard Stephen Felger and Mary Beck Moser (Tucson: University of Arizona Press, 1991).

By the early 1970s the popularity of Seri ironwood carvings coincided with the decline of fishing in the Gulf and the closing of the fish cannery in Old Kino. In response to the loss of jobs and money, a few Mexican fishermen took up the trade and began using power tools to produce similar but more stylized reproductions. These carvings, produced in greater and greater quantities, began appearing in souvenir shops in Nogales and other border towns and were frequently sold as being hand carved by the Seri. Few buyers knew the difference, and no one anticipated the ecological implication of the rapidly growing market for ironwood carvings.

What began as a positive and sustainable economic venture for the desperately impoverished Seri Indians, within two decades became an ecological crisis for ironwood trees and the Sonoran Desert. By the mid-1980s, ironwood carvings became a major economic industry in Old Kino, with numerous cooperatives harvesting ironwood trees in an area radiating hundreds of miles from Kino.

Gary Nabhan speculated on the ecological implications of the cutting of these slow-growing trees, knowing that, as a legume, the ironwood must play a significant role in fixing nitrogen within the Sonoran Desert ecosystem. After receiving a grant, Nabhan employed several Prescott College students to assist in his research. *Ironwood: An Ecological and Cultural Keystone of the Sonoran Desert*, edited by Gary Paul Nabhan and John L. Carr (Conservation International, 1994), includes a paper titled "The Influences of Ironwood as a Habitat Modifier Species: A case Study on the Sonoran Desert Coast of the Sea of Cortez," by Joshua J. Tewksbury and Christian A. Petrovich.

Results of the research indicated that more than twenty species of plants grew in association with the ironwood tree. Even more disturbing was the growing use of mesquite charcoal used for grilling beef at trendy American restaurants. By the early 1990s, large tracts of desert were being chained for mesquite. In this process a chain attached to two tractors is dragged across the desert, denuding it of vegetation, which is then burned in large pits to produce the charcoal. The barren desert is then planted with exotic African buffel grass, *Cenchrus ciliaris,* an annual that produces forage for cattle. In addition, it also creates a dry fuel for wildfires that now annually blacken and destroy huge areas along with native vegetation, which has not adapted to fire. These are only two examples of large-scale ecological changes that have occurred during the thirty years that Prescott College has had a presence in Kino Bay.

Many of these and other changes have been documented by students through papers, senior projects, and group journal entries, which exist in assorted files, boxes, and group journals, and constitute a tremendous resource waiting to be organized and referenced. Prescott College alum Hudson Weaver, who is continuing her graduate studies at the University of Washington after getting a competence in Marine Studies in 1996, is now completing her thesis focusing on cultural and ecological aspects of Mexican fishermen in the Gulf. Her work exemplifies the potential for integrative studies that will enhance our understanding of the Gulf and those whose lives depend upon it.

The first two classes taught in Kino Bay in 1972 focused on marine invertebrates. Students specialized in specific phyla with a goal of creating a reference collection with photographs of the representative invertebrate fauna of the Midriff region. Techniques for collecting and preserving specimens, as well as the taxonomic classification of species, occupied much of our time. Given the amazing ecological and cultural diversity of the region, it became evident to all of us that more varied courses needed to be offered.

The following year, students began enlarging the scope of their projects to include ecological and cultural relationships. Dr. Paul Long, a professor of photography and cultural anthropology, offered a second course, Visual Anthropology, which helped broaden our understanding of the region. One of his students, Tom Sheridan, went on to become the curator of ethnohistory at the Arizona State Museum and is the author of several books, including *Arizona: A History* (Tucson: University of Arizona Press, 1995).

Several professors already mentioned, and Professor of Geology Dr. Douglas Brew, taught a variety of courses that focused on marine environments and cultural studies, and were based out of Islandia Marina in the 1970s. However, the College's bankruptcy in December of 1974 brought an abrupt end to what was becoming a growing presence of the College in Kino Bay. After the resurrection of the College, classes continued in Kino, and in January of 1979, I returned to teach at Prescott College and co-taught Coastal and Cultural Ecology with Dr. Bill Stillwell, basing once again out of Islandia Marina. At that time in the College's history, there were only about sixty students enrolled, and the College owned two vehicles. We were given "Old Blue," a Ford pickup with a camper shell, which carried four people in the front, and eight people and all of our gear for a month in the camper (which, unfortunately, attracted large volumes of carbon monoxide from the ailing exhaust system). We would have to stop repeatedly on our drive to revive and redistribute the human cargo (I share this tidbit of trivia only to point out how far the College has come in the past twenty years).

During the 1980s, I team-taught Coastal and Cultural Ecology every other year with Alan Weisman, who taught a variety of classes in writing and journalism at the College during the mid-70s to the late '80s, and is the author of *La Frontera: The United States Border with Mexico* (New York: Harcourt Brace Jovanovich, 1986) and *Gaviotas* (White River Junction, Vermont: Chelsea Green Publishing Company, 1998). He significantly inspired the importance of having an understanding of Mexican and Seri history and culture as part of our perspective for studying in Kino. I recall one interview, in particular, when Alan translated the stories of a blind elderly Seri man from Disemboque, who told of days in his youth during the early 1900s, when he and other Seris were hunted by Mexican soldiers. As he shared his memories, I observed several elderly Seri women with tears streaming down their brown weathered faces talking quietly amongst themselves. Alan also helped me communicate with several Mexican children, who wished to use my kayak, that they must take turns, and I appointed one nine-year-old boy to monitor the safety of the group. Now in his twenties, Ramon Salis is a fisherman and trusted friend of the College. Prior to leaving the College to pursue his writing career, Alan helped to articulate the need and potential for establishing a permanent field station in Kino Bay.

Another interesting milepost that occurred in 1985 was the enrollment of our first Mexican student, Veronica Behn. She has continued her graduate studies in cultural geography and has assisted on several courses in Kino. It was the fortuitous hiring of Dr. Tom Fleischner and Dr. Mark Riegner that boosted faculty support for teaching in Kino Bay, and their course, Coastal Ecology, augmented the curriculum by focusing once again on the natural history and more scientific interests of the Gulf, which had first attracted the College to the region.

In the fall of 1989, Tad Pfister, a marine biology student from the University of Arizona, transferred to Prescott College at the recommendation of yet another Prescott College alum, Wayne Vanvoories, who had been inspired by the Gulf and continued his studies in biology at the University of Arizona where he has gained national attention for his work in microbiology. Tad had literally grown up in the Gulf, and with his father (who is a veterinarian in Nogales, and was coincidentally born at 220 Grove Ave. when it was a hospital), spent many years fishing and living in the village of Libertad, 200 kilometers north of Kino. His knowledge of the region's natural history and Seri Indians, as well as his love for the Gulf, ability to speak Spanish, and skill at running a *panga*, immediately caught my attention. Tad introduced me to another prominent figure of the Gulf, Dr. Ed Boyer, who for his PhD dissertation had investigated the decline of the sun star, Heliaster kubinijii, from the Gulf in the 1970s, a phenomenon I had observed and wondered about its cause.

In 1991, with a growing interest in developing a permanent field station and academic program in the Gulf that could be utilized by numerous faculty, students, and researchers, and with the encouragement and technical assistance of Alan Weisman, Joel Hiller, and Dr. Garth Hansen, a formal request was made to the Prescott College Board of Directors to purchase a facility in Kino Bay. The recommendation was accepted, and "Casa Blue" was purchased in May 1991 for $150,000. Tad and I traveled to Kino to investigate the new Prescott College Center for Ecological and Cultural Studies, "Centro de Estudious Ecologicos y Culturales." Tad was enlisted as the field station manager and Dr. Ed Boyer was hired in 1992 to become the first director of the Kino Bay Center. After nearly twenty years from that first brilliant sunrise on the beach just south of Punta Ignacio, a dream had become a reality.

As an environmental science major, I enjoyed the opportunity to study specific organisms in depth. At the same time, I questioned the ethics of collecting and killing so many organisms. In the 1970s there was little tolerance given to students who questioned the ethics of killing for science, and most students did not object or question our motives. I also found myself frustrated by the lack of attention given to ecological relationships as well as cultural perspectives that aroused our curiosity but competed with our time to focus on creating an index collection. As my interest and commitment to the Gulf grew, I was determined to demonstrate my competence as an environmental science major by conducting a noninvasive research project.

In January of 1973, fellow student Mark Grinter and I designed an independent study to do an ecological survey of Pelican Island with a primary focus on the vegetation and bird life. Photo documentation was used in lieu of shooting and collecting birds, which at that time was the standard for scientific documentation.

While the final 100-page text of this study was unfortunately lost by the professor, a list of birds and photographs remain as baseline data for further studies. Of particular interest was the high concentration of Osprey that nested on Pelican Island in the early 1970s. We documented seven nesting pairs of these "sea hawks." Large numbers of Brown Pelicans, Blue-footed Boobies, and Double-crested Cormorants were also observed nesting and feeding on schools of fish that frequented the south and west sides of the island. One of our most exciting observations was of a Common Goldeneye. Interestingly, kleptoparasitic behavior was observed between a gull and immature cormorants, where a gull would "dance" in front of the young cormorants causing them to regurgitate their food, which was then ingested by the gull.

During my three weeks of study on Pelican Island, I gained more than lists of plants and birds, observations of feeding behavior, photographs, and journal entries; I came away with a profound sense of humility and respect for the individual lives of the numerous species that inhabited Pelican Island. I observed the harsh reality of life on the barren island where a minor miscalculation in flight could result in a tortured death in the arms of a saguaro, cardon, or cholla, but I also came to appreciate relationships between individual animals and species that reflected an incredible will to live and continue to live and coexist as they have for countless generations, perhaps for tens of thousands of years. I began to understand the harsh, but at times joyful, existence of the Mexican fishermen who frequented the island to clean their catch. I gained a sense of wonder of the island when it was shrouded in a bank of fog, creating an illusion that it was a world unto itself. While it is unfortunate the final written project was lost, the opportunity to conduct this study provided me with a challenge to attempt a noninvasive ecological study with an ethical standard for conducting scientific research. It is my hope that this will become a guiding mission for research conducted at the Prescott College Center for Cultural and Ecological Studies. To my knowledge, this commitment to noninvasive research is unique among academic institutions.

Inherent in this commitment is an underlying recognition that ultimately the College curriculum and experiential opportunities that exist for faculty, students, and researchers should go beyond obtaining knowledge to a gaining of wisdom regarding the Gulf, the Sonoran Desert bioregion, and the varied lives of its inhabitants. Part of this understanding is the recognition that our presence in the Gulf has, and will continue to have, an influence on its future. Going there with a sense of awe, humility, reverence, curiosity, and respect for the varied human and nonhuman life forms that have adapted to and evolved in this incredible landscape should be a guiding ethic for all who live and study at the field station. This was my dream as a student in January of 1973, and my hope for our future role in the Gulf.

The New Century: New Direction

◇◇◇◇◇◇◇

In recording the events of Prescott College's early years, the thirty plus boxes of archival information was so vast that condensing it to a readable history was extremely complex. It is likewise difficult to detail what is happening now because the first years of the twenty-first century are as yet unfolding.

The fall of 2000 did more than usher in the first school year of the century; it also began a new stage in the history of Prescott College. The now well established leadership of the alumni on the Board of Trustees quickly moved ahead to find a new president to be in place before the beginning of the school year. In July 2000, the Board appointed Dr. Dan Garvey President of the College. Garvey, former professor of graduate education at the University of New Hampshire, came to the College after having spent well over twenty-five years as an administrator and educator focused on teaching and research in the area of experiential education. His experience and background were a very good match for Prescott College's innovative and experiential programs.

By the end of his first academic year (spring of 2001), Garvey had involved the community in a long-term, strategic planning process. Rather than vest the responsibility in a small group, he chose to start at the grassroots. Having the entire community participate in the development of various proposals served as a vehicle for all the components of the school to hear one another. Many of the issues that had beset the community could be expressed and many overlooked agendas could be inserted into the plan, as agreement and finances would support. This was by no means the first time a long-range plan had been devised by the College; in every decade from the 1960s to the time of this writing there has been at least one extensive and comprehensive plan formulated. Periodic strategic planning is a very important tool for an institution. It serves to reassess the past, assess the present, and create a direction and vision for the future. While not every aspect of any plan is ultimately implemented—because events overtake plans—the process can refocus priorities and include new opportunities. The 2001 plan was particularly timely in that it gave an opportunity for the community to be involved in the design of the new campus complex.

A Campus

Well before the arrival of Garvey, the Board of Trustees had been working on the issue of "Campus"—what, where, when, how large? Finding an appropriate site to develop a permanent college campus has been a perennial dilemma for the entire college community. They had been plagued with indecision about where to relocate after losing their original grand campus. The school had been very fortunate to acquire the historic Sisters of Mercy convent within a year and a half of the bankruptcy, and also exceptionally lucky to have been able to find a few buildings nearby that were available for lease or purchase. But the school had long passed these developing years when it could easily have been compared to medieval universities that were organized by students in rented quarters. The College had been operating in mostly provisional facilities through the years while its programs expanded and multiplied on a regular basis. It now needed a permanent Campus.

At various times campus search committees of the Board and College community had been formed to evaluate several opportunities, including local summer camps with buildings and acreage, the Granite Gate resort on the edge of town that was in foreclosure, larger buildings in town to recycle, and an undeveloped eighty-seven acre forest site owned by Mrs. Dalke.

Several comprehensive proposals to adapt, rather than move, were also put forward by groups of students and faculty who had begun the task of studying the current facilities and neighborhood. They investigated such aspects as energy use, zoning requirements, availability of existing buildings and land for purchase, budget and tax implications, proximity of student residences and employment, aesthetics, and how spaces affect learning. Their research resulted in an unusual and valuable experiential learning opportunity and became a part of the curriculum.

After assessing all presently available sites for a permanent campus, the 1999-2000 Board adopted a definite plan to stay at its present location in downtown Prescott, centered around "Old Main," the original convent building. One part of that process was the purchase of some of the adjacent buildings already leased by the College, and the other part was to expand the campus westward—away from the busy street—by building new, ecologically sound buildings. Using the findings of the college community's various task forces and requisites from strategic planning proposals, the Board of Directors joined in the school's ecological wish and mission of recycling underused spaces in the heart of town, thus setting in motion the biggest construction project the College had seen since 1965.

Delisa Myles and Maura Garland at Crossroads Center Opening
photo by Travis Patterson

Just thirty yards behind the convent building, adjacent to a creek and nature area, a site was cleared of old buildings (including the Organic Alley Café), and two new larger structures were erected and christened the Crossroads Center. Both are two stories, and together they enclose approximately twenty-two thousand square feet of usable floor space, plus infrastructure. These buildings were designed to demonstrate the College's environmental philosophy by using eco-friendly materials and sunlight, blending aesthetically with the natural landscape, incorporating state of the art electronic infrastructure; and to be very functional in supporting the College's educational needs.

One building has eight classrooms and both large and small meeting rooms; it also houses the successor to the Organic Alley Café, now called the Crossroads Café, which continues to serve organic, locally grown food. It has both indoor and outdoor seating and two kitchens, the second providing catering services for the various conferences, workshops, and campus meetings of both residential and non-residential programs of the College. The other building contains the library (Information Commons). Beyond the still-growing collections and access to millions of texts through interlibrary loan and electronic access to journals, it is equipped with electronic infrastructure to support wireless computing and provide access to the College websites and the World Wide Web.

Studying in the New Crossroads Café
photo by Travis Patterson

The Crossroads Center not only symbolizes a new era in which the College once again has a campus with a permanent presence in the town, but it has also become a community gathering place. Any day of the week you will find students socializing in the common plaza, studying or relaxing between classes, or perhaps having bake sales for their causes. Hand-painted banners, more often than not, hang from the bridge connecting the two buildings, announcing everything from dance performances to vigils to social action community meetings. Behind the Crossroads buildings a gentle creek flows though a small ravine providing a tree studded nature area for outdoor classes. This is bordered by an agricultural test plot, gardens, and three comfortable houses used for auxiliary services. There is also an apartment building with a few units now used as the first "dormitory" since the college left the big campus. Although the slogan "The Southwest Is Our Campus" is still true, the new Crossroads Center is a beehive of activity around the clock.

PROGRAMS

Prescott College's present curricular content in relation to the changing values of today's world is no longer so radical. It is not unique today for a college to offer environmental studies and outdoor leadership programs—there are many such programs in small colleges and big universities around the country. Fifty years ago an environmentalist's major challenge was just to make it known that nature itself was in danger. Now that the danger is generally understood and acknowledged by people, the major mission is more than just to elucidate the issues. A majority of students at all levels, in all programs, come to Prescott College already aware and motivated to action, so the challenge for environmental educators has expanded.

Discussion On The Patio
photo by Travis Patterson

In 2003, Prescott College joined five other ecologically oriented colleges and universities to create the Eco League, a consortium of schools that share similar missions and value systems based on environmental responsibility, social change, building a sustainable future. Many of the schools were original members of an organization known as the North American Alliance for

Green Education (NAAGE), founded by students of Prescott College over a decade ago. Among its many functions, the Eco League provides for students and faculty exchanges and a medium for cooperative environmental education and activism.

In 2005 a new level of graduate studies was added. Prescott College was granted full accreditation to offer a PhD degree in Sustainable Education, which is a remarkable accomplishment for a relatively young college with less than two thousand students. This milestone is the culmination of five years' work by deans, Master of Arts students, faculty, community volunteers, and President Garvey. The accrediting association recognized two strengths, the College's work in environmental sustainability education and its long-term accomplishments in teacher training. The concept of *sustainability* encompasses

Years	Professional development note	Adventure Education	Integrative Studies	Education	Environmental Studies	Arts & Letters	Milestones
1999 thru 2002	Professional Teacher Preparation was added to Curriculum	Adventure Education	Integrative Studies two sub-programs—Cultural & Regional Studies and Human Development		Environmental Studies	Arts & Letters	Resident student body approaches 500. Total college enrollment approaches 1,000+. All non-resident divisions combined into one, called Adult Degree Graduate Programs (ADGP). New President, Dan Garvey, appointed.
2003 thru 2005	Professional Education and Teacher Credentialing Program combined and given status as a separate program	Adventure Education	Integrative Studies: Cultural & Regional Studies And Human Development	Education	Environmental Studies	Arts & Letters	Crossroads Center built and Campus expanded. PhD program in Sustainability Education initiated.

Table 5. Professional Teacher Preparation Added to Curriculum

the creation of programs to train teachers and supervisors to help students learn and practice all of the ways they can contribute to the viability of our and other societies. It also provides a base for research into the causes of societal instability and the remedies to promote long-term stability. The PhD program applies not only in the field of professional education, but also to various fields that promote sustainability of peace, social justice, and environmental health.

Also during this period, the Adventure Education program had taken on a professional educational mission. The program had always been highly visible locally, but now it assumed national leadership through the Association for Experiential Education.

Curriculum Configurations: 2000-2005

From 1999 through 2005 Prescott College has graduated over 700 resident Bachelor of Arts students, 1,400 non-resident BA students, and 330 Master of Arts students, and has granted 350 teaching credentials.

The number of graduates from the external and advanced degree programs illustrates how significant a part of the College the Tucson operation, Indian Teacher Training, and Adult Degree and Master of Arts programs had become. In fact, these operational divisions and curricular programs had grown to such an extent that it had become difficult for them to work closely together or with the Resident Degree Program. They had each adopted different calendars and graduation standards and processes, and appeared to be drifting toward being, in essence, separate colleges. President Garvey has been working to re-establish closer working connections and more uniform standards.

Prescott College's commitment to education and its active participation at every level, from preschool through this new PhD program, continue to provide a wide variety of opportunities for students of all inclinations in addition to furnishing a broad avenue for spreading the school's ethics and philosophy.

Activism Moves into the World Arena

A fresh form of student and community participation has emerged at Prescott College that is different from that of the 1960s, when student activism was in full swing on urban campuses and in the southern states. During the '60s, Prescott, Arizona, seemed very remote from those places. While there were a few students who traveled to other venues where social change was taking place and completed internships and independent studies, on the whole Prescott College students studied social change as scholars and observers—at a distance. In fact, Prescott students of that era who had political and social interests lamented that they felt a sense of isolation, of being "out of the mainstream."

With a permanent downtown campus and expanded opportunities of foreign study, the trend for activism in environmental, political, and social issues has increased considerably. A strong emphasis on ethics had always permeated Prescott College curricula and community life, and while the College seldom takes positions *as an institution*, many classes and scores of groups became active in examining local, statewide, national, and worldwide events and viewpoints. The College encourages students and all members to get involved, make commitments, and try to change the world for the better—without controlling the message or rejecting those who might disagree with the majority.

The practicum course Writers in the Community is an example of the involvement students have with the community. Under the auspices of the Arts and Letters Program, Writers in the Community encompasses the Prescott College philosophy of blending academic study with service learn-

Eco-Friendly Student-run Bicycle Shop

ing. In this course students go out into the community and teach creative writing classes to diverse populations, such as kids at juvenile detention centers or boarding schools, and at veterans homes. This kind of constructive activism grows out of the College's embrace of experiential learning and the character of the students and faculty that this philosophy attracts.

In almost any week of the year there will be events on campus to examine controversies and to organize advocacy or service. And almost any month of the year faculty-led and student-led groups are traveling to the Arizona-Mexico border, Africa, or Latin America, to disaster relief projects (as Hurricane Katrina relief in New Orleans, in which students and faculty raised money to travel to the city to help clean up and rebuild), to environmental restoration efforts, to regional and international conferences, and so forth.

In 1997 a student initiated nonprofit called the Ripple Project was created with the aim to incorporate more community engagement into the Adult Degree Program at Prescott College. Over the years student involvement from both ADP and RDP students has allowed Ripple to grow into a center dedicated to enriching students' academic experiences as well as providing a volunteer force to the greater community. In 2006, Prescott College received a federal grant to fund two full-time Americorps VISTA positions with the Ripple Project.

The Future

Prescott College, like all colleges, is in the business of equipping students to understand the intellectual and cultural worlds, but the world of knowledge (information and theory) does not hold still. What was true yesterday is not true today. The most visible force now radically shifting education is the digital information and communications revolution. Cyberspace is changing the ways individuals and organizations think and operate. Distance virtually disappears and a glut of information appears in its place, information that is often impossible to interpret for lack of time given to assimilate it. Not wanting to become museums of antique ideas and customs, colleges and universities are actively working to adapt not only what they teach, but also *how* they teach it.

In promoting Prescott College, Dr. Garvey uses every opportunity to speak about relevance, and how today's education must prepare students to be effective change agents in solving the immense problems of the future.

Relevance was the educational catchword of the 1960s—and the issue of relevance is even more *relevant* as the College moves into the future. More than ever, educational systems, particularly those privately funded by tuitions and gifts, have no alternative but to meet the needs of their clients, and those needs are changing. A small college that lacks a substantial endowment is always living on a knife's edge financially, but Prescott College has a forty-year record of survival. To continue that survival and to insure future growth, PC's Board of Directors and administration have recently taken steps both to review the College's current position in this changing milieu and to tackle the challenges that are inherent in an unpredictable future.

To continue its role as a leader in innovation will require constant effort and creativity on the part of Prescott College. It is a strenuous and endless challenge. But as Dr. Parker and the other founders observed in the 1960s, the world does not need another *standard model* small College.

In the Fall Community Meeting of 2006, President Garvey announced the formation of the *2010 Committee*. It was composed of thirteen administrative and program leaders who were charged with the mission of assessing the status of the present College and making recommendations for improving and operating a college with a view to the future. The report and recommendations of the 2010 Committee came out in April 2007. Briefly stated, the committee outlined four major areas to be considered: Clarification of Organizational Values, Academic Structure & Program; Faculty; Administrative Structure & Processes; and Board of Trustees.

The Committee acknowledged that the members of the Prescott College community had drifted from a "shared vision, [or] clearly articulated and agreed upon values." And in so doing, they specifically defined their goal as to "engage in a community-wide process to articulate" an "organizational mission" that would also embrace a *"diverse, socially just, and sustainable organization model."* [93]

Concerning future academic planning, the committee proposed to use a more strategic approach to curriculum development by evaluating the viability of each program as it relates to external markets and analyzing data on the choices of students who make up our market.

The committee studied the underlying financial structure of the College to connect how the budget reflects what the College values and supports; the goal being that of taking initiatives and adjusting to the realities of competitive markets while fulfilling the mission of the College.

"One College" emerged as a goal for streamlining the operations of the College. Reviewing the current complexity of managing all of the programs the committee recommended aligning the calendars of ADP/RDP/MAP/PhD. This increased collaboration across the College would hopefully not only ease the workload for administrative offices but also make viable cross-college contracts for faculty.

Other recommendations included offering a resident master's/graduate option, involving graduate students in teaching and research opportunities, increasing non-credit and/or continuing education offerings, creating new orientation opportunities for RDP students, increasing IT support, and investing in labs, classrooms, and student housing.

Beyond philosophical, curricular, and operational change, maintaining Prescott College's eminence as an innovative college in this unpredictably evolving world society will be a challenge. Only time will tell what private colleges that survive will look like in twenty or fifty years. Will young people still want to spend four years taking classroom and field courses? Or will they demand other systems of learning and action? Successful private colleges of the future may well be research institutions or workshops in which only a few courses are offered, where students learn through other structures not yet devised and in many other venues, and most student papers, inventions, and art works are presented to the world through internet journals. The possibilities are manifold and are unpredictable.

A Brief History of the Prescott College Library: 1995-2007

◇◇◇◇◇◇◇

by Linda Butterworth

In 1995 the Library was located at 320 Grove Avenue; Susan Burton was the Library Director, Eve Tallman was the Off-Campus Services Librarian, and Linda Butterworth was the newly-hired Reference Librarian.

The building (now the Sinagua building, housing Environmental Studies faculty offices and classrooms) consisted of two rooms for the approximately 27,000 books and 250 journal subscriptions, one online computer station (a dial-up connection through the Arizona State Library; the number was always busy), four CD-rom compatible computer stations, and four additional computers used to access the book Catalog, to connect via Telnet (pre-WorldWideWeb) to other libraries and electronic sites, and to check e-mail via the Arizona Free Net. The tech services office at the rear of the building had a door leading out to a garden, to a large garage used for storage, and to the creek. There was a 24-hour study room in the back; students were given the 1-2-3 combination at their Library Orientation and took full advantage of the small space, although not always for studying. On several occasions whoever unlocked the door in the morning found students asleep, or engaged in other non-academic activities.

Susan Burton was a sharp, forward-thinking, creative Library Director, fully committed to the PC experiential learning philosophy. She encouraged the staff to teach students to become self-sufficient in finding resources for their classes, and in turning information into knowledge. Susan took a sabbatical in 1995 to prepare a Block course for faculty: the Second Knowledge Workshop. All three librarians participated, and the class was a mix of RDP, ADP, MAP, and CIBTE faculty. For many of them, it was not only an introduction to new, online methods of research, including the use of e-mail, but the first time faculty from different programs had a chance to meet and work together. It was a huge success, talked about for years afterward—but never offered again.

Eve Tallman (currently Library Director at Grand County Public Library, Moab, UT) was not only a superb librarian, but also a world class rock climber who spent summers doing Search & Rescue in Yosemite. Because of this, the Library served as a hangout for many of the Adventure Education students who wanted to line up climbing trips with Eve, ask her advice, or talk about their own climbs. Eve taught independent study classes involving rock climbing, had AE students signing up for work/study in the Library— and along the way these "outdoor types" became quite proficient in using the library and developing solid research skills.

The entire Library staff participated in the semiannual book sale. This event was held outdoors on the sidewalk and in the adjacent parking lot, with proceeds going to the Library's slush fund to be used for such luxuries as new books and office supplies. Eventually the event grew to a College-wide garage sale: items sold included exercise equipment, clothing, and personal photos.

From 1995 on, the Internet and use of online resources shaped the growth of the Library. The budget was minimal; purchasing new books and new journal subscriptions was low priority compared to acquiring access to online journal databases that would be available to not only the RDP students on campus, but to the growing number of ADP and MAP students. Rather than having them call the librarians with requests (e.g., "I need some books and articles on multicultural education"), and the librarians having to do the research, and send out materials they thought appropriate, the students could now access the resources themselves, do their own research, and decide exactly what they wanted. Prescott College Library had unique resources (for Yavapai County) on CD-rom, such as ClinPsyc, Mental Measurements Yearbook, and ERIC. Students from NAU used the PC Library rather than the local NAU branch.

In 1996-97 the Library took an active role in educating the college on the importance of communication and advertising using the [new] WorldWide-Web. Linda Butterworth, Carol Kennedy (an admissions assistant then, currently an Assistant District Attorney for Yavapai County), and John Schmit (an RDP student, later Computer Lab manager, currently Assistant Professor in Film & Video Production, Grand Valley State University) formed the WEBSTERS, dedicated to bringing Prescott College into the Internet Age. They created the first PC webpage, and the Library was able to make a wealth of information available to all students and the greater community.

In 1998, as the campus was being reconfigured to add classrooms and office space, President Neal Mangham decided to lease an old furniture store at 301 Grove and move the Library into it. By this time Susan and Eve had moved on and the Library had survived a short-term director who spent more time on personal issues than on Library issues. Linda Butterworth was the Interim Director and supervised the move with the help of longtime staff members (and former RDP students) Candy Derbyshire and Rick Taylor. They all worked with the architect to design the new space.

The old Library closed in May 1998, and the staff plus assorted student volunteers began packing up the books and everything else. Books, supplies, office equipment—everything—was packed into cartons; each carton had a number, which corresponded to a master list detailing the contents of each carton. Each list was handwritten, as all but one of the computers, all clunky and slow, had been unplugged. One computer was kept running until the last minute—a connection to the book Catalog. As students returned late books, new cartons and new lists were added.

The move to the new Library across the street was scheduled for early summer, and the old Library was packed and ready, but delays and problems started immediately. For one thing, the City of Prescott would not issue an occupancy permit for the building. Because the College needed to begin renovating the old building so classes could be held there in the fall, it was imperative that all Library materials be moved out. Finally, the city allowed the cartons to be moved in, but the Library staff was not legally allowed in the building. Every week or so Lyn Martin, the project manager, told Linda he was meeting with the city to get the permit, and she should have the staff ready to go to work. Every week the meeting was postponed, or the permit denied, and the staff, having come to work ready to begin unpacking the cartons, was sent home.

The summer passed with some work going on in the new Library building (still referred to as Marler's, after the furniture store), but with none of the Library materials unpacked. Occasionally the staff came in and tried to set up office space, and clear work space, but the air in the building was thick with mold and toxins, and everyone quickly felt ill. However, when classes began in the fall, with all the books still in cartons, the new Library was open for business.

Amazingly, the system of finding books in cartons worked fairly well; all the students were very patient, and actually helped unpack and organize when the new shelves were in place. Lyn Martin and his crew were still working on the building—the HVAC system was an ongoing problem, as were leaky ceilings—but the staff settled in. Besides the Library the new building held three classrooms, a computer lab, and the student mailroom, so, although it was inconvenient and dangerous to walk across Grove Ave., the new Library soon became a popular gathering spot.

The new Library lacked the 24-hour study room, and a designated Library classroom, but gained office space and better computer stations, plus a comfortable space for hosting book readings and other events. After a new Library Director, Eileen Chalfoun, was hired in early 1999, the Library was re-energized with new ideas, new staff (Norma Mazur, Lyn Chenier, and Tom Brodersen), and new plans to upgrade and expand Library services, and to take a more active role in exploring new technologies for the Library and the College.

Eileen established a solid, positive working relationship with PC President Neal Mangham, and continued the same when Dan Garvey became president. Her goal was to have the Library recognized for its vital academic role in the community (and acknowledged accordingly in the budgeting process). She and Linda both served on the college's Technology Committee, working to bring the PC hardware up to speed to accommodate the software and online databases necessary for academic coursework, establishing standards for all computer equipment, proposing a laptop computer program for all students, and lobbying for increased IT support. Linda chaired the Public Services section of the Yavapai Library Network, a countywide consortium of thirty-plus libraries, ensuring that the minority voice of the academic libraries was heard by the larger group of public libraries.

An ongoing program of faculty book readings was established: Glendon Brunk, Lon Abbott and Teri Cook, Terrill Shorb, and Craig Childs, among others, read to sellout crowds, with the Library staff providing tasty and original refreshments. The premier event was an afternoon tea. Invitations to the College community and greater Prescott community were sent out, and twenty tables were set up with fine tablecloths and teapots on each table. The staff prepared sandwiches and cookies, and hot water for the tea was boiled in the café across the street and brought back to the Library for pouring. Faculty members Tom Fleischner and Laura Sewell each read from their latest books. It was a memorable and, for the staff, exhausting but wonderful, day.

The librarians met regularly to assess the collection, plan for new acquisitions, and brainstorm ideas about integrating library resources into coursework. Eileen and Linda were voting members of the RDP faculty, and attended faculty meetings and other functions; they used these times as opportunities to further build faculty ties, learn more about faculty interests and projects, and share their own expertise. Linda also attended MAP faculty meetings, and Eileen ADP faculty meetings; again, opportunities used to compare notes on students, and to learn what areas of the collection needed strengthening in support of broadening curricular fields.

Throughout the year faculty members brought classes to the Library.

Linda worked with the students, after conferring with faculty on specific assignments, and introduced them to the online journal databases, the concept of critically analyzing information from print and online sources, and whatever else they needed to both complete an assignment and further the lifelong research process. These Library classes of twelve to fourteen people were usually held in a small front room that comfortably held around ten; with street noise, and sun streaming through the large windows, it made for a less than ideal learning experience. Besides the classroom session, all of the Library's computers would be reserved for these classes, and students could get to work on assignments with Linda and their teacher on hand and available to help and answer questions.

Summers were quiet in the Library, with students off on field courses. The Library, located in a street-front building across the street from the rest of the campus, became a "resting place," literally, for some of Prescott's homeless. They'd come in daily, stretch out on the couch or in a chair, and sleep heavily for hours at a time. One regular was known as Cyclops, due to his one functioning, runny, eye. One day Linda thought she saw Cyclops walk out of the Library with a handful of Eileen's personal books, which were shelved on a cart in her office. She couldn't be sure he had the books, so no action was taken, but a few days later Eileen confronted him directly, asking if he's taken her books, and he replied, "Yes." The books, however, were long gone, although, at the police's suggestion, Eileen spent the next day searching the cemetery behind the Smoki Museum for them; apparently that was where the homeless were living and storing their belongings.

Although there was no room at 301 Grove for physical Library expansion, the staff continually tried to expand services and resources for students, including keeping later hours towards the end of each quarter. The Library webpage, created and maintained by Linda, was updated frequently; handouts, reference resources, subject-specific resources, and pages created especially for RDP courses were available to students on and off campus.

The big news at PC in 2003 was the Crossroads Center: the College was going to build a new structure, for the first time in its history, and the Library, or Information Commons, was the cornerstone of the project. Eileen was on the Planning Committee; after the architect was chosen he and his team met with the Library staff to translate ideas into practical applications. Everyone was enthusiastic and eager to plan a new space, a true Information Commons, a physical space with the flexibility to incorporate small meeting spaces, large community gathering places, individual study spaces and collaborative work spaces, and quiet reading spots. The Information Commons would have the latest technology infrastructure in place to accommodate the wireless laptops students would be using, and there would be a service center adjacent to the Library, staffed by the IT department, available to help students and all employees with computer needs and problems.

Budget cuts were made throughout the planning process; as the plans were finalized and construction began, many of the Library's expectations were lost or revised. Still, the Crossroads Center would be the hub of the campus, and the Library would be in the center of it all. Everyone watched the buildings go up, and the staff toured the new space as often as they were allowed in. The move was pushed back several times due to various delays but was finally scheduled for September 2004, and that's when Eileen realized that no budget provisions had been made for the actual move: who would pack up the Library and physically move it to the new location? After the staff kiddingly suggested a line of people stretching across the street, moving books one by one—and hearing others say "Yes! Great idea!" —they managed to find a moving company available on short notice, and the move itself went smoothly. The Library settled in to the new, unfinished space, while construction workers, electricians, and men with clipboards and hardhats continued to work alongside them.

Nearly three years later, in 2007, the Library has become a fixture on campus. It's not quite what we envisioned, and we haven't worked out all the kinks and quirks of the building yet, but Eileen, Linda, Norma, Tom, Rich, Jim, Geoff, and Bill work every day to ensure that this Library continues to offer the best to our students: the best staff, best books and journals, best online resources, and best environment. Staff and students appreciate the wall of windows on the east side of the building for the views and openness, although the resulting sunlight has faded journals and caused computer screens to be unusable at various times during the day. Our hoped-for tech services/ help center has become The Fishbowl, a mini-computer lab necessary since the proposed laptop purchase requirement didn't happen. Our computers are old and slow, and not powerful enough to support all the programs students need, but we're hopeful a new budget year will prioritize upgrades. We continue to work on providing access to growing collections of scholarly materials through various consortia agreements, and we try to make the access as user friendly as possible. With the addition of a limited residency PhD program at PC, the Library has another constituency to support, although collection development money is limited.

The strength of the Library continues to be its staff: smart, capable, creative, interesting, and outstanding examples of the people Prescott College continues to attract. (More detailed background information on the Library and the Crossroads Center, including photographs and news stories, is available in the College Archives.) L.B.

PART II

Education at Prescott College: Philosophy and Practice

From the beginning Prescott College has been a pioneer in Education at every level from elementary through graduate school. The College serves diverse groups, including spirited resident undergraduates from all parts of the USA and abroad—many of whom seek teaching credentials in addition to their academic degrees. The College also provides educational programs for American Indians on reservations, Hispanics in the Southwest and on the border with Mexico, and people who are unable to pursue degrees through residential programs. The College also evolved innovative modes and philosophies of learning and teaching, emphasizing student motivation and learning through hands-on experience. In this section, pieces written by participants explore important aspect of Education at Prescott College.

By Permission of Prescott College Photo Archives

Students' Expressed Ideals and Motivations

◇◇◇◇◇◇◇

Over the years, many surveys have been carried out to learn what attracts young people to the Prescott College Resident Degree Program and keeps them there. The College has an exceptionally good rate of retention, indicating that its unique approach to education and community building meets the students' expectations.

TABLE OF STUDENTS' EXPRESSED EDUCATIONAL IDEALS AND MOTIVATIONS FOR BEING IN COLLEGE, AND FOR CHOOSING PRESCOTT COLLEGE

Three surveys (2006, 2005, 1974) were synthesized to produce this table of student responses. Results of these three surveys were chosen because they were open-ended, asking students to express in their own words why they decided to attend college and why they chose Prescott College. All statements were accepted and are reflected below. When responses were nearly identical they were combined and listed only once. No statistical analysis was carried out, since students were not part of a structured sample. Items are expressed in students' own words to the degree possible, including those used as subheads.

Prepared by Sam Henrie, Nov. 2006

Learning how to learn effectively and efficiently, including through experiential learning.
- To be competent, skillful, self-reliant.
- To learn and evaluate society's expectations.
- To increase my concentration and consistency so I can do more and better work.
- To learn through direct contact with real phenomena rather than vicariously.

- To learn through working on real life problems rather than abstractions, books, and lectures.
- To learn to use all available resources—college, people, nature—and to maintain that ability after I leave here.
- To accomplish well some task or process.

Participating in a learning community.
- Learning in the company of others—learning from others.
- To discipline my body, mind, and emotions by learning to function within a learning community.
- To work cooperatively with others in small groups to achieve agreed-upon goals.
- To get the support of a college community. Being a functioning and contributing member of a community.
- Physical health—sustenance, exercise, health care.

Social connections—particularly new connections.
- To learn to be a real friend—and to develop some deep friendships.
- To enjoy the support of a college community.
- To develop a new or richer social network.
- To truly love others and enjoy my associations here and now.
- Make friends to share recreation and some leisure pursuits.
- To find love.
- Getting ready to be a link in a genetic/reproductive chain going back to first cell, and going on to endow future generations with my genes and social/personal heritage.

Gain sufficient knowledge and skill base to make the college experience meaningful. Gain a true liberal arts education.
- To get a broad introduction to the world of ideas, history, the arts, culture, etc.
- To gain an understanding of the world by understanding theory and basic principles through the scientific, scholarly, and artistic disciplines.
- To organize my learning under broad categories so I can study many different fields synthetically (avoid narrow disciplines).
- To become knowledgeable of human society, history, world, national and local politics as a foundation for understanding and evaluating what is "going on" in the world.
- To understand the dynamic forces shaping the world.

Learning to see humanity within the broader framework of nature.
- To have experience in wilderness (wild places that have been altered by humans to the least degree possible).
- To get out of doors and into the wilderness.
- To become skillful in outdoor action and wilderness survival activities.
- To learn and practice physical safety when doing dangerous things or in dangerous environments.
- To have exciting and new experiences—adventures.
- To experience many adventures

Working within a curriculum that is an expression of my personal needs, interests, plans, and evolution.
- To earn a degree as a basis for following life interest and many other pursuits.
- To acquire the basic skills of scientific work.
- To earn a degree as a basis for earning a living.
- To prepare myself to be a successful professional person.
- To qualify for further study.

Being free, independent, and on my own.
- To develop a differentiated personality.
- To break free from controls of home, church, club, gang of friends, other influences/controls from the past.
- To have my first living experience away from my region, or my own family.
- To take over the job of achieving my personhood from parents and others.
- Becoming a person—self knowledge.
- To gain independence and breathing room to find out who I am as an individual.
- To get a fresh start.

Passing into early adulthood in a safe and rich environment. To Mature.
- PC is a place to gain full adult capacities.
- To "find myself" and get in touch with my own motivations in order to become integrated and establish a direction.
- To develop a positive and sustainable self-image, learning to live with and love myself.
- To explore and get to know my own mind—how to use it.
- To discover my own talents and interests.

- To understand myself fully, my characteristics, my history and how it has formed me, my talents and interests.
- To achieve a continuity with my past and future—to flow from what I was to what I am into my best potential.

Working toward being a better person.

- To become an enthusiastic, positive, self-actualizing person.
- What criteria of truth, ethics and beauty will I adopt?
- To find my own strengths and weaknesses.
- To accomplish something important in my life.
- To discipline my body, mind, and emotions by learning to function within a learning community.
- To develop a moral-ethical self that is real and integrated.
- To develop "ambitions."
- To engage in the search for the meaning of life, with whatever support I need.
- To find my "bliss"—translating it into a tentative life plan—this means a change in direction in many cases.
- To make the connection between academic learning and my ethical/spiritual life so that learning makes me a more healthy, whole person.

Being of service to other people.

- To work cooperatively with others in small groups to achieve agreed-upon goals.
- To help my fellow students learn.
- To communicate with, advocate and convince, work with others in ways that help them.
- To learn how to teach.
- To earn a degree as a basis for service.
- To become a citizen of the country and the world.

Prescott College's Innovative Principles of Learning and Teaching

◇◇◇◇◇◇◇

(A Presentation at the Inauguration of President Dan Garvey, November 2001) by S. N. Henrie, PhD

WHY PRESCOTT COLLEGE?

The higher education system of the United States is universally recognized as the best in the world, and the best in history. So why create an alternative model? My job today is to outline some of the fundamental innovations in *learning-teaching* that were envisioned by the founders and have evolved in the intervening years, and to suggest how we can build upon that foundation as we launch into the new century.

The founders had a vision: we will educate leaders for the twenty-first century. We will provide an excellent education for a small number of students—students chosen for their capacity to become self-directed, life-long learners. This will be a new kind of college. It will provide a model for change in the higher education establishment.

The wisdom and power of this conception lies in what educators call *the multiplier effect*. Every graduate we send out can influence hundreds of others. Every teacher we train will, in turn, spread the ethics of social and environmental health. Everyone who works with us will see the benefits of our success-based methodology of interdisciplinary, experiential education in action. Though small, Prescott College can have a significant positive impact on the conventional education system. Our graduates, by practicing what they learn here about the world, and about themselves, and about education, can provide leadership that the twenty-first-century world sorely needs.

WHAT STUDENTS ARE ASKED TO LEARN AT PRESCOTT COLLEGE
AS CONTRASTED WITH THE TYPICAL UNIVERSITY

During the 1960s and early '70s, the most striking area of innovation at Prescott College was futuristic subject matter like outdoor action, environmental conservation, and systems theory applied to human problems. Unique curricular organization also set us apart. Instead of conventional departments, the faculty worked through interdisciplinary *Centers* which focused on real-world problems. These Centers brought scholars and practitioners with diverse training together in a "think tank" atmosphere.

Dr. Charles Parker was our founding president, but he stepped aside once our financial and institutional structures were in place, and Dr. Ronald Nairn was brought in from Rand Corporation to be our first operating president. In this choice, you can see the emerging philosophy of the new College. This was to be a college to tear down the ivy-covered walls and challenge students in discovery and reality—thrusting them into wild environments, government internships, industrial planning, foreign service projects, real scientific research, deep self-exploration, etc. This new College would give extraordinary responsibility and latitude to students in creating their own education. It would foster collegial working relationships between students and faculty mentors as they attack real social issues together.

Today our curricular *content* is not so radical as it once seemed. The world has changed around us so that it is no longer unique for a college to offer environmental studies and outdoor leadership programs—there are many such programs in small colleges and big universities (due in part to our leadership in years past, I believe). The College is currently carrying out a Strategic Planning Process, and part of that process should be to reexamine the content we currently teach to see if we still offer the material and experience our students will need to be leaders in the twenty-first century (that is now upon us)!

Conventional colleges and universities teach knowledge (i.e., theory and facts) a bit at a time. They have been responsible for splitting the *universe* of knowledge into smaller and smaller bits. Two processes are employed: *Abstraction*—as knowledge is processed through these systems, the "content" is increasingly purified and divorced from its rich, complex, interdependent natural settings; and *Analysis*—content is pigeonholed into ever finer, more artificial categories that departmentalize each "subject" from all others.

What effect does *abstracting* and *analyzing* knowledge have on the student? The conventional educator might answer that it makes the learning of large volumes of complex information much easier, because it is well "packaged" for teaching and testing. But going beyond mere efficiency or convenience, what effect does it have on the conception of reality which students develop? It focuses the student's mind on the particular, and muddles any overview of the general. Bob Harrill, a faculty member and administrator at PC in the early '70s, told me that he had learned "everything there was to know about seven molecules" when he earned his doctorate in chemistry; then he added, "but I didn't know much about the world." This was Bob's explanation of why he left traditional academia to teach at Prescott College.

The process of *analyzing* and *abstracting* knowledge has an even more sinister effect—it tends to produce specialists and discourage a generalist overview. Specialists are trained to abstract from the whole only their parts of the problem—and then leave the ethical responsibility for the effect of their actions to others—"it's not my department." To illustrate with one example: let's consider the general problem of chemical pesticides poisoning food, water, soil, wildlife, etc. What do the various specialists say and do? Chemist: "I can create chemicals to kill the pests." Chemical manufacturer: "I can make profits, employ workers, and repay investors by selling these chemicals." Farmer: "I can grow higher yields by using chemicals." Grocery chain manager: "I can sell the pesticide-protected, blemish-free agricultural products and increase profits." Medical researcher: "I can demonstrate scientifically that these chemicals damage the soil and are toxic to humans, so I can get published." Pharmaceutical manufacturer: "We can research diseases caused by pesticides and create drugs to cure them." Politician: "by blocking legislation which outlaws these chemicals, I can gain the support (and campaign donations) of both the chemical and pharmaceutical industries, the farmers, and others involved, thus keeping employment high—so I can stay in office." All of these specialists were educated in our system of universities and colleges.

It is not the poor, the uneducated, or tribal people who are destroying the natural environment, but the very people who have had the benefit of so-called "higher" education—an education that has taught them to abstract and analyze, then conquer nature—an education that fails to provide an overview or ethical commitment. As a society, we are very successful in educating people who can create tiny bits of a picture, but the picture, itself, makes little sense—and very few of those involved feel responsible or capable of dealing with our problems at the global level. Perhaps Robert Heinlein was right when he observed, *"Specialization is for insects."* It certainly isn't the complete answer for human beings. But you wouldn't guess that from looking at the standard university curriculum.

At Prescott College we are trying to offer a new kind of education which prepares students to see the *whole* as well as the *parts*—to see things as they interrelate in reality, not as abstract "-ologies," treating isolated problems. We emphasize the ethical implications of policy, asking students to take responsibility for the health of the whole rather than exploiting the part. Another way to say this is that we are attempting to create a *problem-centered curriculum*. To give one example, rather than teach psychology, sociology, and related "-ologies" so that students can take a series of required courses and build up a GPA, at Prescott College these same studies are often synthesized into projects so that students also gain self-understanding, appreciation of others, and communications skills, and perform services within the PC community and in the world. Our students learn in traditional ways, but also by addressing real problems and creating real solutions in the real world.

OTHER KINDS OF KNOWLEDGE, BEYOND FACTS

So far, I have spoken mainly of learning **knowledge**, which consists of theories and facts. Knowledge is the main grist for the mill of conventional education. However, educational researchers and philosophers have identified other types of learning outcomes, that are equally as important—acquisition of **skills/methods/technique**, examination and commitment to **ethics/esthetics**, and what we might call **heuristics or learning capabilities**. To this mix, Prescott College adds **experiential learning**. We try to educate the whole person, so we structure the curriculum to help students learn in all of these aspects.

Since most of us are well acquainted with knowledge learning, and I have discussed the interdisciplinary approach above, I will only add that knowledge has a very short shelf life. Much of what I learned in college is now no longer "true."

Skills-learning is largely ignored at the undergraduate level in conventional education. In good graduate schools—particularly at the doctoral level—students do have the opportunity to learn lab and field research methodologies, studio and performing arts, original scholarship skills, etc., under the mentorship of faculty. At Prescott College, such opportunities are provided—sometimes required—from the freshman year on. All students must demonstrate competence in a Senior Project, which necessarily entails exercising skills.

Particularly in public education, **ethics** and **esthestics** are dangerous territory, strewn with the corpses of issues, causes, and fads. Relativism and neutrality are the academic escape hatches available when students want to explore the many crucial ethical dimensions of learning. There are practical excuses for shying away from controversy and being "politically correct," whatever that might mean at the time. There is a certain comfort in not having to judge the esthetic quality of a student's or a colleague's work. But knowledge is useless, indeed life is meaningless, unless it is informed by ethics and esthetics. As Socrates is quoted, "The unexamined life is not worth living." The best of the private institutions have an important advantage in this realm, and our problems-centered curriculum, our openness to controversial issues, our Socratic teaching puts Prescott College in that league. In my opinion, our open, often raucous, running dialogue on the big issues facing the world—this is our best claim to quality, our essential *raison d'etre.*

Heuristics is a sometimes controversial concept, and here I am referring to those attitudes and skills that a student can acquire to be a better learner. In conventional schools there is little attention to this important aspect of education, except when a student begins to fail—and then learning how to study is considered *remedial,* for *dummies.* At Prescott College we are *success oriented,* which I will discuss in more detail below. Several maxims we commonly use show that learning to learn is an essential aspect of the Prescott College curriculum, e.g., "self-directed learning," "learning is a journey," "lifelong learning," "demonstration of competence," "critical thinking skills."

Powerful Ways to Learn and Teach

Our innovative theory of curricular content is only half of the story—"you can't put *new* wine in *old* bottles." To paraphrase, "you can't teach an integrative, problem-solving, future-oriented curriculum by antiquated, didactic, teacher-centered, creativity-punishing methods.

You have all experienced the *old* bottles. The conventional college teaching methodology, stripped down to its essence, consists of four stages: *input* of facts and theories by lecture, readings, etc.—*memorization* of the material—*regurgitation* of the material on tests—and *rating* of this performance. Divergent ideas are usually ignored or even punished as "wrong" answers. Teachers and books are authorities, and students are taught to inhibit their own emerging ideas in order to score well on tests. Of course there are bright spots, creative teachers, rebellious students who challenge authorities, lab experiments that go "wrong" and stimulate new questions. Let's acknowledge that the conventional methodology is successful in teaching many students who can lay out theories, spout facts on cue, pass tests with high scores, accumulate impressive GPAs, and nail the Graduate Records Exam. I was one of those students and I believe so were all of you. Therefore, I don't intend to berate our educations. No doubt we learned much of value.

But let's look at another aspect, something theorists call *incidental learning.* What does the conventional system teach *between the lines?* Here are some of the lessons we may have learned subliminally: We were taught intellectual conformity, to memorize and repeat the ideas of others without question, that students' ideas are somehow inferior to those of professors and other authorities. We were taught that others ask the questions, and the student's role is to come up with "correct" answers quickly. They taught us how to put on blinders and see only that which has been placed in front of our eyes. In other words, we learned to chop the world of knowledge into tiny, unrelated bits. Since in one way or another we are all educators, we may have learned, probably unconsciously, how to teach didactically and perpetuate the conventional system. But, we are the lucky ones who escaped and found a better way!

More serious than this are the *deficiencies*, the lessons we were *never* taught—unless we taught ourselves. We weren't taught how to apply our knowledge to real-world problems, nor even how to relate what we learned in one course to the materials and issues of another. We weren't taught to ask penetrating questions—particularly questions which don't have ready answers that could be found in a book or dispensed in short form by a professor. Many of the most important questions are still open—no one knows the answers. That's embarrassing to professors, so they make up plausible answers. They did not teach us to doubt the theories and facts being presented to us for memorization—even though a large portion of these theories and facts will be proved false in the near future. In my own lifetime the foundations of physics have been overturned. The same is true of dynamic fields like genetics, paleontology, economics, and medicine. They did not teach us that half of what we might read in a good university library is just plain wrong—that the world of ideas is dynamic and ever-changing. They did not help us to appreciate our own divergent ideas and native creativity. They did not help us learn to communicate about meaning with others, nor how to teach our associates and future students to be seekers and questioners.

At Prescott College, we seek to teach theories and facts, too. But we also try to teach students a certain creative irreverence for the "authorities." We help students understand that questions may be more important than answers—since theories and facts have a short shelf life, but the fundamental questions are valid forever. We lead our students to ask the *real* questions lurking behind superficial treatments of issues, to think deeply, and take themselves seriously as creative learners. We teach students to apply their knowledge to real problems, to make learning relevant to life, to love learning and to become lifelong learners.

Earlier I referred to our slogans about *self-directed learning*, which is not left to instinct at the College. Usually, students need the help and support of teachers, advisors, and other students to become self-directed—which may seem self-contradictory. But the learning journey at Prescott College has been carefully designed and crafted by students and faculty over many years, and has several way stations or stages: continuous personal advising from the beginning, an individual graduation plan presented eighteen months before the intended date, a senior project that demonstrates competence before graduation. In each course, there is also a structure to encourage self-direction: an individual contract containing student-created learning objectives and specifying how their accomplishment is to be evaluated, an accumulated portfolio documenting the student's whole course, and narrative evaluations of performance by the faculty and student. A full description of these and other supporting processes can be found in our Student Handbook and other documents.

To many conventional educators, the term *experiential education* conjures up images of terrified youths rappelling off cliffs, shooting rapids in small kayaks—and that perception is not incorrect, just drastically incomplete. At Prescott College *all* learning programs have substantial experiential components. As Jim Stuckey said years ago, "Our job is to thrust the students into experience." It is easy to imagine this in such subject areas as performing arts or ecological field studies, but how does a teacher structure an experiential component in a more traditional academic field, say, history? You can't travel back in time to allow students to storm the Bastille. To understand how, you must consider what the word *experience* really means. The subject, in this case the student, takes in primary impressions through multiple sensory channels, and those impressions are synthesized and interpreted actively in the subject's mind. Ask: "What do you see? hear? feel emotionally? How can this experience inform and change your life? How will you put this into effect?" These impressions are integrated into a larger fund of life experience, so that the student can find meaning in the new experience. Therefore, experiential learning is not limited to any particular setting or subject matter.

History is just as real as a vertical cliff face, and historians do real work that can grow into an authentic spiritual/intellectual experience with the feel of risk or danger. Historians search and discover; they evaluate credibility of sources. They triangulate and compare facts and opinions. They puzzle over discrepancies and ask deep questions. They use their own accumulated experiences as human beings—their feelings and disciplined thought processes—and they stick with the quest until a picture of an age, an event, or a person emerges in their minds. Then they use channels of communication to provide that picture to others. So what is the difference between a "real" historian and a mere history student? From the viewpoint of an experiential educator or student there is no difference—except in degree of sophistication. If you can describe what a student is doing with a series of active verbs, it's probably experiential education, whether the setting is in open air, a research ship, a sound studio—or in a library. I start nearly every course by saying, "Think of yourselves as an orientation patrol heading into new territory," as I hand out the syllabus, "and here is your map."

I will conclude by talking about a learning principle which I feel may be the most important of all our teaching innovations. Prescott College is *success-based.* American culture also appears to be success-based, so it may surprise you when I suggest that conventional education also promotes *failure*—failure is a necessary component of its methodology.

One of the roles which our society has assigned to schools is to grade and certify graduates, and in the same process to identify and label those who have failed. Grading systems—whether we are grading potatoes or people— necessarily identify both successes and failures; the big one into this bin, the defective ones into that other bin. Without failures there can be no successes; one has to rise above the mass to be recognized and accorded superior value. Conventional schools have developed elaborate systems for labeling and comparing students' performance, and these begin to be used in the early elementary grades and increase in rigor and seriousness as students progress through the various levels. Competition is good, we say—and for the star students it is very good. But the literature of educational psychology and sociology is also replete with cases of students who suffer abnormal and even damaging anxiety when they disappoint themselves and their teachers and parents.

The truth is that these young people *have not failed* just because they can't get the grades that society says they must have. We know by common sense, and from hundreds of research studies, that students differ in their interests, capacities, and areas of talent, yet our conventional schools continue to compare them on one standard. We use so-called *objective* tests—or grade them "on the curve." The curve referred to is the normal curve in which approximately 68% are graded as mediocre, 16% are labeled as gifted or highly successful, and 16% are failures. That's the system, and too bad for those who fall beneath the mean. Again, from experience, which research confirms, we know our conventional system necessarily creates a failure cycle which traps hundreds of thousands of young people every year, particularly in our inner cities and poor rural areas. Failure in school leads to dropping out … leads to failure to find adequate work … leads to …

In the traditional university or college, this perverse logic dictates that the professor who fails the highest percentage of students is considered the most rigorous (quality-conscious) teacher. In other words, that professor is rewarded for failing a higher percentage of students—while the professor whose students learn more, thus exceeding normal expectations, is punished by those who suspect he is a purveyor of poor standards. Those of us who have worked in academia for some time are well acquainted with this phenomenon. We have seen the best and most popular teachers treated as lightweights and panderers, while poor teachers who destroy students' self-confidence and enthusiasm for learning are too often rewarded for their "firmness."

When such an analysis of conventional education is presented, a chorus of protesting voices inevitably arises. Competition is natural and good—it's the way the world works! Survival of the fittest! How can we possibly maintain standards if we eliminate the threat of failure! The grading system is the only way we have to keep the pressure on! *Will students learn if we don't keep pushing them with the threat of poor grades and failure?*

The answer to this last question is known. A century of solid research has produced a surprisingly optimistic answer: **YES, students will learn when the threat of failure is eliminated—they'll learn more and better!** The research clearly demonstrates that *learning is motivated by success*, not by failure. In fact, threat of failure has been shown to inhibit learning. And another body of research, much of it recently conducted in American universities, shows that success-motivated learning is of much better quality than learning coerced by threat. **Success-based learning** is natural and taps the life-sustaining motivations inherent in all healthy human beings. It produces a deeper understanding, which persists over time, and it motivates further learning. Learning driven by threat of failure tends to be shallow and quickly forgotten, leaving only a residue of low self-esteem and resentment against the system and the subject matter.

Prescott College is attempting to create a success-based learning system. We listen to what students say and respect their original ideas. In place of the conventional hunt to ferret out mistakes in students' work, we try to focus on what is right and good in students' thinking—and build on it. It's not that all ideas are accepted as equal in quality or truth-value; we are academically rigorous in the traditional sense. But a Prescott College classroom is a sort of "think tank" in which the faculty and students are on the same side—not in a contest to see if one side can cheat the system or the other side can enforce tough standards. When it works—which is most of the time—it is a transcendent experience for both students and teachers.

To reinforce the success ethic we use narrative evaluations, which generally record what the student has learned, produced, accomplished. These accumulate to become a narrative transcript which is often called a "record of achievement." These transcripts speak eloquently of the achievements of our students—which also constitutes a powerful testament to the achievements of the College.

I'd like to leave you with a quotation from the heroic playwright-president who led the people of Czechoslovakia through their recent struggle for independence from the USSR. He may not have known about our small College, but he caught its spirit when he wrote:

> The role of the schools is not to create "idiot specialists" to fill the special needs of different sectors ... but to develop the individual abilities

of the students ... to send out into life thoughtful people capable of thinking about the wider social, historical and philosophical implications of their specialties. ... The schools must also lead young people to become self-confident, participating citizens.

VACLAV HAVEL

A SAMPLE OF ACTUAL LEARNING OBJECTIVES FROM STUDENTS' INDIVIDUAL LEARNING CONTRACTS FOR VARIOUS COURSES.

Another way to understand what happens in our unique learning-teaching system is to read some learning objectives which students have written and committed themselves to in their courses.

Knowledge Objectives

"I will learn the history of North America in the Colonial Period, and research and write a short biography of one of my ancestors who lived then." "I will learn the basic facts about the physical geography, climate, natural history and ecology of Western Canada." "I will write a research paper, presenting different points of view about the use of wilderness resources." "I will learn the history of oil painting in the Modern Period." "I will learn the names, structure and identifying characteristics of the elements of the standard Periodic Table of Elements." "I will demonstrate understanding of the General Theory of Relativity at a descriptive level." "I will gain an understanding of the Theory of Memetics, as derived from Sociobiology and Evolutionary Psychology." "I will learn how to apply general principles of ecology to human societies."

Skill Objectives

"I will learn to ask penetrating questions." " ... gain skill in judging the validity of ideas and arguments." "I will translate and adapt ideas of general ecology in order to study how political campaigns evolve." "I will compare and contrast the doctrines of Buddhism with those of Christianity." "I will analyze the messages of 100 advertisements for body care products to determine the psychological devices used to induce purchase." "I will synthesize data from three national studies and produce a report which proposes a feasible explanation of high failure rates in inner city schools." "I will locate, evaluate, and report on materials on the Gulf War from a variety of sources, including recent books, journal articles, and internet sources." "I will write an in-depth research paper on organized crime in Russia, using the University of Chicago (Turabian) style."

Ethics Objectives

"I will open-mindedly consider the positions of both the Jews and the Palestinians regarding building of new Jewish settlements in the West Bank." "I will do an objective study of the short- and longer-term results of experiments in decriminalization of drugs in Switzerland, the Netherlands and other countries." "I will write a paper suggesting a balanced use of federal lands, considering the need for recreation, preservation of wild habitats, and economic uses like timber, mining and grazing." "I will reconsider my ideas about professions I might enter from an ethical point of view." "I will carry out a service project tutoring a Native American student in the local public schools, and I will attempt to understand this child's culture, and promote self esteem as a successful learner." "I will actively participate in the local chapter of Amnesty International, writing letters and fundraising."

Esthetics Objectives

"I will study Renaissance sculpture to understand and feel its beauty and meaning." "I will meditate a least a half hour each day, learning to empty my mind and experience self at a deeper level." "I will express my joy and good will for all beings through learning to dance expressively."

Experiential Objectives

"I will experience four different southwest landscapes by participating in four weekend wilderness hikes, attempting to be fully conscious of and sensitive to all life forms I encounter. What I learn through this experience will be reflected in my field journal." "I will visit a Mosque and talk with some of the officials or leaders about what it takes to be a faithful Muslim in America." "I will submit a set of poems I have written to a magazine." "I will wear a blindfold at all times for ten days to experience what it means to be deprived of sight."

[Note: The student who wore the blindfold submitted for evaluation a set of cassette recordings debriefing every day, and a short written appraisal of her learning from the whole experience.]

Professional Education and Teacher Training at Prescott College

◇◇◇◇◇◇◇

by Melissa Doran

Prescott College is a place where activism thrives. Students and faculty here are profoundly committed to creating positive social change and making the world a better place. Education is a powerful tool for this, and for decades students who want to make a difference have sought out the College for this philosophy.

Dan Garvey

When asked to say what image comes to mind when the name Prescott College is spoken, some people would mention aspects like wilderness exploration, kayaking, social activism, or outstanding photography. Many would be astonished to find that a greater portion of the students at Prescott College in the Adult Degree and Graduate Programs (ADGP), as well as the Resident Degree Program (RDP), are engaged in the field of education and teacher training.

Throughout most of its history, and certainly today, the College has been consistently devoted to the best and most innovative education possible, so it should be no surprise that one of its most important achievements has been training thousands of knowledgeable, qualified, and deeply committed educators. The College trains classroom teachers for all grade levels. They are skilled experiential educators in fields as varied as adventure, art, social studies, environment, and in special programs for teaching the underprivileged and in inner city public schools. Prescott College now has graduates who are teaching in communities throughout the country and the world, and many who have stayed to teach here in local communities. In fact many of those very students so often photographed in outdoor gear with huge backpacks traversing remote country, or expertly paddling sea kayaks between islands in the Sea of Cortez, are undergraduates in a program called Adventure *Education*. Most of these students intend to teach, and many are earning standard teaching credentials.

The majority of Prescott College students seeking teacher certification are also working to earn BA degrees through the Adult Degree Program, which is the undergraduate arm of the Adult Degree and Graduate Program (ADGP). These students are dispersed throughout Arizona, the Southwest, across the country, and indeed around the world. In addition to programs in education at the Prescott campus, education and certification of teachers is the foremost program at the Tucson campus, and the College literally pioneered teacher training on several Native American reservations in our state and beyond. All of this demonstrates that professional education in a variety of fields, including teacher training and credentialing, forms the core of Prescott College.

Though educator training has long been a deeply rooted theme at Prescott College, the publicity exploiting the more dramatic aspects of the College, such as images of students climbing a sheer rock face, overlooks the fact that this kind of experiential work is often an essential component of the student's teacher education. Like everything else at Prescott College, classroom learning, independent academic study, and experience in the real world are intertwined. Educators do not teach only from textbooks; true educators are people who share their knowledge and enthusiasm with students in all settings, from pristine river banks, to free schools and community centers, to government systems, and any other venue in which students can be challenged to learn not only facts and theories but also ethical meaning.

Although not associated with the Education program, residential faculty member Tom Fleischner stated it well: "People are drawn to this College because of an unusual style of education and a desire to make the world a better place; the sense that education is a crucial contributor to this cuts across the curriculum." In fact, so many residential students were designing competences around the idea of Education for Social Justice that it has recently been proposed as an approved Competence Area (Prescott College's version of major). Whatever the medium, be it empowering youth through wilderness experiences, creating biophilia and an appreciation for the natural world through environmental education, or working for social justice in a public high school history class, students seem compelled to become educators for the same reasons they were compelled to come to Prescott College: *to create change.*

Over the years teacher training has grown and evolved. Both Resident and the Adult and Graduate Program have been innovators in the field and have created programs unique to the needs of their students.

The Adult Degree and Graduate Programs (ADGP) are community-based programs. The students are required to proactively engage with schools, nonprofit organizations, governmental agencies, or non-formal community-based organizations within their local communities across the country and abroad. The rigorous course work is based on requirements for research, experiential work, and ongoing engagement in praxis within the student's academic program. The ADGP education faculty members have provided scholarly supervision of all aspects of each student's program, plus academic leadership through program development, for almost thirty years. The ADGP students and faculty share a strong commitment to self-directed learning, avid scholarship, and working to make a difference in the world. Dr. Steve Walters, the long-time dean of the Adult Degree Program and Prescott College's leader in education and teacher certification, was committed to fostering an education program that was steeped in the mission of Prescott College. As such, the Education program at Prescott College has been based historically on an underlying foundation of social justice and ecological literacy.

The Adult Degree Program specifically has been a leader in specializing teacher certification to fit the needs of highly diverse and underserved populations and has made great progress in changing the face of education in the state of Arizona through its CIBTE (Center for Indian Bilingual Teacher Education) program. Currently, Native American student numbers are declining within ADGP due to the decrease of federal and tribal funding, non-renewal of previously successful federal grants, and limited scholarship opportunities within our own institution. Prescott College continues to support philosophically the existing partnership with the Navajo Nation Teacher Education Consortium; however, limited reources have curbed the college's efforts in educating bilingual teachers to teach on the reservations.

History of Education Curricula and Teacher Training

The Prescott community leaders who created the first version of the College in the 1960s had a grand vision of Prescott as an important regional center for education at all levels, with a new private college as its crown jewel. Dr. Franklin Parker, the founding President, saw this new College as the most recent in a series of educational institutions sponsored, but not controlled by, the Congregationalist churches, beginning with Harvard in 1647.

One of the early financial supporters of the College, Charles Kettering II, was very interested in the innovative developments in education that were springing up nationally based on new understandings of the learning process and of learners (students). The work of psychologist Carl Rogers, particularly, moved Kettering to promote the creation of a new dimension in the curriculum. Rogers was famous for his ideas about education, championed chiefly in his books *On Becoming a Person* (Boston, Houghton Mifflin, 1961) and *Freedom to Learn: A View of What Education Might Become* (Columbus, Ohio, C. E. Merrill Pub. Co., 1969). Rogers had founded The Center for the Study of the Person in La Jolla, California, and Kettering, attracted by its educational concepts, proposed the establishment of such a Center at Prescott College. A Center for the Person was created, but it wasn't until Dr. Layne Longfellow, a young humanist psychologist and member of the select group at the Rogers Center was appointed chairman that the institution began to take root and grow.

During the first four years, Prescott College was staunchly academic, and did not have any vocational or teacher training programs. After 1970, the Center for the Person dedicated its program to studying all facets of the changing society in new and interesting ways. The alternative, experimental, and experiential new forms of education were a major focus for faculty and students in the Center for the Person. Classes including learning and development theory and the culture, history, and philosophies of education were offered, providing students with a new lens through which to view their own society, but also with options for creating a different kind of society through education.

As yet there was no specific education department, but students were learning about education and teaching in the most natural way possible through their own experiences. Students interested in pursuing teaching as a career were allowed to explore options through internships and independent studies, often facilitated by faculty in the Center for the Person. In the early '70s only one professor, Sam Henrie, taught the educational theory classes, and his wife, Angie, taught methods courses as an adjunct professor. Though it was a small part of the overall academics at the College, there was never a lack of interest, and it was obvious that many students would go on to become enthusiastic educators.

After the "old" College failed financially and gave up its large campus and moved into town, the College emphasized its famous Outdoor Action and Environmental Studies curricula. It was not until 1978 with the creation of the Adult Degree Program that teacher education once again became a large part of the identity of the College.

Adult Degree Program and Education

The Adult Degree Program (ADP) was founded in 1978-79 with only eight students; within a few years it had enrolled forty. By 1984-85 it surpassed 100, and between 1998 and 2006 it grew from 300 to 350. The Adult

Degree Program was created to serve the many adult students who had interrupted their undergraduate studies to work and build families and careers, but now wanted to finish their degrees. It was designated a community based degree program, since most candidates did not have the ability to move or quit their jobs to return to school. Instead they become engaged in the Prescott College curriculum within the context of their own communities.

There was a growing trend nationally of adults returning to school, and the College's educational philosophy was especially well suited to this new group of students. This arm of the College also recognized that adult learners are different from younger students. Adults tend to have the real world knowledge and experience gained from raising families and developing careers, giving them a depth of understanding to bring to the academic curriculum that their younger counterparts may yet lack. Aware of their own needs and values, their strengths and limitations, adult students seek autonomy as well as active participation in their education.

In 1980 the professional education and teacher preparation aspects of the Adult Degree Program were spearheaded by a new arrival to the College, ADP director Dr. Annabelle Nelson. Through her work at Maryhurst College, she had learned how to create life experience portfolios and liberal arts seminars. Nelson created and built the education program from the ground up, and with the help of Pat Dickens gradually built the program into a vibrant part of the college. She created numerous innovative processes within ADP, such as life experience portfolios, the study contract system, systems for recruiting mentors, new student orientations, and Liberal Arts Seminars. The education program grew very rapidly within a few years.

The major leap for the Adult Degree Program, and the whole College, happened in time for the 1988-89 school year, when Nelson had successfully gained state approval for the school's teacher certification program. The application process had begun a year earlier when a student from Wyoming who had graduated with an education degree discovered she was unable to obtain certification in either Wyoming or Arizona. Nelson says she "took that as kind of a moral obligation to get our teacher preparation program state certified." In Arizona, teacher certification programs had been the almost exclusive domain of the three state universities, so gaining recognition for the College's education program was a big step. But beyond that, Prescott College became authorized to recommend students directly to the State Certification Board to receive their teaching credentials. Nelson was also successful in obtaining bilingual teacher training certification for the College.

To have attained these certifications is an unusual and impressive accomplishment for a small private college. Prescott College has worked diligently to use this authorization to train and certify hundreds of teachers and has facilitated their placements as professional teachers in public and private elementary, middle, and high schools. By the late 1980s the teacher training and certification program had also been incorporated into the on-campus resident undergraduate program and the community based Master of Arts Program. In addition, a number of teachers were using the program to enhance degrees already earned, and to pursue careers as school administrators.

Implementing the College's special mission to serve underserved populations, the professional education efforts of the College were extended to other segments of the Arizona citizenry, particularly Native Americans and Hispanics. In 1986 Dr. Annabelle Nelson began a pioneering program designed to meet the needs of Native American schools and educators on several reservations across the state. This new program, the Center for Indian Bilingual Teacher Education, was a branch of the Adult Degree Program.

At approximately the same time that Annabelle Nelson took on the directorship of CIBTE, in 1988, Gret Antilla came, first as an academic advisor in the Adult Degree Program, later moving on to the residential program as education faculty, and eventually becoming Dean of the Resident Degree Program. At that time, the Adult Degree Program handled all teacher training. Residential students wishing to take education courses attended evening classes with ADP students. Antilla recalls that the interaction between the Resident and the Adult Degree students was very positive and helpful to both groups.

When Northern Arizona University (NAU) opened a teacher certification program in Prescott in 1990, many of the local ADP students were lost to NAU's program. Though temporarily impacted by a loss of student numbers, the Adult Degree Program carried on and continued graduating students with teacher certification.

RESIDENT DEGREE PROGRAM AND EDUCATION

At this juncture, the Resident Degree Program quickly added several courses essential for teacher certification and relied on independent studies to supply the remainder. Independent studies were carried out in the form of internships through partnerships with local schools. The RDP education program developed very slowly; devising a program leading to teacher certification required more commitment and ingenuity from the student. Nonetheless, interest in an undergraduate teacher training program continued and several members of the RDP faculty stepped up to further develop the education curriculum in the Resident Program. Environmental Studies faculty member Tom Fleischner considered it a great irony that education had always been an area that cut across all internal boundaries, but did not have its own organized department, in spite of the fact that there was such a strong thrust toward it. He remembers that there was strong support throughout the RDP for starting a formal education program.

In 1995 a cross-College education program was formed between the growing Adult Degree Program and the fledgling residential education program. Unfortunately, the program was closed by the administration shortly thereafter due to budget restrictions.

This setback did not stop the RDP faculty for long, however. In 1999 another Education committee was formed with Environmental Studies faculty member Bob Ellis serving as chairman. Ellis had been at the College for two years and was teaching many of the school's education courses. He mentions that his "primary motivation in elevating Education to Program status was the fact that certification students were not being served. They were forced to take much of their coursework through Independent Studies." A former public school teacher who taught for eight years, Ellis noted, "I felt that the mission of the College could best be served by getting RDP students into schools as certified teachers." To this end a committee of RDP faculty chaired by Ellis met to discuss how the dream for this new RDP program might become a reality. The new informal group has been credited with "supporting and watering the garden" of creating an actual Education Program in the Resident Degree Program. The committee submitted a proposal to create an official Education Program in RDP; it was accepted in the spring of 2001.

Because the Resident Degree Education Program grew out of the school's tradition of experiential education and the Adult Degree Program's community based curriculum, its curriculum naturally tended to be more field based and experiential than other colleges' programs. The residential education program's unique asset is that students are immersed in hands-on educational experiences very early in their studies. After enrolling in their first Foundations of Education course, students were put in schools to observe. Field observation and implementation of student-designed curriculum were essential parts of all education courses in RDP from the very beginning. An average education class in RDP spends at least ten hours observing in classrooms around the state, and some classes such as Experiential Education Practicum spend an entire block course (one month) traveling through schools in the West observing and implementing curriculum. Because of this infusion of practical experience into educational theory, students are better able to synthesize their learning and graduate well prepared to enter the classroom. In fact, student teachers from the RDP program have been described as having "a maturity and confidence that, along with their competence in authentic assessment, experiential education, and best practices in teaching their subject and grade level, make them appear to be more experienced teachers than they are."

The Resident Degree Education Program has attracted highly qualified and ardent new faculty members in recent years, including Maggie Cox, Jordana DeZeeuw Spencer, and Anita Fernandez. Fernandez is a former public high school teacher and was teaching in a public university setting before moving to Prescott College. She states that she was attracted to teaching at Prescott College because of its unique mission and commitment to social justice and by the types of students and faculty the College itself attracts. With a strong background in multicultural education, Fernandez believed that coming to a school with such a social justice emphasis would allow her to begin teaching at a more advanced starting point and get more important cultural sensitivity work done in the field of education. Cox agreed with these sentiments, stating, "The mission of protecting the environment and actively seeking social justice was a match for my life's goals." She also mentioned another reason for joining the College; "I also observed the outstanding quality and depth of authentic tasks the RDP students were doing both in course work and as independent studies and there seemed to be meaningful active learning happening everywhere."

At the time of this writing (2007), the RDP's program in education is heading in many new directions and moving into radically new territory. Student interest is at an all time high, with forty percent of its student body interested in education in one form or another, and more and more students committing themselves to the difficult teacher certification process.

The Prescott College learning community has many facets, including the resident undergraduate program, RDP, the community based bachelor's-level ADP, master's-level MAP, and the PhD program initiated in 2005. In the newly formed PhD program, where the only area of study is education, students can earn a PhD in Education for Sustainability. This advanced degree embodies and showcases what Prescott College does best, on all educational levels. All degree programs now offered by Prescott College have professional education components. The College has both initiated bold and effective roles for itself, in preparing and helping gain certification for classroom teachers, and also been active in creating innovative and experiential education within the communities where it is located and throughout Arizona.

IMPACT ON THE LOCAL COMMUNITY

The Prescott College educators have gained respect and recognition within the City of Prescott and its several surrounding suburbs and towns. Students who graduate from Prescott College with an education degree are the most prevalent alumni population who stay and work in the local community, providing local schools with highly qualified and dedicated teachers. Currently there are at least six recent Resident Degree Program graduates working as full time teachers in local schools, perhaps many more from the Adult Degree and Graduate Program. These teachers also did their student teaching and a variety of other coursework in the local schools, providing citizens with greater opportunities to understand the mission and philosophies of Prescott College, such as liberal arts and environmental sustainability.

The Prescott College commitment to education has affected the community in a variety of other ways as well. Faculty, students and/or alumni have been involved in the formation of four local schools in Prescott: Primavera Academy (a private elementary school founded by Prescott College alum Rebecca Ruffner), Skyview School (a charter school based on the multiple intelligences approach pioneered by Howard Gardner), Mountain Oak (a Waldorf-inspired charter school serving K-8), and Northpoint Expeditionary Learning Academy. Prescott College faculty members, administrators, and board members had instrumental roles in founding two of these schools—Mountain Oak and Skyview. And members of the College community continue to serve many roles in all local schools. Teacher trainees are teaching every school day in Prescott's local public and private schools, in the Tucson area, and on several Indian Reservations.

EXPEDITIONARY LEARNING SCHOOLS (FORMERLY EXPEDITIONARY LEARNING, OUTWARD BOUND)

In recent years the College has found a natural relationship with Expeditionary Learning schools (formerly Expeditionary Learning Outward Bound). Expeditionary Learning's philosophies of integration throughout content areas and emphasis on experiential learning is a natural fit with Prescott College and the two have joined in the Prescott community in many ways. Currently, Prescott is the only community in the nation with Expeditionary Learning (EL) schools from kindergarten through high school. Skyview School, a local elementary charter school, recently converted to an Expeditionary Learning philosophy, as did a section of Mile High Middle School, and the new Expeditionary Learning high school, Northpoint Expeditionary Learning Academy, opened in 2006.

Because of this excellent opportunity, the College has developed Memoranda of Understanding with each of these schools, specifying reciprocal relationships between them. Students of Skyview School and Northpoint Expeditionary Learning Academy have access to certain Prescott College resources, and Prescott College students have opportunities to work in Expeditionary Learning schools in a variety of ways. Graduates of the Adult

Degree Programs are often teachers in these schools and students from the residential program are found observing at these schools most days out of the week. Many residential students have done independent studies with teachers at the schools or have completed their student teaching there. Another way residential students have become involved in Northpoint Expeditionary Learning Academy is through leading wilderness orientations, another natural relationship between the schools. The Expeditionary Learning faculty position of Adventure Coordinator is one that is of particular interest to Prescott College students as it requires an applicant to have both teacher certification and a solid background in Adventure Education. This unique and exceptional learning opportunity that the Prescott College community has with the Expeditionary Learning schools has led to a proposal to form an official partnership with EL. If approved, this will allow Prescott College to award ADGP and RDP students with a special certification with an emphasis in Expeditionary Learning, a certification proving that the student is more prepared to teach in an EL school. Though this is still in the works, two Expeditionary Learning courses have already been offered through the college, and numerous ADGP students have designed studies that include a focus on EL philosophy and methodology, which seems to be a good sign. This would make Prescott College the only school in the country approved to give this type of certification and would make its education program even more highly esteemed.

Mountain Oak School

Dr. Mark Riegner, a Prescott College faculty member in the Environmental Studies department for nineteen years, was one of five local parents who were interested in Waldorf education and wanted to create a Waldorf-inspired school in the community. They held meetings for over a year and Mountain Oak was officially opened in the fall of 1999 as a tuition-free Arizona State charter school. In the years that Mountain Oak has been in operation it has proven to be very successful, with its students consistently scoring above average on the Arizona State Standardized Test (AIMS). Prescott College students have also greatly benefited from having a Waldorf school in the community. It has allowed dozens of Prescott College classes to observe in a nearby Waldorf school and gain insight into this unique style of education, as well as providing students with opportunities to work at the school in a range of different capacities. Students have created gardens at the school and worked as after-school program coordinators, and graduates have gone on to teach at Mountain Oak. Many other faculty members have also been involved throughout the years.

Dr. Riegner explains that one reason Prescott College faculty have been involved with the founding of this and other local schools is that "the kinds of faculty Prescott College attracts are people who take initiative. They are idealists who want to effect positive social change," and that this "flows out into the community from who we are." Because the faculty of the College is so dedicated to quality education, it is "natural to reach out and do this work in the community as well."

Dr. Tom Fleischner, also a Prescott College Environmental Studies faculty member, was part of a group of parents who came together to start Skyview School. Fleischner was part of the original board of directors of Skyview, the first parent-initiated charter school in Arizona. With its focus on multiple intelligences theory and experiential education, Skyview was a natural fit with Prescott College. Over the years many Prescott College faculty members have served on the Board, including Kenny Cook, Paul Smith, and President Dan Garvey. Faculty member Wayne Regina served as the director of the school while taking a few years sabbatical from the College. The formal working arrangement between Skyview (an Expeditionary Learning school) and the College has provided innumerable learning opportunities for Prescott College RDP students and employment opportunities as teachers for ADGP students.

The schools that Prescott College faculty members have had a hand in founding provide the College's education students a chance to observe diverse educational settings. There is a wide enough variety of educational approaches, right here in the relatively small community of Prescott, for students to investigate and discover which educational philosophies resonate for them. Education program faculty member Maggie Cox lists this as one of the major strengths of the Prescott College program.

EDUCATION FOR SOCIAL JUSTICE

Another area that has been growing and coming into its own in recent years within the residential program is the area of Education for Social Justice. Regardless of what it has been called over the years, this has been the heart of what most education students believe themselves to be working for anyway; what has always been done is now finally being formalized due to strong student interest. After a successful RDP pilot course taught in the fall of 2005 titled Educating for Peace, co-taught by Randall Amster, Jordana DeZeeuw Spencer, and ADP student Brian Maher, the program moved in the direction of creating an official competence area.

With a competence in Social Justice Education now available in the residential education program, the working relationships with Expeditionary Learning schools, plus the ongoing connections between Adventure Educa-

tion and the residential education program, Prescott College's Resident Degree Program is building a successful and respected education program.

Between Prescott College's graduate and undergraduate departments,
nearly a thousand students have earned teacher certification since 1984, and
an additional untold number of graduates have gone on to become educators
in wilderness education, in charter schools, and in other educational settings.
Though less than seven years old, the Resident Degree Program in education
has joined the tradition that embodies the very core of what Prescott College
stands for: innovative, experiential, and activist-oriented education.

The Prescott College Center for Indian Bilingual Teacher Education (CIBTE)

by Melissa Doran

Native American education has been dominated by white people since the Bureau of Indian Affairs opened its first Indian School in 1860. By 1887 more than two hundred Indian schools had been established under federal supervision to "civilize" the Indians. A vast majority of these schools were boarding schools, founded on the belief that taking young children away from their families, communities, and language would help to assimilate them into white man's culture. This form of "Indian Education" continued for over a hundred years.[95]

Although there have been many reform efforts throughout the years, including the Indian Education Act of 1972 (which provides money for special programs for Indian children on and off reservations) and the Indian Self-Determination and Education Act of 1975 (which allows tribes and Indian organizations to take over and run Bureau of Indian Affairs programs and schools), effects of these early days in Native education still exist.

Native students continue to have the highest dropout rates (thirty-six percent) of any minority group in the United States, and a disproportionate number of Native students achieve below national averages on standardized tests. Some of the marks of the early years that still exist in schools on the reservation are "Eurocentric curriculum, low student/teacher expectations, a lack of Native educators as role models and overt and subtle racism."[14] Because of the oppressive experiences that their parents and grandparents frequently had in school under a BIA system, education is often looked down upon: "All they remember about school is that there were all these Anglos trying to make them forget they were Apaches; trying to make them turn against their parents, telling them that Indian ways were evil. A lot of those kids came to believe that their teachers were the evil ones, and so anything that had to do with education was also evil ... and now don't want anything to do with white man's education. The only reason they send their kids to school is because it's the law. But they tell their kids not to take school seriously," said an Apache elder.

With these types of experiences, and the fact that education on reservations today [beginning of the twenty-first century] remains a white man's education, with only thirty percent of teachers on the Navajo reservation of native descent, twenty-five percent on the Hopi reservation, and on the Tohono O'odham reservation, a mere twelve percent, it is no surprise that Native people are wary of sending their children to school. (Note: data on percentages of native Indian bilingual teacher on reservations is in constant flux; the information given above is from the early 2000s.)

One solution to this problem is more Native educators. As Peterson Zah, former president of the Navajo Nation and founder of the Navajo Teacher Training Program, said "I knew that if we put Navajo people in classrooms who could instill pride in a culture that for so long children had been told to forget, they would help them succeed." Bilingual teachers could help restore Native languages and would be able to identify with their students on a deeper level.

Because students were not allowed to speak or learn their Native languages in government run schools, many of these languages have all but died out, and reintroducing them in schools may be the only hope for their survival. A 1992 survey of children on the Navajo reservation found that more than half did not understand their native language. "I know we are losing our language and a lot of our culture. That is why I want to go back and share with my Native people. Right now we

Rosilda Manuel, Native-American Teacher

have Anglos and people who don't know anything about our background teaching our children," said Lita Bizaholoni of the Navajo Nation, a CIBTE alum who went on to complete her master's through the Prescott College Master of Arts Program. Luckily this problem was recognized at a national level, and in 1992 President Bush signed the Native American Languages Act, which made it the "policy of the United States to preserve, protect, and promote the rights and freedom of Native Americans to use, practice, and develop Native American languages." This includes the right to bilingual or Native language education, which can only be accomplished with a greater number of Native educators.

According to a report by the Fund for the Improvement of Postsecondary Education, these incongruencies between Anglo teachers and the native population "not only meant that most Indian children were taught by teachers who were not familiar with their culture ... but for many children in Arizona who speak only their native language, communicating with their teachers was difficult if not impossible. To make matters worse, non-Indian teachers usually moved out of the reservation after one or two years." A multitude of problems were arising from the current system, leading Tohono O'odham leaders to believe that it was the prevalent system that was "largely responsible for Native American students' dropping out of school at rates higher than those of any other ethnic group."

Although a majority of teachers on the reservations were Anglo, a great number of Native para-professionals were carrying much of the instructional classroom weight, often doing jobs that the certified teachers could not. These professionals had managed to earn some college credit, but did not have the means to complete a bachelor's degree, thereby disqualifying them from becoming fully certified teachers. Economic difficulties, close community ties and cultural disconnect all play a part in the high dropout rate for Native Americans in higher education. Without a working solution to the higher education dilemma, the general education problem on reservations could not improve.

Dr. Annabelle Nelson

It was upon learning about these problems that Dr. Annabelle Nelson, director of ADP, got Prescott College involved. Nelson came to Prescott College with a deeply ingrained social conscience. Raised by a civil rights activist mother, she held that education was "always about righting social injustice."[62b] And these educational inequities were occurring right "next door" to the College, on local Native American reservations. It should be noted that there are twenty-one federally recognized tribes with approximately 250,000 Native Americans (2000 Census) who live in Arizona, and reservations and tribal communities comprise over a quarter of Arizona's lands. One such reservation, the Yavapai, is located in the very heart of Prescott.[96]

Nelson was very much in sync with what the early planners of the College had in mind when they noted the "proximity of the Indian cultures" and mentioned "the hope that it would be possible in Prescott College to have on the faculty and in the student body those who have first-hand knowledge of the Indian cultures so illustrative of the principle of unity of values and outlook, so necessary in a healthy civilization" in the Symposium.

Having already been an instrumental part of founding the Adult Degree Program (ADP) at Prescott College, Nelson saw a possible solution. ADP, an external degree program, was designed to allow working adults the opportunity to finish their bachelor's degrees in their home communities, through a series of mentored independent studies, which was exactly what this population needed. In 1986 Nelson was approached by Bernard Siquieros, Director of Education of the Tohono O'odham Nation. They met and held a conference on the reservation with sixty teachers' aides and discussed what could be done. Among the participants of this meeting was Rosilda Manuel, who went on not only to graduate from the program, but also to become the Director of Education for the Tohono O'odham Nation.

CIBTT Center (later renamed CIBTE)

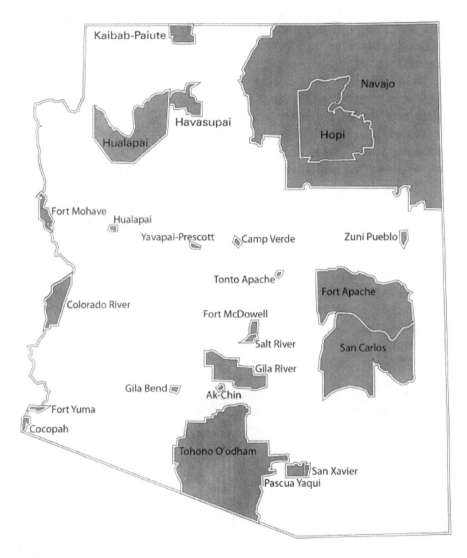

After the meeting, it was decided that a new program, the Center for Bilingual Teacher Training Education, or CIBTE, would be created to serve the needs of adult Native American students. For the next two years Dr. Nelson worked on finding grants to fund the new program, and in 1988 was awarded a large grant of $75,000 a year from the Fund for Improvement of Post Secondary Education (FIPSE). Nearly simultaneously another grant for bilingual education came through providing an additional $225,000. With the money now available the program was off and running. CIBTE began in 1988 with fifteen students.

The Adult Degree Program model was perfect, and the Center for Indian Bilingual Teacher Training was living up to the hopes of all. This new program allowed students to complete their bachelor's degrees and earn their Arizona teaching credentials all within their own communities. This meant not only that students could continue to work and support their families while being in school, but also that strong community and cultural connections would be respected. Rather than fit an imposed mold, CIBTE students were encouraged to use their cultural knowledge and individual strengths. Training, following the ADP model, would be highly individualized and self-directed, with each student working closely with mentors, advisors, and often small cooperative peer groups within their home communities. Students already working within schools could document and use their experiences to further their degrees. This was a crucial piece of the success of CIBTE and of the many teachers who have fulfilled their dreams through the program. For many students, such as LeNora Fulton, who has seven children and works full time, leaving to study at another college would have been out of the question. Through the Prescott College CIBTE program, however, she was able to get her teacher certification.

However, because this distance learning program was so different from many other forms of education the students and their communities had been exposed to in the past, some students heard jokes like "Have you received your mail order degree yet?" Rosilda Manuel laughed them off, saying, "If you only had any idea what this college is putting us through! When you're with an instructor who is very sharp, and you're the only student there, you better do your homework and be up to par with your assignments!"

In efforts to bridge cultural gaps and more fully understand the needs of the students, CIBTE worked closely with an advisory committee of tribal leaders and educators to ensure that the trainees' needs were responded to correctly. As former dean of the program, Fred Shunkamolah, a member of the Kiowa-Osage tribe of Oklahoma, said, "We provide indigenous, tribal education instead of 'Indian' education; we put education into the hands of the tribes and the communities." Cultural beliefs were highly respected at all times, including when it meant the program had to be altered. One class required the dissection of frogs. This being inappropriate to Navajo beliefs, sheep were brought in instead, butchered, and then consumed so that no creature's life was taken unnecessarily.

Although the program was flourishing, Dr. Nelson decided to step down and pass the torch to Bernard Siquieros (former Director of Education of the Tohono O'odham Nation), who became the second director of CIBTE in 1990. In 1992, a Ford Foundation grant was awarded to the Navajo Nation to form a consortium of Navajo Teacher Training programs. "This program was set up to open more doors to Navajo students, holding to the same academic standards, but with more respect and recognition of who they are." Prescott College was a charter member of this Navajo Nation Education Advisory Council, which also includes Navajo Community College (now Dine College), Fort Lewis College, University of Northern Colorado, University of New Mexico, and Northern Arizona University. Although a number of colleges were participating in the consortium, only Northern Arizona University had field based program sites on the Navajo Nation, and only Prescott College had the distance program that allowed students to continue working full time. Many students who started out at NAU and were unable to complete their degrees, due to family obligations or red tape, transferred to the Prescott College program.

Because of the Ford Foundation grant, a large percentage of CIBTE students were Navajo during the first few years and a branch was created in Window Rock to better serve Navajo students. This branch was operated by Carol Perry, who said that the purpose of the program was to "give Navajo teachers the credit they deserve." Another branch was started in Tucson to serve southern Arizona tribes such as the Tohono O'odham and the Pascua Yaqui. By 1995, there were approximately eighty Native American students participating in the program. As the program grew, so did the number of tribes that CIBTE was able to serve. At various points, fifteen different tribes have been represented, including Navajo, Hopi, Tohono O'odham, Absentee Shawnee, Shoshone, Choctaw, Pima, White Mountain Apache, Sioux, Kiowa, Cherokee, Yurok, Pawnee, Pascua Yaqui, Fort Mojave, San Carlos Apache, Puyallup, Hualapai, and Havasupai, eventually branching out beyond Arizona into areas of New Mexico, Utah, California, and even Mexico.

During this time period, although the program was in its prime, there were many administrative changes occurring, including another change in leadership: in July of 1995, Fred Shunkamolah took over as the new dean of CIBTE. In late 1997, the CIBTE program was absorbed, along with all external programs, into the Adult Degree Program. Several years earlier, in 1992, Vicky Young joined the staff of CIBTE as a halftime assistant registrar. She was so interested in the program that she spent the other half of her day volunteering. Over the years her role transitioned and became more and more crucial, and after the merging of CIBTE into ADP, Dr. Nelson said that Vicky, "thank God, became the champion and kept it [CIBTE] alive." There was a fear that upon being absorbed into ADP and without having a program of its own, CIBTE would lose its effectiveness. Although numbers have dropped, Vicky has remained the CIBTE counselor, keeping this unique and important program going within the Adult Degree Program.

In its first ten years, between 1988 and 1998, the program proved to be a tremendous success on many levels. By 1998, over 200 certified teachers, representing twenty tribes, graduated through the Prescott College CIBTE program, with 99.9 percent of these graduates going on to teach either on Native reservations, or in rural areas serving Native populations directly outside the reservations themselves. CIBTE students who had worked as teachers' aides or permanent substitute teachers in the same school for twenty years finally became full-time certified teachers at those schools immediately after graduating from the program. Compared with retention rates in the teens at many other universities, the CIBTE program had an 81 percent retention rate, and of the graduates of the program, 10 percent went on to receive master's degrees. The numbers alone prove the effectiveness of the program, but the work that the graduates have gone on to do in their own communities is a greater measure of the impact.

For many students, it was an opportunity to give back to their community in the most powerful possible way. As graduate LeNora Fulton of the Navajo Nation expressed it, "the highest calling is being a teacher; in the classroom, to your own family and your community." Another graduate of the program, Johnson Brown, expressed that his education through CIBTE had allowed him to continue the work of his ancestors by becoming a teacher.

On a personal level, the program brought about a new found self-respect for each individual. Graduate Elise Flescher, one of many who went on to earn a master's degree after graduating from CIBTE, said, "They brought something out of me that no one else has touched … I'm proud of me."

BIBLIOGRAPHY

Cabral, Elena. "Passing on Traditions, Preparing Children." *Ford Foundation Report*. Fall 1996. May 2006. in PCArchives.

CIBTE Graduation Video. 1994

CIBTE Video.

Marcus, Dora, Eulalia B. Cobb, and Robert E. Shoenberg. Fund for the Improvement of Postsecondary Education, U.S. Department of Education. "Lessons Learned from FIPSE Projects IV." May 2000.

Nelson, Annabelle. Personal Interview. November 2005.

Reyhner, Jon. "American Indian/Alaska Native Education: An Overview." *American Indian Education*. 2006. May 2006. <http://jan.ucc.nau.edu/~jar/AIE/Ind_Ed.html>

Young, Vicki. Personal Interview. April 2006.

The World Is Our Campus: Cultural and Regional Studies

◇◇◇◇◇◇

by Melissa Doran

"The Southwest is our classroom, the world is our campus." This is probably the truest motto of any college in the country. In fact, it is hard to come up with a place that a Prescott College class, student, alum, or faculty member hasn't been. From the top of Mt. Everest to deep within the urban jungles of Latin America, Prescott College has been there.

All of the College's greatest ideals come together in exciting studies in faraway places: self-direction, a passion for creating positive change, self-sufficiency, and a true synthesis and deep understanding of what is being learned. These adventures are the highest form of experiential education.

Although there are few places Prescott College students haven't been, there is one place that they return to time and time again. "Why this institutional love affair with Latin America, particularly Mexico?" asked faculty member Garth Hansen in 1990. Perhaps because of Prescott's close proximity to the U.S./Mexico border. Or perhaps, as he suggests, it is because as a country, "Our very survival is intimately tied to Latin America." Whatever the reason, Prescott College has a rich tradition and history of field courses and independent studies that have been carried out south of the U.S. border since the College was founded. A brief list of these courses includes internships managing a fish farm that supports an orphanage in Morelina, Mexico; hands-on learning experiences

Class Before Native Mural in Chiapas Mexico
photo by Travis Patterson

in tropical biology in the Monte Verde rain forest of Costa Rica; and Spanish intensive classes with students staying in homestays for one month period.

For several consecutive years in the early nineties, students participated in a course titled Mexican Volcanoes Mountaineering Expedition, in which they scaled the three highest mountains in Mexico: Citlatepetl, Popocatepetl, and Ixtaccihuatl, all volcanoes exceeding 17,000 feet in elevation. Students were responsible for planning and executing the entire expeditions. Adventure Education classes have paddled and sailed across the Sea of Cortez in sea kayaks. Since 1991 students have been doing environmental and cultural studies at the Kino Bay Center.

Recently, students have continued the Prescott College tradition of work along *la frontera* (Spanish for "the border") through independent studies, activism, and group courses. Recent independent work has included active participation in the humanitarian aid organization No Mas Muertes—No More Deaths, an organization that provides vital food, water, and medical aid for migrants crossing the cruel Sonoran Desert. Although medical transportation is provided only under life-threatening circumstances, Prescott College ADP student Shanti Sellz was arrested for her humanitarian actions in 2005. Sellz and her partner, Daniel Strauss, had evacuated three migrants in critical condition, in 105-degree heat, to the hospital. They were charged with aiding the transport of migrants, and at this time are still awaiting trial.

Many Prescott College students have participated in this organization, by volunteering for a week, or even an entire summer, patrolling the deserts with No Mas Muertes; and many more have participated in educational campaigns to make others more aware of the issues and deaths occurring in the desert.

Other students interested in human rights along the border became involved in observing with the ACLU (American Civil Liberties Union) during the Minuteman Project beginning in April of 2005. The community first became aware of the Minutemen, a vigilante organization pledging to protect the United States by staking out the border with guns and their own airplane, through participation in the annual Local-to-Global Teach-In at Arizona State University that year. Randall Amster's Human Rights Seminar students had been at the Teach-In and had been shocked at the news of this group's arrival in Arizona. The class took an immediate interest, working closely with ACLU organizer and founder of the legal observer program Ray Ybarra. The group spent every weekend of April side by side with the Minutemen, watching and recording their actions. Through their role as legal observers, this group was able to aid in the protection of the human rights of all, as well as learn through first hand experience in the scorching desert, what it would be like to have to cross it. It gave the students a new understanding, academic and emotional, of the migrant experience. When the Minutemen returned in April of 2006, a group of Prescott College students once again followed close behind, this time as knowledgeable veterans of the patrols.

Independent projects include investigations of the "femicides" in Ciudad Juarez, studies of the World Social Forum in Venezuela, and teaching free English classes at the College for the migrant population of Prescott.

Another place that Prescott College students have been called to recently has been Africa. Students have done several independent studies throughout Africa over the years, including Elana Greene's study of orphan children in Kenya. Greene worked with Urgent Africa, an organization serving orphans of the AIDS epidemic, interviewing 720 children. The information gathered was used to assess how Urgent Africa could best help. The urgency of the situation in Africa soon called several more students.

In 2004 five Prescott College women designed an independent study in South Africa. Andrea Flanagan, Connie Hockaday, Lynsey Markey, Kaitlin Noss, and Ann Radeloff worked with the Topsy Foundation, a South African nonprofit in the Mpumalanga province that provides a holistic approach to caring for children affected by HIV/AIDS. The group created an art room and filled it with paint, art supplies, and paper, and left a replenishing fund. They also wrote a thirty-page volunteer manual. "For me, my main focus was making our art room and volunteer manual sustainable additions to Topsy so that the kids did not have to experience another great loss, so that what we brought to them would be something that kept on giving," explained Hockaday. Although the students were able to give something valuable to the community they worked in, the lessons they gained were even more valuable. "At Topsy I learned that creating true social change is not about solving the whole problem, but rather making room for change for generations to come," said Noss.

The next year the Kenya Project began. A group of students met for nine months during the school year in preparation for a summer block course titled Indigenous People in a Global Context, a course studying the indigenous Maasai people of Kenya and the effects tourism has had upon them. The group studied ethics and eco-tourism and conducted interviews and research, eventually writing a report on their studies. The instructors were Prescott College faculty member Mary Poole and Meitamei Olol Depash, Director of the Maasai Environmental Resource Coalition, an organization the class worked closely with. The two teaching assistants for the class were Kaitlin Noss and Ann Radeloff, who had previously worked with the Topsy Foundation. The Kenya Project was so successful in its first journey to East Africa that a new group began meeting to plan a full eighteen credit summer course to be offered in 2006. The project is an ongoing collaboration between Prescott College and the Maasai people.

The mountains of the world are another place that Prescott College students and faculty can always be found. The strong Adventure Education program has inspired many expeditions around the world, and dozens of Alpine Mountaineering classes have experienced the thrill of being on top of the world. After one such course in the Wind River Range in Wyoming, student Hannah King remarked, "I then realized coming to this incredible place as part of Prescott College's Alpine Mountaineering course not only would give me the opportunity to climb these peaks, but also give me the chance to obtain the foundational skills and knowledge required to climb *all* mountains." She added "The discipline needed to get an alpine start and push yourself physically day in and day out; the judgment and leadership required to make it safely up and down a peak, whether you are cold, dehydrated, hungry or tired; and the confidence you need to deal with exposed unknown terrain are all things that can be applied to so many aspects of our lives."

Prescott College Alpine Mountaineering classes have been all over the world, from the mountains in Ecuador to the ranges of Wyoming. Perhaps the most ambitious of these expeditions was Everest Challenge '98. The Challenge began on May 10, 1998, with three faculty members and six students. Though not all climbed to the top of Everest (Tom Whittaker, Prescott College faculty, did, however, and became the first disabled person to climb Mt. Everest), students participated in service learning activities in other ways. Students Ali Orton and Nathan Barsetti implemented the Access for All Trek, a trek from Katmandu to Everest Base Camp with six disabled people. "The Trek seeks to emphasize the integration of people with disabilities and create a legacy for disabled children everywhere." Students Josh Lewis, Kimberly Schembari, Titiana Shostak-Kinker, and Trevor Wilson joined Prescott College alum Leah Lamb ('97) in an environmental service project removing leftover oxygen bottles littering Everest Base Camp. They lived in Nemche Bazaar, where they worked with KEEP (Katmandu Environmental Education Project) and the Sagarmatha Pollution Control Committee.

Other environmental studies field courses have included a five-week expedition on skis to Scandinavia and Lapland. During this journey in 1991, instructor Mike Goff led the students through the largest wilderness tract in Europe, traversing four major arctic peaks. The students studied the physical geography of Lapland and native studies in the arctic tundra and woodland transitions. Students also explored the English Lake District and the Yorkshire Dells with Goff in a block course a year later. Students have also been on summer expeditions in the Basque region of northern Spain, including a caving expedition in a major European cave system, and a climbing and expeditionary backpacking expedition in the alpine and subalpine environs of the Western Pyrenees and the Cantabrian mountains in 1997. Doug Hulmes has also offered a course titled Explorations in Norway and Scotland: Nature and Culture several times.

*Outdoor Leadership Class
photo by Travis Patterson*

Students have spent entire summer quarters studying contemporary issues and natural history and gaining a sense of place in Alaska, or studying the status of grizzly bears, the reintroduction of the grey wolf, timber issues, and newly proposed gold mines in the Northern Rockies (based in Western Montana). Summers have also been spent studying Contemporary Society, Art, and Politics in Eastern Europe, a class traveling through the Czech Republic, Slovakia, Hungary, and Romania with extended stays in Prague and Bucharest. Steve Munsell also offered a summer course in 2001 titled an Ecotourism Study Tour to Southeast Asia.

Slightly closer to home, students have experienced incredible journeys such as retracing the path of John Wesley Powell's 1869 expedition. Eleven students and three instructors (including course designer Julie Munro) spent three months, starting on October 5, 1992, rafting the 750-mile route along the Colorado River. The class was the first sanctioned undergraduate research trip to be granted a permit through the Glen Canyon Environmental Study (GCES). The class collected data for the GCES as well as studyng research methods and geology, exploring dwellings and rock art of Paleo-Americans, and learning whitewater boating skills and expedition planning. This trip was repeated by a new group of students and faculty in the fall of 2005.

There are far too many places, too many journeys, and too many adventures that have been experienced by Prescott College students and faculty over the years to list them all. Every student travels along a unique path to graduation from Prescott College; some of them stop for a while in Romania to study art and politics, others kayak 3,000 miles from the tip of Baja to Alaska (Missy Miller's senior project). Some go to Yellowstone in efforts to save buffalo from being massacred outside the park gates, and others study religion and culture in Thailand. Wherever you travel, no matter how far off the beaten path (in fact, the farther off the more likely), you'll find us there.

Master of Arts Program (MAP) at Prescott College

◇◇◇◇◇◇◇

In 1990 president Doug North assembled a committee to design a Master of Arts program for the College. Its purpose was to craft a degree-granting program that would allow creative and independent graduate students to develop their own courses of study based on their particular needs and interests. After several months of planning, the committee drafted a proposal for a limited-residence graduate program. The plan was presented to various faculty and administrative bodies in the College for approval and subsequently given the go-ahead by the College's accreditation agency. Dr. Ellen Cole was appointed as the first Master of Arts Program Director, and in January of 1992 twelve students were matriculated into the charter class. The Master of Arts Program eventually merged with the Adult Degree Program in 1997. In 1999, the Tucson Center incorporated the Master's Program and with an expanded faculty began to serve graduate students in Southern Arizona.

MAP presently offers five competence areas. These are in counseling and psychology, environmental studies, adventure education, education, and humanities. Within these five areas students can refine their studies further and have a concentration that is specific to their goals.

Master of Arts students progress through three stages: theory, practicum, and thesis. The majority of students take three semesters (a year and a half) to complete their graduate work. Each student has a graduate advisor to assist and to guide in planning, carrying out, and evaluating all stages of graduate study. The advisor's most important role is to provide support and understanding, while challenging the student to deepen the complexity of her or his thinking.

As students progress through the program, they are required to attend two weekend colloquia every semester as part of the residential component of the program. Typically (2005-06) over one hundred new and continuing students from around the country arrive in Prescott each enrollment period.

Adding to the number of students in attendance are their graduate advisors, faculty, and alumni. During this extended weekend, all MAP enrollees participate in about fifty presentations and workshops. These colloquia provide the opportunity to present ideas and works in progress to peers and faculty and to benefit from the support and challenge of an ongoing community of learners.

Weekends also include conferences with a graduate advisor, individual study planning, consultations with the Library research staff, interdisciplinary workshops, and more.

"One thing that is unique about MAP is how it ties into Prescott College's mission," explains Joan Clingan, the current director of the Master of Arts Program. "This program is committed to social and environmental justice, and every MAP student [is expected] to develop social and ecological literacy. When the program began, the multicultural and environmental requirements could be simply met by reading books or writing a short paper. But now, awareness of social and ecological issues [must] be present in everything they write—every paper. [If not included] they get challenged by their faculty because this is an essential part of their education. It's not a check-off anymore. They come out of the program with a consciousness that is focused on considering how the work they are doing is having an effect on the planet and on society."[58]

Forty percent of MAP graduates are counselors and practicing therapists. Many have become teachers, some even starting new schools. A number have become involved with museums and nonprofit organizations. Several are successful artists. Still others are recognized leaders in environmental work and in social justice efforts.

Joan Clingan shared this account: "One of my favorite stories is about a guy named Kelly who graduated with his degree in Environmental Studies. He applied for a position at the Forest Service, and was up against two other finalists, one with a degree from Harvard and another from a university in the UC system. When our MAP graduate was selected for the job, the man who hired him volunteered, 'Well it is an environmental position; I want someone from Prescott College.'"[58]

At the time of this interview there were about 300 MAP enrollees from throughout the United States, Canada, and even Latin America. And with the advent of the internet, the process of monitoring and mentoring has facilitated the involvement of graduate advisors from beyond Prescott to any place around the globe.

Sustainability Education

◇◇◇◇◇◇◇

In 2000 the College began to contemplate offering a program at the doctoral level, a PhD program that would be similar in process to the MA Program. With the support of the Board and new president, a committee composed of faculty, administrators, consultants, and potential candidates began to meet and plan. Several questions relating to philosophy and resources were addressed: Could the College provide the faculty and learning resources? How would the project integrate into a small organization? Would it divert already fully engaged MAP and RDP faculty from their teaching and curriculum work? Most importantly, what unique capacities did Prescott College have that would justify offering a doctorate? It was also absolutely essential that the program be accepted by North Central Association of Colleges, Prescott College's accrediting agency, and accredited by its Higher Learning Comission.

After nearly three years of deliberation, repeated proposals, and drafts, it was agreed that Prescott did have a unique niche to fill by building upon its leadership in the fields of education and environmental studies. The focus of the doctoral program would be to help teachers, educators, and community activists develop the knowledge and skills necessary to teach the concepts and applications of sustainability—encompassing not just emerging environmental issues and potential solutions, but also the enhancement of several aspects of society and individual life.

Graduates of the program would be professionally prepared to lead schools or government and nongovernment service organizations. The educational focus would embrace both the practice of educating and being educated, and also the study of education as a continuous process of researching, documenting, and implementing positive changes where needed in traditional models and methods. It was believed that the program would also serve to strengthen academic quality at other levels of the College by enhancing existing laboratory and library resources for students to do scholarly research, network, and communicate with each other.

The expectation was that most of the charter group would be people already working in related fields. It was decided that the program would begin as a pilot with about a dozen highly qualified and motivated students, and that it would be a semi-residential program. Students would be asked to spend at least thirty-two days on campus, divided into seven periods of residency.

In 2005 Prescott College was granted full accreditation to offer a PhD degree in Sustainable Education, and began recruiting students.

PART III

Distinctive Curricular Programs and Projects

◇◇◇◇◇◇◇

This section offers a selection of the curricular programs and learning projects that have given Prescott College its unique spirit. The pieces were written by faculty and students with first-hand knowledge of the programs or projects and have not been abridged. There is no attempt here to encompass the whole curriculum, which offers a wide spectrum of liberal arts learning opportunities.

Kenneth Cook describes the College's creative and documentary writing program. This is a sample of the exciting Arts and Letters curriculum, which also offers experiential studies in photography, two- and three-dimensional art, dance, and drama. Both Environmental Studies and outdoor Adventure Education have been major programs at the College from its beginnings, and Douglas Hulmes and David Lovejoy have been key players in development of these two nationally acclaimed programs. Alumna Dr. Diana Papoulias' account of her undergraduate work in Mexico illustrates both the experiential learning and service for which the school is noted. Student Kaitlin Noss' description of students working in Kenya reflects Prescott College's commitment to cultural understanding and social change. Closer to home is the Centaur project, using horses for counselor training, described by student Melissa Carey.

By Permission of Prescott College Photo Archives

History of Environmental Studies at Prescott College

◇◇◇◇◇◇◇

by Douglas Hulmes,
Professor of Environmental Studies and Education

INTRODUCTION

Environmental Studies has played a significant role in the mission and curriculum of Prescott College since its inception. When asked to write the history of Environmental Studies at Prescott College, I was both honored and overwhelmed by the task. The program has impacted and been influenced by so many faculty and students who have been significant members of the Prescott College community. Lives have been defined by their experiences while working for or attending the College, and in no small way have faculty, students and graduates made significant contributions throughout the world. It would be a worthy and daunting task to follow the ripples that began with ideas, idealism, and energy generated from classes, independent studies, senior projects, and post-graduate careers. I am honored to have been a student, and part of this community and the Environmental Studies program, for more that thirty years of my life.

In researching the information for this chapter, I have come across names of faculty and students who were my friends and also challenged me to my

Professor Douglas Hulmes

philosophical roots. We did not always agree, but everyone was passionate and cared deeply about the state of the world and the environments that support the incredible diversity and wonder that defines our existence.

The Environmental Studies program at Prescott College has been and continues to be at the cutting edge of several academic disciplines that fall beneath the shade of its branches. We have and are producing significant contributions that make a positive difference in the world and in human relationships and responsibilities to the environment.

Biology in the Field, 1973

1966-67

Prescott College opened its doors to students in the fall of 1966. Its provisional curriculum resembled that of other progressive liberal arts colleges that year, while the whole College community was designing a more innovative format. It was already well established that the College would be a center for environmental learning and change. This had been one of the strong themes in the Symposium of 1963.

The next academic year, 1967-68, the Prescott College Catalog announced that the curriculum would be organized around four Teaching and Research Centers—Anthropological Studies, Language and Literary Studies, Center for Systems, and Center for the Studies in Civilization. All four Centers were related, staffed on an interdisciplinary basis and supported the goals of a liberal education. Of the four Centers, Anthropology specifically included the environment as a focus.

> The one overriding theme of the Center is Man—man in his relationship to himself, his society, his culture, and his environment. (Prescott College—PC—Catalog 1967, p. 34)

As I write, forty years later, it is interesting to note the patriarchal and anthropocentric tone of that statement, which reflects the cultural and linguistic bias still prevalent in the late 1960s. The Catalog goes on to state,

... By emphasizing the human element, anthropology relates to geography. Geography, botany, zoology, and ecology are the disciplines with which anthropology has concern as studies are made of the interaction of both prehistoric and contemporary people together with the earth on which they live and their ecological adjustments in the utilization of its natural resources. (Ibid., p. 35)

By 1969, Professors Douglas (biology), Johnson (biology), Hargrave (ethnobiology), and Taylor (geology), had joined the faculty. They would go on to be joined by other faculty in 1970 to form the Environmental Science faculty of the early 1970s. Lyndon Hargrave was considered one of the founders of the field of ethnobiology. The mission described in the 1970 Catalog stated that by ...

directing attention to an understanding of human physical and social development throughout the world's time and space, anthropology is a science unifying social and humanistic studies with the natural sciences of biology and geology. Twentieth-century education tends to fracture rather than unify human knowledge. It can produce multitudes of single-faceted experts, but few men of truly broad understanding. Prescott College offers a new means of combating this 'academic schizophrenia'. (Ibid., p. 34)

Specific courses are given as examples of the spectrum of classes offered during the late 1960s: Comparative World Cultures; Introduction to Biology; Ecology and Botany; Bioecology; Plant Taxonomy; Plant Morphology; Plant Physiology; Microbiology; The Earth: Materials and External Processes; The Earth: Structure and Internal Processes; The Earth: Its History.

The 1970s

The early 1970s brought the Center for the Person or, as it was called, the Fifth Center, to the College curriculum, which recognized that

education transcends the academic, that physical, mental, and spiritual growth are mutually interdependent and that man is an entity, not a compartmentalized being. (PC Catalog 1970, p. 9)

A significant change occurred when students were permitted to study in any Center that they chose, concentrating in areas that best suited their individual needs. It was expected that each student would gain at least a conceptual acquaintance with each of the five Centers. It came to be a requirement that each student take two classes from each of the five Centers to demonstrate breadth and integration.

The Center for Anthropological Studies was renamed the Center for Man and the Environment which was

> devoted to the study of man as an organism in cultures, in societies, and having a relation to nature and the universe. (Ibid.)

The new or reassigned faculty for this Center included Dobyns (anthropology), Euler (anthropology), Gumerman (anthropology), Swedlund (anthropology) and Brew (geology). Continuing were Hargrave, Johnson, Taylor, Douglas, and others. Paul Long was brought in as an instructor in scientific illustration.

The Center emphasized teaching through research, using the field as the laboratory and focusing on the Southwest and Northern Mexico. Under the theme Man's Relation to His Natural Environment, courses included: The Evolution of Natural Environments; Comparative World Cultures; Introduction to Ecology and Botany; Bioecology, Population Ecology; Plant Taxonomy; Plant Anatomy and Morphology; Plant Physiology and Microbiology; The Earth: Materials and External Processes; The Earth: Structure and Internal Processes; Mineralogy; Economic Geology; Structural Geology; Tectonics; Invertebrate Paleontology; Regional Geology of North America; Sedimentology, Igneous and Metamorphic Petrology; and Geochemistry.

There was a dramatic increase in biological, ecological, and geological sciences during the early 1970s. At the same time there were few classes that were of an interdisciplinary nature, and the emphasis was clearly in environmental sciences, and not environmental studies.

1972-73

Five Teaching and Research Centers—Arts and Literature, Contemporary Civilization, Man and the Environment, Center for the Person, and Systems and Sciences—made up the programmatic areas of the College. The Center for Man and the Environment aimed at interrelating the natural and social sciences, using an environmental approach as its focal point. While the Center provided areas of service to all liberal studies and science students, it had three major program areas: Anthropology, Biology, and Geology, with Cultural Economics as an important adjunct. This training through scientific method was rigorous and sequential, and its philosophy was considered valuable to students other than those majoring in the Center. The Center's main focus was in environmental science. In addition to professors already mentioned, the 1972 faculty included Belshaw (economics), Rea (biology) and Jane Taylor (biology)—no relation to Vernon Taylor. The faculty of this Center emphasized teaching through research.

> The field is the laboratory and provides, through the great natural en-
> dowment of the Southwest and Northern Mexico, an unparalleled op-
> portunity for students to obtain primary understanding of the basic
> aspects of anthropology, biology, ecology, and geology. (PC Catalog
> 1972-73, p. 32)

In the early 1970s the College boasted the largest ornithological col-
lection in the Southwest. The Lyndon L. Hargrave Collection contained over 300,000 bird bones, feathers, and study skins. The gathering of birds on field courses and preparation of study skins was a common activity in certain courses. The "shotgun" ornithologist was a common sight. Species collection and preservation also became a major focus in invertebrate marine courses held in Kino Bay, Mexico. The geology lab contained a significant rock, mineralogy, and paleontology collection. Most of these collections were the pro-
fessors' private collections, and after the College's bankruptcy in December 1974, the collections were either taken back by the professors, or donated to Yavapai College or the Museum of Northern Arizona. The College maintained a close association with the Museum of Northern Arizona and Grand Canyon National Park, where Vernon Taylor and Robert Euler conducted numerous research projects like the Stanton Cave Archeology project.

I arrived at Prescott College as a seventeen-year-old freshman, in Sep-
tember of 1970. Admissions to Prescott College were quite selective during the early 1970s since Vietnam was forcing young men to secure student de-
ferments in order to avoid the draft. One student was accepted for every nine applicants. My draft number was 16, so attending college was a critical deci-
sion. I was young in age, but academically well prepared and eager to begin my college studies in the environmental sciences, after having been selected to attend a National Science Foundation field ecology program at Foresta Institute near Carson City, Nevada. The selection for this forest program was also competitive, and thirty-five students were selected from across the country. The five-week program introduced me to the field of ecology, and at the conclusion I knew that I wanted to attend college and study ecology. I also was concerned about attending a college that would respect my ethical values regarding the collection and dissection of animals for science, so when I was ironically confronted with a required dissection of a live mouse during my first semester, I seriously questioned my choice of attending the College. My essay, The Story of Mouse, was written as a result of this expe-

rience, which had a profound impact on the direction my education would take.

1973-74, A YEAR OF INNOVATION AND CHANGE

Prescott College adopted a flexible calendar for this year. The academic year was broken into five study periods called blocks. A First Year curriculum was also introduced which included Orientation, September block, October block, etc. Block I was an Education Block where students examined, both intellectually and personally, the philosophy and techniques of educational systems before beginning their own college careers. Blocks II, III, and IV included off-campus activities. In starting the First Year, students were encouraged to explore their connections with professionals working in their fields of study. Block II was titled Man and Nature, and introduced the physical and natural sciences. Rather than being presented as separate units, the material was integrated on humanity, our interaction with our environment, and the dynamics and consequences of this interaction.

General topics included such areas as Man's Encounter with the Environment; Man's Relationship with Other Organisms; Men as Populations; Men in Ecosystems; Ethos, Ecos, and Ethics; Perspectives on Human Evolution; the Scientific Method; Concepts of Health and Ways of Healing; Desert Ecology; the Natural History of the Prescott Region; Ecology and Ethical Choices: Darwin Revisited. (PC Catalog 1973-74, p. 49)

Other faculty offered interdisciplinary classes related to environmental studies. Vern Taylor coordinated a theme area called Environmental Studies, and the term *Environmental Education* first appeared as an interdisciplinary and multidisciplinary approach that covered three broad areas: 1) the total environment and its problems; 2) ecological principles, relationships, and concepts; and 3) skills and concepts for most of the traditional disciplines, from chemistry, physics, and biology to sociology, economics, psychology, and the arts.

Environmental Studies dealt with man's total environment, including its cultural, social, economic, political, chemical and biological aspects. The program demanded that the tools of the various disciplines be used in a highly integrative manner.

Block classes for advanced students included:
Impact of Man on Environment; Geology and Environmental Problems; Desert Ecology; Natural History of the Prescott Region; Organic Gardening and Horticulture; IPSA Council on Environmental Quality; Workshop

in Applied Ecology; the Invertebrates: Past and Present; Ecosystems and Energy Flow; Development and Utilization of Energy; Seminar in Ethnobiology; Natural History of Vertebrates; Environmental Law; Environmental Physiology; Marine Coastal Ecology; Salt River Project; Grand Canyon, an Environmental Study; Quantitative Field Ecology; Marine Conservation, Process, Evaluation and Graduation. (Ibid.)

Prescott College adopted a portfolio system. As a product, the Educational Portfolio was a comprehensive documentation of the student's educational career, including planning, progress, and a thorough portrayal of competence, knowledge, skills, and attitudes in areas of work and study.

Graduation was *competency based*, with a focus on self-direction rather than the accumulation of credits, courses, or years of study. I was the first student to demonstrate competence for graduation in December 1973, and graduated May 1974, after submitting the first ecological survey of Alcatraz Island in Kino Bay. I was offered a Program Director's position for a residential environmental education program, and also was accepted into graduate school to pursue an MS degree in Environmental Education.

1975-77

Bankruptcy of the College in December of 1974 brought a dramatic shift to Prescott College and the focus on Environmental Sciences due to the loss of a campus and lab facilities, faculty, and accreditation, and the reduction from about 450 to 46 students. Over these three years, the number of faculty fell to about a dozen full-time professors with additional part-time and adjunct teachers. Without a campus, the College ran courses out of the basement of the Hassayampa Inn, and students, out of necessity—especially in Environmental Studies—had to rely on the use of private vehicles for field trips.

With the purchase of 220 Grove Avenue in 1976, the College was able to revise its academic program, now based in town. Four disparate and dilapidated vehicles—Bus 31, Ol' Blue (a Dodge pickup truck donated by Jim Stuckey), "the Roach" (donated by Bill Stillwell), and the red Ford window van (provided by Sam Henrie)—provided the College with a limited and incredibly unreliable transportation system that in and of itself provided valuable lessons in patience, teamwork, creativity, and in some cases survival. Epic stories of heroism, ingenuity, self-reliance, stupidity, the genius of Mexican mechanics, and adventure typified field courses over the next decade and would provide insight and exciting drama to the yet unwritten history of what actually occurred during this epoch.

A dramatic downsizing and rethinking of the entire curriculum occurred in the years following the bankruptcy. This change is reflected in the 1975-76 Catalog, which also reflects the corporation name change to *Prescott Center for Alternative Education* (PCAE).

> The faculty of The Prescott Center, although possessing strong academic credentials, tends to defy exact classification. We have no one who would define himself as just a psychologist, or just a biologist. The faculty has a diversity of interests and expertise which in a general way cluster around the study of environments. This should not be seen primarily as an ecological concern. What it does mean is that most questions and therefore most of our studies are formulated with an eye to their connection with how man functions within his environments. Faculty and students concern themselves with self-awareness and expression, community and society, environmental issues and wilderness experience, in an attempt to better understand man's relationship to his world. In this (team teaching approach) faculty are involved with three program areas: Environment and Wilderness, Community and Society, and Self-Awareness and Expression. The Environment and Wilderness program included faculty trained in the disciplines of geology, hydrology, biology, ecology, outdoor action, outdoor leadership, natural history, botany and earth ethics. What we have is a group of people who understand and care about nature and man's relationship to it. (PC Catalog 1975-76, p. 13)

By 1976-77, the College, now referred to as the Center, had reestablished itself at 220 Grove Avenue in downtown Prescott. The Center's programs employed two curriculum models: the project/problem model, and the thematic model.

> The Project/Problem Model moves the student systematically from basic, introductory work to field research, employing a sequence of classes, seminars and research problems. Every sequence is culminated by an intensive field project. The Thematic Model allows the student to build an individualized program from among a selection of courses and field experiences which focus around a unifying theme. Each of these experiences is led by a team of faculty members with differing academic training. Each student's program will reflect his interest and academic progress in several interrelated areas. (PC Catalog 1976-77, p. 12)

1978-79

The Center had now grown to four major programs: Environmental Studies, Human Development, Interpretation of Culture, and Outdoor Action. The Environmental Studies continued to be based on the project/problem model, and was designed to help students examine the technological, philosophical, and ethical implications of humanity's use of the resources nature affords us. Natural Sciences and humanities were combined in a series of preparatory classes, workshops, and seminars, and in field projects that used the environments and ecosystems of the Southwest deserts, coastal regions, and mountains.

The Environmental Studies faculty during these "lean years" included Ken Asplund (ecology), Margaret Asplund Fusari (environmental physiology), Kenneth Kingsley (ecology), Margaret Kursius (desert natural history), Vernon Taylor (geology), and Carl Tomoff (ecology). After receiving my MS degree in Environmental Education from George Williams College, I returned in January of 1978 to teach at Prescott College, and to develop a focus area in environmental education.

There were about sixty students and twelve full-time faculty when I returned. Joanne Maas, Nina Brew, and I helped write a successful grant proposal to the Bureau of Reclamation that funded a Youth Conservation Corps program. It also brought significant revenue to the College to assist in administering the program, as we hired several staff and students. Kevin Kapp was hired as the director of the program. Kevin is the present Superintendent of Prescott Unified School District [in 2006]. The eight-week summer program enlisted local high school students to work on public lands. Prescott College alum Mark Grinter was hired as the work projects coordinator. I was employed in implementation of the Environmental Education portion of the program. Conservation projects were identified on federal, state, and municipal lands. Mark and I had done our senior project together on Alcatraz Island near Kino Bay, Mexico, in January of 1973, were good friends, and worked well together, envisioning integrated work projects and environmental education. The first year of the program was run out of the newly acquired 220 Grove building. After a very successful season, the College was given additional funding to design a residential program that was based at Henry Dahlberg's Mingus Springs Camp, on Mingus Mountain [in the range thirty miles east of Prescott].

The Prescott College Youth Conservation Corps (YCC) program received outstanding evaluations from participants and agencies served. In the spring of 1981, I turned down a position as Interpretive Naturalist for Special Populations at Rocky Mt. National Park, because several members of the Prescott College YCC program had been asked to help train YCC staff throughout the Western Region due to the exemplary integration of environmental education with the conservation projects. One month before training was to begin, U.S. President Ronald Reagan cut the funding for YCC. I spent the summer of 1981 washing windows, but in the fall was hired as a full-time faculty member in Environmental Studies.

1979–80

Returning to the historical narrative, with the leadership of President James Stuckey the College continued its process of regrouping at the 220 Grove Avenue campus.

> It's not the building, though, not the campus that brings us together. The campus is headquarters—our primary meeting and communication place. The real sense of community comes from what we do: our academic, wilderness, social, and day-to-day living activities. We believe in holistic and integrated education. (PC Catalog 1979-80, p. 2)

The Prescott Center College emphasized multidisciplinary studies. Areas of study were not compartmentalized into departments. Professors and students of diverse backgrounds were encouraged to study a community such as Kino Bay, Mexico, for cultural and ecological perspectives.

By 1980 students in Environmental Studies were offered four main com-

Birding In Winter Block
photo by Travis Patterson

petency areas to help structure their programs. These included Natural History with a focus on geology, biology, ecology, and behavior. Environmental Education became a recognized competence and included the theory and methodology for teaching school children, special populations, and adaptive wilderness programs, which utilize knowledge of natural sciences. Field Ecology included theory and techniques of field research and interpretation, math and physical sciences, along with an independent research project. Environmental Studies included a basic foundation in physical and life sciences, experience in the practical application of the ideas of resource management, and completion of an internship or research paper.

> The Environmental Studies Program provides students with experience necessary for understanding the interactions between themselves and their environments. We offer opportunities for students to develop individualized programs leading to careers in environmental studies and education. Students concentrating in other programs may take our courses to become more aware of environmental problems or to gain a basic understanding of this region's natural history. We have an atmosphere conducive to sharing ideas and values. We emphasize the acquisition of knowledge, skills and experience leading to an appreciation and understanding of the natural environment. Since we are also concerned with environmental planning, management, and research, we use scientific methods in studying ecological relationships. ... (Ibid., pp. 15-16)

Courses provided in the Environmental Studies Program included:
Horticulture and Gardening; the Californian Desert and the Desert Tortoise; Concepts of Nature: Landscapes and Mindscapes; Scandinavia: an Ecological and Cultural Expedition; Environmental Education; Environmental Physiology; Plant Natural History; the Southwest: People, Life and Land; Anatomy and Taxonomy; a Cultural and Ecological Survey of Kino Bay, Mexico; Biology of Reptiles and Amphibians; Earth Ethics: Adaptation, the Ecology of History; Environmental Education for Specially Handicapped; Geology; Plant Taxonomy; Ecology of Southwestern Lizards; Prehistory of the Southwest; Field Methods in Archeology. (Ibid.)

Some of the exemplary accomplishments of recent graduates cited in the PC Catalog included research on species of fish in the Antarctic with Scripps Oceanographic Institute (Wayne Van Voorhies); a resident naturalist position at a nearby guest ranch (Dick Hannah); serving as a plant ecologist for the Arizona Natural Heritage Program (Frank Reikenbach); the position of professional wildlife illustrator for the Grand Canyon and Yellowstone

National Parks (Scott Hecker); and the design and construction of a fish farm for an orphanage in southern Mexico (Diana Papoulius—See Diana's account in this book). (Ibid.)

Environmental Perspectives and Whitewater Rafting and Wilderness Explorations of Landscape Studies, and WELS were courses that I developed with David Lovejoy, thus bridging Outdoor Action and Environmental Studies. Steve Munsell, who was working at Prescott College as an intern from Evergreen U. in Washington State, where he was completing his BA degree, assisted in the development and instruction of these classes. They represented some of the longest continually taught interdisciplinary classes of the College's curriculum.

1984–85

By 1984-85 the College's curriculum was organized into five areas: Human Development, Environmental Studies, Outdoor Education and Leadership, Cultural and Regional Studies, and the Humanities.

> These programs are not isolated compartments but frequently support each other. Members of the faculty may and do move freely from one program to another, as do students. Students generally graduate with competencies in one of four areas: Natural History, Environmental Education, Field Ecology, and Environmental Studies. (PC Catalog 1984-85, pp. 7, 15, and 17)

1988-89

The 1988-89 curriculum added Conservation Biology to the program's defined competencies. This concentration integrated the sciences of field ecology with social and economic studies, supporting careers and graduate studies in wilderness and wildlife biology or ecology. The College welcomed two new professors—Thomas Fleischner, to lead the studies in Conservation Biology, and Dr. Mark Riegner to expand our course offerings in Environmental Studies. Riegner's doctoral work was in Ecology and Evolution. Mark and Tom joined Vern Taylor, Dana Oswald, Carl Tomoff, and me as faculty in Environmental Studies. Mike Goff joined the Environmental Studies faculty and provided a significant bridge to Outdoor Action by bringing courses in physical and cultural geography into the Environmental Studies curriculum.

1989-90

By 1989-90 the curriculum was again slightly reshuffled, resulting in five multidisciplinary programs: Environmental Studies, Human Development, Outdoor Action, Southwest Studies, and Humanities.

Environmental Studies emphasized the integration of the field experience into the academic process. The aim of the program was to encourage broad and thorough exposure to and appreciation for the nature of diverse and complex ecosystems, and to provide integrated student graduation tracks that were foundations for unique professions. Beginning students were urged to gain a broad background in the natural sciences so they could form educated opinions and make rational decisions about environmental controversies. Foundation studies included biology, geology, natural history, and weather and climate. More advanced students studied in such areas as field ecology, biology of birds, consequences of technology, and environmental education. Many courses addressed philosophical concerns, such as earth ethics, concepts of nature, and environmental issues and politics. Advanced students were expected to complement their course work with independent studies, internships, and other applied learning experiences.

Environmental Studies students have described the strengths of the program as "field work frequently integrated with class work," dynamic and active class discussion, lots of teacher-to-student interaction, and depth and diversity within a single course. Students generally graduate with competencies in one of four areas. Environmental Education and Interpretation utilizes a strong background in the natural sciences with interdisciplinary course and field experience to prepare students for teaching to a variety of populations, ranging from children to adults, in diverse settings from classroom to wilderness. Natural History focuses on theory and techniques of ecological field research and interpretation, the physical sciences, and includes an independent research project. Human Ecology comprises a basic foundation in the life sciences, diverse courses in environmental philosophy and the human condition, and an awareness of the consequences and processes of resource management. Environmental Conservation integrates the science of field ecology with social and economic studies, supporting careers or graduate studies in wilderness management, conservation biology, and environmental policy. (PC Catalog 1989-90, p.16)

The Catalog included examples of accomplishments of our graduates that reflected the diversity of studies conducted through Prescott College during the past few years. Knowing the names of most of these individuals, I have included them along with the descriptions of their work. Trish Morris was employed as the Director of Education at the Museum of Natural History of New Mexico. Gary Nabhan won the John Burroughs award for Naturalist Writing. Deborah Von Gotten and Veronica Behn were employed by an environmental consulting firm doing research on the southern bald eagle. Several graduates had become teachers, such as Moira Patterson, who taught fifth grade at Miller Valley Elementary School, in Prescott and worked closely with me in the implementation of the Prescott Creeks and Watershed Environmental Education Program, which was already in its tenth year. Maggie Webster became a marine biology teacher on a high school sailing schooner that worked with dyslexic students, and Bob Ratcliff by the early 1990s was quickly climbing the ladder of the Bureau of Land Management in recreation planning, and by 2007 was the Deputy Manager of the National Recreation Program in Washington D.C.

1991

A major event for the College and the curriculum especially for—but not limited to—Environmental Studies was the purchase of the Kino Bay Research Station, on the Sonoran Coast of the Gulf of California (Mexico), now called the Kino Bay Center for Cultural and Ecological Studies. Thanks to Joel Hiller, Alan Weisman, Garth Hansen, Tad Pfister, and many others, the College's first field station became a reality. [Editor's note: Major thanks must also go to the author of this history, Professor Douglas Hulmes, and his family, who were instrumental in securing and developing the Kino Center. In a separate piece included in this book, *History of Prescott College in Kino Bay*, he has described this Center and its educational importance.]

1995-96

The 1995-96 Prescott College Catalog description for Environmental Studies remained the same for several years. Two new competences, Ecological Design and Field Ecology, were added to the more defined competences within the umbrella of Environmental Studies, or "Turkey Tail," as the College curriculum had come to be referred to.

A new description of Kino Bay appeared in the 1995-96 PC Catalog:

One of the greatest geographic features of the Southwestern region is the desert sea, the Gulf of California. Bordered by the famed peninsula of Baja California and the Mexican mainland, the Gulf is one of the last remote and relatively unexplored seas in the world. Located near the small coastal fishing village of Bahia Kino, Sonora, Mexico, our Center for Cultural and Ecological Studies (CECE, the acronym in Spanish) is a field station used by a variety of Prescott College classes such as Coastal and Cultural Ecology of Kino Bay, A Sense of Place (creative writing class taught by Sheila Sanderson), and Field Methods for Intertidal Ecology and Marine Conservation. [CECE] also serves as a launching point for sea kayaking courses as well as a meeting place for various Mexican and American researchers visiting the area. (PC Catalog 1995-96, p. 31).

Tad Pfister, a long-time adjunct teacher, was appointed to be the station manager/field coordinator for the Kino Bay facility. Tad's knowledge of the local areas, the plants, animals, and people of the region was an incredibly valuable addition to the curriculum. He literally grew up with the Seri Indians, the Mexican fishermen, as well as the desert and sea. This experience provides tremendous support to the education, research, and the bridging of cultures.

Several new faculty had joined the Environmental Studies faculty during the 1990s, including Walt Anderson (wildlife biology and resource ecology), Ed Boyer (ecology and evolutionary biology), Tim Crews (agroecology and ecosystem biology), Lisa Floyd-Hannah (biology, botanical sciences, and organismic biology), David Hannah (applied scientific research), Paul Sneed (anthropology, environmental planning, and resource management) and Hans Drake, who taught ecological and environmental politics at both Prescott College and the University of Bremen in Germany.

Walt Anderson added depth and insight to the natural history and ecologic aspects of the program, as well as a significant bridge with Arts and Letters through his talent as a nature artist and photographer. Dr. Boyer brought marine biology to the curriculum, and he also provided leadership for the developing research station in Kino Bay. Hans Drake brought an international perspective to Environmental Studies and Political Science. Dr. Crews provided the expertise as well as energy and determination to create the Wolfberry Farm, which had been a dream for the College for years. The agroecology curriculum and the new CSA (community supported agriculture) for organic produce distribution have flourished since Tim's arrival to the College. Dr. Floyd-Hannah's background and expertise in fire ecology brought an extremely relevant focus to the program; her husband David Hannah brought expertise in GIS (global information systems), adding significant strength to the applied scientific research occurring at the College. Dr. Sneed replaced Mike Goff. He became the coordinator of the Environmental Studies program and provided strong leadership in developing new curricula. He now (2006-07) coordinates the College's PhD program in Education for Sustainability.

1999 – 2001

The College curriculum by the turn of the century was organized into four multidisciplinary programs that included: Adventure Education, Arts and Letters, Environmental Studies, and Integrative Studies. A newly articulated mission for Environmental Studies stated that

> Prescott College is exceptional among institutions of higher learning in that one of our fundamental goals is to promote ecological literacy. Our mission statement calls for education that enhances our world community and environment. (PC Catalog 1999-2001, p. 27)

The program identified four ways to support the mission and goals.

> First, we advance understanding based on a variety of disciplines— from the biological, physical, and social sciences, as well as the humanities—and utilize these insights to illuminate the interrelationships between the human and non-human realms. Second, we teach specific skills in critical thinking, field and laboratory methods, and in oral and written communication. Third, we encourage students to develop a philosophical understanding of and ethical stance regarding human-nature relationships. Finally, we help students develop the ability to apply their knowledge to 'real-world' situations to prepare them for further education and meaningful employment. (Ibid.)

The most common emphasis areas in Environmental Studies included agroecology, conservation, earth science, environmental education and interpretation, human ecology, marine studies, and natural history and ecology. The Catalog articulated four realms of study that further defined the program: life sciences, earth sciences, exploration of personal values, and study of societal values and systems, and directed each student to design competences that include all four realms of study.

A statement on Ecological Literacy also appeared in the Catalog:

> While Environmental Studies is a broad, integrative field that encompasses many disciplines, we believe that ecological literacy is an essential part of the foundation on which an ENVIRONMENTAL STUDIES graduation area should be built. Ecological literacy is the understanding of interrelatedness of all life—human and non-human—in the context of evolution, ecology, and thermodynamics, as well as the context of historical, political, and cultural perspectives. By its very nature, ecological literacy demands expansive, synthetic inquiry rather than narrow specialization. (Ibid., p. 29)

A description of the Wolfberry Farm also appears in the Catalog:

In 1996, Prescott College acquired 30 acres of land to develop a farm
dedicated to education, demonstration, and research in agroecology
… The farm is located 15 miles north of Prescott, in the town of Chino
Valley, a town with a rich agricultural history. The use of this land is
changing, not only because of its growth as a community, but largely
due to agricultural failures. (ibid., p. 38)

Lorayne Meltzer joined the faculty in the fall of 1997, and served as the
co-director with Ed Boyer for the Kino Bay Center for Cultural and Ecological Studies. The Center was for the first time legally recognized by the
Mexican government as *Prescott College, Associación Civil*, the equivalent of
a nonprofit education organization, one of the few U.S. institutions granted
this status.

Bob Ellis (education and teacher training) also joined the faculty in the
fall of 1997, along with Joel Barnes, who had worked as a lecturer for several
years in Environmental Studies. Joel was hired in Adventure Education, to
assist in the development and instruction of the Environmental Education
focus. Dr. Barnes further developed a needed and obvious bridge between
Environmental Education and Adventure Education.

One of the long-term goals had been to begin offering teacher certification in RDP as a means of better serving the residential students who did
not want to transfer to ADP (adult degree program—non-resident) in order
to work on obtaining teacher certification. Bob Ellis, as a certified teacher in
secondary biology with a background in environmental education, provided
significant expertise in the development of the Environmental Education
Competence graduation guide.

By 1999, several new faces appeared in the Catalog and were listed as
Environmental Studies faculty. Lon Abbott (earth science and geophys-
ics) replaced Vern Taylor, who passed away unexpectedly. (Vern had taught
classes in geology and Native American studies for nearly thirty years, and
was clearly a wise elder for many of us who had known him over the years.)
Jack Herring (chemistry and atmospheric sciences) brought significant expertise and experience as an environmental policy analyst, and had worked in
Washington D.C. as an advisor for a member of the U.S. House of Representatives. William Litzinger (biology and ethnobotany) also became part of the
Environmental Studies faculty. Dr. Litzinger's passion for ethnobotany rein-
forced the bridge between humans and plants within the College curriculum.
Dana Oswald, who came to Prescott College with the charter class and had
taught for many years in the Southwest Studies curriculum, moved to Environmental Studies, where her background in anthropology strengthened the
program's general offerings and in particular human ecology. Dr. Oswald also

continually supported and advocated for more courses in ecological design, a curricular area that had been struggling since the early days of the College.

2005-07

The Catalog descriptions of Environmental Studies remained much the same as in the previous few years. One of the most significant changes was that environmental education moved to the newly approved education program in order to provide support for teacher certification classes within RDP. Bob Ellis and I continued to be listed as both environmental studies and education faculty. This was the first year that faculty photos and biographical sketches classified faculty with specific programs in the Catalog.

Environmental Studies defined eight emphasis areas: Agroecology, Conservation Biology, Earth Science, Ecological Design, Environmental Policy, Human Ecology, Marine Studies, Natural History, and Ecology. (PC Catalog 2007, pp. 62-65)

The College expanded in many exciting directions that have increased the influence and opportunities for students and faculty in environmental studies and the college as a whole. Under the coordination and expertise of Dr. Herring, the College joined in a collaborative partnership with Yavapai College, Sharlot Hall Museum, Northern Arizona University, and the Prescott National Forest to create the Walnut Creek Station of Education Research, located forty-five miles northwest of Prescott. This historic ranger station was built by the Civilian Conservation Corps (CCC) before World War II and now serves as a field station for classes, independent studies, research, conferences, and meetings. It has expanded the College's ability to focus on regional resource management issues, while providing leadership for complex management decisions.

The College also formed a formal partnership with Skyview, a charter school that local parents and educators, including Prescott College personnel, had established. Students who have an interest in teacher certification, environmental education, experiential education, or adventure education gain invaluable experience working directly with the Skyview School faculty and students. This partnership expands our relationship beyond the Prescott Unified Schools to provide a supportive environment for innovative approaches to education.

Prescott College became a member of the Eco-League, a national consortium of six colleges and universities that share similar missions and value systems. All of these schools have strong environmental philosophies and curricula based on ecological responsibility, social change, and education of students to build a sustainable future. The Eco-League colleges have high quality programs in environmental science, marine biology, outdoor studies, and education.

> These colleges all stress experiential, hands-on education methods so that students are prepared to take on real-world challenges when they graduate. (PC Catalog 2005-07, p. 96)

During the fall of 2007, the College developed its first international exchange program with Telemark College in Norway. Telemark College (Høgskule i Telemark) is home for one of Norway's most respected programs in Friluftsliv (Free Air Life) as well as Environmental Sciences and has professors from Norway, Sweden, Denmark, and the United States. The Telemark District, in the mountainous countryside, is one of the traditional cultural gems of Norway, a land known for its Viking history, misty fjords, and magnificent landscapes.

Prescott College continues to have a close relationship with the Ecosa Institute, founded by people associated with the College in the belief that design based on nature is critical to the search for a new design philosophy. Located in Prescott, Ecosa offers Prescott College students a one-semester program that emphasizes green-building knowledge and experience.

The only new faculty to join the Environmental Studies program during this period was Jim Brandt (mathematics), who filled an important need by providing undergraduate mathematics to the curriculum. Dr. Brandt's enthusiasm for teaching math as well as his sensitivity to those with special needs was significant. Unfortunately, he, as well as Lon Abbott, accepted positions at other institutions during the spring of 2006, and their contributions will be difficult to replace.

It is also important to note that in addition to the full-time faculty, a number of instructors and adjuncts have given tremendous amounts of energy and expertise to the teaching of courses in Environmental Studies. It would take pages to list and summarize the contributions that all of these dedicated people have made over the years. Their efforts in conjunction with the full-time faculty have helped to create one of the most dynamic and far-reaching academic areas at the College. Since its beginning in the College's early years, the Environmental Studies program has consistently worked to support an interdisciplinary curriculum as well as the overall mission of the College.

The legacy of the program is the hundreds of students who have brought their enthusiasm, creativity, and commitment to making a difference in the world and the environment that supports us. Their stories continue to unfold and are the true measure of our success.

Protein for Nuestros Pequeños Hermanos

◇◇◇◇◇◇◇

by Diana Papoulias, Class of 1979

I went to Prescott Center College to learn the skills I thought I would need to make a difference in the world. I had attended the University of New Hampshire for one and a half years and the University of Massachusetts at Amherst for one semester and was disillusioned with the traditional type of education. I knew what I wanted. I had been reading Frances Moore Lappe's work about food politics and following the demise of the wild fisheries (having grown up along the New England coast). Growing fish in ponds using wastes seemed like one solution to providing much needed protein to meet the new demands that the huge increases in global population would require in the years to come.

I found out about PCAE one afternoon while reading the *Christian Science Monitor.* I knew immediately it was for me. In the fall of 1976 I was enrolled.

I was so fortunate to have the scientific guidance of Maggie Fusari, Carl Tomoff, and Vern Taylor. They made it possible for me to go beyond the current lim-

Diana Papoulias as an Undergraduate

ited resources of Prescott Center and ensured that I would have the necessary doors open to me if I chose to continue my science education in the future.

The opportunity to go to Mexico to Nuestros Pequeños Hermanos (NPH) was an incredible coincidence. At the time, faculty member Alan Weisman was involved in NPH (I believe Alan got involved because alum Adele Piccinati's father was on the board of directors or a benefactor of both NPH and PC), and through his conversations with Father Wasson, he learned that Wasson, founder of the orphanage, was interested in raising fish (he liked the idea of catfish) to help provide low-cost protein for his family of a thousand orphans. NPH had just recently purchased an old sugar cane hacienda vintage late 1800s, with about 120 acres. They would grow corn, vegetables, chickens, pigs, and fruit trees. Alan proposed that I do my student project at NPH and build a fish farm. I jumped at the chance. In 1978 I moved to NPH. I thought I would be there maybe a year. I left in 1982 after the first fish dinner was served to one thousand kids. It took four long years to make it all happen. It was the most incredible experience I've ever had in my life, and still impacts me today.

I began with a machete, cutting down the sorghum on a sloping hillside of about three acres above the onion and bean plots. I spoke little Spanish (despite Pedro Aisa's hard work trying to get me up to speed in a short time). I had an army of rascals to help me who took full advantage of my incompetencies. I had to learn to work within a system that was not only foreign because of culture and language but was even more different yet because it was a small subculture of 'pequeños' (think of a cross between the Lord of the Flies and the Partridge Family), the kids themselves, who had been reared at NPH and who had taken on the various positions necessary to run a large household, a farm, a dental clinic, a medical clinic, a school, … They had their own ways and it took me nearly all the four years to figure out how to work within that system to get things accomplished. Since there was no way I could build the fish farm all on my own, I had to do a sales job to get cooperation from the small ones who were my labor force, to the older ones in charge of purchasing cement, sand, and gravel, to the accountants who held the purse strings. I also had to woo the benefactors who provided funds for new projects like the one I had gone down there to head up. In time I was successful, but there were so many things to learn, and so quickly. Money came in slowly, but as we showed some progress and successes, we were able to get more. Eventually, we got a big grant from a German newspaper that did fundraising for projects like mine by writing a series of stories and soliciting funds from their readership. To engage the kids, I taught a couple of courses in aquatic biology in the school and took the kids on field trips to the local reservoir and streams.

But even so, the project was built on a shoestring. I convinced the manager of the local sugar cane processing plant to come and dig our "grow out" ponds (three at 1/3 acre each) for free. His bulldozer driver didn't pay any attention to my drawings and plans for the ponds, and instead built what he was accustomed to building … three long ditches. The sides were too steep, the ponds too deep … .but it was free and we made it work. Then the ponds didn't hold water. After trying several biological fixes, I found a company in Mexico City that was just beginning to experiment with pond liners. For nearly free, they gave me rolls of the material (six feet wide) that we had to glue together to eventually cover the pond bottoms—a monumental task. In addition to the "grow out" ponds or finishing ponds, there were nine smaller ponds where the little fish were reared. We initially got our fish from the local state hatchery that reared tilapia and also carp. But later we were fortunate to be given some good tilapia brood stock from a producer in the U.S. that produced a high percentage of male offspring. This was great since these fish easily overpopulate their environment and become stunted. We needed to grow edible fish in as short a time as possible. The males grew faster, and with few females there was limited reproduction.

The system was built to take advantage of the rest of the farm … it was integrated, if you will. We used pumped ground water that gravity flowed to the ponds and naturally aerated as it fell into the ponds. The drains of the ponds allowed the fertile bottom water containing dead algae and fish feces to gravity drain to the crops below. The ponds were fertilized by the excrement of the pigs and chickens, since the fish would harvest the resulting algae. We also supplemented the food with corn waste from the *tortilleria* and whatever else we could find—buggy rice, old oats, etc.

With success came jealousy from the townspeople nearby. They helped themselves at night to the fish. Sometimes we would lose half a pond to the nocturnal fishermen. I went on an outreach campaign in the pueblo to teach folks how to rear fish themselves. A few took it on, but most found it easier to throw a baited hook into the ponds at night.

There were a million frustrations and setbacks. So many times I thought I would just bag it and go home. Especially when I was so sick from all the diseases I caught down there. But there was one really important event that kept me from throwing in the towel. It was a late afternoon. The kids had been in school all day. It was wickedly hot; they were hungry and tired and had been sent out to me to work a few hours in the afternoon before supper. They didn't want to be there. We were digging some of the smaller ponds by pick and shovel. The ground was literally like cement. I forget the name of the soil formation now. Our hands were blistered. The tools were too big for the small kids to handle. It was horrible. I had been at it all day and had little patience for their whining and screwing around. Finally I pushed too far and they all just left me there. Except one boy, maybe he was ten. I was so upset. It seemed like we would never finish. I asked him why I got so little cooperation. Afternoon chores were expected in any household. It was only a few hours ... why couldn't they see the benefit of what they were working on? Ezequiel was really blunt ... he said why should we help you, the project isn't really for them, they saw it as being for me, for my ego. That I would most likely give up half way through like most of the do-gooders who had come down there to put up solar panels, or build compost piles, or raise chickens, and all their work would be for nothing. They saw the whole thing as just an opportunity for me to learn Spanish and Mexican culture and feel good about helping little orphan children. This from a ten-year old!!! I was floored. But it really made me take stock of my motives and how my presence and efforts were perceived. He was so right about so much of what goes on by well-meaning folks. I vowed to him then that I would stay involved in the project as long as it took to keep it functioning. And I've counseled many people since who get all starry-eyed about going to "help" the unfortunate.

A couple years ago NPH celebrated fifty years of operation. I went to the celebration and was recognized for my service of over twenty years. After moving back to the States, and to Prescott, I taught a course at PC in Spanish to prepare students to go down to NPH and work at the fish farm for six months to a year. Initially, that is how I kept things going. After a while, I became too busy with my graduate studies to teach the course, and NPH had their older kids take charge during their year of service (NPH has a system by which the kids take time off between primary and secondary school and between secondary school and college to give back a year of service to the house). I trained these kids to do the work to keep the project going. Since leaving, I go and visit a few times a year and call every few months to see how things are going and if I can provide any guidance. Mostly they don't need me.

So since 1978 we've produced about 1,000-1,500 kg of cleaned fish per year to the NPH kitchen. It isn't a huge amount. But we've done it consistently and for nearly pennies a pound. Although chickens and pigs and cows have come and gone, the fish continue to produce—because it was designed to be simple and nearly self-sustaining.

Over the years we have improved things, adding a greenhouse in which we can breed the fish year round, fruit trees like bananas and mangos that grow along the edges of the ponds, goats and sheep to keep the pasture around the ponds trimmed. Students studying aquaculture at the various universities in Mexico come out to do service projects, and learn about our system. In the early years, we had visitors all the time, it was a model project for the country; there was nothing else like it. In fact, when I went looking for some assistance from the state and federal fisheries folks I got laughed at and was told to raise ornamental fish and just sell them and buy fish at the market. Those same fish biologists a few years after were coming to NPH to learn what we were doing.

NPH has changed incredibly over the years as well. No longer are they only operating in Mexico; they now have homes in nearly all the Central American countries and many South American countries as well as Haiti and the Dominican Republic. Wasson is very old now, but still is as charismatic and engaging as ever.

Diana Papoulias, PhD, is a Research Biologist at the Columbia Environmental Research Center and part-time Professor at the University of Missouri. She has been working with the U.S. Geological Survey studying factors that affect sturgeon in the Missouri River. She is doing research on effects of various contaminants that are altering fish reproductive health. In another long-term project she is investigating both fish and wildlife health and its resulting effects on human health along the whole U.S.-Mexico border from San Diego, California, to Brownsville, Texas.

A Short History of the Writing and Literature Program

◇◇◇◇◇◇◇

by K. L. Cook,

The study of writing and literature has been an important aspect of a Prescott College education since the 1963 Symposium in which the foundations of the philosophy and curriculum were laid. The founders enthusiastically recognized the great traditions of Southwest literature and writing, setting goals that would encourage its emphasis in a high-quality liberal arts curriculum. The written word was designed as the vehicle through which students refined their thinking and expressed their learning. The old lecture-test paradigm was abandoned in favor of extensive readings of important literature and small discussion classes. A portfolio system encouraged students to write constantly and benefit from individualized feedback. Grades were deemphasized and narrative evaluations took their place.

While the College was on its old campus (1966 through 1975) writing and literature studies were coordinated by the interdisciplinary Teaching and Research Center for Language and Literary Studies, but they also permeated the whole curriculum, from social studies and biological and physical sciences to wilderness and conservations experiences. Students were reading the best literature in their fields and writing scientific papers, monographs, novels and stories, plays and poetry—and sometimes publishing them. The teaching faculty included excellent writers like Wilbur Stevens, Hogan Smith, and later Alan Weisman, as well as visiting writers of note.

When the College moved into downtown Prescott in midyear 1975, the whole curriculum was integrated so there were no more departments or centers. Alan Weisman coordinated writing for all programs for several years and also pursued his career as a journalist and author, involving students in professional writing even before their graduation. Other faculty and students organized workshops in diverse genres, including nature writing, long

Writing and Literature Class at the Cabin at Sierra Anchas, 1993

and short fiction, speculative and science fiction, scriptwriting, and poetry. Several distinguished writers have graduated from Prescott College over the years (Gary Nabhan, Craig Childs, and Brad Dimock among them).

With the rapid growth of the College in the early 1990s, Writing and Literature instruction was offered under the larger curricular umbrella of the Humanities Program. In 1997, three competence and breadth "tracks" were approved: Creative Writing, Writing & Literature, and Literature. Since 1996, the program has grown to include introductory, intermediate, and advanced courses in all genres of writing (fiction, poetry, nonfiction, journalism, and scriptwriting).

The program is now home to an award-winning national literary journal, *Alligator Juniper*, and an award-winning regional newspaper, *The Raven Review*. Literature offerings include a wide variety of American, world, and cross-disciplinary courses, such as Shakespeare, Literature of the American Dream, Latin American Literature, Family Systems in Film and Literature, Women's Literature. Practicum courses, designed to provide students with hands-on professional experience, include Newspaper Journalism Practicum,

Literary Journal Practicum, Writers in the Community, and New Play Development and Production.

Field courses—such as Travel Writing, The Ancient Peoples: the Literature and Pre-History of the American Southwest, Advanced Fiction Writers' Workshop, Sense of Place: Kino Bay, and Sense of Place: Alaska—have also enriched the curriculum and contributed to the College's overall mission of field-based and culturally sensitive education. Since the late 1980s, Prescott College has also been a co-sponsor of the Southwest Writers Series, which brings ten to fifteen emerging, national, and international writers each year to Prescott for informal dialogues, readings, and other cultural events. Student senior projects in writing include novels, plays, film scripts, collections of poetry and fiction and essays, memoirs, as well as various teaching and service projects.

Since 1987, graduates from the writing and literature area have flourished. They've published books and shorter works in well-respected literary journals and magazines and with independent and commercial publishers. Alumni have also won numerous fellowships, scholarships, and other awards and have been accepted into many of the premier MFA and PhD programs in the country, including the Iowa Writers' Workshop, the universities of Alabama, Arizona, Montana, Texas at Austin, Indiana, Pittsburg, New Mexico State, CUNY Graduate Program, and Bennington College and Vermont College.

Prescott College's emphasis on small classes, innovative curriculum, and strong student/mentor relationships is ideal for a writing and literature program, and is the primary reason that this area of the curriculum has flourished over the years.

The following outline is a much more detailed overview of distinguishing characteristics of Prescott College's writing and literature area. K.L. prepared and presented this for a panel entitled "Developing an Excellent Undergraduate Creative Writing Program," at the 2006 Association of Writers and Writing Programs (AWP) national conference.

PRESCOTT COLLEGE'S UNDERGRADUATE CREATIVE WRITING PROGRAM

Distinguishing Features
- Part of an Interdisciplinary Arts & Letters Program (rather than a conventional English Dept.)
- Maximum enrollment for all courses is twelve students (average class size is ten)

- Professional and pre-professional practicum opportunities in literary and newspaper editing, teaching, and new play development
- Coursework and independent studies in fiction, poetry, nonfiction, and scriptwriting
- Sequenced courses with many courses available at both lower division and upper division levels
- Most intermediate and advanced courses on multi-year rotations to ensure variety during any student's undergraduate tenure
- Co-sponsor of the Southwest Writers Series, which brings nationally known and emerging writers to town for informal dialogues and readings
- Creative writing and literature field courses in Alaska, Mexico, Arizona, and the West Coast
- Award-winning national literary journal, *Alligator Juniper*
- Award-winning regional newspaper, *The Raven Review*
- BFA-level requirements for the competence (major)
- Senior Projects with ambitious quantity and quality requirements (e.g., novels, short story cycles, plays, screenplays, collections of poems, stories, or essays, or a combination of genres)

Graduates

- Alumni have recently graduated from, are currently enrolled in, or have been accepted into top MA, MFA, or PhD programs, including Iowa Writers' Workshop, Montana, Alabama, Pittsburg, Texas-Austin, Arizona, CUNY Graduate Center, Bennington College, Vermont College, Indiana, and Ohio State.
- Other alumni are currently working as journalists, freelance writers, lawyers, teachers, professors, editors, filmmakers, and performers.
- Students and graduates have won many awards and honors, including the Stadler Center for Poetry Younger Poets Prize, the Truman Capote Fellowship at the Iowa Writers' Workshop, the Keene Prize for Best Graduate Thesis at the University of Texas at Austin, as well as publication in major literary journals, including *Hayden's Ferry Review*, *Denver Quarterly*, and *Colorado Review*.

Faculty

- Award-winning poets, fiction and nonfiction writers, journalists, screenwriters, and playwrights
- Faculty members teach 90-100% of all creative writing and practicum courses and mentor or co-mentor all creative writing senior projects

- Current Faculty: Melanie Bishop (fiction/creative nonfiction/ screenwriting/literature), K. L. Cook (fiction/creative nonfiction/ literature), Dr. Reuben Ellis (journalism/literature), Dr. Thomas Fleischner (nature writing), Dr. Charissa Menefee (playwriting/ screen writing), Sheila Sanderson (poetry/creative nonfiction/literature), and Miles Waggener (poetry/creative nonfiction/literature/ managing editor of *Alligator Juniper*)

Literary Journal: Alligator Juniper
- Winner: 2001 and 2004 AWP National Program Director's Prize for Content
- Publishes poetry, fiction, creative nonfiction, literary interviews, and photography
- Offers $500 national prizes in poetry, fiction, creative nonfiction, and photography
- Publishes best Prescott College student work (judged by outside judges) in all genres
- Publishes theme issues every five years (e.g. Nature and Psyche, Scars)
- Staff consists of advanced creative writing students in the context of a Literary Journal Practicum class taught by two faculty editors (one prose writer, one poet)

Regional Newspaper: The Raven Review
- National award-winning college-run newspaper that has a national and regional (rather than primarily campus) focus
- 5,000+ subscriptions
- Students have broken major local and regional stories, including stories on jail inmate abuse, grazing rights, and regional environmental politics
- Staff consists of students in the context of the Newspaper Journalism Practicum class, taught by Reuben Ellis

Southwest Writers Series
- Prescott College has been co-sponsor (with Yavapai College, the local community college) since 1985
- Brings ten to fifteen nationally and internationally known and emerging writers to Prescott for informal dialogues, readings, and occasional workshops
- Visiting writers have included Charles Baxter, Grace Paley, Antonya Nelson, Robert Boswell, Kevin McIlvoy, Bret Lott, Paula McLain,

Al Young, Karen McElmurray, Margo Tamez, John Nichols, Marge Piercy, Jim Simmerman, Mark Sprague, Grace Dane Mazur, Yann Martel, Carl Phillips, Ron Carlson, T. M. McNally, and Melissa Pritchard

Practicum Opportunities

- Practicum courses provide students with opportunities for hands-on professional or semi-professional training in literary editing, journalism, new play production, and teaching.
- Literary Journal Practicum students serve as the staff for the literary journal *Alligator Juniper*. Students learn the criteria for evaluating and running a quality literary journal, and their class experience includes choosing manuscripts to publish, selecting national winners in poetry, fiction, and creative nonfiction, and writing personal rejection letters.
- Newspaper Journalism Practicum students serve as the staff of *The Raven Review*. Students investigate local and regional stories, conduct interviews, write features and opinions, edit, and do all the layout.
- Writers in the Community gives students hands-on experience conducting creative writing workshops in a variety of venues, including local public and private schools, the VA hospital, assisted-living and senior citizen centers, and homeless and women's shelters.
- New Play Development & Production is a practicum that follows the playwriting course. Four to six student-written short plays are taken through the new play development process; playwrights work with student actors, directors, and designers in a repertory-style company to stage full productions.

Creative Writing Competence (Major) Requirements

- Sixteen courses in Writing & Literature Area
- Coursework in three different genre areas (Poetry, Fiction, Nonfiction, Scriptwriting)
- Four Literature Courses (beyond combination writing/literature courses)
- Two Writing and Literature Practicum courses
- Eight upper-division courses (including Senior Project)
- Senior Project (most often an ambitious manuscript of new and revised creative writing)

Creative Writing & Literature Competence (Major) Requirements
- Sixteen courses in Writing & Literature Area
- Coursework in three different genre areas (Poetry, Fiction, Nonfiction, Scriptwriting)
- Seven literature courses
- Coursework in at least two literature areas (American, World, Cross-Disciplinary)
- Eight courses should be upper division (including Senior Project)
- Senior Project (most often a collection of both original creative work and literary analysis)

CREATIVE WRITING COURSES OFFERED AT PRESCOTT COLLEGE
(Does not include literature offerings. Many of these courses are on two- and three-year rotations. LD=lower-division course: UD=upper-division course: LD/UD=available at both LD and UD levels.)

Fiction
- Introduction to Fiction Writing (LD)
- Sudden Fiction: The Art of the Very Short Story (LD/UD)
- Fiction Writers' Workshop: Wilderness Locations (LD/UD)
- Writing as Performance (LD/UD)
- Forms of Fiction (UD)
- Short Story Cycle (UD)

Poetry
- Poem Workshop (LD/UD)
- Vintage Verse (LD/UD)
- Advanced Poetry Workshop (UD)
- Literary-Journal Practicum: Poetry (UD)

Scriptwriting
- Playwriting (LD/UD)
- Screenwriting (LD/UD)
- Scriptwriting (LD/UD)
- Writing as Performance (LD/UD)
- New Play Development & Production (LD/UD)

Nonfiction
- Newspaper Journalism Practicum (LD/UD)
- Magazine Journalism (LD/UD)
- Creative Nonfiction (LD/UD)

- Sense of Place: Alaska (LD/UD)
- Sense of Place: Kino Bay, Mexico (LD/UD)
- Writing as Performance (LD/UD)
- Travel Writing: Journey as Metaphor (LD/UD)
- The Memoir (UD)
- Nature's Voice: Reading and Writing about Natural History (UD)

Practicum Courses
(may take same practicum course more than once)
- Newspaper Journalism Practicum: *The Raven Review* (LD/UD)
- Literary Journal Practicum: *Alligator Juniper* (UD)
- Writers in the Community (UD)
- New Play Development & Production (LD/UD)
- Other practicum possibilities: teaching assistant in a writing and literature course; internship (e.g., for a literary magazine, newspaper, writer, or theatre or film company); community service project (e.g., workshops on writing in the schools, performances for children, volunteer literacy programs, organizing reading series, etc.)

Journalism at Prescott College

by a journalism student (name not known)

Student journalism at Prescott College has evolved through the years from early student-initiated publications to the current *Raven Review*, a fully independent student-published newspaper serving all the people in Prescott and surrounding communities, and reaching beyond through the internet.

While instances of student journalism during the early years of the College are veiled in myth and anecdote, some yellowed and frayed pages can be found in the archives, testifying that students have expressed their reactions to events and issues from the founding of the College in the 1960s. These early publications were often more like newsletters, printed in small formats with on-campus circulations of a few hundred copies. After the College moved into town in 1975, student teams published more formal, and often quite attractive and competent news and opinion weeklies for brief periods, intended for campus and alum audiences. Some are well remembered—*The Pulse, Kokopelli's Seed*—and, rumor has it, *The Sputilator*. Nevertheless, these would expire when the group members graduated.

Other student publications arose from individual or group independent studies and faded away when the students moved on to other projects. *The Granite Mountain Echo* published only two issues. A longer running student publication, *The Word*, was initiated during the mid-1990s, supported by a new course incorporated into the regular curriculum, the Newspaper Journalism Practicum. This course has continued to be the mainstay of student publication at the College to the present (2006). Other new courses and independent studies soon followed, providing students with the opportunity to major in journalism or photojournalism.

In the fall of 2000, student journalism at Prescott College took an important step when students founded *The Raven Review*, the first student publication based on a professional editorial policy and a ratified agreement guaranteeing its editorial independence from the College administration. *The*

Raven Review also inaugurated a new look, going to a larger tabloid size and being printed on regular newsprint paper.

In 2002, *The Raven Review* expanded its circulation to 5,000, taking over the distribution routes of another independent locally published tabloid that served not only the small city of Prescott, but also its neighboring towns of Prescott Valley and Chino Valley. With a circulation ten times that of the resident student body, *The Raven Review* boasted the highest ratio of copy distribution to enrolled students of any college newspaper in the United States.

In 2003, *The Raven Review* won first place recognition in the Scholastic Press Association's annual college newspaper contest, a national award based on content, design, editing, creativity, and art. This award was the first of a series of awards the *Raven Review* would receive in subsequent years.

In 2003 and 2004, student journalists at *The Raven Review* published a series of articles about civil rights violations at the Yavapai County Jail that became part of the documentation of a federal Justice Department investigation of the Yavapai County Sheriff's Department. This was one of the high water marks of activist journalism at the College.

In 2006, student journalists converted the formerly black and white *Raven Review* to color and launched an online version of the paper—ravenreview.com. Students and journalism faculty also began to seek partnerships with other professional news organizations and initiated steps that would create a student news service to syndicate student journalism throughout the Eco League, a consortium of like-minded small colleges to which Prescott College belongs.

Our journalism accomplishments demonstrate the College's philosophy of experiential learning in the real world of ecological and social phenomena, as well as its philosophy of independence and self-direction. We look forward to a future without limits for Prescott College journalism.

The History of the Adventure Education Program

◇◇◇◇◇◇◇

by David Lovejoy

"I find the greatest satisfaction in working with students in a setting where the often lost arts of flexibility, adaptability, and cooperation are critical to safety, sanity, and success. Wilderness provides this, free of dogma, but full of consequences to test one's actions."

—David Lovejoy

The Adventure Education program has long been one of the most prestigious and important aspects of the spirit of Prescott College. Although the program has gone through a great deal of change along with the rest of the college over the decades, much of the original spirit of the program has remained the same. Perhaps the most important of these is the program's unyielding commitment to the out-of-doors. The extent to which this commitment affects the program is evident. As long-time Adventure Education faculty member and Prescott College alum David Lovejoy states, "We, more than any other college program, get out deeper, and stay out longer, than anywhere else. We believe that this depth of immersion has a powerful emotional impact, which fosters respect for the natural, derived from a feeling of kinship with place. As in any kinship, the final result is one of care and commitment to protection of the essence of what has become valued and familiar."

The Adventure Education program, originally entitled Outdoor Action, was founded in 1967 under the leadership of President Dr. Ronald Nairn. Soon after the college opened, Dr. Nairn discovered Outward Bound. Perhaps due to his military background, Nairn decided that this type of program was just what the youth of America needed to become strong leaders of the

High On The Rock Face

future. According to Dr. Jim Stuckey, Dr. Nairn believed that "this is the antidote for the ills of America ... we've got the '60s in full roar, we've got hippies everywhere and drugs everywhere and what you really need is character building experiences, and a good bash up a hill." He believed that "through the medium of the mountains, the seas, canyons and rivers, the qualities of style, compassion, integrity, responsibility, and leadership can be fostered and encouraged."

This new discovery led to the introduction of the Outdoor Action program in 1967 with an inventory of twenty-five sets of backpacking equipment and six ropes. Well-established mountaineer and senior Outward Bound instructor Roy Smith, who has been described as "real hard school," was hired to direct and develop the Outdoor Action program. Roy was the sort of a guy who could plan an expedition on the back of an envelope. Another Outward Bound instructor, Mike Acebo, was also hired to assist in the program and was granted a scholarship to attend Prescott College. An advisory council was formed that included such celebrities as distinguished mountaineer, philosopher, and experiential educator Dr. Willi Unsoeld.

The first Wilderness Orientation was launched in 1968 with the purpose of creating a sense of community. It challenged each student to grow personally, and to demonstrate that involvement in activities such as camping, hiking, mountaineering, and kayaking was relevant to an academic program addressed to the problems of leadership in the twenty-first century. This event made

Prescott College the first educational institution in the nation to incorporate an Outward Bound style program as an integral part of its undergraduate curriculum.

Roy Smith, with the assistance of Outward Bound instructors and advanced Prescott College students, led the first Wilderness Orientation for incoming students, and many of the subsequent ones. The course operated as an adapted version of an Outward Bound course, with students and instructors splitting time between a water component, such as sailing or sea kayaking, and a land component, like canyon backpacking. Although many aspects of Wilderness Orientation have remained the same, there was one major difference between the orientation of 1969 and the orientation of today. As Noël Caniglia said, "Orientation was really a disorientation," a way to knock assumptions out and prime students for real learning. Current orientations are not Outward Bound courses, but are very well designed to orient students to the wilderness and the College. Another fundamental part of Wilderness Orientation that has remained throughout the years is a three-day solo, when each student spends three days and three nights alone in reflection with no distractions, with little gear and often without food. One student described her solo in Paria Canyon as a time when "I got to know myself better, enjoyed being alone—the challenge of remaining alone for three days and nights, the experience of knowing what it is really like to be hungry and to really be a part of nature. ... As a result of orientation I feel I can undertake and accomplish almost anything I want to do or have to do throughout life. ... There is no doubt ... it

Canyon Rafters, Resting on the Shore

was a fantastically worthwhile experience breeding strength, awareness, total appreciation, confidence." Another student had a different growth experience, saying "The solo was pure hell for me, but it was worthwhile. I could have gone back so easily, but I didn't. For once I didn't back out, and now maybe I'll be able to take the next bad thing that happens." These sentiments have been echoed by nearly all those who have participated in solo and Wilderness Orientation throughout the past four decades.

The Outdoor Action program continued to gain momentum quickly. In 1968, it received a substantial restricted endowment contributed by the De-Witt Wallace Foundation, which gave it very many opportunities to expand in every direction. Its mission began to change from extracurricular technical training to an emphasis in developing intentional leadership training and integrating field programs with academic subject matter. The program's expansion was also spurred by a growing national trend toward outdoor experiential education and the growing market for qualified outdoor leaders and teachers.

In 1970, Rhodesian-born Rusty Baillie, of international mountaineering fame, was hired to instruct in the OA program, and eventually to direct it. As a result, Roy Smith's position changed to Director of the Challenge/Discovery program, an external program for the public operating mainly out of Roy's summer home in Crested Butte, Colorado.

In 1971, Dr. Nairn recruited Dr. Jim Stuckey, Bob Godfrey, and a few more Outward Bound instructors and thrust them into a faculty of scientists and scholars who had built reputations in traditional academia. These new recruits brought not only their carabiners and paddles, but new philosophies about experiential education. At this time, however, the College had not yet fully embraced these ideas, and a rift began to form between the two schools of thought. Eventually the tension became so great that Dr. Nairn was forced to literally separate the two schools of thought and create a new Leadership Institute to keep the Outdoor Action department out of the jurisdiction of the academic departments. Part of this separation was about money, not just philosophy. There was deep-seated jealousy over the DeWitt Wallace money.

With the Outdoor Action program safely tucked away within its own institute and out of reach of the College itself, it was free to experiment and continue dramatic expansions. By 1972, the Outdoor Action program was conducting activities for students in whitewater and sea kayaking, rock climbing, mountaineering, search and rescue, sailing, soaring, scuba diving, rafting, and horsemanship. Many of these elements had actually existed before; for instance scuba and horsemanship had actually been phased out by

1972. The program was flourishing, and well-trained students were gradually given major responsibilities for helping with or running field programs, including working as Freshman Orientation instructors and as instructional staff for the Challenge/Discovery program. However, at the time, most of the activities were still extracurricular, and only students in the Outdoor Education or Advanced Leadership Training (ALT) programs were able to graduate with a degree in Outdoor Action.

This first, and extravagant, era of Adventure Education began to draw to a close when Rusty Baillie left Prescott College in the fall of 1974 and was replaced by Mike Goff. The period abruptly ended with the bankruptcy of the College in December of that year. Until then the students and faculty of Prescott College had been involved in countless great adventures, including the first sea kayak crossing of the Sea of Cortez in 1969, rafting expeditions through the Grand Canyon, exploration and mapping of Thunder River Cavern in the Grand Canyon, and successful mountaineering expeditions to Mount McKinley and Mount Kenya. The College also maintained on-call, and deputized, regional mountain- and scuba-rescue units.

After the College barely survived the bankruptcy in January 1974 and moved into town, everything changed, including adventure education. The Outdoor Action program continued on a shoestring budget under the leadership of Director Mike Goff and adjunct faculty member David Lovejoy.

Titiana Leads Rock Climbers
photo by Travis Patterson

Lovejoy states that Mike Goff was the unsung hero of the era, keeping the program alive with his industriousness and survival techniques. He was also responsible for converting all Outdoor Action courses into credit bearing courses. With a minimal equipment inventory of half a dozen ropes, a similar quantity of helmets and backpacks and a few tattered climbing anchors and slings, the College continued to run backpacking and rock climbing trips. For several years following the bankruptcy, the school depended on minimal everything—using private vehicles for transportation on all field courses, begging, borrowing, and requiring students to provide their own outdoor equipment. The College was also attempting to stay afloat through a Summer rafting program in the Lower Granite Gorge of the Grand Canyon, which served outreach and fund raising purposes, and which used students and graduates extensively as guides (this summer program continued until 1984). Lovejoy describes this whole era as "the lean and mean years."

The program did catch a few breaks, however. The College was given back its rescue equipment, which had been tied up in the close of the old campus. This allowed the program to continue training students for the Yavapai County Search and Rescue Team. The program also gained a great ally in new president Jim Stuckey, who had a solid background in outdoor education. Because of the scarcity that tinged all aspects of this period, students were also required to step up in even greater ways than before, and this produced incredibly competent and confident outdoor leaders.

Other changes in this period included centering activities in the Southwest, the integration of the program with academics throughout the college (helped along greatly by alum and Environmental Studies faculty member Doug Hulmes), an expanded breadth of focus for Wilderness Orientation, and a great focus in experiential education in its purest and most genuine form, reflecting director Mike Goff's background and values. This was articulated in the program's mission statement at the time:

"The purpose of the Outdoor Action program is to develop the capacity for leadership, to build character, to heighten sensitivity to the beauty of nature, to challenge one's endurance with rigorous exercise and to encourage teamwork and build trust in one's fellow students through the wilderness experience. The major objective of this program is to help students acquire outdoor skills at a standard of competence, which will enable them to pursue activities independently and to develop for their own practical purposes. These trained men and women will play their part in the developing Outdoor Education programs across the nation."

Despite early financial and student enrollment struggles, the program slowly grew and expanded back to its original strength. This was helped along greatly by hiring highly competent graduates to return and teach at the College on a course-by-course basis. By 1978 the College was able to add backcountry skiing, ski mountaineering, and snow avalanche studies. The program was thriving again, including the acquisition of much more serviceable transportation and better gear. Unfortunately, this period also holds the darkest hour in Outdoor Action's history. In January of 1986, four advanced students, on a group independent study, were attempting to ascend the three highest volcanoes in Mexico. The students were responsible for all logistical planning as well as contingencies and decision making on the expedition. Tragically, near the summit of El Pico de Orizaba (18,410 feet) the climbers suffered a 3,000-foot fall. Student Jerry Webster was killed in the accident (to this date the only fatality in the history of the program), and students Gary Guller and Dave Chianchulli both suffered severe injuries. This incident shook the collective soul of those in the Outdoor Action program and the College as a whole, sparking great changes in the program. The College was dropped by their liability insurance carrier and had to withstand a temporary moratorium on those activities perceived as the most potentially hazardous. Independent studies involving technical skills or potentially hazardous terrain were discontinued, except under strict supervision.

In 1987 Mike Goff transferred to another curricular program of the College, and David Lovejoy became the Outdoor Action program coordinator. Rusty Baillie also returned, having earned a doctorate. There was a significant increase in the number of incoming students, which spurred great changes in the philosophy and goals of the program. It became more formal and structured, and in the eyes of the outside world, legitimate. With this rapid growth in the College, new players were added in 1988, including Steve Munsell and Robin Kelly. In 1989 the program stated its goal to become the very best undergraduate source of well-trained adventure educators and wilderness guides. Lovejoy remarks that "this goal was important because it challenged us to integrate awareness of group behavior, interpersonal communication, and judgment with technical outdoor skills, and to recognize the critical relevance of embedding all of it within a liberal arts education. We had always been known as a college where students could acquire strong technical skills in outdoor pursuits. Adopting this goal impelled us to take a broader strategy, unlike other programs at the College, of a somewhat occupation training perspective." With this came new curricular guidelines, and many practical changes in philosophy.

In 1991 Steve Munsell became the new director of the program, greatly changing the administration of the program. Four years later Steve Pace replaced Munsell. Steve Pace had been program director in the Voyageur Outward Bound School in Minnesota. Under his direction, several large-scale changes in the program were instigated, including a name change from Outdoor Action to Adventure Education, and the addition of human relations and teaching skills training to the Adventure Education curriculum. Advising documents were revised, and three competence areas (graduation tracks) were formalized—Wilderness Leadership, Adventure Education and Outdoor Experiential Education, along with a strong commitment to gender equity.

Since then, the program has only become stronger and more respected as a leader in Adventure Education. David Lovejoy notes that "we are often touted as the program that other colleges wish they had, but for financial, bureaucratic and/or logistical reasons, can't muster the support of their administrators." Field courses remain the strongest aspect of the program, including eighteen credit courses, and students find themselves everywhere from whitewater rivers in California to high alpine summits in Ecuador. Lovejoy believes that the strength and uniqueness of the program still lies in its absolute conviction in "the value of immersion in the natural world where human impacts are much less apparent than in what is considered 'civilized.' In such an environment our connections with our past and our true place as members of nature—rather than controllers of nature—become obvious. We also find this environment one in which enhanced human interactions and self discovery are inevitable."

Graduates from the Prescott College Adventure Program are making powerful contributions to the field in any setting from the Grand Canyon to the Himalayas, and everywhere in between. An obvious and strong passion drives the faculty and students in the program. The Prescott College Adventure Education program continues to be an innovative leader in the field.

New Students Report to the Wilderness, from Prescott Center College (PCAE)—late 1970s and early '80s

◇◇◇◇◇◇◇

It is common practice for wilderness patrols—whether Orientation or other courses and activities—to keep a common journal in which leaders and students write about events that transpire. Here is a sampling of entrees from a group portfolio.

Announcement: "The Prescott Wilderness Orientation, which brought national prominence to the controversial, innovative college is once again in the field. ... Through the efforts of faculty and their programs in the form of the Prescott Center for Alternative Education (PCAE). Although enrollment figures are lower than what was hoped, twelve new students accompanied by four instructors and a faculty member or two are currently working their way down Utah's upper Escalante Canyon.

Last week a forest ranger arrived at his office in Escalante, Utah, and discovered a note jammed into the door crack. Opening the paper he discovered a detailed route plan wrapped around the dollar bill registration fee and this message: "Once again Prescott College—now known as the Prescott Center—is moving through Forest Service lands, well aware of the dangers of flash floods and arduous passage inherent in Utah canyons, in order to orient its freshmen to the equally perilous and joyful activity known as Education."

Students' Reactions to Orientation

"Walking for 80 miles or so through unspoiled wilderness, sleeping under the stars and learning the lay of the land is actually a necessity at the Center ... where classes often take students to remote areas of the field."

"College is a place to change. We're here to learn how to adapt and survive." (Freshman Jim Knaup from St. Louis)

"During times when having a college degree no longer insures one of also having employment, a lot can be said for a school where survival and adaptability rank high among academic priorities."

"You have no place to hide. You cope with what it hands out to you—rain, heat, cold, hard terrain, snakes—you are forced to find out how competent you really are." (PCAE freshman Philip Waite of Topsfield, Mass.)

"All of which means you are gaining self-confidence. You cope with civilization better when you've had the perspective of going without conveniences—your attitude toward flush toilets, electricity and vehicles changes when you've lived without them. Your awareness is sharpened."

"Moving safely and comfortably through the outdoors—and leaving it exactly the way it was found. To the weekend camper, the pains taken by PCAE instructors to cover traces of their passing might seem to be bothersome work, but the results make the extra effort worthwhile."

"In the past I've always camped for pleasure, but this is school. This wilderness we are traveling through is assuming a different shape, maybe even a different meaning by the way the group of us is interpreting it. ... I'm realizing and learning how much I am receiving from other people around me and how important it is to listen. ... Hot sun and seriousness don't always sit well with me; so much nicer just to sit and melt into the creek ... moss is so beautiful." (Tricia Scott, PCAE freshman from Forest Knolls, Calif.)

[Vocational opportunities] "Outdoor instructors are increasingly in demand at schools and programs such as Outward Bound, and those of us from Prescott are some of the best-prepared people in the country because we grew up in an outdoor program integrated with a college education. Everywhere, Prescott is regarded as having the highest standards of competence and safety."

ORIENTATION LEADERS BILL RESSLER AND MIKE ZIMBER
DESCRIBE THE ORIENTATION PROCESS

One of the most difficult aspects of Orientation is moving several strong-minded individuals across the land in an orderly fashion. Each Orientation patrol is a mini-society, where the majority of its members have only recently left their parents' homes.

Starting at 9,000 feet elevation … [our route takes us] from mountain ridges down through ponderosa- and fir-covered high canyons, across streams into great rocky gorges where walls seem so close one instinctively wants to walk sideways. In some spots, the river flows so high that backpacks must be held overhead while wading through chest-deep waters. The reasons for such a journey—as opposed to filling out registration forms and attending President's teas or pep rallies and fraternity-sorority functions that typify the first weeks at most colleges—are [the essential] discussion topics at meals and campfires.

We maximize our immersion in the wilderness simply by minimizing our impact on it. The familiar fire ring—surrounding campfires with a circle of containing rocks, is never used, simply because the resulting scorch marks on rocks remain long afterward as an indication of human intrusion. During Orientation, any rock inadvertently blackened by campfires is scoured clean in the stream. Fires are kindled in shallow pits; later the thoroughly soaked ashes are scattered and the fire pit refilled. All non-burnable garbage, such as aluminum foil, is carried out, latrines are dug deep and covered after using, and toilet paper is carefully burned. Dish-washing is done away from rivers to avoid polluting them.

Morning. A sunrise breakfast, usually consisting of granola or oatmeal and rehydrated powdered milk. After lunching on nuts, dried fruit, peanut butter, or an occasional treat of canned tuna, students work on portfolios—journals of their Orientation experiences, which become the first chapters of a written record that every Prescott student keeps of his education. During Orientation each student becomes proficient at reading a topographic map, administering first aid, identifying regional flora, purifying drinking water, and whatever else is necessary to understanding and using the wilderness. Along with these lessons, students inscribe their daily personal impressions, combining descriptions and insights to form an invaluable and memorable record.

After a week of carrying heavy packs over the slick rock and trudging down rivers, students begin what is considered by many to be the most important aspect of the Orientation: the solo. For three days, each student remains alone in a canyon without food, accompanied only by his or her thoughts. They are supplied with drinking water by instructors who silently check on them each day, and are allowed clothing, twine, a knife, and a piece of tarp for weather protection. Each student has the choice of bringing matches or a sleeping bag—but not both. Books are not allowed, but everyone takes the portfolio and a pencil.

Before taking students to their individual hideaways, Ressler tells them that "solo is your chance to merge your spirit with the wilderness, to clean out your bodies, to appreciate food, shelter and clothing, to learn what it is like to do without. You will miss food less than you think, and if you keep your mind and senses open you'll never be bored."

To have freedom and yet perform safely, to reduce the potential of danger without diluting the spirit of adventure—this is what is taught at Prescott, Ressler and Zimber explained as their students began their solos.

Preventing possible danger from becoming probable hazard is what it's all about—on solo we don't send students twenty miles off without a compass and make them find their way back to camp—the risk isn't worth it. What is worth it is the chance to be alone and totally immersed in nature for awhile. Solo has a unique way of putting your desires—including the desire to get a college education—into a new perspective: it forces you to face your thoughts.

A hot nutritious meal prepared by the instructors greets students as they come off solo, followed by another week of hiking before meeting PCAE vehicles at the junction of Harris Wash and the Escalante River. Students are aware that financial scrambling at the Prescott Center may mean that upon their return they could find an institution structurally different from the one described in PCAE's Catalogs. So far, this information has not been discouraging.

In the wilderness, we live and research outdoors, climb mountains to study geology, or spend weeks learning desert ecology firsthand. Orientation lets these kids—most of whom come from somewhere back East—see what the Southwest is like and become acclimated to working in it. This is their classroom—they have to know their way around and be comfortable working in it.

Surpassing the Safari: Prescott College in Kenya

◇◇◇◇◇◇◇

by Kaitlin Noss, 2006

Our van bounces over unpaved park roads at dawn. A pair of grey-crowned cranes extend their wings near the edge of a precious and dwindling swamp. Just behind them, a small group of zebras take turns bowing to the water or carefully keeping watch for the hunting lions.

We drive away from Mt. Kilimanjaro, its tenacious ice cap turned pink by the rising sun, and out of Amboseli National Park. During our six weeks on course in Kenya, we have seen over a hundred species of birds, come to

Student Andrew Kurz and Mmara woman pose for photograph

know the intimate conversations of several families of elephants, and been woken in the night by the sound of wildebeest bones cracking under hyena jaws outside our tents. The wildlife is breathtaking. But this is not the only reason Prescott College came to East Africa.

This morning we are driving to Kajiado town to present our research to the locally elected representatives of one of the largest areas of Maasailand, the Olkajiado County Council. Each summer a Prescott College class travels to Maasailand and undertakes a research question, which the community has identified as particularly critical through a consensus-based process facilitated by the Maasai Environmental Resource Coalition.

Our trip this year is the second of PC's field study programs in Kenya, developed out of a long-term relationship between Professor Mary Poole and Maasai Activist/Professor Meitamei Ole Dapash. The program works year round, from both Prescott and Maasailand, to support community-initiated projects dealing with clean water, HIV/AIDS, women's micro-lending co-operatives, and culturally competent education.

The Kenya course offers foundational cultural and environmental studies curricula, but the real learning for students comes from the process of researching and writing a paper that will have direct impact on a current issue amongst Maasai people. The research is approached across disciplines, encouraging RDP students from Environmental Studies, Cultural and Regional Studies, Arts and Letters, and Adventure Education backgrounds to get involved and share their particular expertise.

Through this process, students are able to find deep relevance in their coursework, develop authentic relationships within the community they are visiting, and share the benefits of their educations.

At the end of the long dusty drive, our van pulls up to the County chambers and several eager Maasai representatives in suits greet our group of teachers, students, and Prescott College Board members. We are led into a mahogany-paneled room where we will turn over the culmination of our summer's work to the most powerful and recognized governing body for over half of Maasailand. They have been awaiting our finished product, as the issue at hand has become increasingly urgent since we began our work.

This year, Amboseli National Park itself, with its legendary elephants, rebounding cheetah population, and one of the most photographed horizons on the planet, is at the center of the issue Prescott students were requested to investigate. Last November, President Kibaki proclaimed that the park would be given back to Olkajiado Council, who, in fact, hold the legal title to the park, and therefore to the communities that share their surrounding homes with the wildlife.

The presidential decision was hotly contested, especially by international conservation groups who claimed that Maasai leadership was unfit to man-age the prized park. The local Maasai communities recognized the turnover as a political tactic, but saw the opportunity to readdress the issue of govern-mental land-grabs by fighting for the rightful return of park revenues, which communities have suffered without for the past thirty years.

While international non-governmental organizations waged a million-dollar media campaign against the turnover of Amboseli National Park, PC students combed through the Kenya National Archives, interviewed dozens of Maasai elders, surveyed World Bank water projects, and visited govern-ment schools to help bring Maasai perspectives into the debate.

After weeks of living with Maasai communities, taking classes from Maasai experts, and meeting with Maasai university students, our PC class compiled the research and collaboratively wrote a lengthy report on the his-tory and current status of the Amboseli area.

Sitting in the chambers, there is an air of excitement and profundity as the students realize exactly how their class work is part of a larger social action. After Professor Poole presents the key findings, we hand over the document. The Maasai leadership immediately begins to make phone calls to distribute the findings to generate publicity around the Maasai communities' position on the park turnover, to bolster the Maasai lawyer's current court case against the international NGOs, and to disseminate amongst Parlia-mentarians who review indigenous land rights.

"We have worked with many universities over the years," said Tarayia Ole Kores, Chairman of the Olkajiado County Council, "we have helped many students put together dissertations and get their PhDs, but until today, we have not received any tangible product in return."

The benefits of this collaboration are just as tangible for us. Prescott stu-dents were able to participate in a Nairobi press conference on our research findings, stay with Maasai families and learn about their pastoral land man-agement strategies, and spend time in the Amboseli ecosystem while learn-ing about the land from indigenous experts.

Well beyond the typical safari or field study experience, Prescott College students were able to find deep hope in the ability for partnership between seemingly different communities across the globe. At the end of our meeting with the Olkajiado County Council, RDP student Maria Cunha spoke on behalf of the class saying, "We want to thank you from the bottom of our hearts, for helping us realize what a privilege and gift we have in our educa-tions. We want to thank the Maasai community for empowering us to use our education as a tool for social change."

Leap Straight into the Heart of Horses: Centaur Leadership Services

◇◇◇◇◇◇◇

by Melissa Carey, 2005

This spring, Prescott College unveiled its comprehensive equestrian therapy and learning program, Centaur Leadership Services (CLS). Its director, Paul Smith, has taught equestrian-based courses at Prescott College since 1998. "CLS is set up as an independent program that serves both the Master of Arts Program (MAP) and the undergraduate programs (RDP and ADP), as well as the local community," Smith said.

Steeped in History

The official rebirth of an equestrian program at Prescott College comes steeped in the history of students following the trail of Don Quixote on horseback through Spain, and stories of the days when Prescott College not only had a barn but its own racehorse.

"There was a stable where students could check out horses and go riding in the Dells. I even heard stories of playing polo on the front lawn," Smith said of the original Prescott College campus.

When Prescott College was still in its infancy, work with horses was utilitarian or simply for the joy of it. CLS rekindled that joy and function by providing a space for students to explore the powerful, therapeutic horse-human relationship and by bringing the two together to create personal awareness, shared growth, and academic learning.

"We're working with horses more like a contemplative discipline rather than as a hobby. The goal is to work with horses as a means for us to become more fully human, and more effective in our relationships and lives," Smith said.

Smith is the perfect mascot for the program, part rough-and-tumble cowboy and part sensitive Naropa-trained guy. In his block course, Group

Prescott College Racehorse, 1987

Process for Adventure Educators, he bridges adventure education and human development, teaching his students to understand the horse psyche and herd instinct and encouraging them to transfer that knowledge to their work with humans.

"He's brilliantly aware of people. He uses that brilliance in the right moment to emphasize learning," said RDP student Hanna Soumerai. "He's really good at holding an expectation and seeing his students reach their full potential."

A Long Time Coming

Until 1998, when Smith and Barbara Rector, pioneers of Equine Assisted Mental Health (EAMH), offered Prescott College's first Relational Horsemanship class out of Chapel Rock, it had been over twenty years since the College had taught equine-based programming.

Smith and Maria Sonnet reprised Relational Horsemanship in 2000, and in 2002 the first equine-based Group Process for Adventure Educators class gathered in alumni Leif Hallberg's *(RDP '99, MAP '03)* Scottsdale backyard.

"We were camped around the pool with the grapefruit trees," said Smith. The momentum grew, and in 2003, Hallberg and Laura Brinkerhoff were the first students to graduate from MAP with degrees in counseling psychology concentrating in EAMH.

At present, the program offers the country's only graduate program in counseling psychology with a concentration in EAMH.

A Place to Call Home

One of the program's first priorities is to find a place to call home. According to Smith, while the program has had wonderful success without a dedicated facility and horse herd, the benefits of these for both horse and human will be wide-ranging.

"Last year I had a herd of fourteen and I leased eleven of them from Wyoming for January through May, which worked out great," said Smith. "Having our own facility and our own herd, we can do [the program] at a different level of quality and professionalism. That's what we're working on this year."

Smith is looking for a site that will allow the Program to develop and

Centaur Leadership Services at Prescott College

serve the needs of students, clients, and the community. When fully developed, such a site will include:

- twenty-plus acres dedicated to a horse paddock and pasture that would accommodate a small herd, ideally adjoining public lands;
- rotational pasture and paddock space for up to fifteen horses, a covered arena, round pens, supporting barn and out-building, and a student bunkhouse living quarters.

Horse Programs for the 21ST Century

At present, Centaur Leadership Services offers equine-assisted learning and EAMH programs for community youth, and for undergraduate and graduate students pursuing degrees in counseling psychology with a concentration in EAMH. MAP students intern through CLS's Community Mental Health program, which provides equine-assisted psychotherapy (EAP) to local clients.

EAP combines adventure-based practices with gestalt and animal therapies, bringing a licensed therapist and horse professional together to facilitate therapeutic sessions for clients ranging from adjudicated young adults to at-risk and high-risk youth.

As the graduate program continues to attract interest, the challenge, according to Smith, is to keep growth slow to "keep it from being prescriptive." There are now ten graduate students pursuing a master of arts degree in counseling psychology with a focus in EAMH, and more still in the application process.

MAP Alum and Advisor Laura Brinkerhoff said that the new concentration provides the training necessary for those interested in EAMH to practice in a safe and competent manner.

"There's no certification to work with horses in the mental health field. You've got therapists with no horse training and horse people with no therapy training," she said. "Safety is obviously an important part of the work."

CLS also supports students in the Resident Degree Program (RDP) studying competencies in education, counseling psychology, leadership, and adventure education, in addition to those pursing a bachelor's degree in human development with an emphasis in EAMH.

The Group Processing for Adventure Educators course first held in Leif's backyard in Scottsdale has been fine-tuned and expanded, and for the past two years, the class and a leased herd have spent a month at the Walnut Creek Ranger Station in Williamson Valley learning on 200 acres and the surrounding National Forest land.

"We are living with the horses, feeding them and hearing them at night. Your group is your horses and the people, and there are just so many dynamics there," RDP Student Alan Whitehead said of the winter block course. "I was blown away when we were on Group Process and Paul was teaching all these techniques, because we were really getting into the psyche of the horses to see how they respond."

This past spring at Walnut Creek Ranger Station, Smith and Tim Jordan taught the eighteen-credit People, Animals and Nature course that brought twelve students and fourteen horses together to learn about personality theories, relational horsemanship and ecopsychology. The course took place entirely out at Walnut Creek, where Smith and Jordan encouraged students to explore the connections amongst themselves, the horses, and the earth.

As students did so, the horses served as living, breathing representatives of the natural environment, providing direct feedback, enabling them to develop a greater understanding of who they are as people and to work toward building more sustainable relationships with the natural world.

As the programs continue to grow, they will be one part dusty corral and one part holistic learning. "There is definitely a whole new dimension when you have students interacting with large prey animals that directly respond to both the emotional and physical choices the person makes," Smith said.

PART IV

Money Matters

Being acquainted with the economic history of an institution is crucial to understanding how it developed and the motivations underlying the operational decisions that were made, but inserting money reports, tables and graphs, and explanations tends to disrupt the overall story of the school's philosophical and organizational history. Therefore these three chapters about money are presented separately from the general history of the College.

By Permission of Prescott College Photo Archives

Introduction

◇◇◇◇◇◇◇

Reports of financial history usually make dull reading, but the story of Prescott College's creation, its trials in the fiscal wilderness and its eventual re-emergence, is truly a heroic account. When Franklin Parker invented the slogan "Harvard of the West," he obviously was not relating his vision of Prescott College to the original Harvard's financial status. Established in 1636, the oldest private school in the United States held an endowment of over $25.9 billion at the end of 2005. The stability and wealth of private institutions of higher education increases over time, and their tax-exempt status allows them to easily accumulate endowments and properties as the years go by. New independent colleges like Prescott College usually lack substantial initial endowments and face the critical task of creating a reputation worthy to both attract a regular student clientele and to build and maintain a reliable donor base.

Small private undergraduate colleges like Prescott College exist to provide alternatives to publicly financed schools; that is their most justifiable reason for being. They offer freedom to experiment with new curriculum content and teaching/learning methods, and make highly qualified professors available to teach small classes and tutor independent studies. The small size of these schools allows them to appreciate students as unique individuals, and to involve them in authentic field and laboratory work instead of canned exercises.

Society has created tax-exempt status for schools, as well as for churches, charitable foundations, and so forth. Regulations have been designed to allow donors to deduct the full amount of their gifts from their reported income when paying income taxes. Scholarships, grants, and guaranteed loans are available to qualified students who want or need the advantages private schools offer. Nevertheless, Prescott College has had to struggle financially in order to survive and grow. In this section that history will be traced.

Hundreds of financial documents held in the Sharlot Hall Museum and Prescott College Archives, as well as recent financial reports from the current Business and Development offices, have been examined in preparing these chapters. This financial history stretches from the mid-1950s to the fiscal year ending June 30, 2006. These facts tell an absolutely vital side of the history. Without this knowledge, a reader will be left with many false impressions about what happened and why it happened.

In these sections on money, the financial philosophy and history of Prescott College will be framed in terms of themes, because a strictly chronological presentation becomes too complex to follow. Chapter I relates the early planning and building of the first version of Prescott College and its financial dealings. Chapter II traces several innovations that were designed to create governance and a financing system that would be consistent with the College's educational philosophy. Issues of debt and campus development are intertwined and will be discussed together. Chapter III is dedicated to the crucial process of developing revenues to support the educational program of the College.

TECHNICAL ISSUES IN THE PRESENTATION OF MONEY DATA
The Standard Academic and Fiscal Year

An important technical issue is the presentation and discussion of financial figures in terms of the standard academic/fiscal year. Prescott College has always operated on a year which begins on July 1 and ends on the following June 30. Almost all colleges and other schools employ this academic/fiscal year for both planning and reporting purposes. All full-year financial reports and audits of the College are labeled in a fashion similar to this: "Fiscal year ending June 30, 1999." In this book we have adopted a standard format for indicating academic/fiscal years, for example: "1966-67" or "2004-5." And when the period being presented extends to more than one year, we have used a format similar to this: "1984 through 1996," which is meant to encompass the 1984-85 academic/fiscal year through the 1995-96 year.

Inflation and the Interpretation of Money Data from the Past

Inflation can distort perception of financial history. A new Chevrolet Impala Sedan sold for about $21,000 in 2005, while the comparable 1960 model cost about $3,300. The value of a car to the purchaser had not changed, but the value of the dollar had. A 2005 dollar was worth only 15⅓ cents in 1960 terms. Said another way, a dollar in 1960 could buy as much as $6.53 could buy in 2006. The CPI (Consumer Price Index), issued for every year by the U.S. Department of Labor Statistics, is calculated using such pricing information on thousands of consumer items.

Low, controlled, inflation (the reduction of money's unit value) is a necessary feature of healthy market economies, so that every year since the 1930s

American money has eroded a bit in purchasing power. Inflation would give an increasingly false picture of Prescott College's finances the further back in history one goes. To correct for this distortion, most dollar figures presented in these Money Matters chapters will be given in two forms—the actual amounts in the reports, and those same amounts converted into 2005 values by the CPI index of that year. The CPI multiplier was changing slowly during the 1960s due to low inflation, but began to change more rapidly in the 1970s due to factors like the OPEC oil crisis and the Vietnam War.[86]

Sources of data (as reported in text below)	Year	Actual $ amount at that date	Converted to 2005 value by CPI of that year
Cumerford Study of 1960—fundraising potential in the Southwest	1960	$3,000,000	$19,581,000
Cumerford Study of 1962—funds required to found a top-tier college in Prescott	1962	$5,000,000	$31,905,000
Ultimate goal of Prescott College Founding Fund Local Campaign	1962-66	$5,000,000	$31,135,000
Pledges to Prescott College Founding Fund as of Aug. 29, 1962	1962	$1,048,061	$6,687,677
Estimated cash receipts of Prescott College Founding Fund as of Sept. 1962	1962	$143,490	$915,609
Ford Foundation grant of $15,000 to fund Symposium "Emergence of a Concept"	1963	$15,000	$94,575
Tuition revenues received from 80 charter class students (less discounts).	1966	$109,040	$586,232
Charles F. Kettering Family Foundation matching grants to Prescott College.	1968-71	$600,000	$2,714,940
Overall Expense Budget	1973-74	$2,062,018	$7,751,947
Overall Expense Budget	1977-78	$222,247	$642,332.37
Total Salaries—all divisions	1988-89	$849,321	$1,747,401

Table 6. Updating Dollar Values from Different Years in Prescott College History, Applying the Consumer Price Index (CPI)

Table 6 demonstrates the effect of inflation on the purchasing power of dollars. The items in the left-hand column were taken from tables that will appear throughout the Money Matter chapters that follow in order to illustrate the effects of inflation in real situations. As in the first row (Cumerford Study) $3 million 1960 dollars are equal in purchasing power to almost $20 million in 2005. In other words one 1960 dollar was worth as much as $6.52 was in 2005. As time passed, inflation made a dollar worth less and less, so that in the bottom row a 1988 dollar is only worth $1.57 in 2005 values. In the thirty-year period (1960 to 1989), inflation had eroded the value of dollars so they had one-fourth as much purchasing power. This is important to comprehension of a financial history because older money figures represent much greater values than they seem at first glance. In the case of Prescott College's financial history, the reader should appreciate the financial size of the efforts of previous epochs.

Finances of Original College, 1966 through Fall Semester, 1974

◇◇◇◇◇◇◇

Various knowledgeable educators had offered opinions about how much money would be necessary to establish a major college of the kind conceived by Parker. Their opinions varied widely. Some with more fundraising experience considered $10,000,000 to be a realistic goal. Others with more college administration knowledge thought at least $15,000,000 ($95,715,000 by CPI in 2005 values) would insure the new college had a healthy start.

In a January 1956 meeting held in Phoenix and attended by Parker, the United Church of Christ Homeland Missions Board allocated funds to commission a study that would determine whether the Southwest would support a first-tier private college in the Congregationalist tradition. Dr. Wesley A. Hotchkiss from their New York office recommended the Cumerford Corporation of Kansas City to do the study. He indicated it was an experienced fundraising firm, and his recommendation was accepted. However, subsequent research indicated Cumerford was a new company, and this was one of their first commissions. They were not in a hurry; the research took more than three years. According to Cumerford's report, issued to the Board of Home Missions on September 7, 1960, they had interviewed more than 350 people in Arizona, New Mexico, and Southern California—church ministers, business and professional men and women, the "power structure" of major population centers, corporation executives, foundation heads, and representatives of nearly every level of civic, fraternal, or social life in communities throughout the Southwest. Table 7 outlines their estimates of funds that would be gathered from each class of donor.

Categories by average size of gift	Number of gifts expected in each category	Expected yield in 1960 dollars	Converted to 2005 values as per CPI
$100,000	5	$500,000	$3,265,000
$50,000	20	$1,000,000	$6,527,000
$10,000 or smaller to $1,000	180	$675,000	$4,405,725
$1,000 or smaller to $100	1,500	$575,000	$3,753,025
$100 or smaller	7,000	$250,000	$1,631,750
TOTALS	8,705 gifts	$3,000,000	$19,581,000

Table 7. Predicted Yield from Fundraising for a New College in the Southwest

The study concluded, "Prescott would be an excellent location and … Arizona and the Southwest would be able to support the kind of institution of higher education that could take its place among great schools founded by the Congregationalists."[16, 69, 73]

Cumerford was hired to do a second study in 1961, a "needs assessment" to determine how much would have to be raised to get the College started. This round, they recommended a minimum figure of $4,500,000 to $5,000,000 (equivalent to $31,905,000 in 2005 value) to be raised in a period of one year, starting immediately in 1962. But they acknowledged that $5 million might not provide the cushion needed to build the campus and open the doors.[5, 69, 73]

SEARCHING FOR THE REAL RESULTS OF THE PRESCOTT COLLEGE FOUNDING FUND EFFORTS

The Leadership Council created the Prescott College Founding Fund as a legal financial entity on March 21, 1962, but it was underway earlier. The actual fundraising campaign took place in two phases, the first in the local Prescott area, and the second in the greater Southwest.

Phase I, Prescott Area Campaign, 1962: All of the various consultants and planners agreed that *at least* $1,000,000 ($6,381,000 by 2005 CPI-adjusted values) had to be raised from the Prescott community to start with, before seeking funds from the greater Southwest and elsewhere. This initial effort was most likely funded on credit, because a letter to Vic Lytle from Pioneer

Document and date	Donations and pledges, undifferentiated	Notes regarding both costs and balances	Actual cash balances as per report
Balance sheet of the Fund, dated August 4, 1962	Donations were listed as $65,286 (but it is clear from cash balance they were almost entirely pledges, not cash).	Costs not detailed; however the balance sheet indicates an actual cash deficit of $14,803—plus an obligation on a bank loan of $16,285.	Negative balance (cash & credit deficit) of $31,088.
Founding Fund report dated August 15, 1962.	Income in cash donations of $14,350 (plus in-kind gifts).	Expenses— incidental expenditures of $578. Payments to Cumerford of $7,900 and $6,784.	Negative balance (cash deficit) of $912.
Two Founding Fund reports, dated October 30 and 31, 1962.	Income totaling $78,117 (not clear how much in cash and how much in pledges) which includes $15,000 from Ford Fund secured by Parker for the "Emergence … " conference . Possible gain of $13,779.	Expenditures totaling $64,338.	Taking out the $15,000 earmarked for the Symposium, a cash deficit between (best case) $1,221 and (worst case) negative $80,000.
A Founding Fund report dated September 16, 1963.	Cash receipts of $50,075. Signed pledges of $305,750.	Expenditures were not included.	Actual cash money received, positive balance of $50,075.
OUTCOMES	Impossible to separate cash from pledges accurately. Possible cash receipts $143,490	Since two reports do not indicate fundraising costs, it is impossible to determine the total costs; however, what are detailed total $117,014.	Net cash balance between (best case) positive $16,854 and (worst case) negative $42,000.
TOTAL of all reported donations, undifferentiated and ignoring all costs: $528,578			

Table 8. Four Reports on the Prescott College Founding Fund, August through September 1962

Bank of Prescott, dated February 27, 1962, approves a loan to the College of $10,000 at 6% interest. The local Prescott campaign was launched in late spring or summer (exact date unavailable) with the goal of raising $1 million from the community. Parker introduced the town to his ambitious concept of the "Harvard of the West." Parker's genius for public relations and the enthusiasm of townspeople produced a joyful carnival atmosphere all summer.

In this section, existing reports of the actual results will be presented. Unfortunately the records of the ongoing campaign are fragmentary and incomplete, but they are also revealing.

Table 8 summarizes four reports from late summer found in the archives in files designated Founding Fund. These are quite discouraging, but they are contradicted by other reports. Minutes from a Development Committee meeting held in August report pledges gathered by various town leaders who were volunteers in the effort, giving a different picture.

Donor Level	total $$ pledged	Conversion to 2005 value by CPI
LEADERSHIP: those pledging over $50,000.	$637,475	$4,067,728
ADVANCE: between $20,000 & $49,000.	$284,765	$1,817,085
GENERAL: less than $20,000.	$125,821	$802,864
TOTALS	$1,048,061	$6,687,677

Table 9. Report of Prescott College Founding Fund Pledges, August 29, 1962

Table 9 illustrates the technique that was being used to classify pledges by size and encourage donors to give larger gifts, a common method in fundraising. It is worth mentioning that over 120 large gifts were pledged by individuals, organizations and businesses. In 1962, $20,000 was a substantial gift. Modest houses sold for $20,000, which by CPI would be equivalent to $127,620 in 2005 dollars. It is remarkable, also, that 1,200 pledges were on record at this early date. This total, $1,048,061, appears to be the source of the oft-cited *town legend* that a million dollars was raised in Prescott. This sum, in reality, represents all pledges from everywhere made in 1962, but over two-thirds came from the Prescott area. Nowhere in the record does it say exactly how much of this pledged amount was ever collected in cash, and how much remained unfulfilled pledges. Piecing together figures from several sources, it appears that approximately one-third resulted in money collected within a year, and presumably many of the remaining pledges were collected later.

Counting all donations and pledges—including over $300,000 in cash, vacant lots, mining claims, stocks and bonds, a classic rodeo saddle, a concert piano that needed some refurbishing, a prize calf, and 1,199 pledges totaling $1,048,062—by September 1962 the Founding Fund Campaign could and did claim to have exceeded the goal of $1,000,000, although there was very little money in the bank. Only the cash was in a form that could be spent, and there were costs that had to be paid. Evaluating the outcome of a fundraising campaign is a complex business. Donations and pledges ranged from the symbolic small pledges, up to generous ones including eighty "firm pledges" above $50,000. These donations and pledges were all achieved within a matter of months, illustrating that Prescott did enthusiastically support the founding of Prescott College.

The summary given above presents the clearest figures available for the period, and it is easy to see how one participant (an optimist) might think of these results as signaling a great success. Over a million dollars raised in just one quarter, never mind the fact that most of that amount is in pledges, not cash money. A pessimist might focus on the costs of fundraising—nearly all of the cash received was spent on the campaign. After all that furious effort there remained a cash balance of $16,854 in the bank. Who knew if or when the pledges would be paid. A realist would consider the results in the context of the implicit goal for this three-month period—which would have been one-eighth of $5 million—$625,000 *net cash*.

The early campaign had given the impression that Prescott College would be open to students in 1964. (*It's up to you in '62 to open the doors in '64.*) But it was clear by the end of Phase I that this would not only be unwise, it would be impossible. Titles to the tracts of campus land were still being secured; the first set of architectural plans was not accepted by the Board. New plans for infrastructure and buildings were still in development. Cumerford was hardly geared up for the Southwest regional fundraising campaign, and the Founding Fund was about $4.5 million short of its $5 million goal.

Phase II, The Parker/Cumerford Effort to Raise Funds Outside of Prescott, 1960-65

An early document from Cumerford projects a minimum to be raised by December 1961 to be $2,750,000—and by June 1, 1963, to be $4,000,000. As stated in several places, the ultimate goal was to raise a minimum of $5,000,000 before the opening of the College. It also specified the costs and Cumerford's fees—these ranged from 5.8% to 11% in the different phases of the campaign. Most of the Cumerford records in the archives have to do with fees and expenses, rather than descriptions of ongoing activities or results, but that does not mean there was little activity.[33, 69, 74]

Various fundraising plans developed by Cumerford are archived at Sharlot Hall Museum. One 1962 report states that 300 volunteer leaders had been appointed. It contains a list of "kick off" events and meetings in various locations in Arizona and adjacent states. Many cities and towns are listed, but there is no mention of any funding targets or funds actually gathered. The plan appears to give equal weight to cities like Ajo, Arizona, and Albuquerque, N.M.—or to Los Angeles, California, and Nogales, Arizona. The local chairpersons at most of these locations appear to be affiliated with churches or service organizations like the Rotary Clubs or Chambers of Commerce. Not much contact with the "power structure" is apparent in the plans.[33, 67]

To get the Southwest campaign off the ground, Parker was asked by Cumerford to set up and to run the Phoenix office. This entailed considerable sacrifice for him and his family, but he complied. The archives contain records of fundraising costs, which included renting and setting up an office with typewriters and telephones, providing expense accounts as well as living expenses and salaries for fundraisers and other employees, and printing and advertising. Parker was working with a Cumerford employee, traveling extensively, and serving as a spokesman and fundraiser.

Fundraising costs money, particularly if you hire an inexperienced firm from a different region of the country to do it. In yet another document, Cumerford estimated that fundraising costs would be about 10%, leaving 90% net. Assuming their 1960 estimate, it would cost $300,000 to raise the $3,000,000. That would yield a net of $2,700,000 for the College ($17,739,000 in 2005 value).[74]

Behind the scenes, Cumerford continued negotiating their contract to run the campaign throughout the Southwest.

Over time and with successive proposals and requests, Cumerford negotiated different fees. For example, a June 25, 1962, letter suggests a fee of $144,500 plus $46,300 living expenses for their fundraising employees living in Phoenix. Then, in a letter dated August 22, 1962, they requested an additional $70,000 for a fundraiser to reside in Prescott. There are four more reports and letters from the Cumerford Corporation in the archives, each of

---

First phase assessment and organizational budget, $54,000.
Local fundraising, $77,000.
Hiring directors for Public Relations and Pre-Campaign, and also four Associates, $159,000.
Total budget and fees of **$290,000.**

Table 10. Cumerford (Fundraising Corp.) Estimate of Their Expenses and Fees, December 1960 through February 1963.

which states a different fee, in *diminishing* amounts. The contract eventually signed between Cumerford and the Founding Committee, dated September 15, 1962, states that the total campaign budget would be $93,600, and that the fundraising area would include Arizona, Southern California, New Mexico, Nevada, and Western Texas.[33, 69, 74]

However unproductive the fundraising endeavor directed by Cumerford had been, an agreement, dated September 16, 1963, extended their services to March 26, 1964, and reduced their fee to $91,800. Almost immediately this agreement was superseded by another agreement that extended the contract through April 24, 1964, and appears to have further reduced their fee to $56,650. (However, it is unclear whether the constant diminution of fees resulted from new calculations, or simply reflected payments having been made thus reducing the balance.)[69, 74]

The files indicate that Parker had made some inroads in Phoenix and Tucson before he was effectively eliminated from leadership by Nairn and the Board. But the record does not indicate that Nairn followed up on these leads. It could be that a new person on the scene, a businessman named Frank Mertz, tried to follow up, because various letters sent out by Mertz display a letterhead indicating he was the Director of Development. This was only one of several hats Mr. Mertz was wearing; memos and reports from 1965 forward suggest he was also serving as head of the Business Office, and was in charge of some campus operations.[24, 67]

Cumerford and Parker Fundraising, Gross and Net Results

The Founding Fund had commissioned a local auditing firm, Williams and Co., to conduct a final audit, which was issued as a report in October of 1966, eighteen months later. In his cover letter, CPA Williams explained that his firm had "requested confirmation of pledges receivable at June 30, 1965 only" and they had not made allowances for depreciation of the educational plant. The report is very straightforward and easy to understand. For purposes of this writing, various items such as in-kind donations and deferred maintenance costs (which conveniently cancel out) have been ignored.

In other words, after three years of intense fundraising efforts the campaign had a *net* gain of only about $170,000 (i.e. architect's fees paid plus cash in the bank). The report also shows confirmed pledges of $1,091,369, an amount similar to the 1962 pledges, but of course it would not be an identical list of donors since many pledges had been collected and new ones made. These results must be considered in the context of the original target of $5 million in cash, (spendable) money to be raised.

Dr. Parker and the many others who had worked so hard during these years must have been keenly disappointed with the audit results. In a memo

Based on Williams Co. Audit, October 1996
Gross cash donations for the entire 5-year fundraising effort: $568,236.
Money-raising costs for the campaign: < $398,938 >
(mostly living expenses and salaries of the professional fundraisers hired by Cumerford Corporation).
Architecture fees paid: < $126,658 >
Net cash balance as of June 30, 1965: $42,640.

Note: These figures from the accountants' audit correspond well with the total of balances of $33,371 in seven bank accounts at that are reported in a budget report. (The discrepancy of a little over $9,000 is accounted for by other small credits and costs detailed in the report.) This is a report on the Development Fund only; the College had other assets, including the land and buildings, etc.

Table 11. Net Cash Balance as of June 30, 1962

to Nairn and the Board, Parker acknowledged, "We knew we should have had $5,000,000," but Parker felt vindicated in the fact that he had turned over the reins with approx $1,090,000 in pledges—$880,000 of which he felt he was personally involved in securing. And the College now had the beginnings of a campus valued at over $4 million. Here again we see enthusiasm overshadowing real accounting results. The campus was already heavily mortgaged, and that is how it had been built. Most of the actual dollars raised had been spent for the fundraising campaigns. Pledges are like good intentions, but they are not yet not spendable money until they are paid.

Before leaving this part of the financial history, it is appropriate to make some general observations about fundraising. In such campaigns, observers tend to keep their eyes on the gross amount donated, and that is what is reported in the headlines. But it is the *net gain*, after costs have been retired, that is important to experienced fundraisers—spendable money. They have to be concerned with the *ratio* of the campaign's costs to its yield. Unfortunately the final ratio for the Founding Fund cannot be calculated with any degree of certainty because over a million dollars in pledges were not yet collected. On the bright side, experience had shown that a significant portion of the pledges would turn into money eventually.

A more philosophical view should take into account that thousands of people had learned of this future-oriented experiment in higher education and had given or pledged donations, small or large, with good will. Good will is also an important benefit to an organization that promotes social change.

Acquiring the Land for the Campus

Beginning in the late 1950s, as town leaders and the state and national church leaders became involved in evaluating the possibility of a new college in the Congregationalist tradition in Prescott, the topic of campus location came up. They would not repeat the problems that led Grand Canyon College to move to Phoenix. An interesting site was the old Fort Whipple barracks rifle range about six miles north of Prescott.

Parker remembered it this way: "The first negotiation began when we asked a sergeant in the National Guard how often they used the rifle range and land. He told us it was cheaper to send the Prescott unit to the Phoenix range than to maintain the one in Prescott. From there, the Governor got word to the National Guard. We found out the range didn't belong to the National Guard but to the Army, and in further negotiations we learned that all branches of the military had to say they didn't want the land."[67,78]

In another document, Parker continued the account: "Land acquisition started with a letter, dated Nov. 25, 1959, from Governor Fannin, although there had been verbal discussion before. The college site is part of the old Whipple barracks rifle range near Prescott. It was relinquished to the Interior Department by the Army earlier this year."[33]

When the Leadership Council was set up in 1962, Parker took charge of academic issues and fundraising, while Vic Lytle, who was equally active in founding the College, organized efforts to secure the campus land and plan the infrastructure and physical plant. However, it was not just a two-man show; many Prescott leaders were involved, and eventually state and national leaders were important contributors. Securing the land was not a simple matter. Several complications arose and were eventually resolved. The whole process required over two years.

As noted above, it took some digging to find out which agencies actually controlled title to the land. The largest piece, over two hundred acres, apparently was held by the Department of Defense, which had approved its use as a rifle range by the Arizona National Guard. But the DOD could not "give" it to a city or a private educational institution; first it had to be yielded to the Department of the Interior and become surplus public land. Each branch of the military had to certify that they did not want it, which was accomplished. Then the College had to make application to the Department of the Interior. The land was first appraised at $1,000 per acre.

President Kennedy took office in 1961 and appointed Stewart Udall as Secretary of the Department of the Interior. Udall promulgated a new policy for sale of up to 640-acre tracts of surplus federal land to agencies that would use it for education, recreation, and other public benefits. Under this new directive, the price of such land would be only $2.50 per acre, which put it within reach for the College. "The way was cleared for purchase of the land two weeks ago when Interior Secretary Stewart Udall altered government policy." Fred J. Weiler, state director of U.S. Bureau of Land Management's Phoenix office, informed the College that the schedule lowers land costs for public purpose projects, removing what had often been a financial barrier to a community project.[48]

George Rothfuss, Prescott Chamber of Commerce president, announced that the Chamber would pay up to $1,600 toward campus acquisition from a fund originally raised for Grand Canyon College. A dinner was held on January 11, 1962, at which Governor Fannin presented to the College a patent for 160 acres on behalf of BLM, stating that he was "proud of the leadership shown in pursuit of the college." He then "praised the human resources backing the project."[31, 79]

Eventually, under Lytle's leadership, the Board purchased or was gifted several pieces of land totaling nearly a full section, 640 acres (a square mile). The largest portion was from the Department of the Interior, through the Phoenix BLM Office. Forty acres that were key to the integrity of the campus were purchased through the Department of Health, Education, and Welfare, and some small private plots were donated or sold to the College by adjacent ranchers to even out the borders. However, there were two problems that arose before the campus tract was secure.

Yavapai County and the State of Arizona were engaged in enlarging or paving Willow Creek Road, which passed through the southeast corner of the campus tract. The College gladly agreed to cede many acres for the wider right of way. Another complication arose when the County wanted the College to also cede the acreage that lay east of the newly designated county road. It appears that the College did comply, so that the campus site eventually comprised 483 acres.[49]

The second problem was much more difficult to resolve. There were forty acres that all concerned considered essential to the campus which were released to the College by the U.S. Department of Health, Education, and Welfare (HEW) under some explicit guidelines. One requirement was that the College had to break ground and begin construction within the year, or title to the property would revert to HEW. On August 6, 1963, John Gifford, director of the Western Region of HEW, with offices in San Francisco, wrote to the College attorney, John Favour, informing the Board that HEW intended to take action to rescind the title to forty acres in the center of the proposed campus because the College had delayed building on it. Favour responded on August 8, explaining that the College was not granted title for five months after the letter of intent was given, and that construction could not begin in any case because the entrance to the campus tract was blocked by Yavapai County road construction. Gifford did not credit these excuses and informed the College he still intended to start proceedings to take back the property.

A number of remedies were proposed to HEW in successive letters, which were all rejected. Favour, the Board, and all of those who had been involved in securing this land were indignant and determined to overcome this obstacle. Eventually they appealed directly to Arizona Senator Carl Hayden and Secretary of the Interior Stewart Udall, as well as various state and local officials. An accommodation was worked out in which the College agreed to certain deadlines:

(a) On or before March 31, 1964 – selection and employment of design architect. In compliance, the College contracted with John Carl Warnecke and Associates of San Francisco.

(b) On or before May 31, 1964 – Selection and employment of Academic Dean. A letter from the College to Gifford certified that Dr. Mackenzie Brown had been appointed Dean.

(c) On or before October 31, 1964 – Completion and approval of plans of initial buildings to be constructed and a call for bids. The College sent Gifford a copy of a letter dated October 2, 1964, from Warnecke and Associates indicating that a "Pre-planning Report" had been presented to the Board and was adopted October 23, 1964. Warnecke had already informed HEW that the previous schedule was impossible—more time was needed—and a letter dated October 2, 1964, had laid out a new schedule for planning, drawings, etc., almost as it occurred.

(d) On or before November 30, 1964—Letting of contract for initial construction, and

(e) On or before December 31, 1964—Commencement of initial construction. The College did let a contract on August 21, 1965 (eight months past the HEW deadline), to Tanner Bros. Construction Company for "site development."

On March 6, 1964, the HEW Office in San Francisco sent Prescott College a notice by certified mail that upon receipt of $200, the forty-acre piece of land that had been withdrawn would be restored to the College.[48, 67]

Parker later commented, "Both Governor Fannin and Barry Goldwater gave lots of help in these negotiations. ... Stewart Udall was a great help ... he had appointed as his legal counsel an Arizona boy, Max Edwards, who had

Aerial View of the Original Campus

lived in Prescott at one time. So a letter from Fannin to Edwards brought rapid results. Morris Udall also helped a lot at the last in bringing the final results. In fact, there was excellent cooperation from all." In another place, it says "Sen. Carl Hayden also got pulled in."[33, 48, 67]

In the process of fighting this battle with HEW, the town leaders were reenergized and recommitted. The records seem to indicate that it was these HEW deadlines that also induced the Board to mortgage the campus land to the Valley Bank in order to make planning and construction possible within (or close to) the deadlines. This crisis moreover seems to have given birth to a group of wealthy individuals within the Board that came to be called "the Mortgage Trust."[67]

Nairn Takes Charge

When Dr. Ronald Nairn assumed the presidency of Prescott College in June of 1965 he had a rude shock as he examined the books and bank accounts. Adding together all accounts, there was only $33,000 available ($202,537 in 2005 value by CPI). With this he had a staff to pay, a campus to finance and finish building, a faculty to hire, and a curriculum to design in the next year—before the College would see a dollar of tuition money. The million dollars in pledges had to be collected, and that still would not provide enough. The various committees had been working hard and presented him with sheaths of plans, but few concrete accomplishments. The new set of architectural drawings and specifications were nearly completed, but needed to be reviewed before construction contracts could be let. Nairn imposed an austerity regime as indicated in this memo of July 14, 1965, which read: "Soon Prescott College will promulgate its operating budget. This must be allied with the capital commitments arising from the other immediate Problem of plant activation. I need not tell you that relative to the expenditures which lie before us, our financial resources are desperately slender."[28, 67]

The College Newsletter, *Prescott College Progress*, soon announced twenty-two members of the President's Council, which was headed by Senator Barry Goldwater, a very popular Arizona politician who was the Republican candidate for U.S. President in 1964. Twelve had been Symposium participants and the ten new members were mostly from business, industry, and government. The list is very impressive, but there are no records in the Archives of them ever meeting or taking group action. A few of them helped Nairn open doors to money, and also to publicity.

An impressive inauguration ceremony for Nairn was held on campus October 23, 1966. It also presented the College and its students, faculty, and facility to the world of higher education. Among those in attendance were the dean of the College of Liberal Arts, University of Arizona; the presidents of Arizona State University and Northern Arizona University as well as delegates from twenty-three other colleges and universities throughout the nation. Board Chairman Dr. Lawrence M. Gould and President Nairn dedicated the College to its purpose and its future.

The relationship with Senator Goldwater was cultivated by Nairn and the Board. His picture appears in several news articles and public relations pieces by the College. In the archives there is some correspondence between Nairn and Senator Goldwater, but it does not mention actual money. Goldwater may have made small financial contributions, but his main role was to provide visibility and high-level contacts for Nairn—entree to the state and national "power structure" that Parker had been unable to crack. So long as Nairn was able to create and hold up the image of Prescott College as a unique, important, and very high-quality educational experiment, he was quite successful in raising larger gifts.[44, 79]

The scope of his fundraising vision is contained in a letter to James Patrick, president of Valley National Bank and chairman of the Development Committee, dated July 12, 1965, just two weeks after Nairn arrived in Prescott. It was written ostensibly to recommend an academic timetable for recruiting personnel and students, but his main purpose was to specify the campus buildings he wanted, and to give estimates of their costs: Women's Dorm, $260,370; Men's Dorms (2 of them) $351,790; Commons, $416,500; Auditorium, $336,400—$1,365,060 in total ($8,378,738 in 2005 value by CPI). He also mentioned architect's fees and other minor costs. He explained he was sending these figures because Patrick was "the Board member respon-

Year	Overall Budget	Adjusted to 2005 Values by CPI	Money from Tuitions	Adjusted to 2005 Values by CPI	Percentages of Budget from Tuitions
1966-67	$539,200	$2,898,924	$109,040	$586,237	20.22%
1967-68	$667,744	$3,459,813	$266,772	$1,382,238	39.95%
1968-69	$1,671,981	$8,277,133	$368,668	$1,825,089	22.05%
1969-70	$1,424,217	$6,749,843	$462,269	$2,190,846	32.46%
1970-71	$2,367,721	$10,713,669	$512,582	$2,319,376	21.65%
1971-72	$2,638,863	$11,624,947	$560,992	$2,471,330	21.26%
1972-73	$2,462,782	$10,176,785	$1,052,800	$4,350,413	42.75%
1973-74	$2,062,018	$7,751,947	$1,036,350	$3,896,053	50.26%

Table 12. Percentage of Yearly Budgets Supported by Tuitions at the "Old" College, 1966 through December 1974

sible for fund raising"—and suggested "selling these buildings" to be named after donors.[26]

TUITIONS, 1966 THROUGH FIRST SEMESTER OF 1974

The Charter Class had eighty students, who each paid $1,450 for the year's tuition. There were also dormitory and food service charges, but the income was mostly offset by the costs. A very small number of discounts were awarded, so that the gross tuition income was $109,040. Nairn had been predicting 250 students in the charter class. Financially that number would have been a godsend, but in the Fall of 1966 the College was really not ready to receive many more than eighty students. However, it is instructive to see how 250 students would have altered the financial situation of the College in its first year.

The 1966 budget (excluding campus building costs) was $539,200 (equivalent in 2005 dollars to $2,898,901). Eighty students did bring in $109,040, which paid only 20.22% of the budget; 250 students would have brought in $430,160 which would have paid 79.8% of the budget. In other words, with 250 students, the percentages of the budget paid by tuition and from fundraising would have been reversed. As it stood, Nairn and the trustees had to raise almost 80% of the College budget, $430,160 (in 2005 dollars, $2,312,669). That is a tall order for the first year of an infant College. A letter dated June 9, 1967, from Gould, chairman of the Board, to Lytle, says, "The College had a brilliant opening year, but must raise $600,000 by August 1st, 1967." (This date was less than two months away.)[71]

The College Exceeded Its Budget from the First Day

With all of the fundraising contacts and activities described above, one might think that the College's financial prospect was assured, but that was not the case. Money was coming in from a number of sources and going out even more quickly.

Even a few months before the College was scheduled to open, there were still dissenting voices. In a letter to the Board dated November 17, 1965, Hotchkiss, representing the Homeland Ministries, laid out fiscal projections for the academic year 1966-67. He noted that the approved Prescott College Budget showed an anticipated operational deficit of $305,500; institutional tuition grants (discounts) of $35,000; and debt service on a mortgage of the land and physical plant of $78,700—thus creating a total deficit of $419,200 ($2,573,049 in 2005 value by CPI). Fundraising would have to supply $420,000 for 1966-67. Then he estimated that an additional $904,300 would have to be raised for the following 1967-68 year. Speaking for the United Church Board, he reiterated their original position that the College should not open unless it had $4,000,000 in cash or firm pledges.[71]

Of course, at this point it would have been nearly impossible to stop the train, which was hurtling down the track, even though its coal box was practically empty. This was probably the logic of the board of the Southwest Conference of the Church, as they passed a resolution on March 7, 1966, authorizing the first $50,000 payment on their pledge. In the resolution, they outline the College's accomplishments: (a) in-hand pledges of more than $1,000,000; (b) a library of 25,000 volumes; (c) site work on infrastructure, (d) twenty buildings costing $400,000; and (e) half of the charter class recruited. The campus building was underway, mostly financed by mortgaging the land as well as interim construction loans.

Even though there were no students on campus, 1965-66 was a furiously busy year. The second phase of building steamed along. The charter class of students was recruited and admitted. Mackenzie Brown and others were hiring faculty, while Mertz was building an administrative organization. Nairn, in addition to developing his Board and President's Council, was walking tall in his fundraising, courting his donor base and soliciting from notable foundations and private philanthropists. Several significant gifts were announced.

Kettering and Other Major Donors

There were other financial developments during the first operational year. The Church Missionary Board did pay a $50,000 installment to the College in April of 1967. George Farnham, a major benefactor, provided collateral for borrowing an additional $100,000—this was to be "matching." The Board authorized $40,000 for a president's house to be built on campus. It is not specified in the Archives whether the president's house was to be paid for out of the general fund or from new financing.

To achieve the level of fundraising suggested, it was necessary to recruit new financial supporters and Board members who had hefty financial capabilities. Nairn sought to create a network of new contacts with substantial means. On October 22, 1967, the full Board met in an all-day session, and three new members were introduced—a former director of the Barrow Neurological Institute, a prominent cattleman and civic leader, and Charles F. Kettering II. The announcement in Progress stated, "Mr. Kettering, who has a deep understanding and concern for education, is Vice President of the C. F. Kettering Foundation," and adds, "All of these men bring vigor and expertise to their relationship with the College and the Board."[44, 79]

Three gifts totaling $600,000 had been given by the Kettering Family Foundation; $250,000 of this had to be matched on a 2:1 ratio, with the object the raising of $1 million for the College. Mr. and Mrs. George R. Farnham gave $250,000. A $25,000 challenge grant was made by Mr. and Mrs. Harold James of Prescott, and was matched by local individuals. These gifts qualified the College for another matching gift of $75,000 from a Texas foundation. The Scaife Family of Pittsburgh, Pa., contributed $150,000. Mrs. H. H. d'Autremont of Tucson contributed over $100,000. No doubt there were other gifts that do not show up in the Archives.[45, 72]

Charles F. Kettering II inherited a major fortune from his grandfather, Charles F. Kettering, who had been the director of research for General Motors and the holder of over 300 patents on automotive components. He and his family funded the Sloan-Kettering Biomedical Institute and Cancer Research Center, developed the Kettering University, and created the Kettering Family Foundation, which he managed. They had sponsored and funded several large-scale studies related to education and were interested in incorporating the principles of the Human Potential Movement into higher education.

Kettering supported Nairn's fundraising plans, and he finally joined the Prescott College Board of Trustees in 1968. Although records are incomplete, it was announced that his foundation contributed $600,000 to the College; there may have been additional grants. It was generally believe that he had guaranteed to support the establishment of the College up to $5 million. He was killed in a tragic accident on December 12, 1971. Subsequently the Kettering Family Foundation withdrew any pledges or guarantees to the College and withdrew from any further association with it. Within a few months another major donor and leader of the trustees, George Farnham, died of cancer. These losses were demoralizing and knocked the financial foundation from under Nairn's grand plan for the Prescott Institutions.[4]

First Balance Sheets in 1966

Two months before the first students were to arrive, a new balance sheet for the College was issued on June 30, 1966. Its importance lies in the fact that it shows the real financial picture facing the College at the beginning of its first teaching year. Considerable progress had been made, but the financial situation was still tense. Available in the bank for all operations was $152,008—adequate for two months, at best. There were also salable but not very liquid assets, including off-campus lots, mining claims, and stocks, valued at $55,154. The endowment, which could not be spent, consisted of $27,648 on deposit, and stocks valued at $100,000. Pledges of $1,630,330 were on the books, and experience indicated they could possibly yield a third of that amount in a year, with cultivation. The report indicated that in the past year the College had received and expended $914,228 in donations restricted for campus development. Non-cash assets—campus land, buildings and equipment, and furniture—were valued at $894,228, which was less than the amount already spent on construction. The planned campus buildings and infrastructure were less than 50% completed, so that fundraising and mortgage borrowing were being pursued vigorously. Finally, the report indicated that the College had borrowed $100,000 from Valley National Bank.[20]

On September 26, 1966, the Charter Class commenced its studies at Prescott College. Nairn boasted, "The students are bringing remarkable maturity to their studies, to the campus community, and to the honor system which underlies all aspects of life at Prescott College."[44, 79]

The Prescott College operating budget analysis after the first year—July 1, 1966, to June 30, 1967—was prepared by Frank Mertz, the new head of the Business Office. It is twenty-five pages of figures, the first such detailed budget in the record, and is very revealing. Table 13 summarizes the essential figures.

Further explaining Mertz' report, the overall size of the College operational budget had been approved to be $482,000 for the first operational year, 1966-67. At the conclusion of the fiscal year, income had fallen short of the budgeted amount by $148,000, while costs had exceeded the budget by $57,000, thus creating a total deficit of approximately $205,000. Revenues and gifts intended to support the operation of the College brought in only 52% of the budget, and the rest would have to be raised from gifts for campus building or borrowed on the basis of equity. The report mainly dealt with the College operations; however, there is an unsigned hand-written note on the

Net deviation from approved budget, 1966-67

On the INCOME side:
    1) Tuitions & Fees (budgeted $191,750,
    but received only $113,802) deficit of $77,948
    2) Pledges and Other Gifts (budgeted $239,750
    but received only $169,638) deficit of _____$70,112
    Under-funding of approved budget total deficit of $148,060

On the COST side:
    1) Academic Costs, including library, exceeded budget by $12,400
    2) Student Service came in less than budgeted by   <$12,350>
    3) Administrative Costs exceeded budget by $13,300
    3) General Operations and Building & Grounds
    seriously overran the amount budgeted by _____$44,280
    Overspending beyond approved budget: $57,630

Net deviation from approved budget: deficit of   <$205,690>

Table 13. Net Deviation from Approved Budget, 1966-67 Fiscal Year[21, 67]

last page relating to the capital campaign for the campus construction. It says, "Actually $599,652 has been received in payments *or pledges*, but $505,652 is needed to complete the capital obligation."[21, 67]

If less than half the pledges received were actually paid that year, as in previous years, it can be assumed that the difference had to have been made up by borrowing. It appears that adding together the operational deficits in the College's budget and those of the capital budget—campus construction costs—there was a total deficit for the year of between $500,000 and $600,000.

Figures on various Archive documents vary considerably regarding costs of building the campus. The clearest version comes from a report issued in 1966.

Table 14 does not represent completion of all the planned facility. A June 1966 newsletter indicates plans were on the drawing board for more buildings and facilities to be ready by August 15, 1967, for housing and instruction of the 1967 enrollment. It went on to promise, "This is part of an eight-year construction program to enable the College to grow to its ultimate enrollment of 1800."[44, 79]

Land	$224,372
Construction	$1,066,937
Equipment	$168,559
Total	$1,459,868

(converted to 2006 values, $7,848,688*)

Note: The Construction item is further broken down as follows: Lecture-Seminar Bldg., $347,686; Residential Halls (10), $250,000; Chemistry Building, $35,000; Administration Building, $30,000; Carpet $60,000; Theater Seats, $18,500; Audio-Visual System, $12,000; Underground Electrical, $35,000; Gas Installation, $15,000; and Miscellaneous, $120,415; Architects Fees, $40,000; Furniture, $92,000; Landscaping, $10,000.

*If these costs seem to be amazingly low, the reader must remember they represent 1965 dollars. The CPI multiplier for the year 1966 is 5.3763, yielding a contemporary value of nearly eight million dollars.

Table 14. Prescott College Physical Plant, Initial Expenditures[3, 32]

A document dated June 1967 titled *Cash Flow Analysis,* prepared by Mertz, was issued after the first instructional year. It is quoted in full:

"We have a commitment from the Valley National Bank to borrow up to $650,000.00 using the stock of Mr. George Farnham and the anonymous benefactor as collateral. As of May 31, 1967, we had drawn $125,000 of these funds leaving a balance of $525,000 still available.

Other income expected during the summer months:

(1) Minor student fees $15,000.

(2) Payment on pledges $20,000.

(3) Federal Construction Grant $128,000.

"The Federal Construction Grant will be drawn on a percentage basis as the work proceeds. Therefore, the total funds needed by August 1 should be approximately $536,000. We will have about $600,000 in income, leaving a net of $64,000 going into August.

"The only additional income we can project is the balance of the Federal Grant, i.e. $88,000. Therefore, the very minimum we must have in cash for August and September is $425,000.

"It must be pointed out that:

(1) If we don't raise the minimum, WE ARE OUT OF BUSINESS.

(2) If we merely raise the minimum, we have used up all of our collateral and therefore have no more flexibility. We would also incur high interest rates which would add approximately $40,000 more to our operating budget.

"Simply meeting the minimum is fine, provided that the entire $1,268,601 is available prior to December 30, 1967."[10]

OPERATING A COLLEGE WHILE BUILDING A CAMPUS

The financial history of the College between the years of 1965-75 is very difficult to understand or to portray coherently in summary. The first complication arises from the fact that there were two intertwined projects underway: (1) the financing and building of a campus with its attendant fundraising through grants and gifts, and (2) the operation of a College. Each had its own financial life, but in the archival record they are intertwined. Money was transferred from one project to the other at regular intervals, making it hard to follow.

A further complication occurred when Prescott College, Inc., was converted into a legal entity called the Prescott Institutions for the school years 1971-72 and 1972-73. This new structure had four semi-independent divisions, each with its own set of books. They were: Prescott College, the Leadership Institute, the Schole, and the Corporate Center. During these two years, tuition revenues and fees, gifts and grants, and auxiliary earning were distributed among the four centers in ways that seem somewhat arbitrary, and the same is true regarding expenses.

The accounting problem was again compounded in 1973-74 when the trustees decided to reverse the action, to consolidate the institutions and regain the organization's original name, Prescott College, Inc. At this time the bookkeeping of the four institutions was recombined, as well as the academic and management functions. A final complication in understanding the finances arises because some of the financial records of this period have been sealed until the year 2064 at the request of those who donated their records to the Sharlot Hall Museum.

Despite all of these complications, a thorough study of the audits and budgets that are available for these years does yield an overall picture of the financial history. The following two tables represent an attempt to disentangle the operational side of running a college from the building and developing of a campus.

YEAR	Earned by College from tuitions, etc.	Gifts/ grants for operations (not campus)	Total money intake of College	Total year's expenditure for College	Yearly balances (sadly all deficits)	Yearly deficits as % of total expenditure
1965-66	$0	$175,183	$175,183	$175,183	$0	0
1966-67	$113,802	$230,000	$343,802	$539,200	-$195,398	36%
1967-68	$295,750	$190,000	$485,750	$667,744	-$181,994	27%
1968-69	$297,479	$122,718	$420,197	$1,156,984	-$736,787	64%
1969-70	$396,273	$342,232	$738,505	$1,296,951	-$558,446	43%
1970-71	$594,704	$300,000	$894,704	$1,467,907	-$573,203	39%
1971-72	$690,000	$1,043,167	$1,733,167	$2,543,824	-$810,657	32%
1972-73	$958,266	$209,349	$1,167,615	$2,247,415	-$1,079,800	48%
1973-74	$928,856	$255,000	$1,183,856	$2,362,018	-$1,178,162	50%
1974sem1	$500,000	$40,000	$540,000	$1,368,202	-$828,202	61%
TOTALS	**$4,275,130**	**$2,692,466**	**$6,967,596**	**$12,282,043**	**-$5,314,447**	**43%**

Table 15. "Old" College Revenues and Deficits, 1966 through 1975[32]

Table 15 summarizes the essential financial facts related to Prescott College as an ongoing educational enterprise. On the income side are monies received from tuitions and fees, net profits from auxiliary enterprises (e.g. dormitories, food services, bookstore, public events), and yearly totals of unrestricted gifts and grants to the College that were intended for educational operations (not targeted to campus enhancement). A curious income item in 1968-69 came from "borrowing" $55,000 from the College's endowment capital.[66]

The yearly costs of delivering services include faculty, administrative and staff salaries, transportation, communications and utilities, food services in the commons, dormitories, and hundreds of other costs, large and small, that are consumed in the normal operation of a college. The tables speak for themselves in showing that in every year since the College opened to students (1966) it ran a deficit. The cumulative deficit for the decade reached well over $5 million, which is about 43% of the total budget, indicating just how much of each year's expenditures would have had to come from somewhere else.

The 43% overall deficit raises two questions. Why was this deficit situation allowed to continue year after year? And, where did the money come from to keep the operation going for nearly a decade?

As to the first question, there are many reasons for subsidizing a new school. If tuitions had been set at too high a level, perhaps student recruitment would have suffered. Well-established schools have built up a clientele and so they are operating at full capacity, which theoretically brings in enough money to pay the bills. During the first years of any new financial entity there is a learning curve and many adjustments have to be made. As discussed above, the first budget turned out to be very much out of balance, and that can be attributed to inexperience. Yet little was done in subsequent years to remedy the deficit by increasing tuitions or enrollments. There was planning for increasing enrollment up to 1,800 students, but the student body grew hardly at all for five consecutive years. Lack of revenue was apparent; however—in the case of Prescott College—there was an even more potent factor having to do with financial philosophy. There are two approaches to creating a new financial entity—whether a company or a college. The conservative way is to build slowly and usually painfully, making sure the needed money is in hand before launching new efforts. The more daring way is to create something excellent on the risk that financing will appear. "Build it and they will come," as the saying goes. President Nairn was of the second mind. He had great confidence in the marketability of the Prescott College concept to philanthropists, and also much confidence in himself as a fundraiser. Every year the Board would authorize a budget that was out of balance (i.e., it had a line

	Gifts restricted for campus development	Growing campus debt— by mortgaging	Appraised or estimated campus value for year	Transfer of unexpended plant funds
1965-66	$763,335	$100,000	$914,228	
1966-67	$599,653	$350,000	$1,771,969	unknown
1967-68	unknown	$970,175	$3,035,591	661,246
1968-69	$759,348	$1,454,541	$3,599,399	639,210
1969-70	unknown	$1,808,483	$4,005,926	414,447
1970-71	unknown	$2,819,500	$4,812,024	unknown
1971-72	unknown	$3,459,000	$5,236,676	9,257
1972-73	unknown	$3,694,600	$5,275,138	unknown
1973-74	unknown	$3,985,000	$5,300,000	unknown
1974 sem1	unknown	$4,358,000	$5,300,000	unknown
	incomplete	not cumulative	not cumulative	incomplete
TOTALS	$2,122,336	$4,358,000	5,300,000	unknown
in 2005 dollars by CPI	$7,942,206	$16,308,508	$19,833,660	

Table 16. "Old" College Operating Deficits Met by Mortgaging Campus[66]

for half a million dollars or more on the *income side* for anticipated gifts). This was not so irresponsible as it may seem in hindsight, because they always had sufficient pledges in hand to cover their deficits. The budgets and audits both show gift pledges as uncollected obligations, as though they were so secure that they could already be added to the bottom line. However, as mentioned several times, their record of collecting pledges was that they eventually collected no more than a third of those pending in any given year.

Deficit Financing by Mortgaging Campus Asset

As to the second question, of where the money came from to keep the College going: The audits show that nearly every year's deficits were covered by transfers from the campus/plant funds to the operational budget. The figures reporting how much money went to contracts and services to build and maintain the large and spread-out facilities are difficult to interpret forty years later. This is not said to hint at any misappropriation, but simply because some of the old records have been lost or sealed, and the costs of building the campus and operating the College are intertwined. The picture that emerges is that most of the campus land was made available to the College at low or no cost by government agency grants, and the rest was paid for by donations. The infrastructure, buildings, and equipment were also largely paid for by large gifts, but were then almost immediately mortgaged for their full value, and even above their market value.

Through various perfectly legal budget manipulations, money borrowed to create the campus found its way into the operational budgets of the College. Considering the whole decade as an input-output system, the only mystery is that between the costs of operation of the school and the building of the campus, there appears to have been about two million dollars provided that can't be identified as to source. Nairn and the Board appeared to have raised or donated much of this money, and the sealed records at Sharlot Hall Museum would explain at least some of the mystery. It is also probable that money was budgeted which was never spent. And it is certain that a few hundred thousand dollars were tied up in the bankruptcy. In any case, it is a happy outcome that the books ultimately show a positive picture and there is no need to account for a disappearance of funds (which is the more common case when a bankruptcy occurs).

The positive implication of these funds being funneled into operations is that the students were getting a high-priced education at a considerable discount. In every year, the students were paying less than half the cost of the education they were receiving. For example in the 1971-72 academic year, each student paid $2,100 in tuition, while the College expended $5,915 to supply that student with educational services. Some of the advantages this provided were small classes with excellent professors, a high-quality library that was open twenty-four hours every day, extensive opportunities for field and laboratory work, art and photography facilities, wilderness orientation for new students and many outdoor activities throughout the Southwest and northwest Mexico for all students, and a large natural campus with a field house, auditorium, swimming poor, polo/soccer field, and stables.

Unfortunately, this high level of service for such a low tuition was not sustainable, and covering deficits by mortgaging the campus was certainly not a wise policy. One might ask why something in the formula was not changed. The truth was it would not be so easy to do so, and like the fabled bumblebee the College was already in the air and flying—for a while—even though its wings were too small.

The original plan was to increase the student body quickly to provide economies of scale, but facilities were still being built. Tuitions could have been increased, and they were in fact doubled toward the end of the nine-year period. Instead of building a student body of 1,800 by then, which was the original plan, the College student body was still only 450 in its eighth year. Rapid expansion, if it were feasible, might have helped solve the budget deficit problem, but they failed to take into account one principle: if the unit cost of a service is greater than the price charged for that service, the more units the greater the loss. Finally, it must be recognized that private colleges also compete for students, and older well-established colleges are in a position to supplement their students' tuitions from the earnings of large endowments. Prescott College had almost no endowment.

Another often overlooked factor is that the Southwest did not have a strong tradition of private higher education as do the Eastern seaboard, Midwest, Northeast and the West Coast. Expectations of adequate support simply had not materialized, despite much hard work. Prescott College lived on the enthusiasm of the participants, parents, and friends, and the conviction that President Nairn and the prestigious Board members would eventually be able to develop a reliable financial foundation for the sustenance of the College. In the new Prescott College "tradition," they looked at their financial struggle in the same way that a mountaineer looks at an imposing peak. If they had the courage to fight their way to the top, it would be easy going after that.

The Prescott Institutions

If Nairn and the College leaders had decided in 1970 to rationalize the College's finances and rein in spending, things might have gone in a better direction, but they did just the opposite. This was when the Board approved the ambitious reorganization of dividing the College into four separate entities. Arguments can be made that this new organizational pattern had merit, but it cost a great deal of energy and considerable money at a time when the College was on the edge financially.

As can be seen in Table 15, there was a dramatic rise of gifts and grants in 1971-72. This was due to Nairn tapping his national contacts to raise over a million dollars to support his new Institutions. Despite this infusion of capital, the financial situation worsened. Instead of just one institution running a yearly deficit, four did. This extraordinary fundraising effort and the unprecedented expense caused internal rebellion and external burnout. The faculty and staff were tired of this constant change, and they lost confidence. Nairn's impressive accomplishment of bringing in a million dollars of new money had exhausted the patience of many big supporters.

Just a few months after the reorganization, the Board authorized an internal committee, which named itself FRED (not an acronym), to devise a plan to recombine the four Institutions and restore just one College. Only two Catalogs, 1971 through 1973, featured the four Prescott Institutions; the next, 1973-74, was published with the name Prescott College. The Board accepted Nairn's resignation in the May 5, 1973, meeting, and set up a search committee for a new president. It was a perplexing situation because a new president's first duty could have been to close down the whole enterprise.

THE MERTZ AND LONGFELLOW PERIOD

On November 3, 1973, a Board of Trustees search committee recommended Frank Mertz to be president of Prescott College, in spite of his lack of academic credentials. While it was not stated in so many words, Mertz' only mission was to put the College on a solid financial course, and he was given only a year or two to do it. To allow him a chance, some of the Board members had supplied money directly through personal gifts or grants from charitable foundations they controlled. Others had guaranteed loans from banks by mortgaging their own personal assets, since the actual real estate value of the campus had already been mortgaged. When Mertz was appointed, the total owing on such guaranteed debts was $3,985,000. He appointed Dr. Layne Longfellow, who had been director of the Center for the Person, to lead the College's educational efforts.

In the face of this debt and the constant deficits, a heroic person stepped forward and took the whole responsibility onto his foundation, in essence bailing out the other Board members. He was Richard Wilson, and his foundation was the Robert C. Wilson Foundation of Arizona, which was the administrator of a modest fortune based on money from General Motors. Dick Wilson had been an avid supporter of environmental conservation in Northern Arizona for several years, and an active supporter of the College's mission from its inception. By consolidating and taking responsibility for the whole debt, Wilson allowed Mertz latitude and time, though short, to make a final attempt to rescue the College. Mertz' task was doubly difficult, because major donors are loath to invest in a hopeless enterprise, and the word was out—there was blood in the water.

Mertz took several actions: another $400,000 was borrowed, tuitions were raised slightly and student recruitment was assiduously pursued, the annual fund was vigorously pressed, all former donors were approached. Thirty-eight foundations were contacted, requesting amounts ranging from $2,000 to $61,000, with one exceptional request to the Kresge Foundation in the amount of $250,000. All requests were turned down.[24, 72]

Two vice presidents were appointed from the faculty, Dr. Bob Harrill for administration, and Dr. Layne Longfellow for curriculum. The College was reorganized. The academic divisions were eliminated and an innovation called "First Year," which had been planned earlier, was carried out in the autumn semester of 1973.

Few participants, however, were privy to the full depth of the financial crisis facing the College, since much of the deficit from 1972-73 was being passed along to 1973-74 by obscure bookkeeping manipulations. Because of this, the deficit for 1973-74 was shown as $100,000 greater than the previous year—and on the books it appears as the largest ever. All of the cost cutting and revenue enhancement measures Mertz had instituted only bought a half a year's respite.

In the spring of 1974, a parent of two Prescott College students, Mr. John B. Hawley of Minneapolis, donated $100,000; DeWitt Wallace of Reader's Digest came through with a grant of $149,961; and the annual fund brought in a quarter-million dollars. All of this allowed the College to complete the 1973-74 academic year, then squeak through the summer and open in the fall of 1974 with only the first semester tuition payments in the bank. President Mertz faced the year with an iron determination that absolutely everything would be done to keep the College open for the year and turn the situation around so that it would never be threatened again. He claimed full conviction that it could and would be done. He was a man of faith. The Board was more skeptical.[24]

Pressing ahead, making every effort to utilize the fall semester tuitions cautiously, shifting money between accounts as needed, and exploiting ninety-day payment options with vendors, Mertz was able to keep the College afloat until November, but then the unrestricted bank accounts were empty. At that point, salvation seemed to present itself miraculously in the guise of two individuals from Chicago, Hal (or Harry) and Barbara Lowther, whose purported goal was to rescue the school. They wrote over $350,000 in checks to pay salaries and vendors. Within two weeks the miracle was shown to be a hoax as the checks bounced and the couple withdrew. (Since this is one of the most bizarre incidents in the history of the College, it merits its own chapter; "Hal Lenke, Private Eye," by Melissa Doran is presented below.)

Paradoxically, there was College money languishing in restricted accounts, retirement and payroll tax receipts that did not have to be sent in until the end of the quarter. In addition there were two or three hundred thousand dollars of paid second semester tuitions already in the bank, which Arizona law said could not be touched until the second semester opened— just a few days after the holidays. So close, yet so far away. Perhaps, with those funds and the new tuitions for second semester that had been billed but not yet received, the College could have finished the 1974-75 academic year while Mertz and the Board worked to find a financial solution.

Sometime in November, Mertz took an action which, though done with the best of motives, was not legal: he diverted restricted funds to pay some faculty and staff salaries as well as the most critical utilities and suppliers. When he informed the trustees of his action, they felt that they had no alternative but to remove him as President, because the action had put them in legal jeopardy. They appointed Bob Harrill as interim president with the assignment to either find a legal way to keep the College open, or to design a graceful way to close it down at the end of the semester.

In their December 17 meeting the Board learned that the checks written by the couple from Chicago were bouncing and the liability insurance had lapsed, so they were again legally and financially in jeopardy. They decided to close down the campus early the next day. They instructed Bob Harrill to shut down and order everyone to remove their persons, and any of their property they did not want to lose, from the campus because it would be under lock and key by five PM that day, December 18, 1974.

For months, most of the faculty and staff of the College, and many of the students, had been aware that the College was in financial difficulties, but they hoped and believed these issues would be solved once again. Someone would pull a rabbit out of a hat. A Board member, Hamilton Wright, a well-known television personality in Phoenix, pledged a two-week, full-time effort to raise enough money to open in January. But the Board's action had made it real. It was nearly impossible to think of resuming after Christmas vacation, even though new funds would be available. Several Board members

Original Campus Closed Down
photo by Catherine West

left with the belief they would never be returning. Faculty and students organized to continue the College without the campus.

The bankruptcy petition for the insolvent Prescott College Corporation
was filed a month later on January 31, 1975. It was signed by Dr. Robert W.
Harrill as President. The document lists all outstanding obligations, including $69,475 owed various government agencies; thirteen pages of creditors
who were owed amounts between $0-$1200—mostly unpaid salary payments, totaling $60,275; and seven promissory notes, $400,000 to the First
National Bank of Arizona, and $3,985,000 to a Tucson lawyer, Eugene Isaak,
representing the Robert C. Wilson Foundation of Richard Wilson. The outstanding obligations and notes listed above total $4,514,750.[3]

The bulk of the bankruptcy petition, approximately 150 pages, lists the
assets. It assigns a value of "unknown" to all of the real estate and library
resources, and assigns a value of only $964,507 to all the equipment, inven-
tories, bookstore inventory, horses, etc. Here we see the typical resolution of
a bankruptcy: a huge loss of value, assets, human investment, future possibili-

ties and dreams. Certainly the assets of Prescott College far exceeded four and a half million dollars.

During the next year, Judge Johnston sold off the library, the bookstore, and the heavy equipment. The proceeds were used to compensate creditors—including those owed salary. Creditors were paid a percentage of their claims in exchange for releases. Then Judge Johnston and the Robert C. Wilson foundation marketed the campus.

Embry-Riddle Aeronautical University of Daytona Beach, Florida (ERAU) purchased the campus and the assets that remained in January of 1978. Ironically, ERAU paid a minor amount of cash to secure the purchase, and then issued long-term, low-interest bonds to pay off the Wilson Foundation—a process that probably had been available to Prescott College as well.[90] Many well-motivated and sincere supporters of Prescott College, and especially those who had contributed tens and hundreds of thousands of dollars over the nine years of its operation, felt very disappointed about what happened to their dream. However, in reality the people of Prescott had actually achieved their practical and noble goal of making the community of Prescott into a center for higher education. As the story unfolded, these events combined to help found three colleges—Prescott College, Yavapai College, and in the beginning Grand Canyon College, now in Phoenix—as well as a number of private and charter schools at other levels.

UNDERSTANDING THE CAUSES OF THE 1975 BANKRUPTCY

When the College was closed, in December of 1974, there was a great deal of speculation as to the causes. A common theme was that Nairn, with approval of the Board, had wasted a great deal of money building extra structures on campus, particularly his own residence and four other houses, which were not useful for educational purposes. Reviewing the record, it is clear that money was wasted or misspent on many projects, but that was not the root problem. In the period of the closing and bankruptcy, it was popular to blame the Lowther couple from Chicago; however they really did no harm, and the confusion and publicity they caused may have helped the College survive for a month. This analysis of the College finances reveals the real causes. The root problem was that the College did not have a solid financial structure from the beginning, and Nairn, for all his promotional talent, did not build a financial foundation when *and if* he actually had the opportunity. Experience demonstrated that the large and expensive campus, for all its virtues, was not the best setting for Prescott College. At this writing the College in its downtown locations and field stations surpasses its first embodiment in most ways.

Prescott College suffered a financial failure in 1975 such that most observers counted it out. But the College bounced back, vindicating its mission as an innovator of high-quality future-oriented education. It appears to be the only new private college in recent times to have suffered such a financial crisis, and then fully recovered.

Hal Lenke, Private Eye: The Case of the Ironic Rescue

◇◇◇◇◇◇◇

by Melissa Doran

Hal Lenke had made up his mind. It wasn't going to be easy, but neither was the decision to close the school. It was January of 1975, less than a month after Prescott College closed its doors due to bankruptcy. Hal sat at his desk, one of many displaced faculty members of the now-deceased college who had decided to stay and fight. He had moved here recently, enticed by the unique opportunities Prescott College offered in experiential education, and he wasn't going to let this special school die without at least an explanation. While most of the other faculty attempted to find ways to look forward, either in the form of creating a new school, or jumping ship and moving elsewhere, Hal looked back. To try to discover what the Board had missed; what had happened to leave Prescott College nothing but a campus of empty buildings and floundering students.

He poured himself another cup of coffee and picked up the Chicago *Little Tribune*, a newspaper that despite the distance between Arizona and Illinois seemed to always be at his desk these days. He skimmed the paper, half looking for clues, half-heartedly acknowledging to himself that there was probably nothing there. But the Lowthers, the ironic rescuers of Prescott College, were from the Chicago area, so maybe, just maybe, something would come up.

And something did. The headline caught him mid-sip, *Harry Lowther Resigns Post*. He put down the cup of coffee to hold the paper tightly in both hands and quickly read the rest of the article. Harry Lowther was the other half of the husband-wife team that ran Phillips Research Foundation, the nonprofit agency that was going to save Prescott College. Only a month ago, everybody had thought they had found the answer, these people were saints, with impeccable records and a drive for furthering the causes of non-traditional schools that seemed almost too good to be true. As it turned out, it was. Before the deal was finalized problems began to arise. Checks that had been written to faculty and debtors were bouncing, and the banks were getting suspicious. When they wouldn't allow the checks to go through, Harry and Barbara asked for the second semester's tuition to cover their expenses. It was an illegal move the college wouldn't agree to; the Lowthers dropped the deal and Prescott College, thereby effectively closing it. Nobody could figure out exactly what had happened, it all happened so quickly. But now, with a month to go over and over it in his mind, Hal began to wonder if the Lowthers were really who they said they were at all. But they had passed a background check, and they were at the head of a very prestigious organization in higher education—IED, the Institute of Educational Development— how could they not be?

Hal's mind raced as he put down the article and tried to decide his next move. This was the second resignation this week; Barbara Lowther had recently resigned her post as president of Lincoln Open University in Illinois as well. Something was going on, but he wasn't quite sure what, yet. He went through a mental rolodex to decide who to call. He had to call somebody, the newspaper reporter maybe? No, Lincoln Open University. He knew that somebody there could give him some sort of explanation, and he'd just seen in the paper the other day that Barbara had resigned at the will of the LOU board; it had listed the chairman's name, where was it? He fumbled through the pile of a week's worth of newspapers on his desk to try to find the article. After about five minutes of searching and papers falling to the floor, he found it. C. Virgil Martin. He would just call Mr. Martin and see if he could get any answers out of him.

He dialed the operator, and after a number of connections and what felt a little like the children's game of trying to put the square wooden piece into the cutout of the triangle, he finally found the right hole, and was connected to Martin. He introduced himself as a former faculty member of Prescott College, and the chairman of LOU immediately knew the purpose of his call.

"We have about $106 in the bank," Martin said exasperatedly. He explained that the university had been given a $350,000 Lilly Foundation grant, and now it was gone. About half of it had been written in checks for the university, but the other half was unaccounted for. Though nobody knew for sure what had happened to the money, the suspicion around the university was that the Lowthers had either mismanaged it or siphoned it into a personal account. "What I resent about the Lowthers is not the money, it's the damage they did in the Midwest to this idea of a special kind of college. It was the crucifixion of an innocent bystander."

Hal knew the feeling all too well. He too felt as though his own college had been killed. He thanked Martin and hung up the phone, feeling both renewed and overwhelmed at the same time. Another, similar college had fallen due to remarkably similar circumstances, and both failures seemed to trace back to the Lowthers. The connecting piece was the Phillips Research Foundation.

Hal had tried numerous times over the past weeks to contact the Lowthers or anybody at the Phillips Foundation, to no avail. He had given up trying. But he knew that to get to the bottom of this, he was somehow going to find somebody on the inside to let him in on the inner workings of PRF. He thought back to the very beginning of this epic journey, to the man who had introduced Prescott College to the Lowthers in the first place, Barbara Lowther's father, Webb Phillips, Sr.

Webb resided in Sedona, Arizona, only sixty miles from Prescott. When he had first called the college in October of the previous year, it had been an answer to a prayer. Literally, or at least then-president Frank Mertz had thought. An evangelical Christian, Mertz prayed over the task of saving the college every night for months. One night, he had a vision telling him that he would get a contact that would save the school the next day. It was that day that Webb called, directing him to IED and his daughter's organization, the Phillips Research Foundation.

It had seemed like the perfect answer. IED was one of the most reputable organizations in higher education and had previously been run by Samuel Gould, who was himself one of the soundest men in the field of non-traditional education. He, and the rest of IED, had trusted Barbara enough to turn over the entire operation to the Lowthers, thus giving them instant credibility in the field. How could anybody question somebody so highly reputed?

It had been a long day already, but Hal decided to make one last phone call. He called Webb.

Webb Phillips seemed a bit distraught to have to talk to somebody representing Prescott College, but he accepted Hal's need for answers and gave in to a short conversation. He told Hal how he had given his daughter money to start the Phillips Research Foundation in 1972; it had been her dream to work with and fund schools that were trying new, experimental forms of education, and he had helped her. Within a year Barbara had made connections with IED and convinced them to let the PRF take over as the "management arm" of the institute. Since the foundation's inception in 1972, Barbara and her husband Harry had taken over several nonprofits and schools, including not only Lincoln Open University, but Campus-Free College in Washington D.C.; an equestrian school for American Indians in Illinois; Operation

Wingspread, an outdoor-education program for neglected and dependent juveniles through the Illinois Department of Children and Family Services; and the Safer Foundation, which offered rehabilitation services to ex-offenders among others. Hal quickly jotted down names and places of these organizations on a torn piece of scrap paper, all he had handy. He thanked Webb for his help and cooperation, adjusted his horn-rimmed glasses and sighed. If the Lowthers had helped all these organizations, what had gone wrong with their deal with Prescott College?

It was a few days later by the time Hal was able to do any more investigation into the failed school; things were picking up with moving the new College into the Hassayampa Inn temporarily and trying to find enough work to make ends meet. But he pushed aside some of the more mundane tasks he should have been doing to pick up the paper with names of other PRF organizations and ponder again what had gone wrong. Well, he thought, might as well turn over every leaf, I've got nothing else to go on, and he once again started the process of finding phone numbers to small, slightly obscure, organizations across the country.

First, he called Campus-Free College. Hal knew nothing about the college except that, like Prescott College and Lincoln Open University, it was also a non-traditional center for higher education. He was able to contact Dr. Gregory Sinner, the chairman of the CFC governing board. Expecting to hear a success story of the Lowthers' support for the school, Hal instead found another disheartened chairman at another disheartened college who had been let down by the Lowthers and the Phillips Research Foundation. Like Prescott College, CFC had been financially strapped and on the verge of bankruptcy when they were contacted by the Lowthers. They were offered substantial financial support in exchange for control over their fiscal operations, including the collection of student fees and payment of bills. It had sounded good at the time, and CFC began the process of making a deal with PRF. However, while talks were under way, Harry Lowther promised to foot the college's $5,400 October payroll; two months later the college had received nothing but delays and bounced checks. They threatened legal action and forfeited any further connection with PRF. Hal was told the dealings with the Lowthers had been "intolerably unprofessional," and that the college had decided to "firmly withdraw any and all possible arrangements between our two foundations."

Shocked, and at the same time thrilled by this new explosive information, Hal pushed on and began dialing the numbers of other organizations on his list. Time and time again he called small, struggling, or obsolete organizations with the same results. The equestrian school for Native Americans had stayed in business for only a few months, with paychecks being returned to trainers due to insufficient funds. Operation Wingspread lasted only three months before being closed down as the Lowthers had never fulfilled their part of the agreement and had not paid the state of Illinois. Hal's head was spinning. The Lowthers were obviously either con artists or completely irresponsible and unprofessional—but which was it?

He thought back to the meetings the Prescott College Board and faculty members had had with the Lowthers, and how completely together they had seemed—how their credentials and backgrounds were stellar, their motives genuine. It was time to look closer to home, call Ham Wright, chairman of PC's Board, and find out why they had missed what should have been obvious discrepancies in the Lowthers' record.

They had trusted the Lowthers' credentials and their connection with IED to stand on its own, Ham said.

Though Hal had heard that now, in the wake of so many new discoveries, the IED board was pushing for Barbara's resignation, he knew that at least at one point they had trusted her enough to put her and her husband in charge of the institute. That would be his next phone call. Difficult as it might be to find somebody in the organization willing to admit they had made some sort of judgment error, or to find somebody willing to talk at all, he tried anyway. Most of the people who had made the initial decision to allow Phillips Research Foundation to take over were no longer at the institute, but a very kind secretary was willing to look up past records and do some investigation on her own; she would get back to him, she said sweetly.

Hal was not convinced. He didn't think the secretary, soft-spoken and kind as she may have seemed, would really get back to him with any information. After all, this organization must have made a mistake somewhere, and nobody wanted to be the informant. The organization would obviously try to cover up its mistakes if it had made any.

A few days later, however, she did call back. She had found the records of a background investigation that IED had conducted previous to the takeover by PRF. It was clean, the IED board had been impressed by Barbara's record at North Central University in Illinois, her PhD in psychology and her authentic drive for furthering the causes of non-traditional education. They were sure that she had all the credentials, money, and drive necessary to be in charge of IED, and without hesitation they had handed it over. The secretary, sweet as ever, apologized for not being able to be of more help, and wished him a good day. Hal hung up the phone, confused. If the Lowthers did have devious motives, they had obviously stumbled upon them recently. A background check had been done and it had come up clean, impressive even. What next?

Hal was tired, confused and out of ideas. Maybe they were just well-intentioned people, who happened to also be completely inept and incapable of following though. The road to hell is paved with good intentions, Hal thought, as he slumped down in his chair, and threw his glasses onto his desk.

References:

PCArchives, NEWSCLIPS, 1975, file #1246, "Huge Scandal Hits the Academic World," New York Times News Service, 1975.

PC Archives, Oral History Project, Interview of Hal Lenke

The New College

◇◇◇◇◇◇◇

The founders of Prescott Center for Alternative Education, Inc. (PCAE) believed in equality, democracy, and self-direction. They had experienced the contradictions inherent in a traditional structure—that both financial control and decision-making procedures were at odds with community values and democratic decision-making. This mismatch was at least part of the reason the first version of Prescott College was often rife with conflict and eventually bankrupted. The new College's pioneering attempt to resolve such systemic contradictions is an interesting and informative history.

Like the previous chapter, a thematic rather than chronological approach will be used to describe the financial events of Prescott Center for Alternative Education, Inc. (PCAE, 1975-1999) and Prescott College, Inc. (after it recovered its original corporate entity in 1999). From 1975 to 2006, there were periods of stability in which little of exceptional interest occurred in terms of financial policy, revenue, and budgeting. Periods of financial stability will be examined briefly to understand what was working. It is the exceptional times that are more instructive and that more often command our attention. Hence, more space will be dedicated to some remarkable experiments beginning in 1975 that were undertaken in an attempt to adapt the financial management and governance to the school's educational philosophy and practice, which stressed self-direction and democratic community values.

The Nonprofit Corporation—Neither Fish Nor Fowl

Prescott College, Inc. and Prescott Center for Alternative Education, Inc. were both established as nonprofit corporations. Theoretically a nonprofit entity is owned by "the public," but in practice no one knows quite who owns it. Its assets are controlled by a council called a Board of Trustees or Board of Directors, whose members in most cases did not donate the assets, yet are fully authorized to give them away or sell them as though they owned them, so long as they can rationalize their actions by the mission. They have the power to close down the corporation, even when they had no role in creating it. The most important identifier of a nonprofit corporation is its mission—what it was set up to accomplish for the public good. Nonprofits also have the hidden mission of providing a tax shelter for those who set them up and for donors, but they are not allowed to make profits or distribute earnings to them.

In the case of an unaffiliated school like Prescott College, the nonprofit corporation sponsors a community of learners, teacher-scholars and managers, but its commitment to any of them is not binding. There may be traditions of tenure, but in fact any or all of the employees—from the janitor to the president—can be fired at any time and would have no recourse other than to sue to recover unpaid wages or damages to reputation. Legally, those who have built and who operate the educational enterprise are dispensable paid workers. Unlike the stockholders of a *for*-profit corporation, those who invest money, expertise, time and energy into a nonprofit corporation have no real control over their investments. They have no effective vote in electing the Board, and there are no stock options that they can exercise to gain a piece of the ownership—since ownership is vaguely ascribed to "the public." A nonprofit can earn money to support its activities, but this capacity is limited and circumscribed by law. Nonprofits are "ruled" through top-down authority by an executive who is hired and evaluated by the Board.

OLD PRESCOTT COLLEGE CLOSES—PCAE TAKES ITS PLACE

In the emergency faculty meeting, held December 18, 1974, in which interim President Bob Harrill announced to the faculty the Board of Trustees' decision to close the College early, a second version of the College was born. Most of the faculty and half of the students refused to accept the decision of the Board to close the College and formed a group to develop an alternative corporation and school. Dr. James M. Stuckey, who had been a faculty member of the Leadership Institute of the old College, was elected President. The group spent the next weeks accomplishing two goals—reassembling a student body from those who had returned home after their expulsion from the old campus, and creating a new legal/financial vehicle to continue the educational program. On January 28, 1975, the incorporation of the Prescott Center for Alternative Education, Inc. (PCAE) was official. Eleven volunteer incorporators served as the first Board of Directors, until a new Board, elected by the whole community, could be put in place. The new school's operational name was in doubt. They settled on Prescott College II, but were advised by lawyers it was too similar to the old name. Then they adopted the name Prescott Center College, which was opened to students in rented facilities in downtown Prescott.[36]

At this point the reconstituted College had to face a number of hurdles.

The participants had little or no experience running a college or any kind of business. Tuitions had to be collected and accounted for, budgets had to be projected, people had to be paid, curricula had to be put in place, teaching assignments with schedules and room assignments had to be made, vehicles and insurance had to be secured, and so on. They decided that policy decisions had to be made communally. Everyone was considered to have an equal voice and vote. It was a big job, and everyone pitched in as members of a dynamic learning community.

History Of Democratic Salary Distribution, 1974-89

Of the four hundred and fifty students who had attended the last semester of the old College, one hundred and ninety-six returned to register at PCAE in late January for the spring semester. Some had paid a full year's tuition and their second semester payment was tied up in the bankruptcy assets. They were not asked to pay more. No financial aid was available, and a few registered for half-time study at reduced tuition. Once this first semester under the auspices of PCAE was underway and it was known how much money was in the bank—just $251,124 for the whole enterprise to stretch over the next six months—a very critical challenge came to the fore. That was not enough money to pay everyone who wanted to stay with the College, or to pay at more than subsistence level. By common agreement, a finance committee was appointed, and staff and faculty members submitted estimates of how much money they would need to survive until June. Then they divided up the tiny pool of money allocated for salaries according to need. Everyone fell back on family resources, and many took second or third jobs or applied for unemployment benefits. Surprisingly, financial sacrifice and insecurity did not create an atmosphere of fear or defeatism. Instead, there was a revolutionary spirit in the College that first semester, and an appreciation for a taste of a rare freedom to initiate something new and important. The semester was completed successfully, with a $7,000 surplus. The community voted to use it for student recruitment, thus precipitating a decision to continue the experiment for the next full academic year. Tuition was reduced from $2,600 to $2,000 (and did not reach its previous level until 1979).

That summer, agreements were made to hire all staff and faculty who wished to stay and build the new Prescott Center College, anticipating about 125 returning students in the fall. When only fifty-six reenrolled in the 1975 fall semester, those plans had to be scrapped. The budget for the next nine months was $172,952, eighty thousand dollars less than the budget for the six-month spring semester just completed. Another emergency plan was required. Some, whom the Board considered to be essential staff and faculty, were budgeted for a very meager "full-time," nine-month salary. Others, who had additional sources of income, were asked to accept payment as "half-time, half-pay" teachers, with reduced teaching and advising loads.

As the new Center became accustomed to its economic constraints, deliberations about how money for salaries should be distributed began in earnest and a consensus emerged. It was acknowledged that every kind of work was valuable, and beyond that every kind of work was essential to the development of the Center. A school needed teachers, but they couldn't teach if students had not been recruited. The classrooms needed to be cleaned and the equipment needed to be maintained. An hour of work, when considered in terms of human effort, was the same for a president or a van driver—sixty minutes in both cases. It was also recognized that every person, regardless of rank or education, had to be supported financially at least at a subsistence level. Therefore, in 1976 the PCAE Board adopted a policy that might be termed "economic democracy." Everyone who worked at the Center—whether janitor or secretary or president—would receive the same base pay. This base pay level was to be determined by calculating the money available for salaries after other essentials were budgeted, and dividing it by the number of recipients (allowing variations for half-time workers and adjunct teachers).

The base pay for a "full-time" employee was six thousand dollars. Six thousand dollars corrected to 2005 value by consumer-price-index (CPI) was equal to $20,833 before income tax and FICA deductions. In 2005, the poverty level income for a family of four was $19,350. Putting this in perspective, all full-time employees were receiving about what the Census Bureau would have considered poverty level. This salary base was for the nine-month academic year, but was supplemented by additional percentages according to how many months one actually worked. Those who continued working through the summer were paid one-fourth more. Soon an additional percentage enhancement was added as "responsibility pay," which generally meant supervision of other employees. Over the next thirteen years, the equal pay approach was modified progressively, yet continued as a policy through 1989.

The College clearly could not have survived without the equal pay policy. Yearly budgets from 1975 through 1989 were in balance, mostly as a result of very low personnel costs. If one segment of employees—or even one employee—had been paid disproportionately more than the others, all would have justifiably demanded to be paid at parity with their professions. From the faculty point of view, equal pay policy also threw out traditional faculty ranking and tenure practices with their publish-or-perish implications and invidious comparisons. Teachers were evaluated on the basis of teaching performance, rather than conventional criteria. It was a loss to the College that low but equal pay discouraged recruitment of new teachers and other employees who had families to support. The new College was built on the financial sacrifices of those who were building it. With sacrifice came a spirit of adventure and dedication to the mission, which was communicated by osmosis to the students.

The College recovered and then slowly began to grow. It attracted many outstanding students, who appreciated the adventure of creating a college from the ground up. Students were able to exercise their talents fully. Everyone was on a first name basis, and there was little differentiation between participants based on age or status. While accreditation was being pursued assiduously, the learning community also enjoyed the freedoms that not being accredited afforded. The curriculum was very flexible, and students carried out some truly adventurous and real-world off campus field work and independent studies. While safety was very important, they were not constrained by as many rules as would be imposed in a more developed school. Many senior projects were comparable to master's theses. Being relieved of dorm life and food services also had its good side. Most students came to consider the necessity of securing their own housing and sustenance to be an essential part of their educational experience. Altogether, it was a rare experience that not many people can have. Everyone was afforded the same respect; all opinions were considered; planning was mutual. The faculty also experienced these benefits and considered them welcome compensation for low but equal pay. When the College regained accreditation in 1984, some of these features had to change, but others were maintained.

In the real world of capitalist America, it was inevitable that the new College would eventually reinstitute the conventional financial stratification that values one type of work or training over another. The retrenchment was led by the Board and the Resident Degree Program (RDP) faculty. After Bohrson retired in 1989 the Board set a higher salary level as they searched for another president, on the theory that a well-qualified person could not be attracted unless compensation was in a higher range than for other employees. Dr. Douglas North was selected in a national search. After he was installed as president, there was increasing pressure to conventionalize the compensation levels of the whole administration. The *goal* of bringing all salaries in the College in line with the compensation practices in the industry (meaning the higher education establishment) was soon adopted. Although budgets could not support its full implementation, salaries were increased considerably in the next three years and an attempt was made to keep up with the cost of living thereafter.

The Resident Degree Program (RDP) teaching faculty had been asked to suggest to the Board a policy for differential compensation of teachers, and they spent the better part of a decade hammering out the details of a complex, three-tiered salary schema that attempted to reward professional

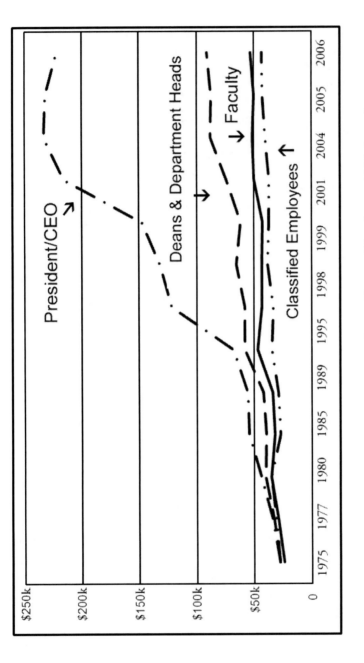

Graph 1. Average Compensation for Different Classes of Employees, 1975 through 2005—Corrected to 2005 Values by CPI. Based on Various Audits and Financial Reports, Including IRS 990 Forms, 1997 through 2006. [104]

preparation and years of service. This turned out to be a thinly disguised return to the three-tier faculty ranking practices of American universities, and the principle of equality very quickly gave way to the conventional pay and benefits hierarchy found throughout academia.

Adopting conventional industry values, student workers earned at the lowest level (about minimum wage); classified workers like secretaries and plant maintenance workers were next; teachers' salaries—although spread out by the new salary schema—were centered at the third pay level; operational department heads including deans were at the second level; and the president was at the top. It should be acknowledged that for the next ten years the spread of salary levels was very modest as compared to many institutions, thus preserving for a while an attenuated form of "economic democracy." Disparate pay was not a big issue during the decade of the 1990s.

After 1999, a growing disparity in pay within the classified staff and professional teaching personnel—and particularly between central administration and all other personnel—tended to erode communal values and stimulate invidious comparisons. This tendency was exacerbated by the fact that most faculty members were still considerably underpaid, and many who had family responsibilities continued to find themselves in the position of sacrificing financially in order to stay at Prescott College.

Graph 1 demonstrates the purchasing power of yearly average salary levels of each class of employees. When a line trends upwards, it means that their average salaries are increasing faster than inflation. When a line is flat it means their compensation is keeping up with inflation, and when downward their compensation is static and its purchasing power is declining. Salary levels for administrators were not generally published within the College after the mid-1990s.

As salaries were differentiated, other conventionalized values emerged, like judging aspects of the College by how nearly they conformed to practices of a group of other schools considered to be comparable. Rather than looking to the College community's own values, needs, and possibilities, decision-makers increasingly justified their actions—including setting differential pay levels—by citing what other schools were doing. Another closely related value change that resulted from disparities of pay was that those at higher pay levels naturally accrued more authority and status, while those at lower pay levels began to feel and to be treated as replaceable education workers. The ethos of community ownership and responsibility gave way to a conventional attitude among many employees, including some from the teaching faculties, and it was openly said that "working at Prescott College is just a job, *not a mission*."

A number of highly qualified teachers left the faculty to take better paid positions in more traditional schools. There were several other inevitable changes that followed. Full financial transparency had to end, and that process progressed to the point that pay levels of individuals became quasi-secret information. In short, the College experienced a general "regression to the mean" in philosophy and practice. The changes mentioned above occurred over time, and most were subtle and unconscious. Such issues were hardly ever put on any agenda for discussion or vote.

Countering any negative effects from conventionalization, many new extracurricular programs and activities were encouraged or actively sponsored. This was very successful in stimulating enthusiasm and commitment among the students. The campus was greatly improved as the Crossroads Center was built and additional buildings were added, creating spaces needed to develop a stronger sense of community. Public relations and student recruitment programs were also expanded and improved.

In 1999, the College recovered its original corporate entity and began to operate again as Prescott College, Inc. It is an interesting coincidence that by 1999 the Board and College were revisiting some of the budgeting and management processes of 1966 through 1975, like mortgaging the whole campus. However, the underlying drift in management philosophy did not indicate that the College would repeat the financial debacle that closed the old College in 1975. Money management was very professional, and there seemed to be little chance that the College would again falter financially.

In summary, the College would not have survived during the decade following its 1975 financial collapse if it had not adopted an equal pay policy. That policy was abandoned in the early 1990s, and the College appears to have generally benefited from stratification of compensation levels along conventional lines. However, these changes have not yet accomplished the promised equity for many employees. Faculty members, in particular, have not yet been rewarded adequately as the College has become more prosperous. When cost of living is taken into account, as calculated through the CPI, most employees have hardly advanced in their purchasing power during the twenty years preceding this writing.

HISTORY OF SELF-DIRECTION AS A MANAGEMENT PROPOSITION,
1975-96

Returning to the 1960-74 period, the College always emphasized self-direction and personal responsibility as key elements of its educational philosophy and practice. However, at the "old College" there was a structural contradiction that militated against this philosophy. Board members functioned in a manner analogous to owners. They were fully authorized to hire and supervise the president, set policy in every aspect of the operation, and decide how the property of the College should be used or disposed of. By contrast, those charged with carrying out the educational program—the faculty, staff, and students—were subordinate and had no voice in most decisions that affected their livelihoods and education. The Board was self-perpetuating, which meant that new members were selected by current members as they saw fit. The Board did not ask for the consent of those who would be governed by them. It changed membership quite often and generally operated at a distance from students and faculty. In Parker's era the membership consisted of national leaders in higher education and religious education, and Prescott-area community leaders. In Nairn's era it was dominated by wealthy philanthropists and state politicians. In both periods the actions of this unfamiliar Board were somewhat mysterious to those who were "in the trenches." This reflected the typical top-down structure, and the Board's absolute authority was not identified as an "issue" because it was customary and legal in nonprofit corporations, as described earlier.

Particularly in the area of finance, the on-campus community held the well-justified feeling that they were dependent. Because the student body was so small, and the physical plant so expensive to operate, tuitions and fees covered less than half of the yearly budgets. The rest had to be acquired by fundraising, which was the prerogative and duty of the Board and president. When fundraising was inadequate, these leaders were forced to mortgage the new campus. The College's continued success was contingent on gifts and decisions of wealthy Board members whom the faculty and students did not know. The main bridge between the working College and the mysterious Board was president Nairn. It was reported that he relished the role of savior, announcing each successive year that he had at last secured the College's financial future. Looking back, a cycle of neurotic dependency had developed which entirely contradicted the philosophy of self-direction and self-responsibility that the College was espousing educationally. By the early 1970s many students had joined the game of speculating whether the old Prescott College would be able to survive long enough for them to graduate.

Table 13 (p. 278) illustrates that the main root of the crash of 1975 was not directly caused by the Board. The grand campus and elaborate college was far too expensive to operate efficiently, particularly with so few students. Tuitions did not pay a high enough percentage of the costs of the "old College" for it to have survived financially. In 1972-73 tuition revenues were dramatically increased due to recruitment of 150 additional students, while mild austerity measures were instituted. The next year the budget was further tightened, even though inflation was rampant due to the OPEC oil embargo. That year students paid half the cost through tuitions, which was a large increase but not enough. The figures for 1974-75 are an average of the final semester of the "old College" and the first semester of PCAE.

When the crash took place in the fall of 1974, there was some inevitable finger-pointing. Nairn was already out of the picture, and many of the Board members had abandoned ship. The remaining Board members appeared to be more concerned with the debts owed to them and the foundations they controlled than they were with the fates of the staff, faculty, and students who were summarily ordered off the campus. A mythology grew up around the crash, featuring two sets of villains. Harry and Barbara Lowther were the immediate culprits in the story. (See account by Melissa Doran, "Hal Lenke, Private Eye," p. 295) Holding a distant second place as supposed "villains" were that band of mostly unknown trustees, who had met in the middle of the night of December 17, 1974, and had closed the campus without ever having consulted those most affected. Complaints about the lack of communication and consultation were partially true, but it is unjust to blame those trustees who had exhibited such good will toward the College, and who had contributed so much to its support. Rather, they should be seen as champions in a failed struggle to create an ideal College.

As described above and in the narrative history (Section I: Prescott Center College [PCAE] from 1975 to 1984), those students, staff, and faculty who persisted and created their own corporation, PCAE, in January 1975 were adamant that their new educational vehicle would be different. There was a powerful feeling of spiritual and financial ownership, and a new sense of effectiveness. The founding group held the keys in their own hands, and did not intend to give them up. They investigated alternative nonprofit corporate structures, including those developed by early Congregationalist and Quaker schools that had charters and governance structures involving their local communities in support and oversight.

New bylaws were written which they believed would guarantee that PCAE would never be put into a contingent position, so that people from "the outside" could never again turn it in unwanted directions or close it down. The principal features designed to insure this were: (1) All participants in the College were designated as "members" of PCAE, including faculty, current students, employees of all classifications, and serving Board members. (2) Before every Board meeting a PCAE Corporation meeting was held to inform the members about pending business. (3) When there were open seats on the Board, candidates were nominated in an open process. There was no official nominating committee, and no restriction on who could be nominated; students and employees of the Corporation were not excluded. (4) All members of the Corporation were given ballots, and trustees were elected by majority vote. (5) Every trustee was equal in responsibility and authority. Students, teachers, and other employees that might fill seats were not elected as representatives of their particular group, but represented the whole constituency of the Corporation. (6) The president of the College was an ex-officio, non-voting member of the Board. Bylaws were updated three times, but the democratic elements listed above were in effect for nineteen years, until the fall Board meeting of 1996.

In evaluating the PCAE experiment in corporate democracy, its educational qualities and accomplishments should not be overlooked. Throughout its history, from the Symposium in 1963 to the time of this writing, experiential education has been a major element in the philosophy of the College. Prescott College is well known for its accomplishments in this method of nurturing learning. Experiential education is based on the theory that real-life experience, working with authentic phenomena in a real context, fosters learning that is authentic and lasting. While reading and other vicarious sources of information are essential to education, it is incomplete without application in laboratory, field, internships, and other settings.

During the two decades that students participated as equals in the PCAE Corporation and filled seats on the Board, thousands of them learned experientially about how organizations function. They participated as more than observers—thinking, doing research, making real decisions, and seeing the results. Perhaps no other contemporary college has provided this kind of direct experience to its students.

The same sort of evaluation could be made in considering the experiences of the whole self-governing learning community, composed not just of students but also of employees, from the most humble to the top leadership, with the teachers occupying a middle position. The Prescott College community also extends into the world through the alumni, parents, friends, and supporters, as well as colleagues at other schools. There is no data that has captured the outcomes of the experiment in self-governance and corporate democracy as it affected all of those individuals, other than the esteem and enthusiasm they have expressed for the College.

The experiment in corporate democracy must also be evaluated pragmatically, by the results it produced in sustaining the College and fulfilling its mission. On these criteria the record is good. Beginning in 1975 with nothing but a reputation and the commitments of the people involved, the whole community, which was governed by its elected Board, built a College. Year after year budgets were shaped and implemented without deficits—until the early 1990s (an account of that is contained in the next section). The College grew to twice the student population of the first version. It pioneered programs to educate underserved populations including Native American and Hispanics, and prepare them to teach in their own bilingual cultures. It developed the field of Adventure Education and prepared undergraduate and graduate students to become leaders in environmental conservation and social justice. It developed excellent programs in humanities and fine arts. Many of the accomplishments described in this book were initiated during the period of full community self-direction and democracy.

From the beginning of this phase there were individuals within the College and affiliated with it who had significant reservations about the kind of communalism and unlimited democracy the founders of PCAE attempted to build. These were supportive people who had the best interests of the corporation and College in mind. Their reservations focused on fiduciary responsibility, circular authority, and a sense of propriety.

There is a legal rationale for investing fiduciary and policy-making powers in an independent board. The board is supposed to insure that the non-profit corporation serves the public interest. Having IRS and state-recognized nonprofit status allows the institution to receive donations from individuals, companies, and foundations without those moneys being taxed—effectively diverting money from government to the nonprofit institution. Hence society does have a stake in the institution, and theoretically an independent board protects that interest. By that logic, the PCAE bylaws weakened the public interest by putting those being paid out of the corporation budget in a position to control that budget and thus benefit themselves unduly from tax-exempt donations. Practically, it would be absurd to claim that anyone employed by PCAE was being enriched; salaries, benefits, and fees were so low and based on equal pay for that whole period.

A similar circularity in authority and power was also a possibility within the framework of the PCAE bylaws in that they placed real power into the hands of employees other than the president of the corporation. In other words, the new bylaws overturned the hierarchy of power in the organization. That power consisted mainly in the power to supervise the work of those lower in the hierarchy, to hire and fire, and to budget and spend money. But many people involved in the organization did not know about "flat" organizational structures or communal decision making, and found it very uncomfortable to disrupt clear lines of top-down authority, regardless of how well the system worked.

Another issue that was occasionally mentioned had to do with the dignity or status of Board members. It was sometimes claimed that wealthy or influential individuals would be unwilling to serve on the College's Board if they had to be nominated and voted on by the whole community and serve on equal terms with students. Although no specific information was available to support this claim, some leaders were concerned that such persons would be insulted or embarrassed, and that the Board's ability to raise money was being compromised. Responding to such worries, it was frequently pointed out that the "old" Prescott College Board—which boasted many wealthy and influential individuals—did not, in the final analysis, properly manage the old College's finances nor redeem it in 1974-75.

Over time, full self-governance became controversial. Some trustees and at least two presidents asserted that allowing employees and students to be nominated and elected to the Board without restriction created an unacceptable circularity—that those who were supposed to be the authorized authorities were ultimately governed by their own subordinates. Under PCAE bylaws, employees on the board could and did evaluate and set policy, thus inverting traditional hierarchical governance. Such conflicts in philosophy created friction at times, and eventually brought down the fully open and democratic self-governance system that the founders of PCAE had designed. It is important to note that during the democratic phase the business of the Corporation and College was carried out effectively, even when it seemed cumbersome. On a rare occasion when an unworkable decision had been made by the full Board, which included several students and employees, the Board's executive committee intervened. But neither curricular disagreements nor financial crises seriously endangered the College until the end of the democratic self-governance phase. The democratic Board had quite ably guided the College as it was reestablished and began to flourish.

However, in the summer of 1996, in the midst of what was generally perceived to be a financial crisis, a Board composed of an equal number of internal and external trustees agreed to change the bylaws to restrict the number of internal members to two—a student, who would be nominated by the student body and a faculty member, who would be nominated by the combined faculties. A more complete account of this change will be presented in the next section.

Concluding this theme, Self-Direction as a Management and Financial Proposition, it is impossible to disentangle the financial implications from educational and community values of the experiment in self-governance carried out from 1975 to 1996. However, certain generalizations seem self-evident. In the first few years, the College depended heavily on the dedication and sacrifices—including financial sacrifices—of the staff and faculty. It is very doubtful those sacrifices would have been made if the community had not been self-governing. This history also reveals that true self-governance has been controversial, and that within the extended College community there has been a lack of consensus in the philosophy and practice regarding authority and governance.

History of Debt and Pay-As-You-Go, 1975–97

In our society, colleges—like most service institutions—are conceived to be *eternal*. They are created to exist and operate, not to end. Certainly in the

1950s and 1960s Dr. Parker, the citizens of Prescott, and the many who had contributed so much of their time, thought, and substance to the establishment of the College did not consider the possibility that their contributions might be for naught. Even as they became aware the financial situation was deteriorating, the students and their families could not quite envisage that this lively institution on its new multi-million-dollar campus could be taken away so easily. By the early 1970s most participants knew that it was going through a severe test, but they also nurtured a faith that it would survive this youthful phase, that certainly wealthy and influential people and agencies would see it through. When their faith was dashed in 1974, after only nine and a half years of operation, a harsh and unbending reality manifested. In the real world of money, when an organization runs out of cash and credit so that it becomes insolvent, it *does* close its doors. All the positive thinking in the world cannot overcome that reality.

The founders of PCAE had lived through that experience and learned the lesson of that unyielding reality in the world of money. As they created a new set of principles and policies, they built in a prohibition of paying for operations through borrowing. The new policy had various names: *no debt*, *in the black*, or *pay-as-you-go*. If tuition and gift income did not equal budgeted expenditures, the budget was reduced. In moments of shortfall, when other expenditures had been cut to the bone, paychecks were delayed or even reduced by mutual consent. Reserved funds like IRS and FICA deductions were never dipped into. Bookkeeping was conscientious, and regular audits were contracted, even though account figures were very small. Of course, one reality that kept the College's managers on target with this no-debt policy was the fact that PCAE was tainted in its credit rating by the bankruptcy of its predecessor. PCAE and the Center College claimed to be the full successor of the old college, and merchants and lending institutions took them at their word.

For the first half decade of PCAE, the no-debt policy was scrupulously followed, even though the occasional delays in payment of bills or paychecks caused mild consternation as well as extra work in bookkeeping. But the College was careful to fulfill its financial obligations. Meanwhile it was steadily building up equity in its property. The biggest equity accrued in its main home, the Sisters of Mercy Convent. The College had invested about $25,000 through its down payment, and then had invested over $200,000 (almost double its purchase price) in renovations. Inflation had steadily added to the equity, too. Based on this equity and a good credit history, the school's bank set up a limited revolving account that could be drawn upon in times of cash-flow shortfall, usually in late spring and summer. This was not seen as a violation of the no-debt policy since immediate income in the form of fall tuitions was virtually guaranteed. With their newly secured line of credit, the College moved away from what some termed "crisis management." Another factor helping to even out the cash flow was the establishment of the ADP (external BA degree division), which had different tuitions cycles. Soon the College's CIBTE (Center for Indian Bilingual Teacher Education) program received sizable grants, also expanding the cash on hand.

Student numbers remained low until 1984. Tuitions also remained low, hardly growing when dollar amounts are adjusted for inflation by CPI. Many observers were very impressed that the College had continued in business and recovered during this period. Much was said about the financial sacrifices of the faculty and staff is such a difficult working situation. On the other hand, participants were not depressed or discouraged. Rather they expressed enthusiasm and hope for the future. The budget for the 1975-76 academic year was $173,000 ($568,921 in 2005 value by CPI) and the total student body was 62. Twenty years later, 1995-96, the budget was $7,334,000 ($9,133,729 in 2005 value by CPI), and the combined student body reached 711. In other words, after two decades the number of students served had increased eleven-fold, while the College budget (corrected by CPI) had increased sixteen-fold. Stuckey, having guided the new College through its infancy, left the presidency in 1983 and joined the Adult Degree Program, where he could employ his expertise in program and curriculum design.

Ralph Bohrson, who came from the Ford Foundation, was appointed president in the summer of 1983. He immediately set out modest goals that were within reach. He wanted to move away from any hint of crisis management. He brought other skills and priorities, emphasizing stability and leaving curriculum to the faculty. He reformed the business and student aid systems, and activated a committee for long term planning. The College was granted full accreditation in 1984. Once the business functions—including financial aid through federal sources—were regularized, Bohrson retired as president in 1988.

Dr. Douglas North was appointed president in 1989, and brought yet another emphasis. He was eager to place the College on the national scene again, and less cautious about finances. A progressive educator who came from Goddard College, he was inclined to move ahead with new projects, particularly in the non-resident programs. Under his leadership the College was accredited to offer an MA degree, and the non-resident Master of Arts Program (MAP) was initiated in 1992 with six students. Another leader, Joel Hiller, dean of the College, was active in off-campus "adult education," as it was called. He was particularly vigorous in developing the facilities and programs in Tucson. A small office was opened in Phoenix, but closed after a few months. Hiller also initiated an application to the State of Arizona to provide a BA-level program for prisoners incarcerated in state prisons, which unfortunately was not funded.

Another initiative was to increase enrollments, particularly in the resident BA program (RDP), while also raising tuitions at rates exceeding inflation. This was successful, and it ushered in a period of accelerated expansion. It was as though a flood gate had been opened and everything the College had been deprived of in its first decade and a half was made available all at once. Tuition revenue was greatly expanded from 1988-89 to 1992-93. With higher enrollments and tuitions, overall income increased by 310% (while

Year	Instructional salaries	Student services salaries	Academic support salaries	Institutional support salaries	Total salaries	Total expense budget	Total PC enrollment all programs
1983-84	$262,113	$42,468	new budget category	$47,548	$352,129	$764,134	160
1984-85	$331,320	$48,846		$49,342	$429,508	$810,461	228
1985-86	$411,051	$45,529		$59,875	$516,455	$975,442	217
1986-87	$509,686	$65,193		$72,641	$647,520	$1,123,191	222
1987-88	$568,577	$101,677		$78,373	$748,627	$1,371,428	267
1988-89	$645,999	$107,618		$95,704	$849,321	$1,747,401	277
1989-90	$938,262	$154,401		$142,752	$1,235,415	$2,753,170	343
1990-91	$1,366,211	$200,894		$145,813	$1,712,918	$3,944,221	343
1991-92	$2,066,455	$280,483	$253,925	$206,029	$2,806,892	$4,759,951	510
1992-93	$2,489,362	$372,478	$311,019	$307,737	$3,480,596	$6,115,323	551
1993-94	$2,824,292	$373,297	$362,068	$354,804	$3,914,461	$7,035,375	609
1994-95	$2,896,448	$442,379	$459,282	$381,485	$4,179,594	$7,559,724	668

Table 17. Total Salary Budget Increase (12 Fold) Compared to Student Enrollments Increase (4 Fold), 1983 through 1995

the overall budget increased by 347%), to well over $6 million in just four years. To cover the growing gap and pay for the many improvements, North and the Board set higher goals for fundraising. Unfortunately the fundraising, for both unrestricted and restricted gifts, improved very little—from about $116,000 in 1988-89 to $303,000 in 1992-93—an increase of only $187,000. In other words, while the fundraising increased, it represented an ever smaller percent of the overall revenue because of the dramatic increases in tuition income and the overall budget. While fundraising represented 6.7% of the budget in 1988-89 when North assumed the presidency, it represented only 4.9% of the budget in 1992-93. In the process of growth and financial expansion, the College was increasingly tuition dependent, and this process has continued to the date of this writing. (The next chapter contains a more complete analysis of revenues.)

The most expensive project underway was the revamping of the College's whole salary structure at every level. As explained above, beginning in 1990, the College sought to bring compensation levels in line with what they believed to be industry standards. Many judgments had to be made to determine what these levels should be. The Board and those who were assigned to do the research gathered comparative data on compensation levels at other colleges and universities, which data appeared to be more germane to their deliberations than the needs of individual faculty members.

Table 17 demonstrates the increases in salary budgets by category and in total over twelve years from 1983-84 to 1994-95. Under the equal base pay policy, total salaries increased from about $350,000 in 1983-84 ($690,000 in 2005 value by CPI) to about $850,000 in 1988-89 ($1,400,000 by CPI). In that same period enrollments increased from 160 to 277. While enrollments increased 1.7 times, salaries doubled in purchasing power as per CPI.

After the new differential salary policy was initiated in 1989-90, total salaries increased from about $1.23 million ($1,945,000 by CPI) to about $4.18 million ($5,506,615 by CPI) in the next six years (1989 to 1995). In other words, while enrollments only doubled, salaries increased by a factor of 2.83, nearly tripling.

This analysis demonstrates that salaries represented the largest factor in increasing the budget and incurring a deficit, as discussed below.

Graph 2 illustrates this process graphically. The numbers used to generate it are actual dollar amounts, not corrected for inflation, so that the increases are more dramatic than they would be if purchasing power were used as data points. However, the spread of the three lines accurately depicts the fact that increases in salary levels constituted the leading factor in unbalancing the budget.

As the analysis above demonstrates, under increasing budget pressure

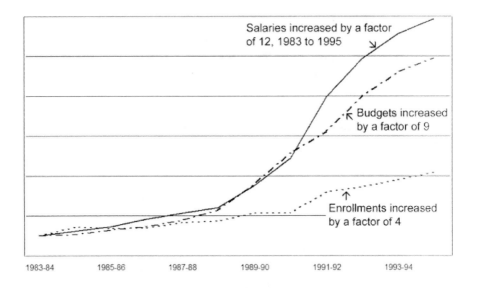

Graph 2. Comparison of Enrollments, Budgets, and Salaries, 1983 through 1995 (not corrected by CPI)

in the early 1990s the fiscal conservatism, which had been maintained as a policy since 1975, began eroding. This was not done consciously as a matter of policy. It crept up on the Board and new president. Projected budgets of the period appear to have been based on anticipated increases in student enrollments in all divisions, steeply increasing tuition totals, and unrealistic fundraising targets (necessary to *appear as* balanced budgets, but never realized). The budget projections appear to have been based on very optimistic estimates rather than a sober examination of institutional history.

One might ask how the gap between income and expenses was allowed to happen and went undetected. Another new controller had been hired, and for three successive years, 1989-93, the Board was given internally generated financial reports that blended incomplete bookkeeping data with optimism. When the Board asked for a comprehensive audit, it was told that the books were in transition and were not in shape to support an audit. That appeared at the time to be a reasonable explanation because a new bookkeeping system had been necessary in order to accommodate the higher level of complexity happening in the institution. It was, however, not reasonable to attribute the problem to the previous president, Bohrson, who was very conscientious in his financial management.

The growing financial deficit was also partially hidden by CIBTE, which brought in over $300,000 each year in grants. At least half of this money was already allocated for Native American students' tuitions, which they paid to the College. Administrative and teaching salaries paid out of these grants increased the size of the budgets, but did little to fill the growing financial gap since additional personnel had to be paid out of the proceeds. Adding to the confusion, most of the CIBTE grant income appears to have been mistakenly posted on the books as "unrestricted gifts." This would have increased that fundraising income category by almost $1,176,000 spread over three years, without increasing dollars available for other operations. This led to a false impression that fundraising was improving at a faster rate than it was. Finally, the financial records from this period were incomplete, and the new controller appears to have been incompetent or negligent. At least it is not clear how these growing yearly deficits were allowed to bridge the end of three fiscal years without detection. It is clear, however, that a situation was developing which was similar to that of the "old College." The College was again overspending and passing deficits across the June 30 ends of fiscal years.

President North resigned during the May Board meeting in 1994. While it was established policy that all professional positions were to be filled through a national search and a democratic vetting process, the Board felt the College community was not ready to open a national search at that time. The Board also was insecure about the financial health of the College. A decision was made to appoint internal administrators to interim positions to fulfill the functions. Joel Hiller, the dean of the College, accepted the interim position of external president, with the charge to raise funds and represent the College externally. Lady Branham, dean of the Tucson operations, accepted the position of interim internal president, with the charge of managing personnel, budgets, and other internal responsibilities.

One of Branham's first actions was to appoint separate deans for each of the external programs—the non-resident undergraduate program (ADP), the non-resident MA program (MAP), and the on-reservation teacher training program for Native Americans (CIBTE). This added some cost, but it mainly was a matter of assigning upgraded titles to people already doing the work. She did this to provide more leadership to the divisions so that she could concentrate on the problems confronting central administration. This did make it necessary to change the way the books were kept in the business office. Branham dismissed the negligent controller and replaced her with her assistant.

North had left the College during a serious financial moment, as the new interim presidents soon discovered. Revenues were increasingly insufficient, but no quick remedy was available. At a college, costs are not so easily curtailed, people have been hired, properties have been leased or purchased under mortgages, and programs have been committed to. Branham worked conscientiously to pare down operational budgets without harming the educational programs. She instituted an austerity program with the full support of the faculty and staff, and the College was able to shave about $500,000 from the 1994-95 budget. Student enrollments had increased by fifty that year, and tuitions were raised on average about $300, so that the budget deficit was reduced even though salaries had increased. Hiller was also hopeful that the College might soon receive substantial support from a major donor. It appeared that the return of conservative fiscal policies would soon eliminate the accumulated deficit.

At this hopeful juncture, however, a second crisis seemed to materialize out of nowhere—or it could be considered a continuation of the first, for it followed precipitously on its heels. Branham learned about new regulations of OE (U.S. Office of Education, Office of Post-Secondary Education), that were to become effective on July 1, 1994. This would require a Single Audit (professional audit of all federally provided financial aid) for the previous year to be submitted in order to maintain certification for the Title IV, Student Financial Assistance Program. While there was no indication of any default at that point (early May, 1994) the College was not ready, and no Single Audit had ever been done. Upon further investigation Branham learned that if a college should fail to comply, it could be "referred for administrative action." She immediately initiated a two-year audit, and intensified the College-wide austerity program.

As the business office worked to provide data for the audit, the hidden problem with the budgeting and accounting surfaced, and it became necessary to change personnel. Branham replaced the controller with an interim business manager. Though a valiant effort was made, the required audit could not be accomplished in the very short seven-week period available. The archives contain a letter from OE, dated February 24, 1995, that scolds the College for missing the previous July 1994 deadline for submitting the Single Audit report, along with a new application for funds. OE allowed the College another thirty days to comply. Price Waterhouse, the accounting firm conducting the audit, then advised the College that they could not produce the required audit at all because the books were lacking certain essential reconciliations with the general ledger, and procedures were not in place in the College to analyze the year-end cutoff of expenditures. This may explain how deficits had been passed along from fiscal year to fiscal year without raising a red flag. Another archived letter from Price Waterhouse, dated April 7, 1995, advised that the College now had a $1.2 million deficit.[47]

The College had been renegotiating its debt situation, particularly the mortgages. As lenders became aware the College was in deficit, they changed their formerly confident attitude. For example, the College received a letter, dated April 14, 1995, from Stockmen's Bank that threatened to raise the interest rate to 22%. Such penalties were avoided because the replacement business manager/acting controller defended the College on all counts, and agencies and banks were convinced to allow more time to restructure debt. Nearly complete financial reports and applications were finally supplied and accepted by the Office of Education, and temporary certification was granted to the College. On July 28, 1995, a complete audit for the year ending June 30, 1993, was submitted, and the College seemed to get back on track to regain full recertification.[47]

It is clear from the archives that it had been the tardy audit, not the growing deficit, that upset OE in the first place, and there is no documentary evidence in the archival record that the College's accreditation was in imminent danger.[47]

The impending crisis seemed to have been avoided by fall 1995. Overall enrollments were up by forty-five students, and tuitions had been increased modestly, yielding a gross tuition gain of over half a million dollars, while the economies instituted, including some deferred maintenance, reduced costs by half a million dollars. This should have stopped deficit spending and retired some of the debt. On the down side, fundraising was reduced—at least on the books—which shifted more of the revenue load to student tuitions.[9]

The year 1996-97 began with another big push for austerity. Branham brought an accountant with extensive community college fiscal management experience onto the Board. This new Board member/accountant soon insisted that the interim business manager/controller Branham had appointed be replaced by himself, and he took over the College's business office. Shortly thereafter, he told Branham and the executive committee of the Board that his analysis of the books indicated the College was heading toward insolvency and bankruptcy, and was in imminent danger of losing its accreditation as well as its certification to participate in the government's student financial aid program. If that were to occur, it would cause the College to close down. He implied that only he had the insight and experience to turn this situation around, and he was taken seriously. Branham felt the community should be informed of the situation, so she suspended classes for an afternoon and convened a community meeting to which students, faculty, staff, and administration, as well as local Board members, were invited. The new Board member/accountant quickly dominated the meeting and gave the same grim message to the whole College, again emphasizing that only he could "turn the [financial] train around and keep it from going over the cliff."

He warned the whole community that the College would have to relinquish its bequest arrangement for "the Dalke property." This announcement was made without the authorization of the Board, which had entered into a legal contract with the Dalke family and their legal team. It was a stunning blow to the College community, which had put great stock in the prospect of saving eighty-seven acres of beautiful forest land on the western boundary of Prescott from commercial development—Mrs. Dalke's dream. The community had anticipated building a campus there, or at least a field station for environmental studies. It was widely promoted and appeared in the College's public relations media, including recruitment and fundraising literature.

THE DALKE PROPERTY

Details of the Dalke bequest can be found in the Prescott College archives, and some aspects are pertinent to this fiscal history. Dorothy Dalke, a long-time friend and supporter of the College, owned a trust in which she had placed this property. She wished the property to remain undeveloped as a green zone, and she felt the College would be able to preserve it, while using a small portion of it for campus facilities. Her legal advisors had worked with the College's administration and legal team to create a contract by which the College would purchase an insurance policy on her life with her trust as beneficiary, so that the property would be deeded to the college at her demise. The City of Prescott government was also in support of the project, even though it would remove from the tax rolls a prime area that could be used for expensive residential and commercial development.

This very public airing of the financial straits of the College by a Board member, who was already in control of the business office, created a surreal atmosphere throughout the College community. Some of the most bizarre incidents in the history of the College followed. Many faculty and students were distracted from their studies to the cause of "saving the College." The new Board member/business manager was the third person in two years to be in charge of the business office and act as controller, and he appeared to act independently and without authorization. He used the authority of controller to stop the Dalke payment, for example. He was reported to have contacted North Central Association and the U.S. Office of Education, representing himself as the virtual president of a failing college, imploring them not to revoke accreditation or disqualify the College for financial aid. However, the archives indicate that it had been the tardy audit, not the debt, that upset OE in the first place—there is no documentary evidence in the archival record that the College's accreditation was in imminent danger.[47]

Because Branham believed these warnings were credible, and the College was really headed for "the cliff," she initiated a secret project, working with all cost center heads, to develop lists of employees, including faculty, who would be suspended without pay when the current year's funds were depleted, which she anticipated might happen within weeks.[25]

Meanwhile, new auditors were to be employed. A memo dated January 17, 1996, from the new Board member/business manager—now also controller—specified that the Peat, Marwick accounting firm would do the 1995 audit.[25]

On February 5, 1996, internal president Branham signed a consulting contract with this Board member/business manager's consulting firm. Since he had also consulted with the local community college in a similar fashion, it appeared that he and an out-of-state partner had created a business network to intervene and aid colleges. A letter in the archives suggested that Prescott College should relinquish some of its legal financial authority to a foundation or consulting firm. This was not done, but in effect it would have bypassed the Board's fiduciary role.[25]

While all of this was happening, the Board's Executive Committee was also developing plans to drastically pare back expenses, including discontinuation of the dual presidency. Many within the community found it difficult to know who was in charge.

The spring Board meeting of 1996 opened and then went almost immediately into executive session, so that the community was not allowed to understand the issues or give input to the Board. When the general session convened an hour later, a motion was immediately introduced and passed to return to a single presidency. The dual presidents were consequently on notice that their presidencies would be terminated by this action; however, they were both invited to apply to the national search. This process further added to the feelings of stress and confusion suffered by the community. The open discussion that followed centered on how to conduct the national presidential search.

One of the most paradoxical aspects of the second "debt crisis" was that the deficit seemed to be increasing with each successive financial report no matter what austerity measures were implemented. As the College ever more drastically cut all daily and weekly budgets, the deficit levels reported by the business office grew proportionately. The faculty appointed a committee to look into this perplexing situation, and they finally uncovered the cause. The new business manager/controller/Board member had implemented an accounting system in which all savings (i.e., budgeted dollars not spent in a given month) were recorded as "internal deficits." In certain businesses any money saved during the first three quarters would be spent in the final quarter of the fiscal year; such a process of internal budget management might make sense in that situation. However, at Prescott College the last quarter was always the most inactive because very few classes met in summer, and in that particular year it was expected that considerable savings would occur in the final quarter. In other words, through an accounting process inappropriate for the situation the deficit was being inflated on the books, and people were being frightened, while in reality savings were accumulating and adequate money was in the bank. When the on-campus faculty became aware of this, they passed two resolutions and sent them to the Board: a vote of no confidence in the internal president, and a demand that the interventionist accountant/trustee be removed from the Board and the business office, and be instructed not to represent himself as "virtual president." The faculty did not want him to be contacting the College's accrediting and financial aid agencies, which was of course the proper role of the president.[18]

At the summer Board meeting of 1996 the chaos of the previous year was addressed by the Board. Branham resigned from the presidency and the College and was awarded a year's salary. Hiller was asked to continue as interim president while the truncated national search was to be carried out. He was also approved for a year's sabbatical with pay. The officious Board member/business manager resigned his positions. And the College was put on a road to financial stability by Norman Traeger, a parent of one of the students, who was a venture capitalist from Ohio. He and his wife offered a proposition that in essence gave him temporary control of most business functions and allowed him to restructure management at the Board and general levels. He offered a modest contribution, and promised a "bridge loan" to extend the budget to the June 30 end of the fiscal year if that became necessary. His offer was contingent on a number of conditions: (1) he would be allowed to restructure the Board membership to include himself and others he trusted, while retiring most "internal" members, (i.e., students and employees of the College including administrators and faculty), (2) he would create and temporarily control a small budget committee with authority to manage the budget, (3) he would screen and approve candidates for business manager/controller, and (4) he would participate in the recruitment and hiring of a new president, chosen from outside the community.

The offer of a modest contribution played no part in the Board's decision. There was some negotiation, but by the end of the two-day Board meeting the offer was accepted with little change. The parent from Ohio, now a Board member and head of an emergency finance committee, moved ahead with considerable energy, recruiting on-campus staff members as needed, reforming the College business office, and vetting candidates for a new controller and a new president.

A new business manager/controller, now designated CFO, was selected and put in place very quickly. She worked with the new finance committee to thoroughly restructure the financing of the College's properties by converting leases to purchases and arranging a comprehensive financing of all College properties through bonding.

The abbreviated search for a new president went forward. Neal Mangham was appointed in January of 1997. He worked diligently to provide leadership to the whole College, which at the time had four divisions. One of the very important decisions taken was to combine the administration and budgeting of all three non-resident divisions under one dean, while maintaining their distinctive operations. Efficiency was improved, but identity of the separate programs was lost. This was particularly harmful to the American Indian teacher training program, CIBTE, which soon fell to just twenty percent of its highest enrollment. Thereafter the on-reservation Indian teacher trainees were served through the regular non-resident BA and MA programs of the College, with no special status or separate financing.

No "bridge loan" was needed, and gradually Traeger returned control of the budget to the new administrative and business leadership. But complete stability and effectiveness had not as yet been achieved. Because the emergency finance committee had put so much energy into its task, the new CFO had gained inordinate authority, which tended to sideline Mangham, the new president. Inadvertently the reform Board had created another divided leadership problem, and the relationship between the CEO and CFO was strained as they pulled in different directions when important decisions had to be made. Within two years they had both resigned, and new searches were underway. Traeger, who had intervened to put things straight, also left and resigned from the Board along with his chosen outside trustees.

At this point, Prescott College alumni who had matured, prospered, and gained experience in the world asserted leadership on the Board. The faculty advised that it favored hiring an interim retired college president for a year or two, but the Board had another idea. They appointed one from their own ranks, Sturgis Robinson, an alum from the beginning years of the College, to be interim president. After that year Dr. Dan Garvey was selected through a national search.

A study of the College's financial records from the late 1990s through 2005 demonstrates that the financial operation of the school has been improved dramatically. The financial records were kept very professionally and audited in a timely manner, and that is not the most important aspect. The financial records give evidence that the College was very competently managed from a business standpoint. Since that time to the time of this writing there has been little possibility that a financial deficit could inadvertently overtake the institution, as happened in the 1970s and early 1990s, to cause such havoc.

HISTORY OF CAMPUS DECISIONS AND FINANCING, 1975-2005

Money Matters Part I contains the financial history of the first version of Prescott College. It reveals that the original campus—483 acres of beautiful virgin chaparral-covered land and nearly fifty buildings and other improvements—was at the center of the financial life of the College. The campus attracted donations of at least $5 million, which would be equal to $28 million in 2005 dollars by CPI. Because tuitions and donations to support general operations and special projects did not cover the costs of operating the new College, the campus was mortgaged in stages over the nine and a half years (1966-75) until the equity was exhausted. At that point the first Prescott College was bankrupt and had to give up its grand home. Since that time the College has not distorted its budget to acquire property, except possibly in responding positively to Mrs. Dalke's offer. Furthermore the College has not abused its equity in properties.

Returning to the legend of the move into the basement of a hotel in downtown Prescott in 1975—the College community realized that what was said as they were expelled from the first grand campus, that a College is people, not land and buildings, was true and prophetic. While being in town offered many advantages, the basement of a hotel was not ideal. The College was again very fortunate to acquire the historic Sisters of Mercy Convent within a year and a half of bankruptcy, and also to find several buildings nearby that were available for lease or purchase as the College grew. One by one the College leased or purchased buildings over the next two decades, financing each new acquisition through conventional mortgages. When the reform Board formed a special finance committee in 1996-97 they worked with a new CFO to rationalize all financial structures of the College. One of their most important contributions was to convert leases to purchases, then roll all the property-related debt into a single financial package. All College properties were refinanced at a very favorable rate by issuing bonds backed up by the City of Prescott in 1998.

By the 1990s the College needed a permanent campus with specialized educational facilities. After much searching, and after analysis of its current location, in 1998 the Board decided the College would stay where it was, surrounding the old Sisters of Mercy Convent building, and would expand westward toward the granite hills and away from noisy city traffic.

Part of that 1998 decision was to build a modern and ecologically sound College center close to the convent building. From beginning to inauguration of the facility took nearly six years. It was the first major building project undertaken since the 1960s, when the original buildings on the old campus were constructed. The new Crossroads Center consists of two large two-story buildings with a community mall between them. It has a footprint of nearly

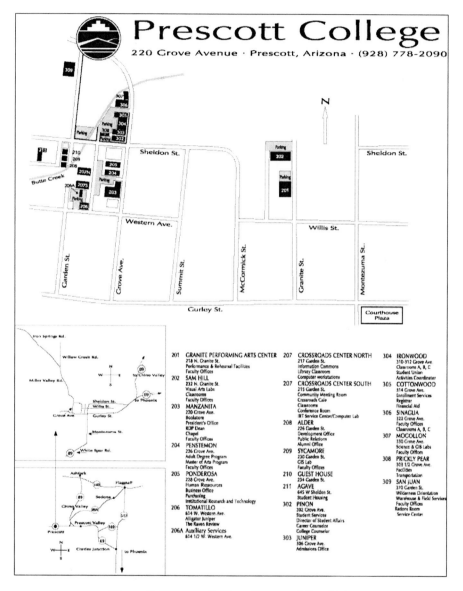

Figure 2. Prescott College Campus Map 2006

an acre, and to the west is an expansion of more acreage with a stream and nature area as well as several buildings housing auxiliary services and a small dormitory.

By 2005-06 Prescott College owned several millions of dollars worth of land and buildings, which were used for all of the many functions necessary to mount a professional effort in higher education. The Prescott downtown properties, now approved as the central campus, consist of approximately nine and one-half acres in the form of an elongated triangle, beginning at 220 Grove Avenue, the College's "old main," (the Sisters of Mercy Convent building) and extending northward two blocks to the bridge over Butte Creek. Along these two blocks, the College purchased seven buildings and was leasing three on lease-purchase agreements. Tracing a campus border along Butte Creek to the southwest, and then jogging to the west at Sheldon Street for half of a long block, then south to Western Avenue, forms the hypotenuse of the triangle. This somewhat crooked border encloses a nature area in the creek arroyo, two houses, a small apartment building and the two newly constructed large buildings mentioned above. Proceeding eastward on Western Avenue for two blocks, the College owns one house and one lot, completing the triangle. In summary, within these borders, encompassing approximately nine and one-half acres, the College owns three large two-story buildings, three office buildings, five converted residential houses, one small apartment building, various utility structures, two building lots, and four parking lots. Nearby, the College owns two off-campus buildings in Prescott—the historic Sam Hill Warehouse, purchased in 1993, which houses a ballroom sized visual arts gallery and studios, darkroom facilities, and faculty offices; and a smaller office complex two blocks from campus. The College also leases a portion of a large building near the Sam Hill Warehouse,

Prescott College Research Station on Kino Bay, Mexico

which it uses as a dance studio. In Tucson, the second campus consists of a large Spanish-style center located near the University of Arizona campus. In Kino Bay, Mexico, the College owns a research station consisting of several research spaces, a four-bedroom home with an additional roof sleeping area, a utility yard accommodating boats and other equipment, and an excellent library to support the kinds of studies going on there.

A Second Bonding

Along with the approval to begin construction of the two new buildings in 2003, the decision was taken to again seek bonding for the whole Prescott Campus, rolling together the previous bond notes and other mortgages that had been engaged. It was a very opportune time, and ten-year bonds totaling $4,305,000 were issued by the College under tax-exempt authority of the City of Prescott. These bonds were purchased by a local bank at the extraordinarily low interest rate of 4.6%. Securing this financing at a point when interest rates were the lowest they had been in years was projected to save hundreds of thousands of dollars over ten years. At the same time, the College undertook a four-year capital fundraising effort, which raised $1,150,523. This total included a single gift of half a million dollars, yet the overall goal was not reached, which is unfortunate since donors are more likely to contribute larger gifts for "bricks and mortar" than for other projects. Nevertheless, these accomplishments provided a much more secure base for the College than had ever existed at the "old College" on its large campus.

The no-debt policy has been restored in a sense, although the College currently carries a debt on its properties of about the same amount that drowned the first College on the old campus. This fact, however, must be put in perspective. Five million dollars is a much smaller amount than it was in 1975 ($5,000,000 in 1975 would be equivalent to $17,350,000 in 2005 by CPI). The current debt load is secured by property that comfortably exceeds $5 million. But most important is a realization that the current debt does not suggest a deficit. The growing yearly income is sufficient to support the increases to operations and therefore the budget is continuously in balance.

Conclusions

This concludes the discussion of some the important financial experiments undertaken after 1975. Most of these attempts to operate in a new way, to reconcile financial philosophy with educational philosophy, were swept away as soon as finances allowed, but some trace of them remains. Perhaps they have conditioned the College to seek economic justice for its participants as it advocates social justice in the larger world.

To achieve fiscal responsibility, Prescott College will
- maintain a "big view" of compensation to include retirement planning and personal development;
- maintain and grow the Board-designated contingency fund as outlined by Board policy;
- engage in business forecasting as a matter of financial preparedness;
- seek revenue from diverse sources and broaden its donor base;
- seek funds from sources that are socially and environmentally responsible;
- invest in an environmentally accountable campus;
- invest in the Library;
- invest in its Field Stations;
- invest in maintaining small class size;
- involve interested members of the community in learning fundraising practices;
- develop adequate scholarship funds to attract and support students with need;
- fairly compensate all employees for their work;
- employ an open process for discussing allocation of resources;
- link the planning process to the budgeting process.

This list of goals was followed by a comprehensive Financial Action Plan to implement them.

Table 18. Financial Goals from the 2001 Strategic Plan

Revenues

Private nonprofit colleges usually get their revenue from only four sources: tuitions, earnings, research grants, and donations. If one wishes to understand the history of Prescott College, it is very interesting and ultimately important to be informed about how Prescott College has fared with each of these revenue sources.

The archived records of revenues from 1966 through 2006 can be examined at the Sharlot Hall Museum and the Prescott College archives, and the College Business Office. The earlier records are not perfect; however, every possible effort has been made to cross-check audits, financial reports, Board minutes, and informal documents to arrive at the data presented here. When audited yearly reports or other records were unavailable, a few of the figures had to be estimated based on proximate data. With this caveat, the tables included in this chapter realistically reflect what was happening in the College financially at each juncture.

Tuitions

The tuition structure of the "old College" serves as a very useful baseline for analyzing the school's tuition practices after it was reorganized in 1975. Table 19 below displays revenues received from student tuitions at the "old College" (1966 through December 1974) and the first three years of the "new College" while there was only one category of students, resident undergraduates (RDP). Therefore there was only one tuition level. This table provides a good analysis of the connection between tuitions and actual cost of education.

Because of inflation, a CPI correction to 2005 values (figures in italics) was essential to make a true comparison from year to year and for contrasting the "old College" fiscal management with that of the new school. For example, $1.00 in 1966 had the same purchasing power as $5.56 in 2005. Table 19 facilitates a true comparison by also displaying all figures adjusted

Year	CPI multiplier	Overall budget	Corrected by CPI to 2005 values	Revenue from tuitions	Corrected by CPI to 2005 values	%age of budget from tuitions
1966-67	5.3763	$539,200	$2,898,924	$109,040	$586,237	20.22%
1967-68	5.1813	$667,744	$3,459,813	$266,772	$1,382,238	39.95%
1968-69	4.9505	$1,671,981	$8,277,133	$368,668	$1,825,089	22.05%
1969-70	4.7393	$1,424,217	$6,749,843	$462,269	$2,190,846	32.46%
1970-71	4.5249	$2,367,721	$10,713,669	$512,582	$2,319,376	21.65%
1971-72	4.4053	$2,638,863	$11,624,947	$560,992	$2,471,330	21.26%
1972-73	4.1322	$2,462,782	$10,176,785	$1,052,800	$4,350,413	42.75%
1973-74	3.7594	$2,062,018	$7,751,947	$1,036,350	$3,896,053	50.26%
1974-75*	3.4722	$1,500,000	$5,208,333	$650,000	$2,256,944	43.33%
1975-76	3.2895	$172,952	$568,921	$116,560	$383,421	67.39%
1976-77	3.0864	$140,124	$432,481	$118,440	$365,556	84.53%
1977-78	2.8902	$222,247	$642,332	$129,720	$374,913	58.37%

*Note: The figures for 1974-75 are an estimated average of the final semester of the "old College"—Fall semester 1974—and the first semester of Prescott Center College (PCAE)—Spring semester 1975.

Table 19. Percentage of Yearly Budgets Derived from Tuitions at the "Old" College 1966 through December 1974, and at the "New" College 1975 through June 1978.

to 2005 values in italics, calculated using the Consumer Price Index, CPI (US Bureau of Labor Statistics). Although the "old College" closed down its campus and operations in December of 1974, this table continues to track operations through June 30, 1978, the last fiscal year in which only Resident Degree (RDP) students were enrolled.

During the first six years, the "old College" received less than a third of its revenue from tuitions. How did it stay in business when two-thirds or more of its revenue had to be derived from non-tuition sources? What were the other sources? It appears that the gap was filled by fundraising and by mortgaging property. From existing records, it is difficult to disentangle these two sources because parts of the campus were under construction during this period and various types of large loans and gifts were being brought in simultaneously.

Academic/ fiscal YEAR	Capital gifts— restricted for campus	Campus buildings costs	New amounts added to mortgage each yr.	Campus mortgage debt cumulative by year
1965-66	$763,335	$1,166,937	$100,000	$100,000
1966-67	$599,653	$505,652	$250,000	$350,000
1967-68	*	*	$620,175	$970,175
1968-69	$759,348	$9,183	$484,366	$1,454,541
1969-70	*	$29,571	$353,942	$1,808,483
1970-71	*	*	$1,011,017	$2,819,500
1971-72	*	*	$639,500	$3,459,000
1972-73	*	*	$235,600	$3,694,600
1973-74	*	*	$290,400	$3,985,000
1974 1st sem.	*	*	$400,000	$4,385,000
TOTALS	$2,122,336	$1,711,343		$4,385,000

*blank cells do not indicate that there was no activity, rather that reliable data could not be found or interpreted.

Table 20. Non-Tuition Revenue at the "Old" College, 1966 through December 1974

The financial picture is confused by creative bookkeeping in which money was moved between construction, maintenance, and College operations accounts as required to keep the College going. (This statement should not be taken to imply that anything illegal or unethical was done.) Another difficulty is that some of the critical financial records gifted to Sharlot Hall Museum have been sealed until the year 2064 at the request of donors. What is clearly established is that by 1974 all the 483 acres of land, the campus buildings, furniture, and equipment—practically everything—had been mortgaged for more than its market value. Even the small endowment fund had been "borrowed from" to support the College's educational operations.

Another source of revenue at the "old College" was auxiliary earning from dormitories, food service, bookstore, and renting campus spaces for activities compatible with the College mission. Further on in this chapter auxiliary income will be discussed in full. Here it is mentioned to complete the explanation of how the college made up a bit of its yearly deficit.

Years July 1 through June 30	Earnings from auxiliary enterprises
1966-68 No reliable data	
1968-69	$153,205
1969-70	$40,092
1970-71	$50,000
1971-72	$50,000
1972-73	$55,403
1973-75 No reliable data	

*Table 21. Auxiliary Earnings from Dormitories, Food Service, Bookstore, etc.,
at the "Old" College*

The old campus was located six miles north of town on a large tract accessible by a newly paved road, remote from rental housing and other businesses. Many students did not have cars, and there was no public transportation. Up to two-thirds of the students lived in campus dormitories, the building of which had been subsidized by federal grants. Most students used the campus food services for most of their meals and snacks. Their rents and food tickets were paid along with tuition at the beginning of each semester. However, this auxiliary income was small and did not come close to filling the gap.

We can infer from Table 19 above that there was a serious attempt to correct the deficit situation beginning in 1972-73 as the student body was increased by 150 students and tuitions were raised by $375 (about $1,000 in 2005 value by CPI), but it was too late. The reason for briefly rehearsing this financial history at the "old College" is to illustrate how important it is to derive an adequate percentage of a private school's budget from tuitions and fees charged to the students.

Tuition income at Prescott Center College, 1975-78

Examining the tuition history during the transitional years of 1975 through 1978, when the College had lost its campus and had only sixty to ninety students, it was actually charging a lower tuition than the "old College" charged, particularly when adjusted by CPI, but the students were paying between 60% and 80% of the bill. The balance of the yearly budgets came from small-scale gift fundraising and grants.

In these transitional years the "new" Center College experimented with both tuitions and matriculation status. Students were offered declining tuition as they progressed and also the opportunity for off-campus studies, as described in this excerpt from the 1977 Catalog:

> By the end of the first year we expect the student to have made significant progress in the ability to find and use diverse resources, in learning to contribute to the design of his [or her] own program at all levels, and in the necessary integrity and rigor of commitment and self-evaluation essential to increasing self-direction. This progress should continue throughout the advanced years.
>
> Because the advanced student needs less assistance in terms of process, he [or she] demands less time and effort from the faculty. Therefore, his [or her] tuition is reduced for the second two years. Tuition is again reduced when the student gains senior status and his [or her] graduation proposal has been approved.
>
> *Non-resident study* [which was charged at about half tuition per unit] is off-campus independent study, which requires no use of campus facilities or direct faculty contact, except on an occasional basis. Faculty involvement will be primarily by correspondence, to evaluate plans, portfolio, or other written work.
>
> *Transfer students*, no matter what their transfer status, pay the first year tuition during their first year at the Center.
>
> *Deferred matriculation*. The college allows delayed matriculation by which a potential student applies for admission during the senior year of high school.[39]

It is not possible to assess whether this kind of experimentation with tuitions actually encouraged students to stay at the College, but by 1980 uniform tuitions were adopted.

Expanding the base by serving other student populations

The next phase of the tuition history features the expansion of the College into non-resident education programs serving additional population groups.

Fiscal-academic years	A Total of students from all pro-grams	B Average tuition paid per student	C corrected by CPI to 2005 value	D Average budget spent per student	E Cor-rected by CPI to 2005 value	F Excess cost per student not from tuitions	G Cor-rected by CPI to 2005 value	H %age of budget from tuitions
Multi-year Averages								
1978-83	118	$2,383	$5,292	$3,040	$6,770	$657	$1,478	78.4%
1983-89	229	$3,700	$6,378	$4,452	$7,637	$753	$1,259	84.8%
1989-92	399	$5,923	$8,510	$9,157	$13,141	$3,234	$4,630	67.0%
1992-95	609	$7,742	$10,186	$11,991	$15,785	$4,248	$5,599	64.8%
By Year								
1995-96	711	$8,325	$10,368	$10,316	$12,846	$1,990	$2,478	80.7%
1996-97	773	$8,416	$10,238	$9,142	$11,122	*$726	$884	92.1%
1997-98	874	$8,806	$10,546	$9,919	$11,879	$1,113	$1,333	88.8%
1998-99	947	$9,267	$10,864	$10,146	$11,894	$879	$1,030	91.3%
1999-00	934	$9,810	$11,123	$11,259	$12,765	$1,448	$1,642	87.1%
2000-01	941	$10,032	$11,060	$11,072	$12,207	$1,040	$1,147	90.6%
2001-02	994	$10,368	$11,257	$11,679	$12,681	$1,311	$1,423	88.8%
2002-03	953	$11,027	$11,705	$13,001	$13,801	$1,974	$2,096	84.8%
2003-04	934	$11,532	$11,925	$13,063	$13,509	$1,532	$1,584	88.3%
2004-05	939	$12,097	$12,097	$13,990	$13,990	$1,892	$1,892	86.5%
2005-06	955	$12,649	$12,257	$14,346	$13,901	$1,696	$1,644	88.2%

Table 22. Percentage of Yearly Budgets Derived from Tuitions at the "New" College 1978 through 2005.

Table 22 displays some interesting analysis in columns D through G. The tuition levels in column B represent a weighted average of tuitions from all the different programs offered. When interpreting the tuitions levels, the reader should take into account that tuitions charged to non-resident students were about half the amount charged to resident RDP students. In the 1978-79 school year the Adult Degree Program (ADP) was recognized as a separate division. ADP grew faster than RDP, reaching two-thirds the size of RDP by 1996.

In 1986, five years after the inception of ADP, its spin-off, the Center for Indian Bilingual Teacher Education (CIBTE), gained separate status. In 1992-93, MAP was initiated with only six students at a lower tuition level, and by 2006 had about 200 students. The PhD Program was initiated in 2005, but is not included in these figures due to its small size.

The first year that the total budget exceeded one million dollars was 1987-88, and RDP represented 61% of all tuitions received that year, but that percentage has meandered downward to 54% in 2005-06 as the other divisions have grown faster.

To summarize, the data on Tables 19 and 22, above, show that students progressively financed an ever larger percentage of yearly budgets, reaching the apex of 92% in 1996-97, then hovering around 90% thereafter.

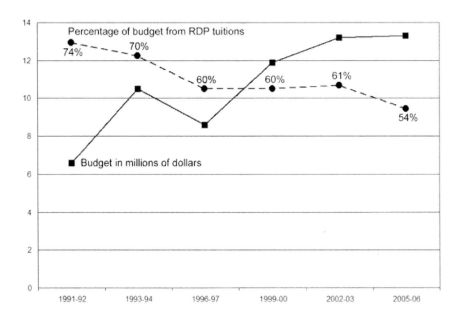

Graph 3. Percentage of College Budgets Derived from Resident Degree Program Students' Tuitions, 1991 through 2006.

Graph 3 illustrates the differential contribution of the resident program as contrasted with the growth of the overall budget. These data imply that the external degree programs—Adult Degree, Center for Indian Bilingual Teacher Education, and Master of Arts programs (collectively know as ADGP)—have grown faster than RDP, and by 2006 accounted for almost half of the tuitions revenues of the College.

The "new" College has increasingly been financed by student tuitions. This trend did not represent a decline in non-tuition sources earnings. Auxiliary earnings, grants, and donations did increase slightly over the years, but contributed an ever smaller *proportion* of the revenue. Another factor explaining why tuitions constituted an increasing percentage of budgets was increased enrollments. While tuition levels only doubled when adjusted to 2005 values by CPI, the size of the combined student body increased ten-fold. In other words, the 90% tuition dependence that has been the case from 1996 through this writing (2006) does not indicate the increases in the College's tuition charges were unjustified. Rather it appears to indicate that other sources of revenue had not grown at the same pace, and were too low.

Some Benefits of Tuition Dependence

To be so heavily dependent on tuitions would seem to be entirely disadvantageous, but there is a bright side. Data to be presented later in this chapter will suggest that there may be an invisible ceiling on *non*-tuition revenues available to Prescott College. For example, Annual Fund donations did not increase in proportion to the growth of the student population. The demise of the "old" Prescott College in 1975 demonstrated that budgeting on the basis of anticipated fundraising gifts is poor policy and very dangerous.

In the early 1990s, president North recruited a few trustees to the Board who possessed or controlled considerable wealth, but the College slipped into debt again and these trustees did not make up the difference. The College's financial history also demonstrates that there was little correspondence between the number of graduates (alumni) and annual donations, which seems counterintuitive. Granted, if donations could be *linked to* increases in enrollments and parent and alumni pools, fundraising would then be more reliable as well as productive in attracting sufficient funds to support growth. Yet through 2005-06 tuition income remained the most reliable source of revenue. Revenue from tuitions is functionally and reliably linked to the growing size of the student body.

Raising tuition levels was not an unprecedented policy at the College. Tuitions were adjusted upward in every year but two from 1966 through 2005. In *unadjusted* dollars, RDP tuitions were increased from $1,400 in 1966-67 to $17,280 forty years later in 2005, which might seems excessive. However, when these figures are corrected to 2005 values by CPI, it becomes clear that the *real* tuition levels were only doubled from about $7,900 in 1966, to about $16,320 (RDP only) in 2005 values. As discussed earlier, in 1966 tuitions paid only one-fifth of the bill, which was unsustainable. By 2005 tuitions paid about 89% of the costs, which presented some difficulties, but the high percentages of budgets provided by tuitions did sustain the College for a decade. Without these increases in tuition income, the College could not have progressed or even survived. Despite the *reliability advantage* of being 89% tuition dependent, there is no denying that *excessive* dependence on tuition income does present several problems that have to be managed carefully.

The Disadvantages of Overdependence on Tuitions

Focusing on the resident program (RDP) for a moment, it becomes clear that there are also disadvantages to overdependence on tuitions. While tuitions have been the most reliable source of revenues, they can also falter if not carefully managed. This danger was demonstrated in the years 2000 through 2005 in RDP enrollment numbers. Before 1998-99, when tuitions were increased, recruitment of new students was apparently not impacted, nor was student retention. For the first thirty-five years when tuitions were increased, the number of students recruited also tended to increase simultaneously. As pointed out above, in real terms—amounts corrected by CPI—tuitions had only been increased by a factor or two or three over this long period. However, after 1998-99 a new phenomenon occurred in the residential program. Registration numbers leveled off and then declined as tuitions were raised. RDP decreased by ninety students between 1998 and 2006. That is a *decrease* in RDP enrollments of about 18%.

Increases in tuitions correlated with reductions in RDP enrollments, 1999-2005. Note that the upward slant of the tuition line has already been corrected for inflation by CPI. It displays increasing tuition in real values as adjusted to 2005 dollars.

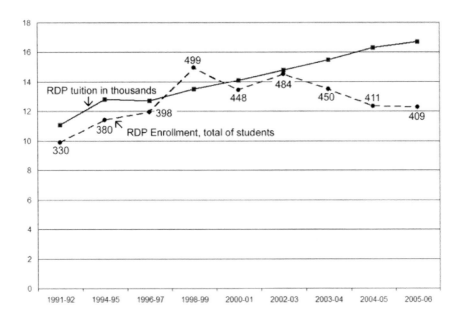

Graph 4. Reductions in RDP Enrollments Correlated with Increases in Tuitions After 1996.

By 2005-06 enrollments were 18% below the 1998-99 level; however despite this decline in enrolled students, the higher tuition levels almost made up for the decline in dollars collected, keeping overall budget revenues from RDP nearly stable. However, the budget does not tell the whole story. Since RDP students are charged a tuition that is higher than that charged to non-resident students, it appears that RDP students with less financial means had been choosing less expensive schools, switching to the ADP non-resident program, or dropping out of college altogether. If that were the case, the College would be obliged to provide more financial aid in order to attract these less affluent students—particularly if it intended to honor its mission of serving underserved populations.

The data show a high correlation between raises in tuitions of RDP and decline in enrollments, but correlation does not prove causation. Other factors than price may have also contributed to the decline in numbers. The whole higher education establishment constitutes a sort of market, and that market is dynamic. The overall economy is changing as well. Since the late 1990s many studies have shown that the American middle class—from which Prescott College draws the majority of its students—is stagnating financially and consciously feeling the pinch. Decisions by middle class parents to send their children to private schools may be more difficult, and accumulation of debt as a result of using both student and family federally guaranteed loans may seem more risky. There are internal factors too; a school with fewer students must trim its curriculum and enrichment projects because it is losing economies of scale. This could lead to a downward spiral in curricular programs and enrollments. Finally, the principle of diminishing returns may be a factor. Enrollments cannot be relied on to continue growing forever, and tuitions cannot be raised indefinitely.

At Prescott College the effects of this temporary decline in enrollments in the resident program was offset to a large degree by increasing enrollments in the ADGP external programs.

While the RDP enrollments decreased by 90 students between 1998 and 2006, ADGP enrollments increased by about 100 students. Therefore, the combined student body numbers stopped increasing, but they remained static rather than decline. Tuitions were also raised for the external programs, but ADGP enrollment continued to grow despite these increases. The net effect of tuition increases was a growth of over $2 million in the overall College budget for the period.

Year	Overall budget	Corrected to 2005 values by CPI	Money from tuitions	Total all students, all programs by year	Average tuition paid by student	%age of budget from tuitions
1998-99	$9,608,020	$11,263,798	$8,776,043	947	$9,267	91.34%
1999-00	$10,515,584	$11,922,430	$9,162,700	934	$9,810	87.13%
2000-01	$10,418,719	$11,487,011	$9,439,965	941	$10,032	90.61%
2001-02	$11,608,925	$12,604,695	$10,305,844	994	$10,368	88.78%
2002-03	$12,389,672	$13,152,518	$10,508,261	953	$11,027	84.81%
2003-04	$12,201,075	$12,617,450	$10,770,534	934	$11,532	88.28%
2004-05	$13,324,691	$13,324,691	$11,793,363	939	$12,559	88.51%
2005-06	$13,732,056	$13,306,255	$12,278,268	955	$12,857	89.41%

Table 23. Total Increases in Tuition, All Programs, Percentage of Overall College Budgets.

The Revenue Enhancement Project

Steven Corey, appointed CFO in 2000, working with the Board, considered the College's tuition levels and stated his opinion that the College had not priced itself out of its market. After a study of tuition levels at small colleges similar to Prescott College, the Board came to the conclusion that the College's tuitions levels were comparatively low, and the reputation of being one of the most inexpensive private colleges in the United States had been one of its major attractions. They also believed that the College should attempt to attract students on the basis of its other fine qualities.

Even though the College's tuition levels may have been in the lower range, the school had been atypical in its heavy reliance on tuitions, and the full disadvantage of overdependence on tuitions also became evident. The majority of independent private colleges have other substantial sources of income. In 1999, the Prescott College Board and administration began working on a comprehensive plan to increase revenues of all types, which became known as the *Revenue Enhancement Project*. Its main features were:

1) to recruit students in greater numbers, thus increasing the tuition base; 2) to raise tuitions of all programs at a steeper rate; and 3) to raise more gift money.[99]

In the early 2000s all three of these approaches were combined in a determined effort to increase the number of available scholarships, grants, and discounts.

FINANCIAL AID

In a typical academic year, 2005-06, 68.8% of students registered in the College (RDP and ADGP combined) were receiving financial aid through one or more of the available sources managed by the Financial Aid Office. The term "financial aid" covers a lot of ground, but can be divided into three types: 1) monies that eventually have to be paid back—these represent the lion's share of all aid available; 2) monies that have to be earned as hourly wages; and 3) monies that are awarded without strings attached, that do not have to be paid back or earned. The figures that will be provided in this section summarize aid given to all students, combining all programs, RDP and ADGP, except when specifically noted.

Graph 5 presents all of the sources of money that went into 2005-06 College budget, totaling $13,910,149. The largest portion, nearly 45%, was

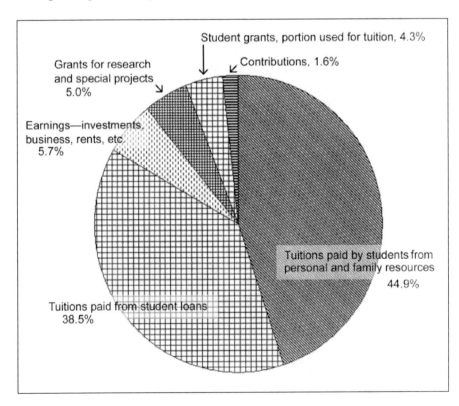

Graph 5. Tracing All Revenue to Its Sources, 2005-06 Fiscal Year

paid out-of-pocket by students and their families. About 38% came from the portion of student and family loans that was paid as tuitions. Not all loan or grant monies go for tuition, because students typically use about 35% to defray living and school-related costs, thus paying about 65% to the College as tuition. About 11% came from sources like overhead charged to research projects, investment income, and business earnings. The smallest portion—about 1.6%—entered the budget from fundraising. However, it is important to note that additional donations were brought in through fundraising, but could not be credited to the annual budget, because they were specifically restricted for such long-term purposes as new buildings or permanent endowments.

Loans to Students and/or Their Parents

By far, the greatest amount of student aid distributed through the College consists of loans to students or their parents, which are federally guaranteed and sold to commercial lending institutions. The guarantor government agencies usually pay fees and interest on the amount owed so long as the student remains enrolled in school full time and earns enough credit to meet guidelines.

In a typical academic year, 2005-06, Prescott College students and/or their parents borrowed a total of $8,212,330 in such guaranteed loans.[47] However, as is customary, that full amount was not retained by the College as tuitions—"rebates" were granted. Data on "rebates" indicate that about 61% of the federally guaranteed loans, scholarships, and grants were retained by the College as tuition in our typical year, so the College retained $5,009,521 while $3,202,809 was rebated to students for their use as living expenses. The overall College revenue was $13,910,149, and more than a third of that income came directly from guaranteed loans, which the students or their parents will eventually have to pay back with interest.

Scholarships and Grants

A much smaller amount of money was provided in grants and scholarships in our typical year, 2005-06. The Single Audit report indicates grants equaled $1,052,019. Work-study "grants" were also listed yet in a practical sense they are not grants but jobs. And they are not listed, as revenue for the College because students use these earnings to pay living expenses, not tuition. In addition to the federal grants, the College itself provided $911,441 to students in the form of scholarships and discounts/tuition waivers, which lowered many students' tuition charges. About $30,000 came from private scholarship funds made available by donors, and the College funded the remainder. Scholarships are awarded on the basis of good academic work, while waivers are awarded by formula on the basis of need or as part of the College's benefit package. A significant portion of the waivers go to College employees as guaranteed benefits, if they are or their qualified family members are enrolled with the intention of earning degrees. However, since such institutional grants/discounts simply move dollars from one column of the budget to another, they do not bring in new dollars.

Summarizing, just over a third of this typical budget was supplied in real dollars by student financial aid of one sort or another. At this point one might ask where the remaining two-thirds of the budget came from in our typical year. About 11% of the budget was gained through fundraising and other sources, and the remaining 45% was paid by students and their families out of personal resources.

Financial Aid from the Student's Point of View

During the decade 1996 through 2006, a little over a third of tuitions received by Prescott College were paid out of students' loans. That is from the College's point of view. Looking at this situation from the perspective

INCOME	2004-05	2005-06	average %
1) Earnings from summer employment	$4,000	$4,000	15.6%
2) Work-study earnings @ $7.25 to $8.00 per hour	$360	$1,944	4.5%
3) Cash from family	$1,200	$1,000	4.3%
4) Stafford loan to student	$2,526	$3,500	11.8%
5) Parent Plus loan to parent for student tuitions and expenses	$16,000	$14,000	58.7%
5) Tuition discount from Prescott College	$650	$1,970	5.1%
TOTAL	$24,736	$26,414	100.0%

EXPENSES	2004-05	2005-06	average %
A) Tuition for two semesters	$16,320	$17,280	65.8%
B) Additional school fees and expenses, including books, course fees, etc.	$1,200	$950	4.2%
C) Living expenses, including rent, utilities, clothing & equipment, auto expenses, gasoline, etc.	$7,150	$8,200	30.0%
TOTAL	$24,670	$26,430	100.0%

Table 24. Income and Expense Budget of a Typical Student Receiving Financial Aid (by permission and anonymous)

of students, about 57% of the money that they borrowed was retained by the college as tuitions, while the remaining 43% was refunded to them for living expenses. Those students who enter and stay at the College by borrowing are grateful, of course, for the opportunity, but it is a big financial commitment.

To provide a concrete example from a typical student's point of view, the author asked an RDP student who was receiving various forms of financial aid to share her 2004-06 personal budget with the readers.

Many who investigate and report on the costs of college concentrate on tuition and fees, books, etc., but fail to take into account that students must also pay for their living expenses. This student, exemplifying the financial situation of the 69% of students receiving financial aid during these years, had to spend about $600 per month for food, rent, transportation, health care, clothing, and other incidentals. Those costs require 30% of her income from all sources. The remaining 70% of her yearly income from all sources, including personal earnings, money from her parents, as well as financial aid, was used for school costs. This student has had to live a very frugal and carefully planned financial life while in college. She and her parents, who she reports are not wealthy, have calculated not just current costs, but also the debt burden they will face after she graduates. Their conservative estimate is that her parents will have taken on over $50,000 in debt, while she will have taken on between $12,000–$15,000 Since her parents own a home, they can borrow more than she can, although she hopes to pay off both loans herself.

Together they will owe at least $65,000 *plus interest*. Monthly or quarterly payments will begin to be charged shortly after her graduation, and will be amortized over a period of years. If, for instance, the amortization schedule were for fifteen years, and the interest rate were 6.5% per annum, the monthly payment on $65,000 of debt would be $566.22. If the full term of fifteen years were paid out, the student and/or her parents would have paid off the principal amount of $65,000, plus interest of $37,000—for a total of $102,000. This is not an extreme case. In fact, those students who are qualified as independent—meaning not family supported—may have to borrow more.

Of the majority of graduates of the resident program who used financial aid, 65% will leave Prescott College with a debt burden that probably equals one- to three-year's salary for a person with a BA who is just entering the professional work force. Those who intend to go on to do graduate work can expect to pile up even more debt. They hope that their additional education results in higher earning power. In a purely ethical sense, the College is mortgaged to its graduates. A minority of full-time RDP students come from families with substantial means or have educational trusts, and for that reason may not need to use loans, or will borrow considerably less.

Since non-resident students (ADGP) live and work in their home communities and have a variety of financial situations, no "typical" student on financial aid could be identified. A slightly higher percentage of ADGP students receive some financial aid. However, since their tuitions are lower, the loans they take on as they earn their degrees are usually less burdensome.

At this point it must be acknowledged that a heavy student debt load is typical in other small private colleges and universities in the United States, so that Prescott College and its students and their parents are not unique in shouldering high levels of debt. Furthermore, students attending tax-supported colleges and universities also accumulate debt. While public institutions have partially subsidized tuitions, their students still have living expenses to pay and often must also borrow student aid funds. It should be acknowledged that interest payments are paid out of the federal tax fund while the student is enrolled full time in an approved program; students do not have to repay these loans until after graduation.

In helping students with these loans, the government has chosen to pay interest rather than give grants. Commercial lending institutions are as much the benefactors of these programs as are the students. They are paid interest out of the tax fund until students graduate, and then the students and their families continue the payments. It has been estimated that the deferred interest paid by the federal government to lending institutions, plus the losses due to defaults, would go a long way toward converting loan programs to grant/scholarship programs. The United States is the only developed and fully industrialized country that allows or requires its talented youth to pay such a large percentage of the costs of higher education, and to be burdened with such high debts upon graduation. The College is dedicated to the goal of relieving as much of this burden as possible through raising scholarship funds and granting discounts.

Non-Tuition Revenues

Non-tuition revenue has made up only ten to twelve percent of the total income of Prescott College during the decade from 1997 to 2006. Although the tuition charged by the College is not excessive, most private schools derive a *smaller portion* of their budgets from tuitions, because they have developed other sources of revenue. It is more typical for small schools to depend on tuitions for 60% to 80% of their yearly budgets. This means they can award more scholarships, have higher expense budgets, build endowments and contingency funds, and be able to finance campus improvements without borrowing.

To compare schools on such financial dimensions is valid, but hides certain unique qualities of Prescott College. Through much of its history, the

College has concentrated on sustainability, and spent its resources creating innovative curricula and teaching systems. It has not expended much time and resources to develop a program of auxiliary enterprises, grant seeking, or large-gift fundraising. Heavy reliance on the students' support through dependence on tuitions is also partially a result of the College's philosophy of independence and self-direction, which is the foundation of its mission. Many educational institutions are very dedicated to values of accumulating property and earning money, which is not a bad thing since money is needed to support their educational activities. However, it is possible for corporate-style goals of raising and managing funds to become the primary concern of a school's directors and administrators, thus subordinating its educational mission. Indeed, some educational institutions do serve almost as fronts for accumulation of real estate and for other profit-making enterprises. Throughout its rather stormy financial history, Prescott College has always chosen the opposite approach. The College has focused on its educational mission, and for that reason in some moments it has skirted the cliffs of financial disaster.

Auxiliary Enterprises

The first broad category of non-tuition revenues is termed "auxiliary income" in the College bookkeeping system. This means money earned from any enterprise that looks like a business. The rubric "nonprofit" that is used to define the College's class of corporation really does not mean that it is prohibited from making money. Rather, it means that no individual associated with the school can be unduly enriched from any earnings. The most promising source of earnings for Prescott College is investment. Amherst College, for example, has an endowment of over a billion dollars from which it earns up to $50 million dollars per year that can only be used for educational, research, and charitable purposes. Prescott College need not wilt in the glow of such riches, but understand that Amherst was a small struggling academy in 1821. Rather, the College should be encouraged that its Board has set aside a small endowment, which is growing year by year. The College is now making some income from investing its "seed" endowment and other restricted funds, which all together add up to less than a million dollars. Referring to Graph 5, 5.7% earnings, in 2005-06 the College took in $783,859, from book sales, food services, investments, etc. For many large universities and older small colleges, these businesses are a significant source of revenues.

Most large schools are in effect major innkeepers and restaurateurs, making significant income from rents and food services. Over the years, federal and state governments have subsidized the building of student housing as well as maintaining and upgrading units. On any large university campus, acres of multistory dormitory buildings have been built. Since they serve thousands of student tenants who are not able to find comparable off-campus accommodations, these buildings—essentially apartment buildings, not really *dormitories*—earn large profits that subsidize the schools.

University bookstores also make high profits, trading in commercial textbooks and all other books and media required by course instructors. The majority of commercial textbooks are designed for mass education systems in which there is a captive market of hundreds of thousands of student consumers. Commercial textbooks are excessively expensive, and are revised or updated at close intervals so that sales of the latest revision will be sustained. Bookstores and other campus outlets also make big profits on sound systems, furniture, computer equipment and software, and hundreds of types of clothing and regalia. Another large source of college and university income is the renting of space for meetings and conferences of all types. Finally, sports teams and events are major sources of income, particularly for universities.

Throughout Prescott College's history, various schemes have been attempted to supplement the budget by providing desirable services and products, but income was usually eaten up by expenses. Because the College's courses have been limited to a dozen students, and are not taught in the mass-education format of lecture, textbook, and objective test, the bookstore carries a multitude of titles, but a very small number of copies of each title. Most students bring their own computers to school, and have not been big consumers of college regalia. In 1992, the Student Union purchased and operated a small natural food restaurant, which served excellent organically grown food. In 2006, the first dormitory building was purchased adjacent to campus; it serves only a few students.

Various schemes to make profits by renting out Prescott College facilities have been tried, but they also failed to yield significant profits. In 1972, when the first College was on the old campus, which encompassed over 500 acres, there was a project to rent out the facilities for conferences and other outdoor educational activities during the summer months. In the two years this plan was in effect, it actually lost money. Perhaps it would have become profitable had the College not abandoned that campus two years later.

In all these cases, earnings have been small or nil because the College has very few and very independent-minded students, hardly a mass-consumer market. The real financial benefit of auxiliary enterprises for Prescott College may come from increased enrollments that result in the College providing more essential services. Otherwise, for all the reasons cited above, it is very doubtful the "auxiliary income" could become a big contributor to Prescott College revenues in the foreseeable future.

Fundraising

Fundraising has become both a science and an industry in America and much of the world. Prescott College has a spotty record in fundraising, as is evident throughout its history.

However, since 1975 and the establishment of the "new" College it has been the conscious decision of the entire College community to *save and conserve* in preference to *earn and spend*. Since this approach is against the grain of common ways of thinking about growth, it has sometimes been seen as a sign of weakness. Having reviewed in depth the history, including financial history, of Prescott College through its first half century, the author believes it is a strength. Furthermore, it appears that this against-the-grain philosophy has been understood and embraced by Prescott College students and most participants at every level. The renewed effort to increase donations, initiated with the Revenue Enhancement Project in 1999, was not an abandonment of that frugal philosophy; since its major focus has become increasing availability and size of scholarships and grants to help students cope with increasing costs of tuitions, special educational projects, and living expenses while at the College.

Nonprofit Status

Prescott College, Inc., and Prescott Center for Alternative Education are both certified as *nonprofit* corporations by the IRS, the State of Arizona and other concerned agencies. The benefits that nonprofit status bestows on schools relate to American tax structures. Nonprofit organizations that qualify—whether churches, foundations, charitable services or schools—are exempted from paying property taxes on their land, buildings, equipment, stocks, investments, and accumulated capital funds. This exemption results in *savings*, but does not produce revenues.

A second benefit of tax-exempt status does result indirectly in revenue. Donors can "write off" donations they give to tax-exempt organizations when calculating their yearly income for the federal IRS, and State and local taxing agencies. Taxpayers' donations, paid directly to the nonprofit organizations they support, are deducted 100% from their reported income, and come off the highest bracket they would pay. Through this system, American individual citizens, businesses, and corporations are given a powerful incentive to donate billions of dollars each year. Americans donate more per capita than do the citizens of any other nation, and we like to believe that we would make generous donations even without these tax incentives. However, experience demonstrates that tax-exempt status is a great advantage in attracting donations large and small.

At the time of this writing (2006) the Prescott College Development

Category	Fundraising Personnel and Institutional Support	Approach to Donors
Type I - Small Unrestricted Gifts, Usually in the range of $25 to $500	2nd level development office personnel, alumni, Board members, students, and community volunteers	Constant general appeals, concentrated Annual Fund Drive
Type II - Larger Targeted/ Restricted Gifts for Well-defined purposes, endowment money, real estate acquisitions and new construction, major plant developments, new infrastructure and technology, major library acquisitions, etc.	President, chief development officers, board members, representatives of the College, people with special relationships with the wealthy potential donors and foundations	The potential donor must be approached and cultivated by a higher-ranking person representing the College, and must be asked for a donation to fulfill a well-defined purpose. Donor usually wants public acknowledgement.
Type - III Bequests People of means, designate the College to be beneficiaries of their estates upon their decease	SAME AS TYPE II	SAME AS TYPE II
Type IV - Grants for Research and Development Projects 1) Projects should involve students for experiential learning; 2) costs of the project, including personnel time, should not exceed the financial and educational value to the College.	Usually faculty members who need extra funds for scientific research, larger-scale art works, expeditions, centers for social action, etc. They will fill the role of principal investigators and/ or project managers.	Seek grants from government or private agencies engaged in the activity the grant seeks to accomplish.
Type V - Scholarship Funds A large-scale effort to raise gifts of any size to a Scholarship Fund. Student grants offered based on 1) need-testing and 2) high academic performance.	All of the methods outlined above, (except for R & D grants), and all of the personnel mentioned, should participate— including faculty and students.	While many potential donors shy away from contributing to a fund that supports general operations, they will be attracted to the idea that supporting students is targeted, contributing directly to the education of individuals.

Table 25. Comprehensive Fundraising Schema

fundraising office uses a software system designed for nonprofit fundraising departments, which is somewhat different in its categories from the software used by the Business Office and the rest of the College. Both systems are designed to place gifts in categories/accounts for purposes of accounting, but neither of their charts of accounts adequately differentiates how the funds are solicited. For the purpose of this explication, a non-standard set of categories will be used which do highlight modes of solicitation. When data are presented they come from both the Development and Business offices, as well as the archives. Audits for the years since 1996-97 may be requested from the Business Office, but the Development Office does not issue yearly reports at this time.

Small-Scale Unrestricted Gift Fundraising

Over the forty years of its operation, Prescott College's fundraising efforts have been most consistently successful in soliciting small-scale, unrestricted gifts. The term "unrestricted" means that a gift was not earmarked for any particular purpose by its donor—the money goes into the general fund and the College can use it for whatever it decides. Usually, small gifts—under a thousand dollars for instance—are unrestricted, while larger gifts are most often "restricted" for particular purposes.

Every year the College has received numerous small unrestricted gifts, and its main method of solicitation has been an annual fund drive. The average yield for all years 1966-2006 was $179,345. When corrected to 2005 value by CPI, the average yearly yield was $397,044. That means that Prescott College has received small, unrestricted donations that total over $15 million during forty years of operation. That is a significant gross amount and was greatly appreciated, and it has been well employed by the College.

However, sophisticated donors and professional fundraisers are also interested in the cost of raising funds. They speak of the *net* yield, the total dollars received less the fundraising costs. For several reasons, Prescott College accounting records and yearly budget reports have never been set up to isolate fundraising costs from other administrative costs. For many years there was not a separate development department since most fundraising was done through the President's budget, and several employees as well as many volunteers contributed only part of their time to fundraising. In the mid-1990s, a separate office for development, alumni relations, and publications evolved, but this office had several functions, so that the salaries and other expenditures used solely for fundraising cannot be isolated. However, a rough estimate can be made for the years 2001 through 2006, excluding large targeted gifts for the new Crossroads Center. With a margin of error of + or − 10%, the cost of raising small, unrestricted gifts was 39%. In other words, the

College invested about $390 to raise each $1,000, so that the net yield would be about $610 per $1,000. A 61% net yield is quite good, considering the small size of the operation. Major nonprofit educational organizations boast an 85% to 90% yield, when they operate on a vastly greater scale.

"Old" College Years	(1) Unrestricted Gifts e.g. Annual Fund	(2) In 2005 Dollars by CPI	(3) Unrestricted Gifts as Percentage of the Overall Budget
1966-67	$94,000	$505,376	17.43%
1967-68	$175,000	$906,736	26.21%
1968-69	$389,700	$1,929,208	23.31%
1969-70	$305,050	$1,445,735	21.42%
1970-71	$200,000	$904,977	8.45%
1971-72	$200,000	$881,057	7.58%
1972-73	$51,877	$214,368	2.11%
1973-74	$200,000	$751,880	9.70%
1974-75	$15,000	$52,083	1.00%

Table 26a. Unrestricted Gifts as Percentage of Annual Budgets 1966-1975

A careful study of Tables 26a and 26b reveals two surprising trends. Column 2, where yearly small gift totals are corrected by CPI, shows a declining trend. The highest gross yields were in the "old" College between 1969 and 1974, the year that first incarnation of the College failed financially. There were other bumps between 1991 and 1995, which happened during a period when the College budget was stretched dangerously. During the decade from 1996 through 2006, the yearly unrestricted gift yields, in CPI adjusted 2005 dollars, has hovered around $200,000. Some questions must be asked about this trend: Why the downward leaning in real values—particularly taking into account that the number of alumni, alumni parents, and those acquainted with the College in other ways has increased steadily year by year? Why the leveling off after 1995? Is there some sort of "invisible ceiling" that the College fundraising effort has hit?

The second surprising trend is that unrestricted gifts represent an ever-smaller percentage of the overall budget, declining to about 1.5% after 1999. Graph 6 below shows that this is not mysterious. It is simply an artifact of the comparison with increasing budgets, which exceeded $14 million by the year 2005-06. But why doesn't the gifts line track the other lines upward?

A tentative answer may be found in the "principle of diminishing re-

New College Year	(1) Unrestricted Gifts e.g. Annual Fund	(2) In 2005 Dollars by CPI	(3) Unrestricted Gifts as Percentage of the Overall Budget
1975-76	$29,229	$96,148	16.90%
1976-77	$33,939	$104,750	24.22%
1977-78	$78,585	$227,124	35.36%
1978-79	$145,000	$382,586	69.71%
1979-80	$143,000	$339,667	46.35%
1980-81	$146,689	$318,197	39.33%
1981-82	$102,256	$208,686	25.29%
1982-83	$119,390	$234,098	23.21%
1983-84	$131,000	$246,241	21.95%
1984-85	$224,767	$407,926	28.59%
1985-86	$137,000	$244,207	16.83%
1986-87	$146,250	$251,289	15.18%
1987-88	$407,000	$671,617	29.68%
1988-89	$115,466	$181,836	6.61%
1989-90	$134,904	$201,650	5.92%
1990-91	$245,425	$352,116	6.22%
1991-92	$358,218	$498,911	7.53%
1992-93	$303,186	$409,711	4.96%
1993-94	$110,419	$145,480	1.38%
1994-95	$448,619	$575,153	5.73%
1995-96	$167,120	$208,120	2.28%
1996-97	$141,875	$172,597	2.01%
1997-98	$218,914	$262,172	2.53%
1998-99	$197,359	$231,370	2.05%
1999-00	$169,614	$192,306	1.61%
2000-01	$137,378	$151,464	1.32%
2001-02	$166,201	$180,457	1.43%
2002-03	$166,201	$176,434	1.34%
2003-04	$192,206	$198,765	1.58%
2004-05	$210,056	$210,056	1.60%
2005-06	$215,906	$209,211	1.57%

Table 26b. Unrestricted Gifts as Percentage of Annual Budgets 1966-2006

turns." It is possible that the increasing cost of recruiting new donors—particularly those who have less connection and weaker motivation to give to the College—may have made it comparatively less desirable and profitable to grow the donor base proportionally. Only careful analysis and planning can answer such questions.

Whatever the case, small-donation gift solicitation has another important function. Apart from funds received, gifts at this level create the additional benefit of sustaining and spreading good will. The donor pool is maintained and increased by keeping contact with alumni and parents, making friends, extending invitations to the community to attend enjoyable events, and even through solicitation phone calls and letters. Social research has demonstrated that people like to be asked for small donations by institutions they believe in, and they expect to give small gifts in the final quarter of the calendar year. Unrestricted fund drives like the Annual Fund build good will and support for the College as a social institution.

In summary, the history of the College seems to indicate that small unrestricted giving can be increased, possibly by a factor of two or three, but it would most likely prove unprofitable to invest a great deal more money and effort in this category of fundraising.

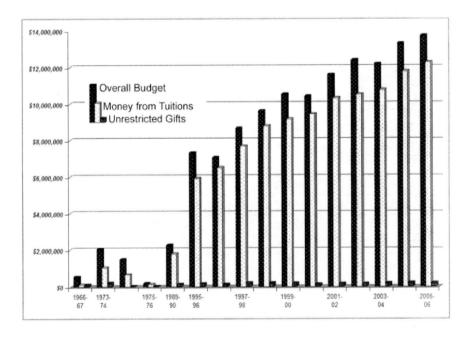

Graph 6. Tuition Income Compared with Unrestricted Gift Income 1966 through 2007

Large Restricted Gifts

Large-scale gifts and grants—ranging from thousands to millions of dollars—are usually restricted, meaning the donor gives the money only for a well-defined purpose. This category of fundraising is the primary means of raising endowment money, funding real estate acquisitions and new construction, and even supporting major plant developments like new infrastructure. It is also often made available to fund such projects as library acquisitions or adoptions of new technologies.

Prescott College has a very spotty history in obtaining large scale targeted gifts. The records of fundraising in the "old" College have been sealed until 2064 to protect the identities of donors who contributed during that period, but the names of several large-scale donors are known. The first operational president, Nairn, raised a dozen or more gifts in the three hundred thousand to six hundred thousand dollar range, which were used to start construction and later to make up budget deficits, but he returned to a small number of big money donors a bit too often. None of those benefactors have come forward again. The Hulmes family made generous gifts to support development of the Kino Bay Center in Mexico. And between 2001 and 2005 several individuals gave generous gifts in support of the new Crossroads Center, the largest being a half million dollar contribution by an alum, Sam Walton. In all such cases, the gifts were arranged through efforts of an individual representing the College working with a donor. In all cases the donor was honored and given appropriate recognition. These were bright spots in an otherwise poor record for attracting large scale gifts. The College's meager record in this area is evidenced by its small endowment, and the fact that most of the campus has been financed by mortgages and bonding. No exact figures for current large-scale donations are provided here because full data are not available

One of the possible causes of the College's poor performance in attracting large-scale gifts is that the College has changed presidents and Board members too frequently (see appendix). However, its forty-year longevity and the esteem and good will of the many who have been touched by the College should provide fertile ground for seeking future large donations, and the Board and President have expressed their intention to raise more large-scale gifts.

Bequests

Bequests are a distinctive form of large-scale gifts in which a person designates a nonprofit entity as a benefactor in his or her will. Since the restoration of the College as PCAE in 1975, the leaders have been more absorbed with supporting current operations than securing a distant future.

Cultivating bequests has been given a lower priority, because they yield nothing at the moment.

A few bequests had been promised to the "old" College, and these became a matter of dispute between PCAE and Embry-Riddle Aeronautical University when ERAU purchased the old campus and all its assets, including the defunct corporation. These bequests were intended to have Prescott College as beneficiary, but legally they were assets of the old College and thus became part of the disposition of its assets. An accommodation was worked in which both parties shared any benefits. This resolution allowed ERAU to return another asset, the name and legal Corporation, Prescott College, Inc., which was yielded to the College in the late 1990s.

In 1991, a landowner and friend of the College, Mrs. Dorothy Dalke, placed nearly a hundred acres of beautiful pine forest adjacent to the town into a trust for the purpose of creating a green zone on the western border of Prescott. Mrs. Dalke believed in Prescott College's conservation mission, and worked out a contract through which the College would eventually acquire the property, with the guarantee the College would never develop the property commercially, but use only a small portion of it for campus purposes. Dr. North, then president of the College, and Joel Hiller, dean of the College, should be acknowledged for their work in securing this arrangement. Mrs. Dalke's legal advisors had worked with the College's administration to create a contract by which the College would purchase an insurance policy on her life with her trust as benefactor, and the property would be deeded to the College at her demise. The College's only obligation was to pay for a life insurance policy that would compensate her family for the loss of the tract of land. In 1996, during a real or imagined financial crisis (see the previous chapter), the community was told that the College would have to relinquish this bequest arrangement. Later, efforts were made by alumni and the community to restore the original bequest arrangements. However, the newly reformed Board decided not to pursue this opportunity, and the "Dalke Property" was relinquished.

In 2007, it was announced by President Garvey that a bequest had matured and the College would receive $1.3 million.

Joel Hiller, Director of Development, has pointed out that in many cases the College is not advised about bequest arrangements in the wills of wealthy friends, and may from time to time be surprised by these acts of generosity. However, if the College would take a long-term view, bequests could be the vehicle through which an adequate endowment can be accumulated.

Grants for Research and Special Projects

There are various reasons for an institution like Prescott College to seek grants and contracts to carry out research, service, or development projects, and the College has hosted a number of such efforts. However, almost every year after the mid-1980s the College has provided a venue and business services for funded projects developed by faculty, students, and sometimes outside researchers. Faculty members who need extra funds for scientific research, larger-scale art works, expeditions, centers for social action, etc., write project proposals and submit them to appropriate private and governmental agencies. These faculty leaders serve the role of principal investigators and/or project managers. The Development and Business offices help to identify potential supporters, produce grant proposals, follow up, etc. When necessary, the Business Office advises the applicant of procedures for creating contracts with governmental or private agencies.

Prescott College, like other schools that enjoy nonprofit status, is not prevented from earning money by means of educational projects. Nor is it prevented from retaining a net surplus from projects that it might take on. It is often the case that schools house projects that are not directly initiated by the personnel of their institution, in which case they may receive rent and overhead payments.

Three criteria have been followed at Prescott College: 1) projects should involve students; 2) costs of the project, including personnel time, should not exceed their financial and educational value to the College; and 3) projects should advance the College's mission or its educational potential. In other words, the College should not allow itself to become a loose nonprofit R & D "job shop" to which any project can attach itself. However, there seems little danger of that.

Prescott College has been relatively inactive in this realm of fundraising, with the notable exceptions of the Center for Indian Bilingual Teacher Education (CIBTE), which was the largest project to receive outside funding in the College's history. CIBTE earned grants and contracts for almost two million dollars from federal and private sources. The CIBTE project was closed when all external divisions were consolidated. It spawned an even larger-scale project now administered by the Navajo (Diné) Nation. Other projects the College has sponsored or accommodated include Project SEE, a cultural development project on the U.S.–Mexican border; a NASA research project housed on campus; and a number of small grants for various environmental research projects. Two planning grants were submitted to the U.S. Office of Education in the 1980s, but were not funded.

Many such projects consume most of the money granted. However, other small schools do supplement their budgets by going after grants that support faculty, college-sponsored conferences, and other valuable educational efforts. Government agencies and private foundations often recognize and allow the host college to earn reasonable financial benefits and to be compensated for rent, overhead, and other services. This sort of revenue enhancement requires a great deal of coordination and planning. Because research and service grants have both educational and financial potential, it would be worthwhile for the College to consider encouraging them more actively.

Funding Scholarship and Tuition Grants

Over many years kind donors have established scholarship funds, some with one-time gifts and others as revolving accounts. It is important to acknowledge these scholarship endowments, so they will be listed here by the names of the grantors: Boyce, Bremmer, Cartledge, Clowes, Ebarb, Ellis, Goodman, Haide, Hearst, Kemp-Garcia, Kanup, Maas, Morris, Quitobaquito, Reed, Simpson memorial, Stuckey, Tufts, Wells Fargo, Windsor, and Wright. In the year 2005-06, a total of about $30,000 was awarded to Prescott College students in small scholarships from these funds. This becomes a foundation of good will that the College can build upon as it seeks to increase scholarships and grants.

As noted above, the Board and administration initiated a Revenue Enhancement Project in 1999, with the purpose of building a more secure and diverse financial foundation for the College. At that point RDP was still growing and was at its apex enrollment. But then RDP enrollments began to wane, and the College managers began to suspect that the second of the Project's goals, "2) to raise tuitions of all programs at a steeper rate," might be in conflict with its first goal, "1) to recruit students in greater numbers, thus increasing the tuition base." Therefore, it was decided to further focus on the Project's third goal, "and 3) to raise more gift money."

In the early 1990s a decision was taken to combine all revenue enhancement approaches in a long-term, large-scale campaign to increase the amount and number of available scholarships and grants to students. Specifically, the College would direct all unrestricted gifts to a scholarship fund. This was a key decision that responded to the history of over-dependence on tuitions. The money raised allows the College to attract more students by offering scholarships and grants. From potential students' point of view it helps them enter and stay in the College. And that, in turn, helps the College maintain its excellent educational programs.

An established fact in the fundraising world is that many potential donors shy away from contributing to a *general fund*, because they cannot be sure how their contributions will be used. They often feel that supporting the day-to-day operations of an organization is somehow a misuse of their gifts. From their experience in business, they believe an organization should already have developed and funded its budget. They feel that gifts should go to enhancement and innovation, not mere maintenance. These same wary potential donors might be attracted to the idea that "supporting a student" is targeted. If they can be assured that their money will contribute directly to the education of students who are service-minded, who will work for positive change, who will return the gift to the world upon graduation, and continue contributing throughout their lives, the wary donors' resistance can be converted into enthusiasm.

In this way the goals of raising more gift money and of increasing tuition levels become directly linked to the goal of providing more financial aid, thus making it possible for students with limited means to afford the College. As Steven Corey, the CFO explained, "As for financial aid, we are already engaged in a multiyear process to increase our financial aid by exponential amounts. Whereas financial aid grants and discounts represented 4% of tuitions in 2004, it is planned that 24% of tuition will be paid by grants to students who qualify by 2009."[15]

Conclusions

What can be learned from this short exposition of the forty-year history of Prescott College's various efforts to finance its operations?

1) **Tuitions Revenues:** Because of its rocky financial legacy from the 1960s and 1970s, which resulted in a lack of endowment, the College has been over-dependent on tuitions. The Board and administration initiated the Revenue Enhancement Project in 1999, but even this plan was mainly based on raising tuitions at a steeper rate.

2) **Financial Aid:** Prescott College has served a population that mirrors a cross-section of the American class structure, so that two-thirds of its students need financial aid to enroll and stay in the College. Lacking an adequate financial foundation, the College's financial aid program has depended on federal financial aid, mostly in the form of guaranteed loans. Therefore, more than half of the graduates find they have accumulated a significant debt. A commitment has been made to address this problem (see item 7 below).

3) **Institutional Grants and Scholarships:** Since the number and size of *funded* scholarships from both governmental and private sources is inadequate to meet students' need, the College's commitment to increase aid is mainly dependent on discounting tuitions. This entails transferring money between accounts, but does not add any revenues to the budget. A significant portion of the discounts go to employees and their immediate family members as a guaranteed benefit. The college is working toward the goal of awarding 25% of total tuition in grants to students in need of aid.

4) **Unrestricted Giving:** Each year the College has received a thousand or more small gifts, adding up to between $150,000 to $400,000. In the early years when the budget was smaller, such amounts represented a significant percentage of yearly revenues, but since 1996 the same totals have represented

only about 2% of the College's income. It is not completely understood why unrestricted gift income has not tracked the constant upward trend of the yearly budget. It has also been difficult to isolate the real cost of raising these funds; however, from triangulations of budget detail figures it appears that the cost is about 39% of the intake, give or take ten points, leaving a net gain of about 61%. Unless unrestricted giving can be increased by orders of magnitude, it will not be an effective means for solving the College's fundamental financial problems. However, small-gift fundraising is extremely important for public relations, and it has the potential of contacting and cultivating friends who may eventually become major donors.

5) **Large-Scale Restricted Giving:** Securing large gifts is about the only means of building a solid financial foundation. One gift of a million dollars equals five years of small gifts, and the cost of securing it is proportionally much smaller. It is not uncommon for small colleges with unique missions to receive sizable gifts restricted for endowment, campus building programs, endowed chairs, research laboratories and projects, and other purposes. However, such gifts seldom appear serendipitously. They are the culmination of clear direction, considerable planning, and cultivation of potential donors. **Bequests** are a variant of this category of fundraising.

6) **Research and Service Project Grants.** A small nonprofit private College is an excellent platform for creating and securing funding for research and service projects, and Prescott College has hosted a number of these. The largest was CIBTE, which was self-funded through governmental and private foundation grants of over two million dollars. Since these grants require considerable work in locating sources, preparing proposals, doing the contracted work, and then reporting results, they cannot become big net earners for the College, but they may bring in new funds in the form of overhead, salaries and, as in the case of CIBTE, tuitions from new project-funded students. The value of such projects is mainly the enrichment of the educational side of the College, as well as enhancement of the College's experience and reputation.

7) **Targeted Fundraising for Scholarships:** The College has recently (early 2000s) committed itself to increase scholarships and tuition grants to students at a scale that is at least commensurate with increases in tuitions. Institutionally funded scholarships, grants, and discounts do not add to the general fund, but are a process of redistribution. The more new money the College can raise for financial aid, especially in forms that do not obligate students and/or their parents with additional debt, the more beneficial the policy will be in creating a sustainable financial foundation. Giving for this specific purpose of helping a student gain an education and become a contributing citizen could be a major new theme in Prescott College fundraising.

PART V

Humorous, Outrageous, and Touching Accounts of Prescott College Life and Adventures

Prescott College people are great storytellers and letter writers, probably because there is a powerful community feeling born of the Orientation experience and nurtured by the small seminar-discussion format of classes, and countless extracurricular activities. The College encourages informal portfolio writing as well as formal papers, and features student and faculty accounts in its various publications. The following unabridged and unexpurgated pieces are typical of the sincere (but sometime irreverent) culture of the College.

By Permission of Prescott College Photo Archives

My Experience

by Melissa Doran, Class of 2007

I came to Prescott College in much the same way as everybody else, with a vague notion that I wanted to study something environmental. "Ecopsychology," I remember telling people when they asked what I was going to study. I always wanted to be the one doing something different, and majoring in something nobody had ever heard of (myself included, really) was one way to do that.

I remember the first time I came across Prescott College. I had been plugging along at some grimly average state university, walking around everyday wondering what had become of me. Why was I suddenly merely one within the masses, sitting amongst people I didn't know in crowded lecture halls? So I got online, determined to find something better, something that suited *me*. I did a college search for schools that offered various environmental studies, sustainability studies, urban revitalization, community development, all these sorts of obscure majors. And only one kept coming up time and time again. Prescott College. I remember looking at the website that very first time, and the first thing I saw was "Who Studies Here? Environmentalists, artists, educators, and activists." That was all it took. The more I looked into it, the more I knew it was the *only* place that I wanted to go. Coming from a humble working class background, there was only one thing holding me back: Money. But I applied anyway, and despite knowing that going to this little college would put me in debt for the rest of my earthly life, I came.

But of course, I went to visit first. Before I shelled out several grand a semester I wanted to see what I was getting myself into. The first time I came to Prescott, and walked excitedly to the campus, I was so disappointed I cried. All the high hopes and expectations I had had, everything I had envisioned from afar in Detroit, all came crashing down that first night. I cried and I started going over options in my head again. Community college it would be. How stupid I was to think that this college could be everything I had built it up to be. There was no campus to speak of, a couple little buildings next to the Dept. for Economic Security.

My boyfriend and I begrudgingly went to our meeting with the admissions counselor the next morning, our minds having been made up the night before, but Amanda Hanson immediately changed them. She explained the concept of the school, the ideas of experiential education (students were always out *doing* things, the size of the campus wasn't really that important), self-direction, small classes (there was an intentional 14-person cap on every class—so that everybody could fit into the vans for field trips), etc. She offered me cookies with sincere apologies that they weren't vegan. We walked around the tiny campus, saw posters of all the things the students were organizing, and realized, yes, this is all that I thought it would be after all. There was something to be said, I thought, for a college with more 15-passenger vans than buildings.

I spent the summer scared out of my mind about Wilderness Orientation, having never done anything like it before, and being far too small to possibly carry the 80 lb. pack they suggested. But the summer ended and before I knew it I was at my first day of class. Ha. First day of "class." Yes, this place surely was different. I stared around the group that had gathered in a circle at Sam Hill Warehouse that Sunday afternoon, and my first instinct was to RUN. It was worse than I expected. Everybody around me had dreads, and they had all done NOLS. Or sailed around the world. Or had worked as outdoor educators for years already. I've never even *been* backpacking. Who was I kidding?! I thought to myself, as I called my boyfriend crying; telling him there was just No Way I could do this. I briefly considered breaking my leg so I wouldn't have to go on Orientation, but I wussed out on that too. ...

And thank God I did. It turned out to be the greatest experience of my life. From the first day meeting my group (which consisted of not only people my age, who have become lifelong friends, but Gabriel, in his late twenties, Alan, in his late thirties, and Stuart, in his mid-forties), I knew something life-changing was happening. By the time we were on the bus being carted off to the wilderness, I looked out the window and realized two things. One, I was home. And two, that I wanted to major in Education for Social Change. I'm not sure that I even knew what that meant yet, but I had ideas in my head of what it meant. I spent the next month in the wilderness perfecting the idea, which two years later, I'm still pursuing. Never before had I known what I was going to do so passionately and pursued it so unyieldingly.

On Orientation, I learned my own strength and potential. I was made aware of the absolute power and unbelievable beauty of nature. I learned how strong a bond between strangers can become, so quickly, in the wilderness.

I learned these lessons through 4:30 a.m. hypothermia and crashing head first onto a boulder, through floating on my backpack down a canyon creek, staring up at the brightest blue sky I've ever seen, and from watching a flash flood rise around our ankles after a night of monsoon thunderstorms, and having to immediately run to higher ground and climb mountains in the rain. Orientation changed my life.

For the past two years I have thought that I would not return the following semester. I just Could Not afford it. But every semester, I find a way, and put myself further and further into debt because it is worth it. Because there is no other college I want to be at.

My first year was spent evolving as a person, becoming independent again, and becoming a member of an amazingly tight and strong community. It was spent discovering my passions, with both hits and misses. I soon discovered, however, the things that truly called me. No longer was I depending on some vague notion of what I wanted to do (ecopsychology was dropped), I knew exactly what I wanted and found teachers who nurtured those passions, exposed me to new information, and most importantly inspired me to do great things, make great changes. I discovered that teachers were friends here, and that they are not only teaching, but they are doing incredible things in their own lives, through their own activism.

My second semester I took two classes that would solidify my educational path—Human Rights Seminar with Randall Amster and Writers in the Community with Melanie Bishop. Not only did Randall quickly become a friend, but he was the activist I always wanted to be, and more. The critical moment of this class, however, was at the annual Local-to-Global Teach-In in Tempe, Arizona. Members of our class had stayed at Randall's friend's house the night before, and that day Randall was on a panel discussion with Ray Ybarra and state representative Kyrsten Sinema. Ray spoke of his new project with the ACLU, legally observing the Minutemen group that was on its way to Arizona. This group was an armed racist vigilante group that was coming to Arizona to patrol the borders and "protect" the country from "illegals." This struck an immediate chord with our entire class, and we decided to make it our project. On the way back to Prescott the next day I sat next to a friend who was in what I referred to as the "activist elite" at Prescott College. There was a certain group of about ten individuals who knew the ropes and who just Got Things Done at the school. They were my role models; I wanted desperately to be like them. I remember talking with this friend and telling him how I wanted to get involved, but I didn't know how, and he encouraged me. The next month was spent working in the hot desert sun, side by side with Randall, Ray, Kyrsten, and several members of our class, working for the

ACLU, making sure that everybody's human rights were respected. Suddenly I was becoming an activist, I had passion, I was teaching others. This was the beginning of coming into my own as an activist.

That semester was also spent working closely with my friend and co-teacher Will Waterman, teaching a creative writing class to "troubled" teenage boys at Blue Hills Academy twice a week. Through Writers in the Community, we had been teamed up with these boys, and had dedicated ourselves to inspiring them and helping them find empowerment through writing. We threw conventions to the wind, told them that grammar and spelling didn't matter to us; we wanted them to find themselves and their strength through writing. We sat on the floor, we brought kayaks to the desert to inspire stories, and by the end of the semester, we listened to eight boys proudly read what they had written before a crowd. And I knew that this was what I wanted, to inspire change in individuals through teaching.

By my second year at Prescott College, I was right on track with my own goals. I was on track for a degree in Education for Social Justice, I was running the Amnesty International chapter and working with border issues, and I was part of an incredible community of people who constantly inspired and supported me. I was made to do things I didn't think I could do.

Over the two years that I have spent here I have not only discovered who I wanted to become and what I wanted to do, but I have found countless role models who encouraged me along the way, both students and teachers, but all friends, and I have become that person. I am confident and sure of my goals and myself, and this, I believe, is the greatest accomplishment of education.

Note: Melissa Doran, one of Prescott College's outstanding alums, graduated in December 2007 and is establishing herself as a professional educator. Melissa has written other articles included in this book under her byline, and she served as researcher and editor as well.

Student Letter to the Prescott College Community through Dan Garvey

◇◇◇◇◇◇◇

April 15, 2007

Dear Friend and Family and Teachers,

If you are receiving this message you have made a difference in my life and I care to share with you some thoughts.

I just got homesick. Not just now, really it was closer to five minutes ago as I began to read all the Prescott College messages in my PC e-mail inbox, but I guess that is not the point. The Kenya Project Thrift Store, community lunch, class registration, parties, rock climbing, frisbee, birds, spring, waking up to the chatter of house finches under a palapa roof. Friends. These things are the point.

In the past three years I have pondered what "home" is. I have pondered it a lot. Is home a place? A town? A building? A piece of property? A deserted beach on the Sonoran coast? An estuary, knee deep in mud, staring at strange avian wonders while my closest friends stare at me, wondering, "who is this guy? " and "where did such excitement come from?"

In the past three years at Prescott College, I have been all over the country and some places outside the country, and everywhere I have found a home. Even with homes everywhere, I find that not all of them are for me, not all of them are my Home. So I ask again, what is home? Or maybe more specifically, what is my home? Can you have more than one? Can I have a home in Maine and a home in Arizona? A home in Bahia de Kino and a home in Amboseli? A home on a snow-capped peak towering over forest and stream and a home on desert slick rock under the coyote's moon? The answer that I return to each and every time that I ponder this question is No, it does not quite work that way.

For me, my home changes. It splits and morphs, travels and stays

Abram Fleishman (right) and Douglas Clendaniel birding at Watson Lake
photo by Travis Patterson

grounded. It holds me and comforts me during times of frustration and sickness, and laughs for the sake of joy. Sometimes it is nowhere to be found and other times it is right there in front of me, begging to be seen, to be acknowledged. My home is my people, and my connection with those people. Without the connection, my people turn into ordinary people, and fade into the backdrop of life. Where else can you find such care and compassion, such unconditional love, than at home? But remember, home is never constant.

My people are never sedentary. Even my parents have moved great distances in the past year, changed their lives, and they continue to shape who they are—a reminder of the lucid dynamic nature of Home. After more than thirty years in Maine they just moved across the country, three thousand miles, to Oregon. After years and years as a science educator, my mom decided to be trained as a yoga teacher and movement "healer." My sister is going to graduate school for a degree in psychology. My friends are graduating from college and traveling and going back to school and getting jobs and getting married and having kids and buying houses. And me? Where am I?

Well, I am adrift. I am away from my Home. Away from my people. Right now, as this boat rolls and pitches towards *its* home, I am sitting *consciously* removed from that vortex they call Prescott, or Putney, or Days Meadow Farm, or the ocean, or Home. I have seen more than sixteen people come and then go from this boat, but none of them are my people. For the first time, I am *consciously* separated from "my people." *Consciously* alone, with no one operating on my frequency, functioning at my level, thinking in tandem, feeding off our mutual excitement for biodiversity, sculpture, bicycles, music, birds, strawberries, or the most simply incredible fact that we exist at all.

The key here is the *consciously*. Think about that. Pause for a moment and think about implications of the word *consciously*. Stop and reread the paragraph if you need to, but understand what I am talking about.

I am talking about an awareness. I am talking about a growth of self. I am talking about brand new, never before known realizations, not new experiences. Just an acknowledgement of something that has happened before, and will happen in the future, though it is my hope that the next time will be "planned."

The mutualistic excitement that I mention above is something I value in my people. The mutual realization that you and I both have something great to gain from each other. Share the load and it might be lighter, and you might be able to lift bigger things. The mutual willingness and desire to learn from both peers and elders is something that I have come to realize is not normal or common, yet it has been ever present in my life.

I have been lucky in my education—and just so you know, *my education is synonymous with my life*—so I know what I am talking about. I have been surrounded by like-minded, generous, idealistic, altruistic, generally happy people. From my beginnings at The School Around Us, to Putney, Outward Bound, NOLS and finally Prescott College, I have been blessed. Not just with the content of those programs, but instead the people conveying that content and the students with whom I have shared the experiences. These people have seen how good something is, and instead of the "normal" or "American" reaction of trying to have more of that magical something for themselves, they turned around and tried to share it with anyone and everyone who will listen. In this case, that something is knowledge. The excitement for the transmission of knowledge that my teachers and peers hold is unique and precious, and in truth, it is the reason I am still a student at Prescott College. Through my time here on the research vessel *Pacific Storm*, I have become aware of just how unique and, possibly, how valuable it is to hold excitement in teaching and learning.

Traditional academia is a subject I know almost nothing about. I have never spent time in a classroom that the instructor was a Mister, or Miss, or Doctor, and my learning environment consisted of a desk. My teachers were always Peter, or Lorayne, or Dave, and they had kids and families, and lives. They were always willing and happy to meet me almost anytime of the day to talk over schoolwork, or life, and they have always been there to listen. The difference between Prescott College, or Putney, or NOLS, and traditional education is that at Prescott College, Putney, and NOLS, your teachers are your friends. They interact with you, when appropriate, as peers. They guide you through a scholastic voyage, and they check in with you along the way to make sure you are still there. And if you are not right behind them for some reason, they will slow down and sometimes come back and help you so you do not fall behind.

I have now just spent a little over two months with traditional academics. Not academics in the sense of learning but academics in the sense of people. PhDs who are researchers, not professors. The information they produce is not for the general public or their institution; it is for their funders. They go where the money is, not where the greatest need for information is. They are opportunistic and successful and have busy fast-paced lives. And most of them even seem happy. They are not conservation driven, and not environmentally oriented.

It has been surprising to comprehend the opportunistic nature of the scientists on this trip. Perhaps ever a little disenchanting at times. Though through this experience I have gained a greater motivation to study and eventually do research in areas that I want to study. I am even more driven to find money for projects that I think are important, not some donor. I understand the difficulty in achieving this goal; however, I also sense the value and importance of such goals. I have come to realize conservation, and more so restoration, is what I believe in and am inclined to pursue. Applied restoration biology. Repeatedly it has been pointed out to me that most of conservation is done by a select few. It is those few that have inspired me. Whether I go into science or I go into education I want to make a difference, and I am beginning to understand the sacrifice that must be made to succeed.

I have been told that *education is a journey, not a destination*, and I have no doubt that it is true. The accumulation of experiences and knowledge never ends, and for me it is just beginning. I need to thank you for listening to me, and maybe actually hearing what I have said. The message in this letter is that I miss my community, my people, my home.

Sincerely,

ABRAM FLEISHMAN

PS: I saw a blue whale the other day...

Note: At the time of this publication, Abram was a senior in the Resident Degree Program, intending to graduate in Spring 2008.

Out of Arizona

by Joanne Motichka, Class of 1974*

What am I doing here? I thought, racing towards my destination and now having to down-shift into second gear as my 1965 Volvo's carburetor chokes in the thin desert air. A wrong turn off route 40 and onto 89A has me crawling along the scenic route, stuck behind a trailer, going about five miles through the town of Jerome and over Mingus Mountain. My AAA trip tick states there's still 60 miles left before I touch down on the Prescott Prairie and find the sprawling college campus that will be my home for the next few years. Worried how late it's getting, I figure room registration will be closed by the time I arrive and I'll end up sleeping in my car again, or under it, depending on whether the sun sets in Arizona or not.

Once off the mountain range I floor it trying to make up for lost time. Speeding across the flat terrain dusk approaches and the sunset mellows out into a spray of dusky rose and tangerine—intensifying the bedrock to a deeper shade of red. The Granite Dells. As I study this foreign landscape I realize somehow I've been here before—well almost—in a movie theatre when I watched an epic drama where views of earth looked just like this from the mother ship.

The opening shots of Stanley Kubrick's Space Odyssey 2001 were filmed near the Prescott College Campus when it opened its doors in 1968, and as I drive past the spot where a tribe of sleeping apes awoke at dawn, moved in slow motion, swinging their clubs, I realize my Space Boogie had just begun. Back east, sun-drenched, luminous landscapes and horizons with apparently no end could only be seen in the movies or on TV programs such as *Bonanza* and reruns of *Planet of the Apes*. I descend even lower, to an altitude of 5,300 feet above sea level, and a series of rusty rock formations jutting towards the

*These events took place in 1972; piece was written in 2005

sky comes into view as does a wind-whipped wiry tumbleweed, which crosses the dusty road and bounces off my car's fender like an out of bound basketball. Void of vegetation the two Twin Peaks in the distance are scorched dry and wrinkled like a pair of crinkled tits.

I pull off to the side of the road to study my map, take a piss and wipe the yuk off my 122S Volvo's windows that interferes with my vision. Only five miles away now from my target I look around—at a horizon that never ends—and wonder what kind of bugs end up on your windshield here? In the land of Lorne Greene and Jesse James who played out Kings and Wild Bandits, I too would have to play out a part on the Ponderosa Prairie. My eyes skip over the tops of cactuses and burn like the orb visions that remain after one stares into the blinding sun and must then look away if one wants to see anything at all again. In this vast openness there may be freedom, but there is also a peculiar type of emptiness. Prescott is a very small town of 16,000 inhabitants and doesn't have a movie theatre; a concert hall and the few 'art' galleries on the side of the road offer bright oil paints on black velvet. There's plenty of knick-knack stores, Indian outposts, and cowboys to empty bars on whiskey row, but if you're a cultural junky it might be hard to get a fix. Shops sell snakeskin pointed cowboy boots that look uncomfortable (but are absolutely the bomb) and wide brimmed straw hats that give men a "Mexican edge." If you want to brush up on your game of pool without chalk the most used cue sticks are racked at the Piñon Pines or the Palace Bar.

It hasn't rained in years.

I take a deep breath as I switch out of flip-flops and into a pair of Keds. Pulling sand particles that are caked and parched within my nostrils I keep wondering, what have I gotten myself into now? I reenter the car cabin, depress the clutch and turn the engine over and pick up the trail.

Newly posted arrows point to the Prescott College parking lot, which is in the middle of nowhere. Situated on a sprawling 620-acre parcel of high prairie plateau, Prescott College was different from the school I was supposed to attend in Missouri—which housed 4,000 students and a variety of ethnicities. Instead, PC has 400 enrollees and the only race represented there is white.

In 1973 seventy-eight percent of students attending the nation's public schools were white and twenty-two percent were minorities, which meant that college enrollment consisted of even a higher percentage of the Caucasian tribe. Back then the word *minority* was a category that primarily included blacks and Hispanics, though on all federal applications, there was the proverbial slot for "other." While it might be understandable that some mixed-heritage students would rebel against a school's effort to get them to identify themselves as one race or another, thirty-five years ago immigration and intermarriage were far from defining race across the country and rare was the institution that pretended to be integrated.

Terminating discrimination and segregation (which eventually led to minorities being quicker to get scholarships than whites) was a part of my era's 'social responsibility' efforts maturing and many of its leaders developing programs to unite people of all colors. After the restless racial sixties—the Newark Riots, Martin Luther King's and Malcolm X's assassinations—injustice had taken its toll on our society. I too, had been a recipient of discrimination, landing in prison wrongfully where some of the inmates and most of the matrons were black. Upon release, as an under-aged juvenile delinquent and an orphan, I would reside in a variety of mixed communities where I attended schools and shared needles, knives, pens, and books, with many blacks. By then "black" was the politically correct term for "that other race," having replaced negro or nigger. "People of color" was a term used by bigots trying to 'erase' black from the societal palette, and by the nineties, "Afro-American" replaced them all.

A milestone in the black-white confrontation was fully in place at Windsor Mountain—a private prep high school I had been fortunate to attend. They had instituted a program for minorities called *ABC*: standing for A Better Chance.

The headmaster was white and the assistant headmaster black. Known for accepting smart students who deserved a good education but could not afford it, the school had a reputation for its desire to provide schooling for those who needed it the most and accepted many students regardless of race or wealth. The school's philosophy was to teach children the ability to find success in solving problems through tolerant, nonviolent, workable school democracy in an era when conflict, drugs, and violence populated world headlines. The students' Bondy Clan wanted to increase the possibility of giving peace a chance by prioritizing equal rights for all people, particularly children and Afro-Americans.

By the time I arrived there, the stoners had taken over.

But Windsor Mountain had more to offer than the freedom to experiment with mind expanding or physically crippling substances. The Windsor charm resided in the fact that the campus felt like home. Relationships developed there were difficult to find at other institutions, because the wide range of student 'types' attending did not exist at other schools. For many, the campus was a safe environment. And while many students were upper middle class, others were very rich and often the offspring of famous rock stars and singers—such as Harry Belafonte, Judy Collins, Thelonius Monk and Sidney Poitier—mixed between the black and white trustafarians were also poor children from Europe and Africa. Bussed in from Harlem (and often kicked out of the public school system) scholarships were given to dozens of Afro-Americans residing there. *Every* student at Windsor was given a second chance at a good childhood if they had missed it the first time around with their original parents, foster parents, or caretakers.

"Adjust, but don't conform" was Windsor Mountain's official school motto.

I made my entrance one glorious fall day much as a prisoner arrives in a black Ford with a gold emblem embossed on both front doors: State of New Jersey. Officially I was a ward of the state.

Many similarities existed between Prescott College in Arizona and Windsor Mountain in Massachusetts. Guidance counselors at Windsor often pushed Prescott to the more neurotic juniors worried about their next move after graduation. Both schools were relatively small and specialized in the development of the individual while offering a stellar education (if the student selected their entrees from the regular academic menus). A sense of freedom (which came out of the spirit of each school) prevailed and co-ed students co-habited with a sense of honesty and integrity hardly visible in the world we know today. Because Windsor and Prescott College had so much in common, PC was a natural stepping stone for many wealthy or upper class students and was referred to as the Harvard of the West.

"It's cool man, cool," Libby Lourie, a younger student at Windsor Mountain mused, flipping through the pretty Prescott College Catalog printed on double weight bond rag paper, color pictures by Jay Dusard—photograper extraordinaire—and a presentation royale one day in our dormitory. Like most juniors, Libby was preoccupied about which college to attend after she left Windsor's nourishing and nurturing womb. I, on the other hand, a senior, was already packing up and preparing myself for Washington University in St. Louis—a prestigious school for the arts and sciences—which I was scheduled to attend in the fall, having already paid my non-refundable room deposit.

Somewhat of a visual junkie, it was obvious to me that the gray skies of Missouri couldn't compete with the colorful canyons presented in the images Libby and I were reviewing that fateful springy day. Flicking through the PC Catalog I spotted phrases such as "creative intelligence," "independent curriculum," and "students get to do their thing." From the photos, Prescott College looked like a posh place, and unlike my current campus in New England, it did not have a reputation for experimentation with herbs, chemicals, glue and let's do drugs instead of high school. The student population was more concerned with politics and the future of the planet, while the Center for the Person at Prescott helped them gain access to horses, kayaks, and long health-affirming expeditions in the great outdoors. The weather was nicer than Massachusetts, so many classes met under a tree; Orientation was held for twenty-five days in the wilderness and students often practiced flipping kayaks in the heated outdoor swimming pool. The school, known for its Outward Bound Discovery Program and its dedication to environment preservation, specialized in field trips and student directed learning, which meant classes were often comprised of two people: you and your professor.

Prescott's unofficial motto was "education is a vacation, not a destination."

But unlike Libby, whose family had a mansion estate on primetime waterfront property in the exclusive Watch Hill community of R.I. and a townhouse on the Upper East Side of Manhattan, I was broke, homeless, on welfare and Medicaid, and received a $3,500 stipend for tuition each year until I graduated college, courtesy the Rehabilitation Commission of New Jersey. In those days $3,500 could buy a decent education, but Prescott College was more expensive than Washington University and put low-income and minority applicants at a distinct disadvantage in the competition to matriculate there. There were probably lots of very talented students from poor and moderate-income backgrounds who could never consider a school like Prescott—including myself.

I calculated that even if I played up the welfare card, I'd still be shy $1,800 for tuition.

I applied anyway. Vibrant with the endless possibilities and dreams the world seemed to be providing Libby and me (considered equals at Windsor) we were joyous as the sun settled over the spruce and pine trees, splaying shadows of all shapes onto our laps, and we reviewed the PC application. After all, we were young. We were raw. And we were beautiful.

But unbeknownst to our young naïve minds—as the ropes of destiny pulled us to the western frontier—they were also hanging if not strangling these two great institutions. In the next few years both Windsor and Prescott would become mere sinkholes of good intentions as they both collapsed into bankruptcy.

The Application Process vs. Financial Aid

Reducing the pressure and stress of admissions the PC application was unconventional and designed with a slant towards the personal. Prospective students were inspired to express themselves in essays that could hardly be contained within the spaces provided and required additional sheets of paper. I have always been reluctant to answer inquiries related to race or religion, but found even stranger PC 's mandatory mug shot. A curious order indeed when one considers driver's licenses in the '60s and '70s didn't even require a photo ID. What's up with that, I wondered? What do they want to know about a person through their photograph?

Perhaps I misunderstood the reason for the photo ID. I'll never know. But I did realize one thing: blacks were more likely to receive scholarships and financial aid than whites and I needed all the help I could get. As someone familiar with the system, opportunities needed to be taken any chance they presented themselves. According to the Prescott College Catalog, Creative Intelligence was a virtual and virtuous course offered; so why not begin the class early, before I arrived? Maybe I could go undercover and my race and appearance didn't have to be specified on this application? Perhaps my image should be unrecognizable and I could identify myself in a different category all together? Perhaps I could apply as a black person?

An exhibition of my self-portraits using charcoals was about to close in the Berkshires when I contemplated PC. A reviewer had written that the expressions on the faces exhibited were defiant, sullen, resigned and, intentionally or accidentally, made an unhappy comment about life. "These are today's alienated youth." What I would often capture was an appearance (perhaps exhausted by nutritional neglect, sleep deprivation, and the after affects of drug use) which would not only resemble aspects of my character, but also reflect those of others. While waiting in long lines in welfare buildings with mostly Afro-Americans I'd study their features, and when I found a seat, I'd pull out my sketch book and start drawing as we all waited our turn for some windowless room to open up (where we could discuss our progress with a social worker or probation officer). My sketches were exaggerated, and sometimes it was difficult to differentiate who I was drawing from the self-portraits I created the night before in my dorm room. The similarities between my subjects and *myself as object* were blurred as we experienced a comparable fate: sometimes the disappointments in our lives were on display in sunken sad eyes that communed with cameras, or some individuals, but mostly our own reflections in lavatory mirrors as we sought relief (or shelter) waiting for our names to be called. My favorite self-portrait at the time depicted myself incarnated as a black queen of the Nile in the dying state.

What colors did I use to paint this image? I thought to myself as I now studied the blank spot on the Prescott College application that begged for a white, black or 'other' check mark. Was it red or yellow? Didn't I use multiple colors? And couldn't I just paste this self-portrait in the space provided and substitute it for a "real" photo? Wasn't that "black" Negroid image as truthful, as representational as any other one that could be captured on film?

Nowadays the federal Education Department has proposed new regulations that allow students to circle as many categories regarding race as they want on any college application. But back in the '70s you were either black or white, or even less so, Hispanic. There wasn't even an option for Native American or Alaska Native.

But there was the mysterious "other." And so after some deliberation, I taped the self-portrait to the application, pointed my pen to the line that said "other," checked the box and scribbled in "Mixed Media."

It was late in the day, on August 28, 1973, when I finally came upon the last arrow directing me to turn into the Prescott driveway where I soon docked my insect-coated Volvo against a horizontal log in the parking lot. I was dehydrated, hungry and sporting a very sore ass from this six-day race across America. The sun settling down for the night produced a twilight that did give the campus a Kubrick-Zone effect, and if one squinted, the four hundred students, receiving room assignments by the flag pole and registering for *what three week outdoor excursion they might take*, could be those hairy apes, moving slowly, stacking kayaks on top of sports vehicles and lifting paddles instead of clubs as in Odyssey 2001. As I slowly opened my car door into a wind tunnel, I contemplated several impending obstacles:

Matuschka (Joanne Motichka) made up as Faux Black

1. How to tell the school I needed $1,800 and
2. How to convince my teacher and student advisors that not under any circumstances was I going on Orientation.

"You have been assigned the Grand Canyon Hiking Excursion with white water rafting down the Colorado River," Lee Stuart (my student advisor) informed me, after handing me my "welcome packet" in the commons.

"I can't go." I almost shouted back above the din of arriving student confusion. The Solo (a book of matches, some water, and if conditions warranted a sleeping bag) was less acceptable to me than flying to the moon on a kite.

"No," I said. "No. I can't go."

Adamant, Lee reminded me that Orientation was a mandatory requirement at Prescott College—one I likened to dragging a dead elephant through a swamp by its tail. Lee, having never met someone with considerable inertia on this issue, summoned a school official, and this individual happened to also by coincidence be my teacher advisor, a man named James Stuckey.

"I need to start my studies straight away." I interrupted before Stuckey and Lee began their pitch. "I don't want to miss out on Dr. Bruce's lectures on the Far East, a course that is not being repeated the following block."

Quickly Stuckey realized persuading me to take the trip of my life was hopeless, knowing I would probably rather fly to the moon on a kite. While he, like Lee, was stunned that I was refusing to go on Orientation, an opportunity of a lifetime and the reason *most* students applied to PC in the first place, Stuckey smiled and did not persist.

"You're going to skip the ultimate trip," Lee said disappointedly, as she walked away disappearing into a small sandy puff of a tornado. As I watched her fade into the sunset, knowing my mission was accomplished, a gusty gale arrived, blowing both my Arizona road maps and Prescott College welcome packets out of my hands.

As I scrambled and stomped on the loose pages flying about I must have looked, for I certainly *felt*, like a yo-yo in a windstorm, knowing a much tougher persuasion lay ahead. The next feat to be tackled had to be more successful than the last if I wanted to secure a key to a dorm room. Talking my way out of orientation was one thing, but asking a stranger for free money was entirely different. Lee had handed me a note to trot on over to the business office after I received my river trip rations and packed them into a backpack, which I conveniently failed to bring along... What wild card could I now pull from the deck of destiny that would boost my credit by 1,800 smackeroos?

Knowing I had taken a big chance—arriving in debt and without a checkbook—I could be told to go away. So I began to panic. I could not give a bogus and bloated claim that I was black even with my newly developed desert tan or predict I would surpass Michael Jackson at the whitening game he'd perfected some ten years later. Sure, I could argue that PC was advantaging those who were already advantaged by pointing to the Corvette Stingrays in the parking lot, and mention that I had never received anything more than a Cabbage Patch doll, a bottle of Tab and a pan of stale French fries from the State of New Jersey at the annual Christmas dinner.

I also could have stated many very talented students from poor backgrounds could be attending this school if Prescott College broadened their applicant pool by giving out *minority scholarships* just like the headmaster at Windsor Mountain had done.

But I didn't.

Instead I played the long shot. Willful suspension of failure allowed me a certain knowledge that some things just work themselves out. I'd wait till luck, life's most sympathetic friend, would come along.

The businessman waiting for me in a brightly lit office room with cow skulls and snakeskins for decorations had both my application and self portrait in hand as I spoke in a quiet, steady, almost nervous tone. Perhaps he was amused as I reverted to being a kid at a Coney Island concession stand without the proper change to purchase that big pink puff of wispy cotton candy. There I stood in front of him, still digging and searching for pennies in my back pockets, knowing not a cent was there.

"I have no parents and nowhere to go on vacations, holidays, or weekends, and I am willing to work off any of the money I owe the college during those times, or any other time my studies permitted."

My audio presentation combined with a visual included flashing my previous grades and flipping through sketches in an art portfolio.

The Prescott College vendor gleaned that I was a serious student and wanted the opportunity to matriculate at Prescott. To my delight, he took my offer and presented me a few opportunities.

First he handed me a slip of paper titled *grant* that effectively shaved $600 off my tuition. Then he opened a metal filing cabinet and selected a folder labeled *work study* and offered me a variety of jobs. (I selected one as a switchboard operator working the graveyard shift.) My career as a telephone operator would put me back in the black, provide a little pocket money for gas, art supplies, and more quarters for the pool tables at the Piñon Pines.

The Green Ghetto

Three types of student housing existed on campus, and these levels appeared to illustrate the lucky and the luckier.

Décor and feng shui have always been an important aspect of my life, and what my home looks like may be more important than what I may look like waking up in my makeup after a late night out on the town. Initially I was assigned to the "middle level" generic dorms at the center of campus which were impossible to decorate. Desks and bunk beds were built in, even the lamps were stationary. The room resembled a railway car and there was no way to rearrange the furniture. If you liked the feel of ice-skating in a telephone booth—here was your chance at the mini-Olympics.

The next level of dorm living was classy pads—actual houses—originally intended for visiting professors with all the modern conveniences, including poker parties on weekends and pizza deliveries late at night that the wealthier students could enjoy. These dwellings resembled rambling ranch style living, high on a hill, with spectacular views of sunsets and mountain ranges. Hotel Service appeared to be included. Laundromat off the kitchen. Barbeques on weekends. And of course, an easy stroll to the heated outdoor pool where one could spot, if they cared to, the run down Green Ghetto.

The Green Ghetto was the most undesirable place to live, because this grouping of scanty shacks were propped up on stilts, much like the way seaside homes stand on sticks so that water may flow underneath the dwelling in inclement weather. The same was true here in the sea of sand at the Green

Ghetto. The winds shifted mounds of earth below the Ghetto floors while the flapping plastic acted as insulation to keep the exposed pipes from freezing. Resembling a barracks, or a battleship bobbing up and down on turbulent seas, flapping sails were replaced by flapping tarps.

One could hardly find silence high on the hill, where coyotes took up moaning as the wind whipped through flimsy insulation that slapped against the cheap clapboard.

The Ghetto was cold: the commons were never occupied and the tarps fluttered incessantly through the night. The steep sandy hill one had to ascend to reach it, the long haul across campus to find it (combined with the wind whip factor) kept the population at the Green Ghetto declining ever since the complex was erected.

Because the Ghetto was less desirable than the other dorms, I was able to secure a suite consisting of two rooms and a private bath. Once unpacked, my crib took on the appearance of a Christmas tree, or a Christmas Card as every week I redecorated it as if I were competing in a national contest: string lights, lanterns, and hanging Indonesian puppets. Avocado plants, tapestries. Skulls and feather bouquets.

A typical weekend at Prescott College might include:

1. Shooting some pool at Piñon Pines
2. Modeling for art class in Jerome: earning 15 bucks
3. Seeing a new Felini movie
4. Having my IUD removed
5. Writing a term paper on Jesse James
6. Square dancing
7. Belly dancing

Nighttime: Listening to Mozart before bed. Mozart is supposed to make you smart.

Known for its Outward Bound Discovery Program and its dedication to environment preservation, PC specialized in field trips and student directed learning. To experience a more collective communal learning setting, I took up play production and joined the theatrical department, landing major parts in all school productions. I also took Kung Fu, wrote a term paper on the *Noh* theatre, made masks to illustrate my thesis, and acted in a one-woman play in front of one professor. On the weekends I rode horses up to Twin Peaks—studied the Indian petroglyphs and observed the constellations, as Arizona is well known for having some of the best star gazing on the globe.

And about once a month I'd write a progress report to my social workers in New Jersey, usually requesting a bigger book budget or clothing allowance.

I was so grateful for the money my social worker, Connie Frailer, would send me. Somehow she'd always finagle something out of the State, even if it were just a check for sixty-two bucks, which then could purchase dozens of paperbacks and eighteen music albums. Muddy Waters. John Lee Hooker. Blind Lemon Jefferson. The Mississippi Delta blues. Sonny Boy Williamson and:

"A-wop-bop-a-loo-lop-a –lop- bam-boo!"

When students came to Prescott to study it was because they chose to, not because they were dropped off, kicked out of other schools, or abandoned by their parents. Isolated away from society, they were able to do their thing, and exploration and discovery were a part of the curriculum. From the beginning, entering students were in charge of their educational decisions and the college did not get in their way. This method imbued pupils with a sense of independence, freedom, and self-esteem, and often an interest in carrying on the school's mission long after leaving College.

I was thankful and grateful for the opportunity I had been afforded, via my social workers and Prescott's generosity. PC, much like Windsor, appeared to be an academically rigorous school with a caring community in which everyone shared in the process of learning. Additionally, a commitment to learning in the spirit of inquiry and discovery provided students with the unique potential for fostering responsive and responsible citizenship.

But Prescott College was doomed much the way Windsor Mountain's fate would eventually force it to close its doors as well. By the time I arrived in 1973, the administrators were selling off the horses, asking teachers to take a pay cut (or no pay), cutting the heat to the outdoor pool, and, like many other great private institutions of that era, about to go bust. Unfortunately Libby Lourie—my dorm mate at Windsor, who initially introduced me to Prescott—found her way there one year later and a full semester after I had left. She would lose her tuition, thus observing bankruptcy taking its toll on students' and teachers' morale in both states—as Windsor folded the last semester she had attended.

So in the late spring of 1974 I packed up my books—took half the Prescott College library with me—weighted down my olive-colored Volvo and along with another student who would share the wheel and driving expenses, we headed back east.

At twenty years old, I had just done a giant U-turn across country and was feeling a bit like one of those spin tops which bounced, bumped, and lost its balance, waddling off the wrong side of the curb.

As we pull slowly out of the college parking lot, my eyes scan 360 degrees to study the dry and deserted landscape we're leaving. Pretty soon my memory will put this view away and begin focusing on the long gray highway carved into granite, snaking its way from the flat desert plateaus of Arizona to the high hills of Colorado. Sitting on the passenger side, my eyes skip over the mountain tops and settle again on the burning sun. Suspended over a distant mountain range, glowing with a faint snicker of endless possibilities that the world one day might provide—I can't help thinking of Phoenix, of that bird that burned, its wings becoming quite crispy as its body turned to ash and it twitched until its little heart could pitter patter no more. But even after death had apparently come to this mythological bird, something spectacular happened after the coals stopped glowing, and the fire ceased smoking, and the ash became cool. In this heap of nothingness, of gray white chalky ash, the bird rose eternally young and flew away again. Will that happen to Prescott College?

Toby downshifts into second and my car returns to its bronco style of dodging tumbleweed—much the way skateboarders avoid traffic cones as we slowly make our way up Mingus Mountain.

And there I was, imagining myself going *up up up* and away as I leave Arizona behind and prepare for my journey east. The sunsets, and in tandem I lay back knowing that this particular view—that we're driving away from in 1973—would never be seen again quite like this. There was a sense of sadness in our hearts as our journey began. Much like people who are in the Army together and go through wars simultaneously—the only way to survive that feeling of emptiness that often accompanies loss is to walk away, throw a grenade over your shoulder, and never look back. With tears in my ears, I didn't realize it would be decades before I would return. Our final destination would be far from this sprawling endless horizon. We will drive straight through the long days and short nights, catching naps in the car or under picnic tables at rest stops. The last stop, where we will say goodbye forever, will be where the action never sleeps: the NYC Port Authority train station on 42nd Street. We will walk away from what initially bonded us together, a race across America—a college on its way to closing—and evaporate quickly into a city with its decrepit piers, graffiti-covered subway trains, abandoned warehouses, Lexington Avenue hookers, and hyper drag queens. Unlike Prescott, NYC had a gritty integrity and, as the late Peter Jennings put it, it was a container of dreams: its culture and society a muse to artists, hipsters, inventors, and entrepreneurs. The Big Apple was not only a beacon of optimism and energy, but also a dynamo stick of liberty.

And when Toby and I hit it—he in need of a shave, a slug of Listerine, and spray of deodorant, and me, desperate for a sip of coffee, a splash of musk oil and a hair brush—NYC, much like Prescott College and Windsor Mountain, was about to go bust.

My haggard co-pilot picked up his knapsack and made a wild dash to catch a bus to Vermont. As he descended into the labyrinth and tunnels of the train station, I realized I had no idea where I'd land that night. First I would have to find a rest stop, then a job, and afterwards a place to crash for the summer before attending the School of Visual Arts that fall. My pinky flicked the right hand signal and slowly I steered my ship—my beloved Volvo tanker—out to Jones Beach. There I would crawl under a blanket and lie among the partly rotten fish and clam feces while the breeze brought in the wild smell that accompanies street beggars sleeping under boardwalks who haven't worn shoes for years.

Back amongst my tribe, I couldn't help thinking the east coast is where every conceivable religion and race lives side by side and without even blinking you can find cultural differences at either end of a toothpick. Slowly I maneuvered my vehicle to one of the many parking lots at Jones Beach. After finding a safe spot under a super nova streetlight I got out, stretched, and noticed a mixture of goo—butterfly wings, leaves, rust and sticks—coating the hood, bonnet and grill of my beloved Volvo. The windshield wipers had cracked and fallen off—a result of un-use, having baked in the Arizona sun for one year. My car was in as much need of a bath as I was.

Wiping off the glass with a very stained off-white t-shirt, I thought of the irony as the cloth magnetized insects to its fibers:

Sometimes you're the windshield and other times you're the bug. Life or death often unfolds beautifully, like a wild orchid, misplaced in the forest.

Last Word

Twenty-six years after my journey out of Arizona, I was invited back by the Prescott College to receive the Javelina Award at the reunion of 2000. In combo with these events, the Alumni Association offered a river-rafting trip down the Colorado. Believing this was my opportunity to experience Orientation—the voyage that I had missed in 1974 when I was a teenager, bent on rebelling against mandates and authorities—I was eager to sign on. This Grand Canyon trip would be the mini-version of the one I had been assigned to twenty-six years earlier; unbeknownst to me it would turn into a rush and rescue mission where many could be seen hanging onto cliffs by the tips of their fingers while others almost drowned. But that's another story.

The organizers of the 2000 awards ceremony informed me that I was last on the line-up to receive the Javelina Award and asked if I could say a few words. Knowing those up at the podium last get to blab the longest, I wanted to know who my audience was comprised of. Ironically, the roster of participants attending the ceremony, reunion, and the alumni river rafting trip represented one race: *the white man,* with the exception of the all black female R&B band that was imported from Phoenix to provide entertainment for the evening.

At the time I was temporarily residing in South Philly and lived on the fringe of the black ghetto where I was once again absorbed with racism, issues of globalization, and America's advertising culture that had consumed the nation. There seemed to be a Starbucks and Staples on every other corner. The Gap had taken over Madison Avenue in NYC. The "right to shop" was in full swing and my collection of advertising propaganda using the words *global this* or *one world that* had grown from a few pages to several loose-leaf binders.

Despite the fad of going global and the attempt to blend characteristics of cultures, there were reasons—*at least to some*—why "race still mattered." While nowadays the federal Education Department is proposing new regulations that allow students to circle as many categories as they want on their applications to identify their heritage—and not all job applications require classifications as to race and gender—equality and globalization are not one and the same, and the waves of discontent clashing on several shores rocked many peoples' boats. Was globalization a good idea after all? And how did it affect culture, and the various races at large? Do we really want to all be one color by the year 2070? Dress the same, looks the same, fuck the same, and wake up to the same coffee from Starbucks? Often the blending of cultures blurs out many of the characteristics of one. While not everyone was dominated by a consumer-driven advertising world (which seemed united in one mission: to make one marvel over its own magnificence) those who I noticed living in poverty in South Philly belonged to one race: Afro-American. While some global efforts convince citizens into trying to pretend that you are not black, and I am not white, and we are all climbing the same mountain, breathing that same pine-soaked air beneath a glowing moonbeam in a country that doesn't pretend to be segregated—in a country that doesn't revel in racial discrimination—many of its citizens still wear bigotry like a badge on their breast blazers. Truth is expensive, hypocrisy is cheap, and it's amazing how the lack of one often affects the profitability of the other.

Unbeknownst to me, a compelling notion would materialize into an obsession, the night I prepared my acceptance PC speech, that would last for several years and materialize into a significant body of new work that I would later title: "Don't Globalize This." If there were no blacks attending Prescott College's activities—or attending the school—perhaps I could appear as one and explain that I was the first faux black woman to apply to Prescott in the '70s? Maybe now was the time to fess up and explain how I had fudged my application to gain admission. Surely it would get some laughs. If nothing else it would give me a chance to brush up on my illusionary skills.

Once I arrived in Arizona I headed to the nearest costume shop, the prop shop, Halloween Shop, where I'd purchase an Afro wig, brown powder compacts and several tubes of black facial make-up to cover my entire body.

It was time now to really show up at Prescott College as a black woman. I had nothing to lose.

When it was all over, I found out that my costume—my disguise or ruse—was so effective that those who had never met me and didn't hear the whole speech actually thought I was black. For those, like Stuckey, who knew me, many got a kick out of my presentation and appreciated my theatrics, which led to a point. As for the all-black female R & B Band, it took some doing for them to warm up to me. But for myself, this piece of educational theatre would inspire an important set of photographic images where I would pretend that the proud individualism of blacks and whites is not crushed and twisted into an unseen gray and that really nobody can tell the difference because nobody gives a damn. True to my art, lesson one was: "Why the color of your skin still matters."

Notes: 1. Joanne Motichka resides in Manhattan and uses her professional name, Matuschka. She is an internationally known artist and art photographer. One of her photographs appeared on the cover of the New York Times Sunday Magazine *and has been rated by Time-Life as one of the most important photographs of the twentieth century.*

2. Matuschka did not participate in Orientation in 1972, but later thought better of it and joined an alumni-sponsored three-day raft trip on the Colorado River through the lower Grand Canyon. She describes this trip as disastrous, and wrote another hysterically funny piece about getting capsized at rapid #232 titled "The Dunking of Dan" (Dr. Dan Garvey, President of the College), which is in the PC Archives.

Letter from Lee Stuart to Sam Henrie

◇◇◇◇◇◇

(Class of 1975) April 28, 2002

I heard about Prescott from my aunt who was a pediatrician in Phoenix. I was attending an elite girls' boarding school outside of Philadelphia, and was being heavily courted by the Ivies, as they had just recently begun admitting women. I was also being heavily pushed toward Smith College by my grandmother, as I would have been the third generation of my family to go there. For myself, I had narrowed the choice to Middlebury and University of Rochester, and was leaning more and more toward U of R, where I planned to become a chemical engineer. Then my aunt called me and said she'd heard of "this very interesting college they had started in Prescott" and invited me out to visit her in Phoenix for Thanksgiving, during which time I could go check out the school. It sounded like as good a plan as any, and I always enjoyed visiting her, so probably the Monday of Thanksgiving week in 1970, I found myself at the flagpole at the driveway of Prescott College.

I must have looked suitably lost, with my letter in hand, telling me where to go, as the buildings on the campus were mostly indistinguishable. A passing student (Jeff Schwartz) said to me, "I guess you're new around here. What are you looking for?" I showed him the paper, and it turned out that I had an hour to go before my interview, so he invited me to accompany him to his calculus class, after which he would take me to my interview. I went along, and attended the class being ably taught by Keith Yarborough, and then Jeff took me to my interview—with Robert Bruce! Robert Bruce was of course wonderful and affable, and I felt highly encouraged. Jeff agreed to come back afterwards to show me the Field House, and then I was on my own. I wandered around, checking the place out, and somehow found my way over to the Commons for dinner (unmemorable).

The practice in those days was to put prospective students in a dorm suite so they could meet "real" students and get to know the college from their perspective. But with me, the admissions office had made a mistake—all the people in my dorm, taking advantage of the Thanksgiving break, were away on a Grand Canyon field trip, and the place was entirely deserted. I settled down to my high school assignment for the holiday—reading *Crime and Punishment*. Deep in Dostoyevsky, around 9 p.m., there was a loud banging on the door. My heart pounded. WHO was at my door?? WHAT should I do?? Visions of mayhem crossed my mind, not helped by Raskalnikov. BANG. BANG. BANG. More knocking. Finally, I answered the door. Raw amazement. There stood Jeff, and about four other students. "Hi!" he said, "It's Thanksgiving and we're staying on campus, and we knew that everyone in this dorm was away and we got care packages from home, and so we decided to bring our party to you!"

That settled it. The next day I withdrew my applications from consideration at all other colleges to which I had applied. It was Prescott or nothing for me, simply on the basis of friendliness, interest, openness, generosity, hospitality, and the enthusiasm Jeff and his friends had for Prescott and for me.

I completed my PhD in ecology in a joint (and quite Prescott-ian) program between the University of California at Davis and San Diego State University in 1984, having done most of my research in Alaska. My own emphasis was on soil-plant relations and the construction of large-scale mathematical models of various tundra ecosystems. I had a magnificent time, but in my dissertation year my mentor died, and to take my mind off the grief, while finishing my degree, I helped set up what became an international nonprofit organization called World SHARE. Basically SHARE (Self-Help and Resource Exchange) was a cross between a food co-op and a buying club, where we organized thousands of families to enroll through their churches, unions, tenant associations, whatever, and pooled their monthly fees to purchase food directly from farmers and growers at a tremendous discount. The families also had to perform community service (a lot of which focused on breaking down the bulk purchases, as in 40,000 pounds of potatoes, into family-sized portions) as part of their participation in the program. SHARE started in San Diego, and I took it with me to Blacksburg, VA, while I had a post-doc at Virginia Tech in the biology department, and then to the South Bronx where I was invited after completing the post-doc at Tech but before I knew what my next steps were. I thought I would be in the Bronx six months, but it turned out to be seventeen years.

I was frankly overwhelmed at the conditions in 1985 in the South Bronx, and setting up SHARE was a tremendous challenge. But in short order, six months, I had 3,000 families enrolled, and by nine months, 11,000 from 250 churches and neighborhood organizations were members, and so I had to stick around to manage what I had created. I had also realized that there were a lot more people able to teach introductory ecology and such in universities than there were willing to stand in the South Bronx, the center of urban poverty in the United States, and say, "ENOUGH of THIS!" So I took a radical career turn, to put it mildly, and aimed my intellectual firepower, systems thinking, and world-class stubbornness at the South Bronx.

Partly due to the success of SHARE in the Bronx, the program went national and then international. At its height, with affiliates in about 35 U.S. cities, we were buying over a million pounds of potatoes a month and actually grew to impact the chicken futures market, because we were also purchasing a million pounds of chicken a month, and that kind of production means you have to get them hatched the right number of months before you need them. Anyhow, it was very wild and wonderful, and as the first program in the South Bronx to run on time, cleanly (politically and in the sense that we could actually eat off the warehouse floor it was so clean), and without government money, I am able to take partial credit for the turn-around in the South Bronx, which is truly one of the most amazing urban stories of our time (though relatively unknown).

I was recruited from SHARE (which continues in the Bronx to this day as a self-supporting nonprofit organization with a budget around a million dollars a year, not a penny of which is from the government) by the Industrial Areas Foundation (IAF), which was forming an organization (South Bronx Churches—SBC) to begin to build a power base for local people and institutions that had been abandoned by the public and private sectors. The leader of the foundation of SBC, who recruited me and who became my mentor, was Jim Drake. Jim had been national director of organizing for the United Farm Workers (remember the grape boycott—that was Jim's brainchild) and had also established a pulpwood cutters' cooperative in Mississippi before joining the IAF to work in the Rio Grande Valley of Texas, and eventually the Bronx.

It's hard for people to imagine, but during the seventies, New York City actually had a formal policy, "planned shrinkage," where they would close services in places like the South Bronx (and by services I mean fire stations, hospitals, and schools, and essentially stop prosecuting crimes) to save money for essential areas of the city (i.e., the Manhattan financial center). Well, this policy was remarkably effective, and left the South Bronx a wasteland of burned buildings and abandoned lots, with two enormously successful industries: criminal activity and the care and maintenance of poverty. The goal of SBC, and the IAF, was to develop a local organization and local leaders with sufficient power to tackle any issue they cared to, and to hold the New York City government as well as private interests accountable for the restoration of the South Bronx.

SBC started by holding about a thousand individual meetings with people in the churches, and, as is always the case (I've since learned) when you ask people what they want to make their lives better, it came down to the big five: housing, education, health, work, and safety. The next thing we did was to get one hundred thousand signatures from adults in the South Bronx to support this agenda.

I became "lead organizer," that is the professional staff member, for SBC in 1992, just as we were breaking ground on the construction of what we called our "Nehemiah Homes." We had borrowed $3.5 million from Episcopalian, Catholic, and Lutheran sources to act as our construction bank, and successfully convinced the City (through mass rallies of upwards of five thousand people and other equally subtle techniques) to allocate about forty blocks of long-abandoned land on which to build. The long and the short of it is that I have been mostly responsible for this effort since then, and as of October, we will have finished about 750 new homes (180 of which also have rental apartments, so it's 930 new dwelling places), all owned by local families earning between $25,000 and $45,000 a year, and have completely reclaimed huge sections of the South Bronx. We've leveraged the $3.5 million into over $81 million in homes, we have paid back all of the $3.5 million, and unspent contingency funds are in excess of $1 million, so SBC is itself now endowed for whatever it wants to do next.

During the same time period, SBC decided to challenge NYC's horrific Board of Education, and force them to establish an academic high school in the South Bronx. At the time (early nineties) the high school graduation rate was less than 50% in the South Bronx, and the college acceptance rate was about 3%. This was the result of many things, not the least of which was the attitude expressed by a high level Board of Education official with whom we met early on in our quest to start the new school: "Do you really believe that these Black and Latino children can all go to college?" The leaders of SBC persevered, and through thick (very thick) and thin (very thin), we managed to get the Board of Education to open a new high school with a mission of preparing students for college: the Bronx Leadership Academy High School. The parents voted in a dress code, the teachers voted out the most potentially damaging parts of their contract, and after a disastrous first year when the school suffered with poor professional leadership, the school has been remarkable. Led now by Katherine Kelly, whose mother taught at Morehouse and who has built a remarkable staff, the school gets about 5,000 applications for 125 seats each year. SBC continues to provide "protection" from the still too prevalent forces in government and in society that seek to destroy excellence and success. In a rousing example of conquering all: last year our 87 graduates received 280 letters of acceptance to college (we also organize the colleges to come recruiting), and this year, even with a (relatively) tiny student body of 500, our girls' basketball team won the city-wide champion-ship. We do very well in chess, fencing, and debate as well. Everything that happens in Bronx Leadership could happen in any New York City school, and finally the Board has taken notice: we are now part of a project to create ten such schools.

As to how Prescott College prepared me for this work? The idea of tak-ing a stand, making it happen, figuring it out, solving the problems, build-ing the teams, evaluating the results, searching for the humor as well as the profound, remembering that it's the journey not the destination, and always looking for the next thing to do, come immediately to mind. I'm at the "next thing" point right now. We have built on all the available land in the South Bronx, the schools work is in the able hands of another, and I am on the prowl for what's next. I have possibilities of working on similar projects in Boston and Connecticut, and have in mind the creation of a highly entrepre-neurial and self-supporting nonprofit organization to multiply and expand on what's been accomplished so far. In that sense, I'm still on the journey, though how sweet the temporary destinations have been—to be able to say that nearly one thousand families in the South Bronx have decent places to live and thousands of students are getting an opportunity for education they otherwise would not have had as a product of my life—this is indeed a privilege, and, as part of the stage was set at Prescott College, I thought you'd like to know.

The Story of Mouse

By Douglas Hulmes, Class of 1974
and subsequently Professor of Environmental Studies

He was just a mouse. Make of it what you will, whether an overly an-thropomorphized encounter between a human and a "lower creature," or a window opening into a world that can be—imagined or real. Nevertheless, the story that I share is as true as any experience I have known.

I found Mouse, or perhaps we found each other, one day not long after I had been given the directive to obtain a mouse for the purpose of science. The exact purpose was for a laboratory experiment. More precisely, we were to find a live mouse for the purpose of performing a dissection for our lab final and thereby observe a living, beating heart, thus concluding our study of biology.

For me, there was no hesitation; I scooped Mouse off the sidewalk. His brown and white quivering body squirmed at first against my closed fingers, but soon he relaxed and offered no more struggle. I carried him back to my dorm room and placed him in a makeshift cage. With whiskers and nose in nervous motion, he explored the prison intently, while his black eyes searched the freedom beyond, and then focused on his captor.

It was obvious from his appearance that he was not a wholly wild mouse. His brown and white markings were not like those of the native deer mouse, *Paramiscus maniculatus*. He appeared to be more likely an escaped hybrid mouse of unknown ancestry.

I will not make you wonder longer. There was no way that I would have dissected this mouse, or any mouse for that matter. In response to the in-structor's directive to find a live mouse for dissection, I flatly refused, stating that I was ethically and morally opposed to such an activity, and that I would do anything else to demonstrate my comprehension of the material.

My instructor's response was surprisingly cold. "You'll fail!" I stood my ground, stating that I felt he was being unreasonable given the fact that I had made high marks on all of the proceeding tests and assignments. After an awkward silence, he relented and asked me what I would do in place of the dissection. It was finally agreed that I would write a personal essay on my refusal to dissect and reasoning behind it. And with that agreement, I began a philosophical journey that has opened a universe of ideas and history of human thought to which I had been previously oblivious. But those lofty ideas you must discover on your own, for it was in fact the mouse which truly opened my mind to wonder.

I kept Mouse safe in a cage for two weeks, or until the laboratory exercise, justified for the "sake of science," was concluded. It was my intent to release Mouse back to his fate in the world. When the time came, however, I could not coldly thrust him out, for I had become attached to him. I concluded to give him a choice. I would let him live in an open shoe box in my room, and he could come and go as he pleased, either stay with me in my room, or venture back to the world beyond via a large crack beneath the door.

I turned in my paper the following week. Admittedly, it was not a brilliant piece of work, yet it was an honest and sincere argument conveying my personal convictions concerning a reverence for life that I held. And they were my ideas, for I had not yet discovered that there were philosophers who shared my convictions, that I could be a serious student of science and have feelings, yes, even reverence, for life. I felt that I could study biology and learn what I needed to know about morphology and physiology without having to dissect a live mouse. I also suggested that biology, which means the study of life, has been turned into the study of dead animals in most high school and college classrooms, and that dissection has, in part out of convenience, replaced the study of the animal as a living animal. The study of animal parts and internal systems has its place, and has obviously increased our understanding of important aspects of biology, but what has it done towards our ethics regarding other forms of life?

My five-page essay of feelings received an eight-page response from the instructor. I was somewhat gratified that I had provoked such a lengthy response, although it proved to be rather condescending. He admitted that he had once felt as I did, but had come to realize that in fact life was a form of energy and as such could not be created nor destroyed, simply altered from one form to another, and if society would condone it, he would see nothing essentially wrong about dissecting a live human being.

I finished reading his response, picked Mouse up, and held him as tears ran down my cheeks. I felt desperately alone. How could I possibly continue my studies in the biological sciences if my ethics and emotions were deemed contrary to what was expected of the serious student of biology?

It was the end of the spring term. I drove home to the Midwest. Mouse accompanied me. I spent the summer as a volunteer science teacher working with elementary school children. I was committed to showing them the wonders of nature while trying to promote the idea of respect for life. At one point I was asked if we could dissect an animal. My initial response was to say no, but when I found a bird that had died when it flew into a window, I decided I could satisfy their curiosity and also demonstrate that one could dissect animals without having to kill them specifically for that purpose.

The summer proved to be rewarding and also humbling. One day when I was showing the kids the wonders of the microscopic world of pond water, I discovered that my message of respect for life had been thoroughly understood. I had three samples of water from different locations. Several students waited their turn to gaze for their first time into the microscope. We finished looking at the first sample. I was feeling especially good about their attentiveness, and eager to show them the next sample. I took the slide from its mount, and not thinking, wiped it on my pants. Immediately a second grade boy who was next in line, looked up at me and said, "you killed all those animals." His eyes still haunt me as I write these memories years later. I admitted my error, apologized, and thanked him for telling me. While incredibly embarrassed, it felt good to admit my error, something I have tried not to forget as a professional teacher. After class I asked the boy if he would like to go with me and return the water samples and microscopic animals to their homes. He eagerly agreed.

Mouse returned with me to the Southwest in the fall. I enrolled in several more science classes, eager to increase my understanding of the natural world. Mouse took up residence once again in his open shoe box in the corner. He was soon making his nightly sojourns into the closet, exploring my clothes drawers, chewing holes in my socks, and often carrying loose items that he found soft or interesting back to his nest. Occasionally he would venture into other rooms in the dorm, but would always return to his shoe box to sleep away the day. On one occasion a dorm mate handed Mouse to me with some disgust in his voice, saying that he had found Mouse in bed with him during the night. On another occasion I opened the door to find Mouse and two deer mice performing some kind of social behavior in the middle of the floor. Surprised, Mouse ran to his box, and the two wild mice ran out the door.

While it may sound incredible to most biologists, who unfortunately have never experienced a mouse the way I did, Mouse came to respond to me in some rather amazing ways. He would frequently come out to play with me while I was studying, would often come when I called to him, climb up into my hands, and seemed to enjoy being scratched behind his ears, while his eyes became rather glazed and contented looking.

I fed Mouse seeds, vegetables, peanut butter, and cheese. I was curious one night when I saw a cricket on the carpet. I called to Mouse, I could hear him chewing on something of mine in the back of the closet. He came into view, actually seemed to squint his eyes, took three pounces, the like of which I had never seen him take, landed on the cricket and bit off its head. He proceeded to devour it. I had suddenly discovered something I should have known all along, Mouse was not a vegetarian!

Mouse continued to amaze me. One night when I was reading in my bunk bed situated above my closet, I heard him rustling in one of my drawers. Not wanting to have to climb down from the bed, I called to him. He appeared out of the closet and looked up towards me. My ski pole was hanging on a nail next to the bed. I reached down and tapped it on the floor next to him. To my utter amazement, he hopped up on the basket. I swung it slowly back and forth. Mouse jumped off, ran in a couple of circles and then jumped back on. This time I carefully lifted the ski pole with Mouse on the basket up eight feet to my bed.

While I cannot "scientifically" prove that any of these events actually occurred or would ever happen to someone else, I can honestly say that I have tried not to embellish them. I also believe that Mouse could distinguish me from a stranger who entered my room, and seemed to prefer certain friends over others.

When Christmas break came, I was faced with a dilemma. I would be flying to Chicago, and then on to Florida to visit my grandparents. I felt I had to take Mouse along with me. I did not have a cage that was small enough to fit into my carry-on bag, so I punched holes into the lid of a coffee can, filled it with tissue and food, and placed Mouse into it. I was a bit nervous, especially, that he might be discovered if my bag was searched. Unfortunately, I did not anticipate a problem at the ticket counter. When I opened my bag to get my ticket and seat assignment, all hell broke loose. Mouse had chewed a hole in the lid of the coffee can and was sitting on top of the lid when I opened the bag. The lady at the ticket countered screamed, "You've got a mouse in your bag." I panicked and ran off into the crowd, hearing her yelling that I had a mouse and could not take it on the plane with me.

As fate would have it, I had gone to the wrong airline counter. I purchased some Christmas wrapping paper and covered the can to make it appear to be Christmas cookies. The lady saw me once again and started screaming, "There he is," but fortunately the airport was packed with Christmas travelers and I made it onto the plane with Mouse securely wrapped.

I returned to college for the spring term. Mouse and I had become quite a pair, and I must say, I felt a bit smug now that we had become fairly well known on campus, and even the most serious biology students were taken by Mouse. He was, after all, rather amazing and very well traveled!

One night I returned to my room late after studying in the library. I thought it was a bit strange that my door was ajar, but horror filled me when I turned on the light and startled a large yellow cat who bolted out between my legs and ran down the hall. I glanced into Mouse's shoe box. It was empty. My heart was pounding as I chased after the cat, grabbed it, and saw, to my worst fears, a mouse tail sticking out of its mouth. I can say with little remorse, I choked the cat until it released Mouse into my hand—but it was too late. I placed Mouse's lifeless body back into his box. I felt a sickening numbness overwhelm me.

It was too late to bury Mouse that night. I climbed up to my bed and lay there, not able to sleep, sickened by what had happened. Just as I was about to fall asleep, I heard something. I climbed down out of bed, turned on the light and searched to discover the source of the sounds. To my utter amazement, Mouse was in his box looking up at me. Mouse was alive! He had only fainted.

Mouse didn't leave his box for three days, and he never again left the room. He died of natural causes during his second summer in Illinois.

When I reflect on all that I felt I learned and experienced while sharing my room and life with Mouse for 1 1/2 years, I can honestly say he profoundly influenced my life. For if it hadn't been for those experiences, I would likely not have been as committed to read the philosophies of Joseph Wood Krutch, Henry David Thoreau, John Muir, Albert Schweitzer, Aldo Leopold, Barry Lopez, John Steinbeck, Terry Tempest Williams, Peter Singer, and many others, kindred spirits who have felt and known compassion for other forms of life beyond the human species. They believed in something contrary to Descartes and the mechanistic theory that has influenced much of Western Civilization, religion, science, and philosophy for nearly four hundred years. The mechanistic theory postulated that nature, including all animals except for man (and some literally believed only white Christian men), was functionally little more than a machine, and that animals did not possess any capacity for consciousness, memory, or ability to feel pain, and certainly did not possess a soul. Furthermore, followers of Descartes and others during the "Age of Enlightenment" believed that it was humans' (man's) destiny to control Nature, and that Nature could be controlled through knowledge and technology. In response to the arrogance that humans are above the laws of nature, these more recent writers and philosophers believe in an ethic or regard for Nature, and that there is a quality or essence and complexity of life and nature that perhaps will never be fully explained by math, chemicals, or dissecting trays, and that each individual life, even that of a mouse, brings forth unique qualities true unto itself. Perhaps that is the essence of the soul, and should at the very least demand our respect and perhaps even reverence.

Letter Sent by Jeff Kiely to Ted Rose*

June 13, 1977

Dear Ted,

For your records on what's happening with people: I am currently work-ing with the Ramah Navajo Adult-Education Program. In the past year I have been the Instructional Coordinator, and in the coming year I will be the Program Development Coordinator.

The Program is doing quite well and expanding rapidly. It's a fabulous context. A corollary involvement here is that I am living in a cabin now (since early March) in the Navajo woods, and there are a number of little projects I have in mind, such as a Solar-Sustained Greenhouse, etc. A couple of anec-dotes for your book and/or movie:

I entered Prescott College in my junior year and, like us all, had the bounty of being introduced to its spirit through Orientation. The entire 3-week experience was immensely powerful, healing, cleansing, and filled with joy and meaning. A couple of things stand out: (1) I was on solo on the shores of Lake Powell, looking for something to occupy myself with on the second day of the 4-day stint. While walking around the shoreline, I picked up some odds and ends, notably a fine, long, boat-line (vinyl rope, or some-thing), which I rolled up and slung around my neck. Presently, the shoreline no longer offered a ledge to walk on (actually I was in the middle of a former cliff, now submerged by lake water). With conspicuous bravado and glee (as though someone were watching), I decided to continue around the shoreline anyway, making rock-climbing moves and neat maneuvers in order to stay out of the water. I finally came to a place where there was nowhere else to go, and there was no way I could duplicate my previous maneuver—which had gotten me into the predicament. I decided to divest myself of my clothes and boots, which I tossed about fifteen feet up on the cliff above me. So there

*Both alums who graduated in the early 1970s

I was in all my ridiculousness, naked save for a blue rope slung around my neck, trying to figure out what to do. At length I plunged from the cliff into the lake, and swam to a stretch of flatter shoreline. The task now for this silly figure was to return to the place on the cliff where the clothes had been flung. Ever-so-gingerly (man, was that sandstone rough on the feet!) I tiptoed my way to a place on the top of the cliff overlooking the forlorn sight of my clothes, which were a good twenty feet or so below. Painfully I eased my way down the side of the cliff, which was at a steep angle, and finally made it to my shorts and shirt; my boots, though, were still further below, on a ledge punctuating a still-more-severe incline. By some means or another, I got to the boots and enveloped my grateful feet in them. Imagine my consternation, though, when I started to think about getting back up the cliff—slippery sandstone, mind you, and distressingly close to the perpendicular.

I found a couple of hand- and foot-holds and inched my way up. At one point, though—and who was there to cry out to?—it seemed that I could go no further, and my grasp was slowly diminishing: At this point, a newspaper headline—printed in my paranoid imagination—appeared before my eyes: "Prescott College Initiate Dies in Fall from Cliff." Needless to say, I wasn't too confident in my ability to execute a 25-foot back dive—wasn't even sure where the water was in relation to my present position. Fortunately for me and my progeny—and for this story—a heroic sentiment surged within me, and in response to the eerie headline I uttered the cry, "No way!" and scampered and jumped and scurried and clawed and lurched and grasped, and finally made it to safety. ... When I got to the top of the cliff, I paused to reflect on the event, looked around sheepishly to make sure there were no witnesses to the drama, and slinked away to sleep away the rest of the afternoon.

On the day of gathering following the 4-day solo, there was jolly camaraderie, and happy explosions of conversation charged the atmosphere. That evening we sang camp songs, Beatles songs, and made up a few. So buoyant was the occasion that before we went to sleep we agreed unanimously to wake up at dawn and jump off the 30-foot cliff on which we had camped into the lake. ... Dawn began to break—not too many hours later—over our camp. I suspect there were still smiles of contentment hidden in those sleeping bags as the first couple of us began to stir. I could hear the whispering: "Are you gonna do it?" "Forget it, man—no way." "Hey, you think we ought to do that thing?" "You're crazy! Go back to sleep." Meanwhile, a major battle was raging within me. A voice urged me to have at it; after all, who else would dare to be the first to jump off the cliff? Another voice, though, reminded me of the warmth and pleasure of the sleeping bag when compared to the chill of the water and of the morning air. The first voice was heard again: "Just think. When will you ever have such an opportunity again? Maybe never! Give it a go!" But then the adversary: "Ah, but this bag is so warm, and I'm still sleepy. Nobody's going to do it, anyway." The first voice urged: "But if you do it, you'll remember it the rest of your life—it's so far from the hum-drum everyday life, so removed from the complacency of comfort and respectability: It'll be a victory … a joy …"

By now, I was slowly crawling out of my night shorts and inching my way out of the sleeping bag. The whisperings were more frequent now between the curled up forms within the sleeping bags sprawled around the camp. Mostly negative. Finally, with heart pounding and body tense with anticipation, I popped out of the bag and started for the edge of the cliff. The whisperings became shouts: "There he goes!" "He's gonna do it." "What the … ?" The lake water was still a grayish blue—rather cold-looking—not yet enlivened by the sun's rays. I almost hesitated. My heart pounded faster, my body tensed even more in expectation of a scary leap.

The edge of the cliff came closer—the experience had become almost surreal. With a surge and a banshee scream, I leaped from the cliff. My whole body was a wild grin as I soared through the chill dawn air. My God! I wasn't even jumping! I was diving! After several intense seconds I hit the water, knifing down through it to about fifteen feet below the surface. I was grinning so broadly that I almost choked on my way back up to the surface. Once at the surface, more whoops and yahoos and screams burst from my lungs.

Thirty feet above me, silhouetted against the dawn sky, sleepy figures appeared. One of my whoops was answered by one of those figures, which leaped awkwardly from the cliff. Then another, and then two more—trying to hold hands in mid-air! Men and women both, others screamed and jumped. Soon the water was filled with whooping and hollering maniacs—sharing the raw joy of Life. A silly, insignificant little event on the shores of a man-made lake in the desert. … But life hasn't been quite the same since.

If I think of any more, I'll let you know. Best wishes in everything. You're warmly welcomed here in Ramah any time. Just let me know when you plan to head this way.

Your friend and brother,
Jeff Kiely

Note: Jeff Kiely has dedicated his life to education, particularly working with Native Americans as an educator in western New Mexico. Ted Rose has been active in developing various projects to connect with alumni and continue the Prescott College service ethic beyond the College.

PCArchives, file: Society of Prescott Students (SOPS) 1977.

Ritual of the High Rappel

by Kent Madin, Class of 1975

[Preface: "The high rappel is a fairly spectacular 130-ft. face in the Granite Dells. New students walk off it backwards, generally trembling and perspiring heavily, and finish up at the bottom with a shit-eating grin and the sense that there must have been a good reason for doing that ..." Dr. Layne Longfellow was a new professor at the time.]

On the high rappel, Layne didn't like the altitude. He certainly didn't think much of the idea of backing off the mountain tied to some very thin ropes. It was one thing for these fresh folk to be initiated through fear, intimidation, peer pressure, and guilt. As a psychologist he understood what was going down here, after all, and while it might be valuable for the students, he knew what was best for him.

It was like a doctor taking his own temperature. How do you argue with a psychologist's professional opinion of what's best for him? And besides, Layne said, "I don't really think this is the right time for me to do this," and "I'll wait because we might not have time for all the students to go ..."

I didn't really know what to do with him. None of the JDs [juvenile delinquents] at Minnesota Outward Bound [where Kent had gotten his training] had been capable of such sophisticated shuck and jive. I just did what old Pete Lev does in the Outward Bound movie (when in doubt, fall back on Standard Operating Procedure).

I began the litany of "Are you going to do it?"

Layne: "squirm, squirm."

Kent: "Are you going to do it?"

Layne: "rationalize, squirm."

Kent: "Are you going to do it?"

Layne: "rationalize, squirm, pull rank."

Kent: "Are you going to do it?"

Layne:" rationalize, squirm, pull rank, hesitate, intimidate."

He didn't do it—at least not that day. Though he did later on. That doesn't matter. What matters is that the tone was set between Layne and me from then on. We did a little dance around each other whenever we met after that. Wilderness Boy and the Guru trying to figure out where the other is at. I think he figured I had him by the balls because of the rappel, while I figured he could get me by the balls by putting on his psychologist's X-ray glasses and seeing who I really was.

And the most memorable time for me at Prescott was graduation. Because it also happened to be my birthday, and the people I love had given me the first genuine SURPRISE!!! party of my life and the wind was blowing across the field and some idiot had placed the chairs facing into the sun again—just like last year.

Layne spoke at Commencement, and I hadn't seen him for a long time. He told this story about his first non-rappel (his version), and said that I was finally graduating. And then he got all the people in attendance to sing Happy Birthday to me.

I have trembled with fear, and shivered with cold, and shaken with rage, and quivered with excitement. I have even sat in a Niagara cyclo-massage chair. I have had my knees go like a sewing machine on a hard move, climbing. When I stood to acknowledge my birthday serenade, for the first time ever, I fairly resonated with love.

Thanks, Layne

Note: Kent Madin became an outstanding outdoor educator. He was one of a team of Prescott College graduates who founded the Boojum Institute, which ran outdoor adventure programs in the Western USA, Baja California (Mexico), and the Sea of Cortez.

PCArchives, file: Society of Prescott Students (SOPS) 1977.

No Sea Shanties at Cat Point

by Mike Goff, Prescott College Faculty Emeritus

An emerald sea lies athwart the rifting gulf that threatens to tear the peninsula of Baja California from mainland Mexico. It is called the Sea of Cortez. The gaping maw of this gulf opens south of the Tropic of Cancer, gobbling at the Pacific Ocean around the old Spanish Main.

At its northern terminus the gulf pinches out in a maze of shallow wetlands and tidal lagoons reaching almost to the Arizona state line. But the active rift rives northwards, troubling the topography of California all the way to San Francisco as the infamous San Andreas Fault.

The bleak marshland at the head of the gulf is the remnant delta of the once mighty Rio Colorado, architect and excavator of the Grand Canyon. Before the dams went in, rich effluence, eroded from the American Southwest, flowed into and blended with the nutrient wealth of the Sea of Cortez as epic flood tides roared up the gulf. The Rio Colorado no longer reaches the sea; its waters are consumed entirely by cities, farms, and casinos upstream.

However, the awesome setting for the Sea of Cortez is staggering to behold. The gulf in which it is enfolded is a vast cleavage torn into the Sierra Madrean volcanic field of northwestern Mexico. Rifting and opening of the Gulf of California began a few million years ago. This breach was invaded by the Pacific Ocean, flooding the young rift valley to great depth. Today, this splendid bathtub sits within an enormous, dynamic basin, still subject to earthquakes and marine vulcanism.

The Sea of Cortez is enclosed east and west by steep, parallel mountain chains block faulted from the old volcanic plateau into rugged hogback ridges. From pine-clad heights, the evergreen sweep of the highlands descends abruptly to the shoreline. From the mainland interior river drainages disgorge into the sea through canyons cut deeper and more rugged than the Grand Canyon of the Rio Colorado.

The entire gulf region is one of the planet's richest life zones. The tropical waters of the Sea of Cortez are home to a startling array of marine fauna; giant squid, toothed and baleen whales; an abundance of sport and edible fish and shellfish. Great white and hammerhead sharks are common, also the enormous but harmless whale shark. Dolphins and sea lions vie for the attention of eco-tourists, and manta rays flash briefly airborne on primeval fin-wings.

Sea and shoreline are wintering grounds for a variety of migrant wading birds and waterfowl that join the native boobies, sea-bound ospreys, and cunning frigate birds for their southern holidays. Great bobbing rafts of brant, northern divers [loons], diverse ducks, and milling grebes idle away the shorter days on oil-calm waters.

The gulf region lowlands lie within the surprisingly fecund Sonoran Desert. Meager summer and winter rainfall nurtures an astonishing mass of arid land flora. Diverse plant types form mosaic clusters of different species, which the cactus family dominates. Saguaros are sixty-foot, branching, succulent, spiny columnar monsters. Chollas rise bush-like with thorny limbs and the ability to release a nightmare of spiny pads on passersby. Agave and yuccas form a ground cover of the stabbing persuasion, such as shin daggers and spanish bayonet. In Baja, the spiny, fluted columns of organ pipe cactus keep company with cedrus, or boojum, a thirty-foot upside-down carrot-like form, festooned to its whip-tip with twiggy thorns that sprout mouse ear leaves briefly, in the rainy season. Among the enchanted cactus colonies, woody thorn bushes make their unwelcome appearance: cat claw acacia and wait-a-minute bush.

Spring rains herald the desert orgy of blooming and fertilization. Awash in rainbow brilliance, the desert becomes a perfumed Eden before the fall. Intoxicated moths, bees, and hummingbirds by day, and bats by night, sup nectar in their frantic round of symbiotic pollination.

This jeweled sea is named for Hernan Cortez. In the early fifteen hundreds he initiated the Spanish conquest of Mexico. By 1530 the conquistadors reached the northern end of the sea in their search for slaves and plunder. On the mainland, they encountered the Aztec high culture extending northwards alongside sophisticated agriculture. On the Baja Peninsula, however, the aboriginals hunted, fished, and foraged. A savage disposition toward the invaders and missionaries won them two more unholy centuries of freedom.

Even today, despite a torturous road running the length of the peninsula, the Baja coastline of the Sea of Cortez remains inaccessible and remote through most of its cliff-bound desert entirety. A few fishing villages occupying sheltered coves and the odd rare spring provide sanctuary and a few provisions for small boats. These attractive coastal waters have become a magnet for sea kayaking expeditions. It is on such a venture that our tale unfolds.

Punta Gato (Cat Point), Baja California, Mexico

Four days out from the fishing village of Loretto, we end a long day's paddle close to Cat Point. There are ten of us, students and instructors, bent on a coastal survey and marine study on the Sea of Cortez. Tired and hungry, we point our boats to shore, riding light swells to an attractive beach. We set up camp close to shore to catch the evening breeze. Sheltering sand dunes undulate inland while nearby the rocky point promises good fishing.

As the harsh desert light mellows, a few of us make for Cat Point. We cross the rocky promontory and descend coarse cliffs jutting from the deep water. The barnacled rocks at our feet are awash in the suck and blow of tireless waves. Aye, a good spot to fish.

Our tackle is crude; heavy line wound onto a plastic bottle. But my lure is a wicked device. The barbarous hook is concealed amongst long white hair cut from the tail of a Hinkle mountain deer and bound to its shank. At the point of attachment, an enamel lead ball has a blood red dot for each eye. It looks like a good fish meal. A Thors cast shoots line and lure from the bottle, arcing far out into the bay. SPLOSH.

Rewind; the white nymph is returning in seductive, graceful jigs just at the surface. A gentle tug as the sea bass mouths on the lure, then the hook strikes and the fish careers off on a hopeless, frenzied dash. It follows the line into shore, at last, back arched, gills flared and great gob gaping.

The short bewitching twilight of the desert casts brooding shadows over the rainbow rocks as we head back to camp. The day ends beneath a black sky prickly with the glitter of stars.

It has happened before, animals of the night slipping under my shelter in search of a snack, or just plain curious. But this creature trampling across my chest is no lightweight. Am I awake, or is this a nightmare? It's too close to my face. I want to brush the vagrant aside where it can make its exit. With a sweep of my arm I make rude contact with a hairy, muscular beast.

The sudden, sickening pain of dagger fangs going through my hand draws a scream of terror that shatters the night. Screaming, screaming. In my agony I am being hauled across barnacled rocks; dragged screaming into that deep green pit of the sea.

But this is no nightmare. My screams are more than a yell for help, more than an instinctive weapon of defense. I feel the terror beyond fear, the paralysis of being prey. My unhinged mind is singing the ultimate swan song in screams that thrill the executioner.

The Beast Will Not Let Go.

I am kneeling now, in my sleeping bag, trying with all my strength to back out of the dreadful confines of my shelter; out into the starlit night. But I cannot draw away. The Beast will not let go.

It has uttered no sound and I catch no rank smell from it. But now, in the gloom I can make out its crouching cat-like form.

My left arm separates me from this animal that has shown such fury, and its nearness terrifies me. I scream helplessly.

People are approaching; I hear their anxious, hushed whispers. Reaching my tent they call out, frantic and alarmed. My attacker responds. I feel its wet gums pressing torn flesh as fangs are withdrawn. Hope; I throw myself backwards out into the starlight, rolling up onto my knees before a tense half-circle of friends. My mangled hand is dripping blood onto the sleeping bag still skirted round my waist.

"Be careful, there's a cat in there!"

It's 2 AM and my friends so rudely roused form a motley band of half-dressed miscreants armed with kayak paddles and fishing spears. They surround me where I kneel on the soft sand like a confessor before his interrogators. But their questions are garbled and confused and I'm in shock.

The nylon shelter quivers, raising a murmur of alarm as a bobcat, big as a boxer dog, ducks under the fly sheet into the open. The bobcat glares defiantly; it is so close, too close. Then it springs.

My companions turn and run, splattering down the wet sand at the waters edge. In the rear, Robin stumbles and falls as the cat hits her square between the shoulder blades. The runners turn and beat the animal vigorously. Free from my sleeping bag I join the group and grab a paddle. One of the lads had slipped on his hiking boots when roused by my screams. Now he gives the cat a smart kick. Finally, it slinks off, but we can see it glowering from the cover of a desert shrub. The attack on Robin got our blood up, and some of the lads favor a spearing match, but with discretion we hold off.

When the bobcat disappears into the shadows we huddle by the sea and lick our wounds. Robin's back is raked by deep scratches and my hand has swollen like a rotten turnip. The attacker looked old and malignant, its behavior vicious and untypical. We are convinced the cat is rabid. Our situation is serious.

After an uneasy night three volunteers set out overland to contact another kayak party a mile away, to ask for assistance. They return with alarming news. During the night the bobcat paid them a visit and attacked one of the guides, severely lacerating him around the head and neck before being driven off with rocks and paddles. How peculiar: he too is British.

Our two groups unite to discuss an evacuation strategy, and this large

group assembled on the beach attracts the attention of local fishermen net-
ting off shore. They know about the demented bobcat and are willing to
transport the injured to the nearest road head. The remainder of the group
agree to continue their coastal traverse to La Paz, where we will all rendezvous in four days' time. They are of course apprehensive about remote beach
camps and plan to make for fishing settlements each night.

The kindly fishermen procure enough fuel for the long boat ride to Loretto. I feel relieved at this sudden rescue but concerned about further delays
if we have contracted rabies. It takes six hours to motor up the coast to Loretto, but when we arrive, a bus, decked out in the finest Mexican livery of
shiny chrome and interior bead-work, is waiting to deliver us to the medical
facilities in La Paz, six more hours along the mind-bending Baja highway.
The bus is comfortable, with traditional mariachi music thundering out of
ancient speakers, to the delight of local passengers. But the interior decor of
religious icons, especially the eternal pained smile of the Virgin of Guadal-
upe and a much bloodied Jesus pinioned to his cross on the windscreen, does
suggest, perhaps, riding a hearse to a final destination.

In La Paz we are treated at an emergency military post. Our wounds are
cleaned and tetanus shots administered. The doctor, who is fascinated by our
experiences with the cat, assures us that the onset of rabies after infection is
quite slow and does not require immediate vaccination. However, we have
an appointment at the general hospital next day. We are much relieved by
this news, but I can't help wondering if I'll wake in the night frothing at the
mouth and growling at Robin.

The general hospital, when we arrived, is under attack by that multitude
of mothers and babies that are such a focal point of Latin America. The staff,
coping very well, is able to give us immediate attention. First, two doctors
explain in detail the course of treatment we could receive at that facility.
There would be a rather complex sequence of injections of the Rabies vac-
cine using the most advanced French product in eight simple intra-muscular
injections over six weeks. If we left the country after treatment started, we
could take the remaining doses in an ice chest and have them injected at our
country of residence. (In the end, Robin and I each take our two final doses
back to the United States and I have my last injection in Moorefield, West
Virginia.) The injections and wound dressing come thick and fast, beginning
that day. Our injuries soon begin to heal, and after the rendezvous we move
some distance down the coast to a reef which is the most northerly coral
bed known. We spend the remainder of our sojourn diving and recuperating
with scheduled visits to the hospital. All drugs and treatment at the Mexican
medical facilities we visited are free. Robin delivers a large consignment of

colored pencils, paint boxes, and coloring books to the children's ward by way of appreciation.

A group of vigilantes armed with shotguns and rifles left La Paz heading for Punta Gato. They were too late. A few nights after our altercation with *Felis rufus*, the animal attacked a Mexican fisherman sleeping on the beach. He rolled it in his blanket and stoned it to death with big rocks. Coyotes dragged its corpse away and ate it.

Evolution of the Prescott Environment, or Roots and Dimensions of Modern Me

by Maggie McQuaid, Class of 1975

[Note: Here are two pieces by Maggie. In the first she describes her feelings about her first years at the College, and the second was written after her graduation. They were both included because together they afford a sort of before-after account of how students can change as a result of the Prescott College experience.]

DIARY ENTRY: SEPTEMBER 10, 1969

"... I don't really know if I'll be able to fit into life at Prescott or not. I don't think I'll be able to make it in such an advanced school. The total idea of the place is so tremendous, so ideal, that a little nobody like me will probably have no place there. ..."

That was a diary entry written the night before I came here. All through that summer, I was tremendously excited about coming to Prescott. From the idea I had received from the Catalog and from the man who interviewed me, I thought that this school was a highly advanced, highly stylized Utopia. I had gotten the idea that this place was the hope and salvation of the entire American college system. My parents, ardent disciples of my interviewer, kept telling me that my time here was going to be full of challenge, involving great disciplines and sacrifices, but the end product would be worth it—I would be an EDUCATED PERSON.

I retained the image of this being a Super-School for quite a long time. My trip here was the classic story of the Girl Going Off to College. There were the inevitable tears at the airport, staunched only when I discovered that the handsome-gorgeous-mysterious-looking guy sitting next to me was also going to Prescott. As the plane ride continued, I made my first big discovery about Prescott, which was the very diverse backgrounds that Prescott students were from. One of the new students I had just met was the son of a Berkeley professor, another was the son of a small town businessman. However, after talking to more and more kids, I found that, despite their different backgrounds, we all had something in common—our parents were all educated, contributing members of the middle and upper classes. Even the students here on scholarships and work loans were from educated, middle-America homes. I noticed only a very few students from minority groups. So, I learned Prescott Truth Number One: Almost all my classmates were from the same homogenous group—white, middle class, suburban.

My next surprise, a pleasant one, came about in the next three days, before we went off on Orientation. I had assumed and almost feared that the students here would all be golden, glorious people (after all, anyone at this educators' paradise would have to be.) Everyone, I thought, would be able to do the pre-Orientation stress tests beautifully, everyone would be worldly and sophisticated, in short, there would be no place for me. I had been a "freak" for most of my life; a long childhood bout with polio had made me weak and clumsy, something I had countered by turning into myself. Other children's teasing during elementary and junior high school really made me believe that I was different, and I let it show during high school. Although I was more accepted there, I was never really into anything. I stood off from other people by my rebel philosophies, by my refusal to conform, by my insistence upon acting in the way that I wanted. By the time I graduated, I was sure that I *was* different from anyone else. I now desperately wanted to be accepted by others, but doubted that I would be. My surprise came when I found out that so many other people at Prescott College were also "different." I found out that people here were willing to accept people for what they are rather than what they should be. My patrol assistant, still one of my best friends here, told me that everyone here was a "freak," that's why everyone got along so well together. For a long time, it was this colony of freaks, this warm, accepting atmosphere, that was my salvation, and only lately have I realized what a potential trip it might be.

Orientation passed rather happily. I hated it in the beginning, got to enjoy it later on, and now look back at it very longingly. It was good for me, gave me a new view of where I belonged in the world, and more importantly, it gave me new confidence in myself. Because I was always very sick, or recovering from being sick, when I was younger, I was coddled and pampered and made to think that physical achievements weren't at all important. On Orientation, I found out that they were indeed important to me, and finishing Orientation was one of the most important things I've ever done. Rock climbing at the beginning of the program was almost impossible for me, and it took me a long time and many tries before I could even begin the climb. But when I got to the top finally, all winded and bruised, I took my first great delight in doing something difficult. I felt, as I reached the top of the climb, that I had reached the top of the world.

Orientation over, the time had come to enter the big wonderland that God, my parents, and admissions had ordained for me. I was excited about the whole concept of the school until I returned home for Thanksgiving vacation and talked to some old friends. Most of my high school friends were attending school at California state colleges, and I was anxious to talk to them. I found out, first with shock and then with concern, that they were learning more than I did, that they had a wider choice of freshman subjects to choose from, that they were much more aware of the world's problems and issues than I was. For a while, I shrugged it off, thinking that I was at fault, not the school. When I came back and started talking to my friends here, I found that they had felt the same things when talking to their old friends. This encroaching fear of inferiority, of the school being something less than the Catalog had written it up to be marked the advent of my doubts of this school.

Christmas vacation showed me another facet of Prescott life that I had not been aware of. Again talking to friends back home, I was at a loss for things to say. While my girlfriends talked of football games, sororities, and dating, my mind wandered to hiking, kayaking, the moratorium, the ecological crisis, and the wild country that I was used to. They talked about Sigma Delta, I talked about Outward Bound; they bragged about their new cars, I spoke longingly of my new pack and frame. The result of this was a total lack of communication on both parts, and another startling revelation on my part—Prescott College breeds its own little group of people. We at Prescott are truly at ease only with each other. Instead of getting a worldly, widespread outlook and position in life, we are brought up in a closed, warm, secure, stagnant place! I was shaken by the truth of this, and I returned here again to find most of my friends disillusioned by the same thing.

Winter quarter has quite a bad reputation around here, and throughout fall quarter I was thoroughly amused by the horrible tales of the dark moods brought about by winter quarter. It wasn't nearly as bad as I had imagined, but I did feel the frustration, the depression, the general "down" that was so widely felt here. This was due, I think, to the isolation of this place, an isolation so vast that it could conceivably be the main reason behind the school's failure.

I took off quite a lot during winter quarter; many people did, just to try to retain some awareness of an outside world. It is vitally necessary to get away from this place once in awhile, because the whole atmosphere here tends to trap and mentally strangle people.

DIARY ENTRY: MARCH 18, 1970

"God, I've got to get out of here. I can't seem to think for myself anymore. Every idea I have has been passed on to me by someone else here. I've got to go away somewhere and think for myself for awhile."

Spring break came just in time for many people. Things seemed to be getting to a breaking point, and spring break gave people ten days of greatly needed rest. Spring quarter seemed easy at the beginning and is ending up as a rather dull period of time in which to get all sorts of business, college and personal, over with. Spring quarter is probably one of the most tranquil; all the people who wanted out left over spring break, and the remainder of the students seem to sit by quietly, awaiting the end. There have been none of the traumas of winter quarter, and not as many of the exuberant pranks of fall quarter. It had been an evidently romantic quarter, due to the warm weather and prevailing winds, and in the words of one observer, "little" couples are popping up all over the place. The patience and tranquility around here are definitely due to the knowledge that the horrors of the year are almost past and that everyone will have a three-month period in which to recuperate.

Still, the problems mentioned before will begin all over again as the next academic year starts. In my opinion, the biggest problem is the isolation here. Because we are isolated, we draw closer together. To an extent, this is good, we get to know each other closely and to realize the worth of each other and to really depend on one another. When we leave the campus for a prolonged time, we really miss each other. It is not uncommon, when far away from this place, to look about at the people we are among, and silently wish to see a familiar face from Prescott. As the year passes, we continue in this intimate atmosphere and it becomes a nightmare. Because we are so close, everyone else's business becomes our own. We begin to know more about people than we wish to. It is impossible (almost) to have a romance around here. Chances are the object of your romantic affection will have been the object of someone else's affection. It's always hard to meet and face a one-time lover, and doubly hard in the close quarters around here. One of the instructors has called Prescott "an incestuous place" and rightly so. Because of the closeness here, when you hurt one person, you hurt many; you cannot act or react without many people feeling it. Eventually, the ideas that motivate people become all the same, nobody can think thoughts that are truly his own. Our set of values loses its perspective; instead of worrying about the war, we hold meetings protesting the pet policy; instead of helping the resistance movement, we protest the bulldozers on campus.

The people here, too, contribute to the closeness of the Prescott microcosm. I love the people here dearly, but we have all been too long in this atmosphere and have all gone in similar directions. The kids here are one little group, not at all like people in the "outside world." I tend to laugh at students elsewhere, with their concern for fraternities and sororities and keeping up with the image set down for them. But who's to say that we are any better. We have a fraternity here—Outward Bound. We are compelled to keep Prescott College true to its image—that of a liberal "hippie school." We somehow think that we are better than other students, but in truth we aren't. We have merely redefined our roles as college students. Too many people, myself included, are too dependent on this school—we could not get along elsewhere.

After all this criticism, I am wondering why I'm coming back next year. I am returning not only because of my dependence here, but because this is the one place that seems to want me.

I can be a "freak" here without anyone objecting. I can act in the way I like, and make people laugh, not at me but with me. This is a numbing, isolated place, but I like it here. Later on I may have to pay the piper for my stay here, but the love and the warmth I've known here will make anything worthwhile.

Letter from an Alum

◇◇◇◇◇◇◇

by Maggie McQuaid, 18 de julio 1977

Dear Prescott Alumnis, Alumnas, and Alumnose,

I'm writing this by light of kerosene lantern, listening to the latest in a series of monsoon season rainstorms pound on the red tile roof above me. Having crawled out from under my mosquito net to write this, I am braving moths, mosquitoes, and bats, and risking malaria, encephalitis, and possibly vampiric transformation. I can't think of anyone I'd rather risk it for than you guys.

I spent all day tromping through the jungle, weighing and measuring rural farm kids to determine their extent of malnutrition. Now I intend to do some weighing and measuring of my life, to determine what to put in this letter.

Here I am in the Peace Corps, in the old town of Pespine, deep in the jungle-ish depths of southern Honduras. I am doing nutritional social work with the national ministry of health; doing a malnutrition study, helping set up infant and child feeding centers, and teaching courses in nutrition, sanitation, and first aid to farm ladies. I like the work—despite the heat, the sweat, the absence of electricity and running water, and the illnesses (malaria once, amoebic dysentery ever since I've been here), this is a good experience. I'm getting older, tougher, and uglier, but the old Prescott College optimism still shines through at times.

It's taken an experience like this to make me realize how much I owe to the times and the place that was Prescott. The intense degree of self-reliance, the ability to open up to and trust others, the willingness to put one's thoughts, beliefs, and body down on the line—I learned all these things at Prescott, and I use them every day.

MAGGIE McQUAID (CLASS OF 1975)

References

PRESCOTT COLLEGE ARCHIVES

The materials related to the history and philosophy of Prescott College, loosely termed the PCArchives, exist in diverse formats and are distributed among several depositories in different campus locations. No master locator system is yet available (2006–07), but the materials include: (1) Catalogs and photographs and some historic documents, letters, etc., in the Archives Room in the Information Commons (Library); (2) an almost complete collection of *Transitions* magazine and many other alumni materials, photographs stored as JPG files, in the Publications and Alumni offices; (3) financial records and Board minutes and reports in the Business Office and President's Office; (4) all sorts of data stored electronically in the Information Technology Office, including two databases: BookMaster (which has 1,214 entries having to do with PC History) and NewsClips (which has 228 news clippings from all epochs—but mostly early—about Prescott College) and numerous electronic files located in the College's storage drives (5) a large body of historical materials of all types, many cited here, have been stored in file folders or other appropriate containers and placed in boxes; however, these include materials that are temporarily unavailable due to a remodeling project at the College's facility, Sam Hill Warehouse.

1   Accreditation Report, 1984.
2   Audit of Founding Fund by Williams and Co., 1966.
3   Bankruptcy Petition for the Insolvent Prescott College Corporation, January 31, 1975. #1967.
4   Biographical information supplied Pat Mroczek, Chief Public Relations Officer, Kettering University 2007, and supplied by Larry Meyers. Charles F. Kettering II File.
5   Board of Missions Study of 1962.
6   Board Minutes, May, 1994.

7   Board Minutes, May 26, 1990.

8   *Breadth of Liberal Arts Knowledge Mission Aspect.* Clipnotes Database #214, 1964-65.

9   Budget Report, 1995-96.

10 "Cash Flow Analysis of 1966-67 Fiscal Year, June 1967." Frank Mertz Box.

11 Center for Indian Bilingual Teacher Education (CIBTE) Box.

12 Charter Catalog and Bulletins, Fall 1966.

13 *Chronicle of Higher Education.* August, 1975. Newsclips database.

14 CIBTE Grant Proposal. CIBTE Box.

15 Corey, Steven. Personal interview. March, 2007.

16 Cumerford Study. 1960. Early Documents Box.

17 Dalke Bequest Files.

18 Faculty Resolutions, April 1994.

19 Faculty Resolutions, April 1996.

20 Financial Report, June 30, 1966.

21 Financial Report, June 30, 1967.

22 Founding Fund Files.

23 Founding Fund Newsclips File.

24 Frank Mertz Document Files.

25 Letter by Internal President. "Financial Aid Re-cert," Jan. 24, 1996.

26 Letter from Nairn to James Patrick, July 12, 1965.

27 Master of Arts Program Catalogs and Bulletins, 1992-93.

28 Nairn Memo, 1965.

29 Nairn, Ronald. "A New Enterprise in Education," *Progress* newsletter Vol. II.

30 News clippings and correspondence of Dr. Bleibtreu.

31 Newsclips, 1960-66.

32 Old College Revenues and Deficits, 1966-75.

33 Parker Files, 1960.

34 PCAE Financial Reports for 1975.

35 PCAE Incorporation Papers.

36 PCAE, Jan. 28, 1975. File 262.

37 Policy Statement, Spring 1975.

38 Prather File.

39 Prescott Center Catalogs, 1975-76-77.

40 Prescott College Catalog, 1970.

41 Prescott College Catalog, 1973-74.

42 Prescott College Freshman Orientation Brochure, 1968.

43 Prescott College, Inc. Petition for Bankruptcy.

44 *Progress* newsletters 1 through 4, 1965-66.

45 Record of Gifts Received, 1966-71.
46 Report to Prescott College Board of Directors, Covering Period from July 1, 1968, through June 30, 1969. Found in box 1969.
47 "Single Audit Report." June 30, 2006.
48 Weiler, Fred J., State Director U.S. Bureau of Land Management, Phoenix Office. 1960s. File Land Acquisition #1.
49 Yavapai County Records; Prescott College Archives, files: Land and Campus 1962-65, Land Reconveyance 1971, Properties Donated 1963-74.

Prescott College Oral History Project

The oral history project was initiated in 2003 by Rick Taylor, an alum who was employed as a librarian by the College. When he left the College to pursue graduate studies, the project was continued by Sam Henrie. The format was that the interviewer posed questions and initiated a dialogue, which lasted between a half hour and two hours in each case. The dialogue was audio recorded then transcribed. Transcriptions are held in the Prescott College Archives, President's Office.

50 Interview with Anne Dorman. May 31, 2003. Interviewer: Rick Taylor.
51 Interview with Betsy Bolding. May 30, 2003. Interviewer: Rick Taylor.
52 Interview with Bob Harrill. October 11, 2006. Interviewer: Sam Henrie.
53 Interview with Dan Garvey. 2004. Interviewer: Rick Taylor.
54 Interview with Doug Wall. May 15, 2004. Interviewer: Sam Henrie.
55 Interview with Jim Stuckey. April 19, 2003 and June 13, 2003. Interviewer: Rick Taylor.
56 Interview with Jim Stuckey. 2006. Interviewer: Sam Henrie.
57 Interview with Hal Lenke. 2006. Interviewer: Sam Henrie.
58 Interview with Joan Clingan. May 2007. Interviewer: Sam Henrie.
59 Interview with Joel Hiller. January 10, 2003. Interviewer: Rick Taylor.
60 Interview with Layne Longfellow. 2007. Interviewer: Sam Henrie.
61 Interview with Noel Caniglia. 2004. Interviewer: Rick Taylor.
62a Interview with Vicki Young. 2006. Interviewer: Sam Henrie.
62b Interview with Annabelle Nelson, 2005. Interviewer: Sam Henrie.

Sharlot Hall Museum Archives

The files and documents related to Prescott College that are conserved in the SHMArchives are generally placed in file folders or other appropriate containers and are stored in acid free boxes. There are also interview recordings and newspapers stored on microfiche. The separate boxes are listed in the card file. However the individual documents, books or recordings, etc., are not listed separately.

63 "1964 Prescott College." Founding Fund Financial Reports, Box 79a and 164.

64 "All in s Day's Work." April, 1995. Database 330, File 164.

65 "Arizona's Educational Treasure." Phoenix *Gazette*, March 5, 1963. Parker Collection.

66 Audits for years 1967 through 1973, Box 164.

67 Box 79a.

68 Box 79a, file 2.

69 Box 79a, file 3.

70 Box 79a, file 17c.

71 Box 79a, file 14a.

72 Box 79b, file zzc.

73 Box 164, file 7.

74 Box 164, file 10.

75 "Cumerford Study of September 7, 1960." Box 164, file 10.

76 Franklin Parker Speech. Box 79a.

77 Lytle Records.

78 "Notes from Board Luncheon." January 12, 1963. Box 79a, file 7.

79 Parker Collection, Vol I. New article, January 11, 1962.

80 Prescott College *Progress*. April, 1965. Box 79a, file 2.

81 Prescott Free Academy and St. Joseph's Academy. File card reference.

82 Sprague Letter to Franklin Parker. September 23, 1960. Box 164.

OTHER SOURCES

83 "21st Century Frontier at Prescott College." *Time* magazine, October 11, 1968.

84 Anonymous alumni quotes. Prescott College Alumni Office Archives.

85 Arizona *Republic*. Sunday, December 3, 1972, B25.

86 Bureau of Labor Statistics, *U.S. Department of Labor*, http://www.bls.gov/cpi/ (November 14, 2007).

87 Burnes, B. "Kurt Lewin and the Planned Approach to Change: A Re-Appraisal." *Journal of Management Studies*, 2004.

88 Carey, Melissa. "Leap Straight into the Heart of Horses: Centaur Leadership Services." First published in Prescott College *Transitions*, Fall 2005.

89 Charles Franklin Parker, ed., *Emergence of a Concept: A Dynamic New Educational Program for the Southwest*. Available through Prescott College Library.

90 *Financial History*. Request directed to Embry-Riddle Aeronautical University Office of the Vice President.

91 Franz, Agnes. Historic Prescott An Illustrated History of Prescott & Yavapai County. San Antonio, TX: Historical Pub. Network, 2004.

92 Kuralt, Charles. "On the Road." CBS Television. Summer 1969. Prescott College Alumni Office Archives.

93 Office of the President. "Final report & recommendations of 2010 Committee."

94 "PC Future Unknown—Foundation Agreement Questioned." The Paper. Prescott, AZ, December 24, 1974.

95 St. Charles, Joe, and Magda Costantino. *Reading and the Native American Learner. Research Report.* 2000.

96 Survey of Arizona Native American (Indian) Tribes and Reservations: Arizona Indian Tribes Economic Development Research Program, 1986.

97 The Higher Learning Commission, North Central Association of Colleges and Schools, 2007. <http://www.ncahlc.org/index/>.

98 U.S. Department of Education Publications, November 13, 2007.

99 Revenue Enhancement Project, President's Office files.

100 Prescott College Catalogs and Bulletins Collection 1966-74, Information Commons Archives.

101 Prescott College Catalogs and Bulletins Collection 1975-84, Information Commons Archives.

102 Prescott College Catalogs and Bulletins Collection 1985-2007, Information Commons Archives.

103 North Central Association Accreditation Reports of 1978, 1980, 1982, 1984, 1990, 1999, 2007, President's Office files.

104 IRS 990 reports filed by Prescott College 1997–2006

Appendix

◇◇◇◇◇◇◇

Members of the Board of Trustees/Directors and Presidents, 1966 through 2005.

Ann Lawrie Sloan Aisa, 1967
Rick Alexander, 1981–84
Marc Appleton, 1996–99
Andrea Arel, 1984–85
Fred Arndt, 1993–95
Thomas E. Arnold, Jr., 1985–87
Ken Asplund, 1975–77
Jeff Baierlein, 1992–94
D. Higgins Bailey, 1977–80
Robert Baillie, 1972–73
Donald Baker, 1989–90
Joel Barnes, 1981–82
Ronald E. Barnes, 1968
Michael Barr, 1986–90
Timothy A. Barrow, 1967–70
C. Newton Bellm, 1968–70
William Black, 1990–92
Herman K. Bleibtreu, 1971–72, 1974–75, 1981–90
Ralph Bohrson, President, 1983–89
Betsy Bolding, 1986–2005
Sharon E. Bonelli, 1993–95
Linda Bosse (Singh), 1993–97
Doug Boyd, 1996–2000
D. A. Bradburn, 1975–86
Lady Branham, 1992–94, Co-President 1994–96
Sidney B. Brincerhoff, 1971–72
Phil Brown, 2003–04

George Bullard, 1992–95
Grace Burford, 1998–01
Marilee Caldwell, 1973–74
Dan Campbell, 1991–96, 2004–05
Vernon L. Campbell, 1968
Buchanan Cargal, 1967
Alton J. Cathey, 1968
Ray Ceo, 1995–97
Judy Clapp, 2003–05
Steve Clark, 2000–01
Steven W. Clarke, 1971–72
Stephen Congdon, 1968–70, 1972–73
Virginia Conner, 1975–76
Allen Cook, 1984–90
David Corkett, 1985–86
Jay Cowles, 1975–82
John Cowles III, 1976–77
Tim Crews, 1996–98
Rev. William Crews, 1996–00
Kenneth M. Croft, 1971–72
Richard B. Crowell, 1967
Mike Crusa, 1979–81
Henry Dahlberg, 1976–78
Timothy A. Daines, 1987–88
Jeoffrey Dann, 1977–80
John J. Daugherty, 1976–77
Charles (Bud) Deihl, 1996–98
Anne Dellinger, 1998–00
Steve DeMocker, 1990–91
James DiMilte, 1972–73
Mary Divers, 1988–90
Henry F. Dobyns, 1971–72
Jess Dods, 1997–01
David L. Dollins, 1969–70
Anne Dorman, 1997–05
Mark Dorsten, 1998–99
John (Jack) Dougherty, 1969–70, President 1970–72, 1975–76
MaryAmelia Douglas-Whited, 1992–93, 1994–95
Connie Dowdy, 1992–97
Russel Duncan, 1981–82
Charles Dunlap III, 1982–85

Jay Dusard, 1974–75
Fred DuVal, 1996–97, 2003–05
Tony Ebarb, 1982–86
Henry A. Ebarb, 1999–02
Donald Ehat, 1973–74
Todd Esque, 1981–82
Kendrick Estey, 1990–94
Robert C. Euler, 1971–72, President 1972–74
Alvin C. Eurich, 1967–68
Betty Everall, 1976–77
George R. Farnham, 1966–70, 1972–73
John M. Favour, 1967–70
Richard A. Fennessey, 1972–73
James E. Fletcher, 1972–74
Erica Ann Flood, 2004–05
Hugh R. Fordyce, 1991–95
Ruth Foreman, 1990–94
Carla Myers Fox, 1969–70
William Fulkerson, 1981–84
Glen Gallo, 1984–86
Lisa Garrison, 1995–96
Dan Garvey, President, 2000– (still serving at time of publication)
Anne Gero-Stillwell, 1978–79
Larry Glenn, 1988–91
Ron Goldfarb, 1979–81
Charlotte Tsoi Goodluck (Grosjean), 1969–72
John Goodson, 1975–84
Laurence M. Gould, 1966–70
Michael Green, 1981–84
Charles H. Greene, 1966–72
Joseph Griffin, 1979–93
Lincoln Hanson, 1979–81
Barbara Harber, 1982–90
Robert Harrill, 1974–75
John Hays, 1982–91
Becky Hazeltine, 1975–76
Scott Hecker, 1979–81
Elizabeth Ann Heil, 1969–73
Samuel N. Henrie, 1974–75, 1977–82, 1992–97
Jack Herring, 2000–04
Taylor T. Hicks Sr., 1973–74

Joel K. Hiller, 1979–82, Co-President 1994–96, President 1996–97
Robert Hobson, 1988–92
Robert Hoffa, 1987–92
Lynn Holaday, 1993–95
Wesley A. Hotchkiss, 1966–70
Doug Hulmes, 1982–87
Jeanne S. Humburg, 1971–72
Frederic B. James, 1966–70
Lee James, 1968
Janie James-High, 1995–97
Melissa Johnson, 1982–84
Lee Jones, 1967
Maya Jones, 2000–02
Amy Joseph, 1975–76
Robert T. Katckiffe, 1978–79
Michael Kelley, 1971–72
Charles F. Kettering II, 1967–71
Robert Kieckhefer, 1968–70
Ken Kimsey, 1979–91
Jeffrey Howard King, 1975–79
James Knaup, 1979–82
Felix Knauth, 1972–73
Otis Kriegel, 1994–95
Robert J. Kriegel, 1991–95
Jay Krienitz, 2002–04
Mrs. William LaFollette, 1971–72, 1974–75
Al Lessik, 1975–76
Ann Brown Linsky, 1975–93
Layne Longfellow, 1975–81
Glen R. Lord, 1972–73
Marc Lord, 1995–96
David Lugers, 1974–75
Rev. Everett B. Luther, 1966–73
Victor H. Lytle, 1966–67, 1969–73
Joanne Maas, 1975–77, 1981–93
Richard Mahoney, 1996–98
T. Keven Mallen, 1972–73
Carla Malvick, 1988–90
Neal Mangham, President, 1997–00
Richard Markham, 1978–86
Lloyd Wesley Mason, Jr., 1969–70, 1972–73

Ann Maxey, 1986–87
A. Lee Maynard, 1972–73, 1975–77
David McCarthy, 2000–05
Karen McCreary-Williams, 2000–05
Eileen DeCoursey McDuff, 1989–90
David Meeks, 2004–05
Lawrence Mehren, 1984–85
Frank A. Mertz, 1967–70, President 1974–75
Austin Meyers, 1979–80
Edward Miller, 1974–81
Oscar C. Mink, 1973–74
Janet Mize, 1975–77
David Moll, 1984–85
Janice Jones Monk, 1990–95
Nancy Moore, 1990–96
Letitia Morris, 1977–81
Robert Mosier, 1985–92
William Mulland, 1974–75
Steve Mumme, 1995–97
Steve Munsell, 1991–97
Austin Myers, 1980–81
Ronald C. Nairn, President, 1966–70, Trustee 1971–73
Florence Nelson, 1982–86
Vernon L. Newell, 1973–74
Kathleen Newman, 1976–79
Aaron W. Newton, Jr., 1971–73
Alan Nichols, 1977–79
Jan Nisbet, 2004–05
Joseph J. Nold, 1976–79
Doug North, President, 1989–94
Leonard Ossorio, 1972–73
Dana Oswald, 1988–91
Fred Ouweleen, 1974–75
Charles Franklin Parker, 1966–70, 1979–82, Founding President 1962–65
Alan Paskow, 1974–75
James E. Patrick, 1966–70
Derek Peterson, 1989–90
Ted Pickett, 1979–81
James Pittman, 1996–97
Richard S. Planchard, 1974–75
John Platenius, 2000–01

Frank Plaut, 2003–04
John Powell, 1992–96
Bill Prather, 1995–97
Alan Prehmus, 1976–79
Lucille Preston, 1969–70
Fred Quweeleen, 1974–75
William Rapp, 1982–92
Robert Ratcliffe, 1976–80
Frank Reichenbacher, 1975–80
Carol Retasket, 1992–93
John Rice, 1973–74
Hank Richter, 1977–81
Idelia Riggs, 1979–94, (Emeritus 1990–94)
Sturgis Robinson, 1997–05 (Interim President 1999–2000)
Thomas F. Robinson, 1998–02
Roe William Roe, 1983–86
Shannon Rosenblatt, 1982–84
Jack Rubel, 1967–72
Alan Rubin, 2002–05
Lester W. Ruffner, 1979–80
Rebecca Ruffner, 1977–84, 2000–05
Daniel Salcito, 1990–93
John Sanafa, 1978–79
Beverly Santo, 1991–92
John Schafer, 1977–78
Joe Schaffer, 1975–76
Adam Schantz, 1966–70
Grace Wicks Schlosser, 1999–2000
Henry E. P. Schmerler, 1990–95
Andy Schmookler, 1974–75
Phillip Schulch, 1973–74
Allison Scott, 1997–98
Gerald Secundy, 1998–05
Martin E. P. Seligman, 1990–95
John Shafer, 1976–77, 1978–80
Jo Sharp, 1974–75
Thom Shelby, 1995–97
Derek Smith, 1992–94
Hogan Smith, 1973–74
Paul Smith, 1982–85